דוד וסרשטיין

ירושלים תשמ"ג

(מאלבון)

THE ANCIENT ARABS

Nomads on the Borders of the Fertile Crescent
9th-5th Centuries B.C.

ISRAEL EPH'AL

1982

THE MAGNES PRESS, THE HEBREW UNIVERSITY, JERUSALEM

E.J. BRILL, LEIDEN

Distributed by
N.V.Boekhandle en Drukkerij V/H E.J. Brill
Oude Rijn 33a, Leiden
Holland

ISBN 965-223-400-1
Printed in Israel
at Mishlat Foto & Offset Services Ltd., Moshav Shilat

To Ilana

Prov. 31:10-31

PREFACE

The Hebrew text on which this book is based was written in 1971. In the meantime, several scholarly papers have been published, some of them rather detailed, touching upon topics treated in this book. I did not, however, consider it advisable to curtail my discussion and the original comprehensive framework has been preserved. Where these new studies are relevant, they are mentioned, and my own comments appear in the notes. The English manuscript was completed in 1977 and has been brought up to date to that year (though there are sporadic instances of more recent updating).

The sources for the material dealt with in this book are variegated in kind and origin. The inconsistency in spelling of proper names is thus inherent: some names derive from traditional sources, while others are from sources in which spelling systems widely differ. I have incorporated all these "as is", making no effort to impose a unified spelling "at all costs". Biblical names are generally given according to the Revised Standard Version. When, however, the Akkadian or West-Semitic spelling is relevant, and the traditional spelling might be misleading, adjustments have been made — often using letters and symbols not found in the traditional English, for example, 'Ephah, Qedar and Tema'.

Professor H. Tadmor, who followed the book through all the stages of research and writing, has kindly read the manuscript and made significant comments on both content and structure. My colleagues, Professor M. Cogan and Dr. N. Na'aman, have also contributed remarks which have led to various improvements. Mrs. Evelyn Strouse edited the English style, and it is only thanks to her unstinting efforts and well-tempered argumentation that the book has reached its present readable form. The Research Authority and the H. Rosenberg School of Jewish Studies, both of the Tel Aviv University, have assisted in enabling the several retypings of the manuscript. To all the above, my gratitude cannot adequately be expressed.

I.E.

CONTENTS

INTRODUCTION

A. THE PURPOSE AND HISTORY OF THE RESEARCH

This book proposes to investigate and describe the relations between the nomads of northern Sinai, northern Arabia and the Syro-Arabian desert, and the population of Palestine and its environs, as well as between those nomads and the great Near Eastern empires which ruled the western part of the Fertile Crescent in the 9th-5th centuries B.C. The study focuses mainly on the political and ethnographic aspects of these relations, and deals, to a lesser extent, with social and economic matters.

The investigation of the nomads within the described geographic confines was only made possible by the decipherment and publication of the Assyrian and Babylonian documents which relate to them and remain our chief source of information about the nomads during the discussed period. The pioneers in research of any dimension on this topic were Fr. Delitzsch (*Paradies,* 1881), F. Hommel (*Geschichte Babyloniens und Assyriens,* Berlin 1885) and E. Glaser (*Skizze,* 1890). Their work was limited in the main to locating and identifying the nomads mentioned in the Bible and in Akkadian sources. For purposes of comparison they also made use of names in Greek and Latin sources, and to a lesser extent those in Arabic (e.g. al-Hamdāni and al-Bakri). Much of their work is faulty by present-day standards and therefore unusable, primarily because of errors in reading cuneiform texts and the mechanical identification of various groups by phonological similarities, without sufficient regard for geographic logic.

A generation later saw the second stage in the development of research, marked by the works of A. Musil and Hommel (*Ethnologie und*

Geographie des alten Orients, 1926), which also account for geographic and social factors relating to the nomads. The documentary basis was likewise expanded by the publication of new sources and critical editions of texts previously available only in preliminary publications (e.g. the inscriptions of Assurbanipal). Of particular value was the contribution of Musil, who in the years 1896-1902, 1908-1915 traversed the deserts from the Negeb and northern Arabia through Wadi Sirḥān and the Syrian desert to the Euphrates. To his diaries on these travels Musil added numerous appendices, some of them elaborations of specific topics, including discussions of various groups of nomads and the history of the principal oases (*Northern Ḥeǧâz,* 1926; *Arabia Deserta,* 1927; *Middle Euphrates,* 1927; *Palmyrena,* 1928; and *Northern Neǧd,* 1928 are especially important to our subject). In these discussions Musil made extensive use of biblical, classical and Roman-Byzantine sources. He even included material culled systematically from the itineraries and other works of Arab writers and geographers, most of which have never been translated into any European language. The vast amount of material cited in these books is extremely important for a knowledge of the geography of the region and various aspects of the life of its inhabitants. At the same time, Musil's work, because of his ignorance of Akkadian and his consequent dependence on secondary sources, is marked by a number of flaws in the chapters dealing with the Assyrian and Babylonian periods.

A useful tool for the systematic study of the history of the nomads was made available when T. Weiss-Rosmarin, in her doctoral dissertation ("Aribi und Arabien in den babylonisch-assyrischen Quellen", *JSOR* 16[1932], 1-37), prepared an index of the majority of references to the various groups of Arabs in Babylonian and Assyrian sources. It is not, however, an original contribution to scholarship, since it confines itself to an alphabetical listing of already known material, and does not re-examine the texts or make an exhaustive analysis of them.

A new phase in the study of the nomads, and one embodying a substantial change in approach, began with the work of W.F. Albright. In two articles which dealt with the Dedan and Massa' tribes ("Dedan", *Alt Festschrift,* 1953, 1-12; "The Biblical Tribe Massa' and Some Congeners", *Levi della Vida Festschrift,* 1956, Vol. I, 1-4) as well as in numerous notes included in his other studies, Albright applied his general critical method to the study of the nomads and their history. He views the matter at hand within the general framework of ancient Near Eastern and biblical research, utilizing the resources of epigraphy, linguistics and archaeology. Thus, Albright sought to take advantage of the conclusions of archaeological research in southern Arabia, and of the implications of the Lihyanite and Thamudic inscriptions discovered in northern Arabia, in order to establish chronological starting points for historical research. He also called attention to new areas of research likely to deepen our understanding of the problems connected with the investigation of nomads. So, for example , the works of G.W. Van Beek on the cultivation, processing and marketing of spices in southern Arabia,[1] which were prepared at Albright's instigation, make an important contribution — despite their reliance on classical sources — to the recognition of one of the basic factors affecting the relations between the nomads and the Near Eastern empires during the period under discussion.

All the previously published research on nomads of the 8th to 5th centuries B.C. has dealt exclusively with particular problems. Our study is the first published attempt to encompass all the complex data on the nomads at that period in order to formulate a clear and complete picture of their organization, their geographical spheres and their relations with the countries of the Fertile Crescent. The method adopted seeks to follow the path pointed to by Albright in the conclusion of his article on Massa': "The material already available makes it certain that we must analyze our complex material with the greatest attention to basic philological and historical principles".[2]

In accordance with these principles, this work is based fundamentally on a critical analysis of the sources, made by carefully examining their texts, the circumstances of their formation, their classification and their usefulness for the purposes of historical research. The book begins with a study of all the Akkadian and biblical sources. Various Akkadian documents — among them letters, passages from inscriptions of Tiglath-Pileser III and Assurbanipal, as well as Babylonian chronicles

1 Van Beek, in R. Bowen and F.P. Albright, *Archaeological Discoveries in South Arabia*, Baltimore 1958, 139-142; idem, *JAOS* 78 (1958), 141-152; idem, *BA* 23 (1960), 70-95.

2 Albright, *Levi della Vida Festschrift*, 14.

— have been reconsidered and conclusions drawn which differ from the conventional ones. The same method has been applied to the classical and North Arabic sources. Special attention was also paid to basic geographical data, unchanged for thousands of years, which may have had politico-military and economic implications.

A number of constantly recurring phenomena are discernible in the history of the relations of the nomads with the sedentary population and the political authorities controlling the western part of the Fertile Crescent in the first half of the first millennium B.C. These pivotal phenomena can be more clearly understood if the basis for them is outlined:

1. At the end of the second millennium B.C. — following both the establishment of centralized authorities in southern Arabia, which made it possible to cultivate, process and distribute spices on a large scale, and the domestication of the camel, which could then carry Arabian produce over great distances — there was a striking change in the nature of the contact between the nomads and the sedentary populations of the western part of the Fertile Crescent. Previous contact had been confined to attempted nomad encroachment with their flocks upon the settled parts of the country and the efforts made to repulse them, and the conflict over grazing areas of the cultivated land. It now developed that the nomads became important for the maintenance of Arabian trade because of their location along the long trade routes. Profit from this key branch of the economy and interest in its uninterrupted operation generated new, commercially based, relations. Especially affected by this change were their relations with the political bodies (the local-national ones and later also the empires) which ruled the region. These economic considerations had demographic and administrative implications as well.

2. The gradual deterioration of the border kingdoms and their disintegrating borders created opportunities for the nomad infiltration.

3. The inadequate manpower in the empires controlling the western part of the Fertile Crescent during the 8th to 5th centuries B.C. led to the integration of nomad tribes into the imperial military and administrative establishment in the region. The Arabs grew increasingly indispensable, particularly when the Asiatic empires embarked upon the conquest of Egypt. The absolute dependence of their large armies on camels for the supply of water in the Sinai desert added a new element

to the relations between the nomads and the ruling powers.

This book proposes, then, to describe and examine political, demographic and economic *processes*. We must emphasize, however, that, because of the few sources available, it is not possible to undertake systematic clarification of the *history* of the nomads and their tribes, but only their *relations* with the political authorities and sedentary populations in the western as well as other parts of the Fertile Crescent in the 8th to 5th centuries B.C.

B. DEFINITION AND DESIGNATIONS OF THE NOMADS

As used herein, the term "nomads" refers to all the populations in the deserts of northern Sinai and northern Arabia and in the Syro-Arabian desert. Most of them raised camels[3] and sheep,[4] lived in tents and unfortified temporary camps[5] and moved from place to place with their flocks, sporadically raiding the permanent settlements in the regions adjacent to the desert.[6] For the purposes of this book, the term "nomads" is applied to oasis dwellers as well. The oases — some of which, like Tema' and Dumah (Dūmat al-Jandal, al-Jawf),[7] served as economic, administrative and ritual centers — were the permanent homes of thousands of people engaged in cultivating the land and in crafts. Although from the socio-cultural point of view it is hard to describe this population as nomadic (a distinction made particularly in classical Arabic sources), we have adopted in this book the terminology

3 See Jer. 49:29, 32; Tiglath-Pileser III inscriptions: K 3751 rev. 5; III R 10, 2:20, 25; ND 400:27; Esarhaddon inscriptions: Nin. A iv 17, 21; Frt. F. rev. 2; Assurbanipal's Rm. viii 114, ix 5, 36-37, 42, 46, 52, 65; ABL 547, 631; Herodotus III 9. Cf. also the Tiglath-Pileser III and Assurbanipal reliefs.

4 Isa. 13:20; 60:7; Jer. 49:29; Ezek. 27:21; I Chron. 5:21; Rm. viii 114, ix 5, 42; ND 2644. Cf. also the Tiglath-Pileser reliefs.

5 Isa. 42:11; Jer. 49:29, 31; Ps. 120:5; Cant. 1:5; and also the Assurbanipal reliefs. About the epithet *āšibūt kuš/ltāri* see below, 3.

6 Cf. Job 1:15; ABL 88, 547; the Assurbanipal inscriptions: B viii 39-40; K 2802 iv 8-10; Rm. vii 102-106, viii 15-16, 71-72.

7 The people of Tema' (uru*Te-ma-a-a*) are included among the nomads who brought their gifts to Tiglath-Pileser as a sign of submission (III R 10, 2:27; K 3751 rev. 3); Dumah is described as the Arabs' fortress (Esarhaddon, Nin. A iv 1: uru*A-du-mu-tu āl dan-nu-tu* kur lú*A-ri-bi*); It is likewise mentioned in connection with Ḫazael and Te'elḫunu in Sennacherib's time (VA 3310 rev. 25 ff.):

of the biblical and cuneiform sources which do not distinguish and do not enable us to distinguish between the sedentary population and the other desert dwellers.

1. The most common name for these nomads in the sources dating from the first millennium B.C. is "Arabs". The term appears first in Assyrian sources in the Kurkh Monolith Inscription of Shalmaneser III, composed after the battle of Qarqar (853 B.C.), and is frequently found thereafter in cuneiform documents dating from Tiglath-Pileser III on. In the Bible it begins to appear in texts dealing with the Solomonic era, but these references seem to stem from a later age (see pp. 62–71).

In cuneiform sources the name has the following forms: ^{kur}*A-ri-bi,*[8] ^{kur}*A-ru-bu,*[9] ^{kur}*A-ra-bi,*[10] ^{kur}*Ar-ba-a-a,*[11] ^{kur}*Ar-bá-a-a,*[12] ^{kur}*Aŕ-bá-a-a,*[13] $^{\text{lú/kur}}$*A-ri-bi,*[14] ^{lú}*Ari-bi,*[15] ^{lú}*A-ru-bu,*[16] ^{lú}*A-ra-bi,*[17] ^{lú}*A-ra-bu,*[18] ^{lú}*Ar-a-bi,*[19] ^{lú}*Ar-ba-a-a,*[20] ^{lú}*Aŕ-ba-a-a.*[21] The forms עֲרָב (Jer. 25:24; Ezek. 27:21; II Chron. 9:14) and עַרְבִי (Isa. 13:20; Jer. 3:2) in Hebrew; *Arabaya* in Persian;[22] "Αραψ, 'Αραβ(ε)ία and 'Αραβίη in Greek and *al-'Arab* in

8 Tiglath-Pileser: Rost, *Ann.* 154, 210; III R 10, 2:19. Sargon: *Lie,* lines 123, 188. Esarhaddon: Nin. A iv 1, 6; Nin. B ii 18, 46, 49, 51; Frt. F rev. 2. Assurbanipal: K 2802 iii 3, iv 8, 13, *passim*; Rm. vii 83, 102, viii 4, *passim*; B viii 4, 8; K 2664 v 6; K 3405 rev. 3; *AfO* 8 (1932–1933), 200:79.

9 Tiglath-Pileser, Rost, *Ann.* 240; Assurbanipal, Rm. ix 71; Cf. Esarhaddon, Frt. B rev. 8: [ ] *A-ru-bu.*

10 Nab. H_2 i 43, 45; Cf. Naqš-i Rustam Bab. line 15; BM 21946 rev. 10. All these texts are Babylonian.

11 III R 8, 94: Sargon, *Lie,* line 121; ABL 631:3, 7.

12 ABL 547 rev. 10. For the *pa-bá* sign in Neo-Assyrian see K. Deller, *Lautlehre des Neuassyrischen,* Wien 1959, 241.

13 ABL 88 rev. 4, and see the previous note.

14 Esarhaddon, Mnm. B, 7.

15 Sargon, *Winckler,* 110:69; Sennacherib, BM 113203 line 28; Esarhaddon, Nin. A iv 1, 4, 6, 12; Assurbanipal, B viii 23. See also *A-ri-bi* without any determinative, ADD 1115 i 6.

16 Esarhaddon, Nin. A iv 24, 28.

17 Sargon, Nimrud Prism, Fragment D iv 42; Sennacherib, VA 3310 rev. 22.

18 ABL 262 obv. 10.

19 ABL 260 obv. 10.

20 ABL 414 rev. 7; Nbk. 287:9; M(ichigan Museum Collection) 422:21; CT XXII 86:7.

21 ND 2644:9 Nimrud Letter XXIII (*Iraq* 17 [1955], 142).

22 Naqš-i Rustam Pers. line 27.

Arabic show that the base form of the name is *Arabu.* The frequent use of $^{\text{kur/lú}}$*Aribi* in the Assyrian royal inscriptions implies that this spelling represents an alternative base form which does not, however, appear to have been taken over in non-Assyrian sources. Its only approximation seems to be the biblical form (הָ)עֲרָב (I Kings 10:15; Jer. 25:24; cf. בית עֶדֶן=*Bīt Adini*). All the other forms of the nominative are variants resulting mainly from a change in the final vowel and the coloration of the penultimate by the ultimate vowel.[23]

The almost simultaneous appearance of the term in sources independent of each other at opposite ends of the Fertile Crescent and its persistence in Greek, South Arabic and Classical Arabic indicate that "Arab" was the designation that the nomads applied to themselves. To explain or derive the meaning of the term "Arab", the early Arabic dialects should be examined, even though it is not yet possible to find there a satisfactory etymology. In any case, ערבה (*'arābāh*), one of the Hebrew words for desert (Isa. 35:1,6; Jer. 17:6, etc.), which does not occur in Ancient Arabic or Akkadian, cannot, as some scholars suggest,[24] provide an etymological base.

As stated, the term "Arab" designates a desert dweller, a Bedouin (cf. Jer. 3:2 "By the waysides you have sat awaiting lovers like an Arab in the wilderness"; Sargon, *Lie,* lines 120-121; ^{lú}*Ta-mu-di* ^{lú}*[I-ba]-a-di-di* ^{lú}*Mar-si-ma-[ni]* ^{lú}*Ḫa-ia-pa-a* ^{kur}*Ar-ba-a-a ru-ú-qu-ti a-ši-bu-ut mad-ba-ri,* "The people of Thamūd, Ibadidi, Marsimani (and) 'Ephah, the distant Arabs, who dwell in the desert"). In the inscriptions of Sargon this term is applied even to nomads in Media[25] who had no ethnic

23 This occurence is common in Assyria. For its definition and for examples see note 407. There are some who think that the term ^{lú}*urbi* also indicates Arabs (this opinion was offered once again and in great detail by D. Neiman, *JQR* 60 [1970], 237-258). For refutation, as well as explanation of the term as meaning a special kind of warrior, see Eph'al, *JAOS* 94 (1974), 110 n. 16.

24 For the assumption of affinity between "Arab" and *'arābāh,* cf. e.g., J.A. Montgomery, *Arabia and the Bible,* Philadelphia 1934, 28; L. Köhler (-W. Baumgartner), *Lexicon in Veteris Testamenti Libros,* Leiden 1958, 733, s.v. II עֲרָבָה.

25 Sargon, *Lie,* 30:188: ^{kur}*na-gi-i [ru]-qu-ti ša pat-ti māt A-ri-bi ša ni-pi-iḫ* ^{d}*Šam-ši*^{si}, "far-off territories on the confines of the land of the Arabs, where the sun is rising".

connection with the nomads of the Syrian desert and were probably not even Semites.[26]

In the Assyrian royal inscriptions the term "Arabs" is applied specifically to the Qedarites,[27] the people of Sumu(')ilu,[28] and to the people of Idiba'ilu (biblical Adbeel),[29] Thamūd, Ibadidi, Marsimani and 'Ephah.[30] According to the descriptions in the Assyrian sources, however, the term likewise fits other groups mentioned in this book in connection with desert regions and with the characteristic life style of their inhabitants, such as the people of Tema', Sheba, Massa', uru*Ba-da-na-a-a,* uru*Ḫa-at-ti-a-a,*[31] the Me'unites, the people of Nebaioth and apparently lú*Te-e-me* as well.

It is instructive to note that not one of the thousands of inscriptions found in southern Arabia and produced by the kingdoms which existed in the region from the beginning of the first millennium B.C. (among them Sheba, Qataban, Ma'īn, Hadhramaut and Ḥimyar) contains the slightest hint of a connection between these kingdoms and the term "Arabs". A survey of the epigraphical material from the kingdoms of southern Arabia, especially in the works of W. Caskel and M. Höfner,[32] shows that the term "Arabs" (*'rb, 'rbn*) appears relatively late: in the region of the kingdom of Sheba not earlier than about the first century C.E. and in Hadhramaut never before the third century C.E. In these documents the term refers to Bedouin who came into contact with the kingdoms either as auxiliary troops or as enemies. In the course of time it began to appear in royal titles such as "the king of Sheba and Ḏu-

26 M. Streck, *ZA* 15 (1900), 353-354.

27 Cf. in the Assurbanipal inscriptions m*Ia-u-ta-'* *mār* m*Ha-za-ilu* *šar* kur*Qi-id-ri/Qa-da-ri* (Cyl. B [Streck], vii 87-88; B [Piepkorn] vii 93-94) = m*Ú-a-a-te-'* *šar* kur*A-ri-bi* (Rm. vii 83).

28 Cf. in the Assurbanipal inscriptions m*Ú-a-a-te-'* *šar* kur*Su-mu*-AN (*AAA* 20 [1933], 86:113) = m*Ú-a-a-te-'* *šar* kur*A-ri-bi* (K 2802 vi 15; Rm. viii 93, ix 2, x 21). For the names and titles of the kings mentioned in the preceding two notes see pp. 51-52, 165-168.

29 Tiglath-Pileser III, Rost, *Ann.* 240; see also pp. 93, 215-216.

30 Sargon, *Lie,* pp. 20-22, lines 120-121.

31 The last five groups are mentioned in the inscriptions of Tiglath-Pileser: Rost, *Ann.* 219; III R 10, 2:27 f.; K 3751, rev. 3 f.

32 Caskel, *ZDMG* 103 (1953), *28-*36 (= G.E. von Grunebaum [ed.], *Studies in Islamic Cultural History* [1954], 36-46; Höfner, in F. Gabrieli (ed.), *L'Antica società beduina,* Roma 1959, 53-68.

Raidān and their Arabs", i.e. the king of the two countries and the ruler of the Bedouin tribes living within their confines and considered to be the king's subjects.[33]

The decline and fall of the kingdoms of southern Arabia in the third and fourth centuries C.E. was accompanied by increased percentage of Bedouin in the population of the region. From then on, the concept "Arab" broadened gradually to encompass most of the population groups of the peninsula. The term coined by Caskel for the process, *die Beduinisierung Arabiens,* is most apt.

This investigation of the distribution and use of the term "Arabs" indicates that it was originally a northern concept exclusive to the cup of the Fertile Crescent and to northern Arabia. As the Bedouin expanded into the territories of the sedentary populations of central and southern Arabia, culminating in the conquest of the settled land by the desert, so the term "Arabs" expanded to designate the people of the region.

It should be added that the term "Arab(s)" in this book has no linguistic meaning, even though many personal names in the following pages are typically Arabic.[34] There are too few sources for us to define what language or languages were used by the "Arabs" or to know whether other groups, such as those designated "Aramaeans", used the same languages.[35] Our information about both groups during the 9th - 5th centuries B.C. mainly derives from indirect sources, in a language other than their own. Because of this we do not refer to documents in which personal names gentilically undesignated appear, even such names as ^{m}*Arbaya* etc.[36]

2. "The People of the East" (בני קדם): The term Land of Qedem

33 Caskel, *ZDMG* 103 (1953), *32-*34 (= *Studies in Islamic Cultural History,* 41-44): Höfner, *ibid.*, 60 ff.

34 Such as Abiyate' (='*byṯ*'), Gindibu', Uabu (= *Whb*), Uaite' (= *Wyṯ*'), Yauta' (=*Ywṯ*'), Zabībe, Yati'e (=*Yṯ*'), It'amra (=*Yṯ*'*mr*), Karibilu, Amme'ta' (='*myṯ*', on this spelling see p. 58.

35 On the Aramaeans in the 12th-8th centuries B.C. see Brinkman, *Post-Kassite Babylonia,* 267-285. For an analysis of "Aramaean" and "Arabian" names see R. Zadok, *On West Semites in Babylonia during the Chaldean and Achaemenian Periods,* Jerusalem 1977.

36 *APN,* 28; *NBN,* 15.

(="the land of the east") is first encountered in the story of Sinuhe, ca. twentieth century B.C., which distinguishes between the Land of Qedem (*Qdm*), Retenu (*Rṯnw*), Cush(?) (*Kšy*) and the Lands of Fenkhu (*Fnḫw*).[37] The statement that Sinuhe reached the Land of Qedem after leaving Byblos and continued his wanderings from there to Upper Retenu indicates that the name Qedem here refers to a region on the western border of the Syrian desert.[38] The name has the same meaning in the Bible in the description of Jacob's journey to Harran, during which he crossed the Land of the People of the East (ארץ בני קדם; Gen.29:1 ff.). In other biblical references the term apparently lost its original meaning and was used generally to refer to the nomads in the desert regions east of Palestine (Judg. 6:3; 8:10, etc.). The prophetic literature tends to use the term People of the East rather than the term "Arabs" in reference to the nomads of the Syro-Arabian desert (Isa. 11:14; Jer. 49:28; Ezek. 25:4, 10).

The People of the East are known in the Bible for their wisdom (I Kings 5:10; cf. also "the proverb of the Easterner", משל הקדמני, in I Sam. 24:13); possibly also the words of Agur, the son of Jaqeh of Massa', and of Lemuel king of Massa' (Prov. chaps. 30-31), that is, the leaders of a nomadic tribe in the Syrian desert were considered to partake of this wisdom.[39]

The Bible and the Akkadian sources use two other typological terms to refer to the desert nomads:

3. The tent-dwelling proclivity of these nomads is reflected in the term *āšibūt kuš/ltāri,* "tent-dweller(s)", which appears in both Neo-Assyrian and Neo-Babylonian literary texts. It is frequently preceded there by the name of an ethnic group such as *Su-te-e a-ši-bu-te kul-ta-ri šá a-šar-šu-nu ru-u-qu,* "The Sutî, tent-dwellers, whose country is remote "

37 A.H. Gardiner, *Notes on the Story of Sinuhe,* Paris 1916, 169, 172, 174; *ANET,* 19-20.

38 In contrast to the opinion of J.A. Wilson and W. Helck, who consider Qedem (=the east) a vague and general geographic term for a wide nomadic area (*ANET,* 19, note 10; Helck, *Die Beziehungen Ägyptens zu Vorderasien im 3. und 2. Jahrtausend v. Chr.,* Wiesbaden 1962, 45).

39 For a survey of all the biblical and extra-biblical references to the Land and the People of Qedem (= the east) see Eph'al, *Enc. Miqr.,* VII, 26-29; see also idem, *JAOS* 94 (1974), 114-115.

(Asarhaddon, Nin. A, v 15); [lú]*A-ra-me* [lú]*Su-ti-í a-ši-bu-ut kuš-ta-ri,* "Aramaeans and Sutî, tent-dwellers" (Sargon, Prism D, vii 57-58).[40] Thus the territory of desert nomads is designated in a Neo-Babylonian epic text as *māt kuš-ta-ri* (BM 82684 ii 13).[41] The same literary connotation is preserved in "the kings of the west who live in tents" *šarrāni*[meš kur]*A-mur-ri-i a-ši-ib kuš-ta-ri)* in the Cyrus Cylinder (line 29), occurring as it does in the comprehensive list of the kings who surrendered to Cyrus. The same term is used in the description of Gideon's pursuit of the Midianites by "the way of the tent-dwellers" (דרך השכוני באהלים, Judg. 8:11).

The term "tent-dwellers" is not exclusive to the nomad groups or to the period discussed in our study: in the Bible it refers to Javal "the father of those who dwell in tents and have cattle" (Gen. 4:20); the first section of the Assyrian King List — reflecting a tradition going back to the nomadic phase of the West Semites who settled in Mesopotamia — concludes with the formula "total of 17 tent-dwelling kings" *(šarrāni āšibūtu kultāri);* similarly, the term ('ἴΑραβες σκηνῖται refers in works of classical authors to various Bedouin groups in the Fertile Crescent and within its cup (see, e.g., Strabo XVI, 753, 767; Pliny, *Nat. Hist.,* V 65, 87; VI 143). Thus it appears that the term "tent-dwellers" did not necessarily, in various periods, designate a particular ethnic group, but a way of life.

4. "All who dwell in the desert that cut the corners of their hair" in Jer. 9:25 and also Jer. 25:23; 49:32. The Arab custom of cutting the hair in a circle with the temple shaved is also known from Herodotus III 8.

C. THE CHRONOLOGICAL FRAMEWORK

Our investigations extend from the middle of the 8th century to the middle of the 5th century B.C., a period long enough to trace the gradual and lengthy — though uniform — development of relations between the nomads and the political authorities and the sedentary populations. The basic features of this process were evident initially at the beginning of our period, when Syria and Palestine were under the control of the Mesopotamian and Persian empires. During this time,

40 C.J. Gadd, *Iraq* 16 (1954), 192.

41 D.J. Wiseman, *BSOAS* 30 (1967), 33.

Syria and Palestine were integrated into the empires, as the politico-national entities — first in Aram-Damascus and Israel and later in Judah and the kingdoms of Transjordan — were gradually eliminated. The broader the chronological framework the more fully understandable are the administrative, economic and demographic results of these fundamental changes in the structure of the political bodies in the region.

Our study ends not at the close of the Persian period (332 B.C.), when the economic and political organization of the area changed radically under the Hellenistic regimes, but in the middle of the 5th century B.C. This early terminal point was chosen chiefly because at this time contemporary sources for the nomads cease; all information on them for the rest of the Persian era comes from classical authors centuries later. Ending in the middle of the 5th century B.C. also relieves us of having to investigate the appearance and identity of the Nabataeans. The clarification of these questions would require recourse to sources and research tools other than those adopted for this work, and is, indeed, a subject unto itself.

D. GEOGRAPHIC LIMITS

1. As noted, this study proposes to investigate the nomads' relations with the sedentary population groups of Palestine and Syria as well as with the political authorities in control of the region. An underlying assumption is that Arabian trade existed in the 9th-5th centuries B.C., and that the nomad groups near its lengthy routes, as well as the governing bodies of Palestine and its environs, were interested in maintaining uninterrupted trade. These matters are part of a more general system which must be studied with reference to the entire Fertile Crescent. It should be noted that in the period under discussion some of the groups moved great distances from the eastern edge of the Syrian desert to the neighborhood of Palestine and Egypt. For these reasons, the geographic borders of our study encompass all the desert areas of northern Sinai, northern Arabia, and the Syro-Arabian desert, including the Middle Euphrates region and the western districts of Babylonia.

By way of introduction, it is worthwhile considering a number of basic geographical facts:

Most of the desert areas in the region under discussion have no insurmountable natural obstacles and seem to be passable (except for the Nafūd desert). In fact, however, traffic through them was limited, and determined by the location of oases and water sources and whether they were not more than a day's walk apart. The main beast of burden in the desert was the camel, which can cover more than 100 kilometers without drinking. The scarcity of water sources and the limited grazing considerably restricted the movement of military bodies and of great merchant çaravans for most of the year, even along the main desert routes.[42] This applies especially to the Fertile Crescent kingdoms and Egypt, whose camels were so few that transport was based on other animals and on infantry. The best time to travel in the desert was the rainy season, when grass and water were available in areas generally arid. And indeed, most of the dated sources indicate that both military and commercial journeys took place during Kislev to Adar/December to March.[43]

The deserts were inhabited by tribes of sheep- and camel-raising Bedouin, moving with their flocks in a delineated area. They made contact, at regular intervals, with a sedentary population (including the inhabitants of the larger oases) and acquired supplies such as grains, weapons, clothes and the like in exchange for the yield of their flocks.[44]

Drought is much harder on the population of the desert and its border regions than on that of settled areas. In time of drought the desert dwellers attempt to encroach upon the settled regions with their flocks, and therefore the pressure is especially great on border zones. Whether the Bedouin succeed or are pushed back to the desert depends on the strength of the authorities in the border areas and upon their concept of government. Thus the attitude of the Assyrian empire, for instance, toward Arab penetration of the eastern borders of Palestine and southern Syria was considerably different from that of the

42 E.g. Musil, *Arabia Deserta,* 535-536.

43 For example, BM 21946 rev. 9-10 (the raids of Babylonian military units on the Arabs in the Syrian desert during the months of Kislev-Adar in the 6th year of Nebuchadnezzar); Nabonidus Chronicle, col. i 14 ff. (the beginning of Nabonidus' campaign to Tema' in Kislev in the 3rd year of his reign); *GCCI* I, 294 (the dispatch of a camel bearing food for Nabonidus from Erech to Tema' in Adar in the 5th year of Nabonidus' reign).

44 See Musil, *The Manners and Customs of the Rwala Bedouins,* New York 1928, 44-45; cf. likewise Ezek. 27:21: "The Arabs and all the princes of Qedar were your favored dealers in lambs, rams and goats, in these they trafficked with you".

kingdoms of Israel and Damascus; see pp. 94-100.

2. Because various military and economic matters discussed in this study devolve upon the road network in northern Arabia, we shall describe its essential points and note some historical conclusions. These routes are charted by means of the large oases, which were hubs of economic activity and often also of administration and worship.

As noted above, the great sand desert of Nafūd (about 57,000 km^2) is difficult to traverse, and, except by a detour east or west of it, impossible from the southwestern part of the Arabian peninsula, the home of myrrh and frankincense and other goods, to the countries of the Fertile Crescent. The branch-off point for the road from southern Arabia to these countries is Yathrib (Medina), from which the following routes set out:

Route 1: Yathrib-Ḥā'il-an-Najaf (about 1060 kms.). At the northern end this road forks into secondary routes leading to points farther east, such as ad-Diwanieh, as-Samawa and even Ur.

Route 2: Yathrib-Khaybar-Fadak-Tema' → a) Dumah-Babylon (in all 1530 kms.); → b) Tabūk-Ma'ān (in all 860 kms.); → c) The western part of Wadi Sirḥān (an-Nabk or Bā'ir) - 'Ammān.[45]
The three alternatives after Tema' were all main routes.

Route 3: Yathrib-Dedan (al-'Ulā)-Tabūk-Ma'ān (760 kms.)

We do not know whether in the first half of the first millennium B.C. the goods of southern Arabia reached the Persian Gulf zone via Route 1, but references to spices and gold in the booty and tribute taken by Sennacherib and Esarhaddon from the Arabs in the Dumah area indicate that large quantities of these goods did reach Babylonia via Route 2.[46]

As to the western part of the Fertile Crescent , Tema' and Dedan (al-'Ulā) were clearly important stations along the alternative Routes 2 and 3, both of which start at Yathrib and converge at Tabūk. All goods

45 For accounts of Arab geographers and writers on the use of the 'Ammān—An-Nabk (or Bā'īr)—Tema' branch, see Musil, *Arabia Deserta,* 516-518.

46 Sennacherib: K 8544 rev. 5; Esarhaddon: Heidel Prism iii 6-8 (cf. also Nin. A iv 20-22).

passing through Tabūk continued to Ma'ān. From there, the roads forked westward to the ports of southern Philistia and apparently also to Egypt, through the "central axis" of the Sinai peninsula.[47] Another branch continued northwards from Ma'ān to 'Ammān and then diverged to Tyre (through the kingdom of Israel) and Damascus. As we have seen, a branch of Route 2 also connected Tema' with 'Amman by skirting Tabūk and Ma'ān to the east.

Tema', it can be seen, was a central station on the Arabian trade routes both to Babylonia and the western part of the Fertile Crescent, while Dedan (al-'Ulā) was central only on the route to the western part of the Crescent.

The Elath-Ma'ān-'Ammān-Damascus route absorbed all the goods arriving from southern Arabia by sea or land and destined for the countries of the western part of the Fertile Crescent, Asia Minor and the countries of the Mediterranean. The three trade centers fed by this artery were Gaza, Tyre and Damascus. There is no doubt that the wars in Transjordan were in great degree fomented by the huge revenues and the politico-economic status resulting from control of this route. This consideration was certainly at the bottom of the aspirations of the kings of Damascus, whose initial goal was the domination of the crossroads in Gilead where the roads to Tyre branch off, and whose final goal was control of the 'Ammān-Ma'ān-Elath section as well. Their aspiration was fulfilled only in the time of Rezin, some two years before the final dissolution of Aram-Damascus (II Kings 16:6).[47a] Control by a single political authority of the three western outlets for Arabian trade (southern Philistia, Tyre and Damascus) — a situation which obtained during most of the period we are concerned with — eventuated in considerable influence on the conduct of the Arabian trade, because all the parties involved were compelled to come to an arrangement with it.

We have no written data or archaeological finds from the first half of the first millennium B.C. relating to Arabian trade to the western part of the Fertile Crescent.[48] The published surveys on the conduct of this

47 Y. Karmon, *Studies in the Geography of Israel* 6 (1968), 58-59.

47a For a different interpretation of II Kings 16:6 see H. Tadmor-M. Cogan, *Biblica* 60 (1979), 491-499.

48 Some scholars believe that a South Arabian stamp, published among the objects from Bethel, testifies to Arabian trade connections with the kingdom of Israel in

trade — the most detailed of which are those of Grohmann and Van Beek — are based mainly on hints and general descriptions in the works of classical authors such as Strabo and Pliny.[49] Up to now, the enormous amount of material gathered by Musil from itineraries and other works of medieval Arab writers has not been used for the study of the Arabian trade routes.[50] These sources show a ramified network of routes to Mecca and Medina travelled by Moslem pilgrims from Iraq, Syria and Egypt. Since the Arabian trade involved considerable costs paid at every station along the routes,[51] there was undoubtedly a desire for economic profit and political advantage from alternative utilization of the various trade routes. It is therefore obvious that research into the factors affecting the Arabian trade demands thorough study, not only of medieval Arabic sources, but of the routes from Medina to the countries of the Fertile Crescent.

The shortest route from the west to the east of the Fertile Crescent goes through Wadi Sirḥān and is about 1200 kms., as compared with the 1800 kms. through the Crescent itself. The importance of Dumah (Dūmat al-Jandal, al-Jauf) lies in the fact that it is the largest oasis in the bottleneck of Wadi Sirḥān. The inscriptions of the Assyrian kings regarding Sennacherib's wars against the Arabs indicate that the Assyrian army reached Dumah,[52] proof of its exceptional mobility in the desert. Nevertheless, it must be assumed that the army arrived at

about the 9th century B.C. (G.W. Van Beek-A. Jamme, *BASOR* 151 [1958], 9-16; 163 [1961], 15-18; J.L. Kelso, *AASOR* 39 [1968], 89), but Y. Yadin objects convincingly that it was found not at Bethel but in South Arabia (*BASOR* 196 [1969], 37-45). On the dispute over this question see also Van Beek-Jamme, *BASOR* 199 (1970), 59-65; Kelso, *BASOR* 199 (1970), 65. Among later objects indicating contact between South Arabia and southern Palestine, one should mention a 6tn century B.C. inscribed Minaean monogram on a jar at Ezion-geber (Tell el-Kheleifeh), stratum IV (N. Glueck, *Yediot* 31 [1967], 125), and a painted South Arabic monogram, probably from the 3rd-2nd centuries B.C., on a storage jar from Tell Jemmeh (Van Beek, *IEJ* 22 [1972], 246).

49 A. Grohmann, *Südarabien als Wirtschaftsgebiet*, II, Wien 1933, 116-124; Van Beek, *JAOS* 78 (1958), 145; idem, *BA* 23 (1960), 75-77.

50 Musil, *Arabia Deserta*, 516-531; *Northern Neğd*, 205-212; *Northern Ḥeğâz*, 326-331.

51 An instructive description of the transport of incense from southern Arabia to the Mediterranean Sea and of the payments for water, fodder, lodging and customs duties at the posts along the marketing routes in given by Pliny, *Nat. Hist.* XII, 32.

52 see pp. 118-121.

Dumah during a suitable season, and was relatively small, just large enough to overcome the local Arabs. We have no information, however, about the movement of large military units and war machines from Babylonia to the western part of the Fertile Crescent through Wadi Sirḥān, making it apparent that the difficulties of terrain outweighed the shortening of the distance.

PART ONE
THE AKKADIAN AND BIBLICAL SOURCES

The Akkadian and Biblical Sources

This study is based on sources of various kinds: historical (including annalistic and other Assyrian and Babylonian royal inscriptions, Babylonian chronicles, parts of the historical books of the Bible, and classical works as well), administrative and economic documents, a treaty between Assurbanipal and the Qedarites, short commemorative inscriptions from North Arabia, prophetic literature, etc. Each of these categories is further divisible.

Also in our possession are reliefs from the palaces of Tiglath-Pileser III and Assurbanipal, occasionally depicting their dealings with the Arabs. The chief value of these reliefs lies in their inclusion of material and cultural details generally absent from written sources or at best barely hinted at. Relevant details are referred to in the notes.

The Akkadian documents constitute our chief source material from the point of view both of general information and chronological data. They are described in Part One where each of the sources is evaluated in order to determine its proper use.

Important information, especially ethnological, is to be found in the Bible. The considerable heterogeneity of the various biblical sources demands special examination of each of them in Part One.

It seems unnecessary to deal separately here with the classical and North Arabian sources, which are described in other parts of the book according to the following criteria:

1. Some of the classical works containing information about the Arabs, such as those of Diodorus Siculus, Strabo and Pliny, postdate the period dealt with here by hundreds of years, and there is no way of determining whether the economic and demographic conditions they describe apply to our period. This is a vital point, because the emergence of the Nabataeans and the onset of the Hellenistic era marked the beginning of crucial changes in the political and social structure, administration and economy. Historical conclusions with chronological implications have therefore been based only on classical authors such as Herodotus and Xenophon, who were contemporary with our period. At the same time, the later works are useful for typological comparisons.

2. Since the North Arabian inscriptions do not constitute a uniform body of material which can be treated inclusively, each inscription and its problems is considered where it appears in the context of our historical investigation.

Chapter I

AKKADIAN SOURCES

1. ROYAL INSCRIPTIONS

A. THE MONOLITH INSCRIPTION FROM KURKH OF SHALMANESER III

The Monolith Inscription from Kurkh contains details of the first six years of the reign of Shalmaneser III, including his battle at Qarqar in his sixth regnal year (853 B.C.).[53] At the end of the list of the coalition leaders and their armies opposing him at Qarqar, chief among whom were Adad-'idri (Hadadezer) of Damascus, Irḫuleni of Hamath, and Ahab the Israelite, come Gindibu' the Arab and his 1000 camels (III R 8 ii, 94: *1 lim* anše*gam-ma-lu ša* m*Gi-in-di-bu-'* kur*Ar-ba-a-a*). The Monolith Inscription is the only documentation of the battle of Qarqar listing the allied armies and their composition, and the names of most of the leaders; other later inscriptions dealing with the same battle note only the names of Adad-'idri and Irḫuleni, and refer to the rest vaguely as "the twelve kings of (Ḫatti and) the seacoast".

B. INSCRIPTIONS OF TIGLATH-PILESER III

The inscriptions are in two distinct groups:

1. The Annals, in which the chronological sequence is retained in the account of each consecutive year;

53 On the battle of Qarqar see A. Amiaud-V. Scheil, *Les inscriptions de Salmanasar II, roi d'Assyrie,* Paris 1890, 40-41. For translation of the Monolith Inscription from Kurkh see *AR* I, § 594-611; *ANET,* 277-279. On the nature of this document see A.T. Olmstead, *Assyrian Historiography,* Columbia, Miss. 1916, 22-23; H. Tadmor, *IEJ* 11 (1961), 144-145.

2. Non-annalistic inscriptions usually called "Display Inscriptions" (*Prunkinschriften*)[54] and, more recently, Summary Inscriptions.[55] These are arranged geographically, or in accordance with the importance of various events in particular districts, rather than in strict chronological order.[56] The details of wars and other events derive from the Annals; these inscriptions are therefore of some help in the reconstruction of broken or missing passages of the Annals. The fragments of Annals which have come down to us are few and incomplete and contain little on the Arabs. Most of our knowledge is therefore based on the Summary Inscriptions, the Annals providing a chronological framework. Our description and evaluation of the sources will take into account the distinction between the two types of inscription.

1. **The Annals:** Tiglath-Pileser's Annals, incised on stone slabs, were removed from the walls of his palace at Calah (Nimrud), where they were first installed, to be re-used in other structures. They were discovered by A.H. Layard, partly in the Southwestern Palace whose construction was begun in the days of Esarhaddon, and partly in the Central Palace. Because the slabs were neither found *in situ* nor in their original order, and because they constitute only a small portion of the Annals, with far more missing than available, problems have arisen in regard to the order of the slabs and the continuity of the text. A critical edition — the only one so far — of Tiglath-Pileser's Annals was published by P. Rost.[57] It is quite deficient from the methodological point of view: Despite the existence of several series of Annals, Rost presented an eclectic version based on the fragments from various slabs and on reconstructions of missing passages; the beginning and end of each slab are not indicated, nor are parallel versions supplied. The text

54 The basic distinction between the Annals and the "Display Inscriptions" was first made by Eb. Schrader, *Zur Kritik der Inschriften Tiglath-Pileser's II, des Asarhaddon und des Asurbanipal,* Berlin 1880, 13-14. In the same vein see also Olmstead, *ibid.,* 32-35.

55 For this term see Tadmor, *Iraq* 35 (1973), 141; L.D. Levine, *Iran* 11 (1973), 2.

56 The attempt of E.R. Thiele, *The Mysterious Numbers of the Hebrew Kings*^{2}, Grand Rapids, Mich. 1965, 104 ff., to show that in the Summary Inscriptions of Tiglath-Pileser events appear in chronological order does not stand up under detailed analysis of all the historical inscriptions of this king.

57 Rost, *Die Keilschrifttexte Tiglath-Pilesers III,* Bd. I-II, Leipzig 1893.

is given consecutively and does not show the disjointed condition of the annalistic material. Parts of the text in his edition also suffer from unfounded reconstructions and emendations. H. Tadmor recently examined the copies, now in the British Museum, of the slabs which Layard and G. Smith made when they were discovered, and classified the Annals in five series (each representing a hall in the palace of Tiglath-Pileser).[58] Tadmor also determined the extent and location of the gaps in the various series.[59] His research shows that the order of events and their chronology in Rost's edition is often erroneous as a result of faulty methodology. In our consideration of the passages from the Annals dealing with the Arabs, we have adopted Tadmor's classification of the various slabs and editions:[60]

a) **Rost, Ann., 150-157** (= *ITP*, Ann. 13:10—14:5) — **This passage** occurs in two series of Annals, as follows:

Series A — divided between two slabs:

Rost, *Ann.* 149-155 (Pls. IV and V) = Lay. $69b_2$+$69a_1$

Rost, *Ann.* 155-161 (Pls. VI and VII) = Lay. $69a_2$+68b

Series B — divided between two slabs:

Rost, *Ann.* 141-152 (Pl. XV) = Lay. 50a

Rost, *Ann.* 153-164 (Pl. XVI) = Lay. 50b+67a

Lines 150-157 deal with the tribute to Tiglath-Pileser paid by various rulers in the west, among whom was Zabibê, queen of the Arabs. Line 157 begins a new detail preceded by the date: Tiglath-Pileser's ninth *palû* (regnal year). The tribute in lines 150-157 can therefore be set in Tiglath-Pileser's eighth *palû,* which was 738 B.C.[61]

The same tribute is also mentioned on a broken stele of Tiglath-

58 Tadmor, *Introductory Remarks to ... the Annals of Tiglath-Pileser III, Proceedings of the Israeli Academy of Sciences and Humanities,* Vol II, No. 9 (1967).

59 *Ibid.,* 18-19.

60 I am most grateful to Prof. H. Tadmor, who was kind enough to let me have copies of Lay. 66 and Lay 29b from Layard's notebook before their forthcoming publication; and also for his help in clarifying various matters connected with the investigation of the Tiglath-Pileser inscriptions. In those cases where this study departs from his opinion the responsibility is entirely mine.

61 For a detailed discussion of the time of this tribute and its place in the history of the kingdoms of Palestine and Syria, see Tadmor, *Scripta Hierosolymitana* 8 (1961), 248-265; M. Weippert, *ZDPV* 89 (1973), 26-53.

Pileser recently found in Iran, in which the record of this episode is generally similar to that in the Nimrud Annals.[62] In the stele, however, the Qedarites (who do not appear in the Annals) are mentioned along with the Arabs, and the name of the king of Tyre is given as ^{m}*Tu-ba-ilu* instead of ^{m}*Ḫi-ru-um-mu,* as in the Annals.

b) **Lay. 29b** (=Rost, *Ann.,* 229-240; *ITP,* Ann.18) — This slab is part of Series C_1. Line 230 mentions districts of the land of *Bīt* ^{m}... . Despite the difficulty of reconstructing this toponym, a comparison of the slab with Lay. 72b+73a (partly parallel to Lay. 29b, see below) seems to indicate either that lines 229-230 are the end of a passage describing 16 districts of the kingdom of Damascus, or that the description of Tiglath-Pileser's campaign in Galilee starts with line 230 and continues in lines 231-234. From line 235 on, the text is fragmentary, with more missing than extant, and the contents are largely guesswork. Lines 235-237 state that Mitinti of Ashkelon broke his oath to the king of Assyria and met his death in the aftermath of the defeat of Rezin (apparently after a local *coup d'état)* and was succeeded by Rukibti.[63] Of the next three lines we have only the following framents: "(238) ... and he implored me. 500 ... (239) ... and entered (TU-*ub*) into his city.[64] 15 cit[ies] ... (240) ... Idibi'ilu the Arab (*[I]-di-bi-'-i-lu* ^{kur}*A-ru-bu*) ...".

Although it is difficult to draw definite conclusions because of the fragmentary condition of the text, it seems unlikely that the last three lines concern the punishment of Ashkelon for the Mitinti revolt: annexing 15 towns from its territory to that of Idibi'ilu the Arab.[65]

62 Levine, *Two Neo-Assyrian Stelae From Iran,* Toronto 1972, 18-20; cf. idem, *BASOR* 206 (1972), 40-42; Weippert, *ibid.,* esp. 29-32.

63 Although in Layard's copy of Lay. 29b appreciable portions of these lines did not survive, including the names of the kings of Ashkelon, it is possible to reconstruct part of the text, as was done by Rost, after G. Smith, *Assyrian Discoveries*², London 1875, 283-284 (Eleventh fragment). The method of reconstruction is important for the assumption that the list of tributaries in K 3751 rev. 7'-12', is made up of various lists and does not refer exclusively to 738 B.C.; see also note 76.

64 TU-*ub* may be read *ērub*^{ub}, "I entered", or *īrub*^{ub}, "he entered". The difference is important for an understanding of the event discussed in these passages, but we cannot decide which is the correct reading.

65 See, e.g. S.A. Cook, *CAH,* III, 382; Alt, *Kleine Schriften,* II, 237, note 5; III, 420, note 1, with whose opinion we disagree; and in contradistinction, Tadmor, in *Military History,* 267-268.

There was no common frontier between Ashkelon and the territory of Idibi'ilu, who lived on "the border of Egypt",[66] since the kingdom of Gaza lay between them. The more probable inference is that lines 238-239 still deal with Ashkelon, and perhaps report the amount of the gift (500 ...) which Rukibti gave Tiglath-Pileser in return for his consent to rule in Ashkelon, while line 240 begins a separate passage on Idibi'ilu the Arab, of which only the first few words are extant.

c) **Lay. 72b+73a** (=Rost, *Ann.* 191-210; *ITP,* Ann. 23) — This slab is part of Tadmor's Series C. Layard's copy of it contains a fragment of another slab erroneously joined to it, either by Layard or by the original scribe. This fragment, which is placed at the end of the lines of Lay. 72b + 73a and duplicates in part the account of Lay. 29b (Rost, *Ann.* 229-237),[67] will henceforth be referred to as "line endings". In Rost's edition the fragment was not presented separately, in Tadmor's it is Ann. 24. Only a few signs survived from each line; what has been saved, however, is of importance because of its reference to the kingdom of Damascus, the Galilee and Ashkelon.

Lay. 72b+73a, except for the last line, is devoted to a description of Tiglath-Pileser's war against Rezin, in the course of which the Aramaean army was beaten, Rezin was besieged in Damascus, various cities including Rezin's birthplace were conquered, and captives and booty taken from them. The description ends with a tally of 591 ruined cities in 16 districts of the kingdom of Damascus. What we have of Rost, line 210, the last on the slab, says: "Samsi queen of the Arabs, who violated the oath (that she swore by) Shamash..." and evidently the continuation of the text deals with Tiglath-Pileser's reaction to Samsi's disloyalty.

In the detailed description on this slab of the actions against the kingdom of Damascus there is no explicit reference to the conquest of Damascus proper and the slaying of Rezin (cf. II King 16:9), which can be dated 732 B.C.,[68] or to the annexation of Damascus to the Assyrian

66 Cf. K 3751 rev. 6; and also Lay. 66:16 (= Rost, *Ann.,* 226).

67 See Tadmor, in H.Z. Hirschberg (ed.), *All the Land of Naphtali,* Jerusalem 1967, 64, note 22 (Hebrew).

68 The Eponym Chronicle, *RLA,* II, 431, notes that the main activity of the Assyrian army in 733-732 B.C. was "against (the land of) Damascus" (*ana* [kur]*Dimašqa*), and it is reasonable to assume that the capture of Damascus and Rezin's death occurred in the final stages of the war, i.e. in 732 B.C.

provincial system. The date of the events recorded on the slab, including the section in Samsi queen of the Arabs, should be as early as 733 B.C. when the war against Damascus began.

A comparison of the structure of the last two slabs in regard to the topics covered gives us the following picture:

Lay. 29b	**"Line Endings" in Lay. 72b+73a**	**Main Text of Lay. 72b+73a**
The kingdom of Damascus **(or Bīt Ḫumri)**	Damascus	Damascus
The kingdom of Israel	The kingdom of Israel	—
Ashkelon	Ashkelon	—
Idibi'ilu	—	—
		Samsi

The discrepancy in the topics covered, although apparently contradicting the assumption that the various series of the annals of Tiglath-Pileser are parallel recensions of the same text, each of which was affixed to the walls of different halls in his palace,[69] can be eliminated if we assume one of the following:

a) One of the slabs should be classified as a Summary Inscription, in Tadmor's terminology, rather than Annals; consequently in only one is a chronological account given. This assumption is difficult to accept, for both slabs clearly exemplify annalistic writing, such as listing town names and the number of prisoners taken.

b) The two slabs do not refer to the same period. Since the report in Lay. 72b+73a accords with the events of 733 B.C., it is possible that Lay. 29b refers to the end of that year or, which is more likely, to 732 B.C. This assumption makes it necessary to set Tiglath-Pileser's campaign to Galilee described in Lay. 29b at the end of 733 B.C., or in 732 B.C., close to the time of the *coups d'état* and replacement of kings in Samaria and Ashkelon.[70] It also dates the campaign against Samsi to

69 On this assumption see Tadmor, *Introductory Remarks,* 10 ff. (In his final edition, however, Tadmor has modified his views).

70 For the dating of Pekah's death and Hoshea's rise to kingship in 732 B.C. see

733 B.C. after she had broken her oath of allegiance to Tiglath-Pileser; in other words, before Damascus had finally been subdued by the Assyrian army, a campaign apparently not connected with the later assignment of Idibi'ilu to the Egyptian border.

2. **Summary Inscriptions:** All the available Summary Inscriptions of Tiglath-Pileser touching on the nomads on the borders of Palestine were found in Nimrud. Two (III R 10,2 and Lay. 66) were written on stone slabs and displayed on palace walls, three (ND 400; K 3751; ND 4301+4305), on clay tablets, were probably drafts for an official Summary Inscription. Every one of the five texts is defective, but the surviving sections all follow the same literary pattern, and large sections of the actual wording are identical (see pp. 33-35). It is therefore possible to reconstruct the missing parts in each by referring to the others. A comparison of the identical passages also permits improved readings of signs and correction of errors made by editors who published each of the texts separately. The clay tablets have dividing lines which separate the various items, thus making it possible to distinguish between various episodes written successively on the stone slabs (where no mark either between or within the lines indicate that one episode has ended and another has begun). This distinction is especially important in the Summary Inscriptions: Since they were arranged in geographical, rather than chronological, order, it is easy to err and assume a connection between episodes concerning adjacent regions, when actually there is a time difference involved.

First we shall describe the Summary Inscriptions and their contents, stressing the parts which concern nomads. We shall subsequently provide a reconstruction of the passages on nomads by putting together the fragments of these inscriptions.

a) **III R 10, 2** (=Rost, *Kleinere Inschriften; ITP,* Summ. 4).[71] This is a 38-line inscription on a stone slab, describing in detail Tiglath-Pileser's

Tadmor, "Chronology", *Enc. Miqr.,* IV, 287. As has been said above, there was a connection between the removal of Mitinti from the kingship of Ashkelon and "the defeat of Rezin" (Lay. 29b; Rost, *Ann.* 235-237). But it is not clear whether this statement refers to Rezin's final defeat, in which Damascus was captured and its king put to death (see note 68), or to a previous defeat on the battlefield as a result of which Rezin retreated and was besieged in Damascus; see also pp. 83-84.

71 Rost, *op. cit.,* 78 ff.; cf. *AR* I, § 815 ff. The text begins with Ḫatarikka and lacks the

activities in Syria and in Palestine and its environs, divided as follows:

lines	1-8:	Northern Syria, the coastal cities of Phoenicia and the kingdom of Damascus;[72]
	8-15:	Gaza;
	15-19:	The kingdom of Israel;
	19-26:	Samsi queen of the Arabs;
	27-33:	The surrender of various nomad tribes;[73]
	34:	The assignment of Idibi'ilu to the Egyptian border;
	35-38:	The text is fragmentary and its subject unclear.

b) **K 3751 (=II R, 67)** (=Rost, *Thontafelinschrift; ITP,* Summ. 7).[74] This is a clay tablet, about half of which has been preserved, inscribed on both sides, summarizing the first 17 years of Tiglath-Pileser's reign (cf. obv., 5). On the obverse, which begins with the introduction

introductions usual in the Annals and other Summary Inscriptions of Tiglath-Pileser, indicating that III R 10,2 is part of a larger inscription which covered a number of slabs.

Tadmor has found in G. Smith's notebooks the original drafts of the text on which III R 10,2 is based. Certain signs in this draft vary from those in the final III R 10, 2 publication.

72 On the reconstruction *[māt Bīt* ^m^*Ḫaza'i]li* in line 7, and the conclusion that lines 6-8 refer to the kingdom of Damascus, see Tadmor, *IEJ* 12 (1962), 114-122.

73 G. Smith's reconstruction of the left part of line 27 in III R 10,2 has ^{lú}ÉRIN-'*-a-a a-na šepâ*^{II}*-ia ú-šak-niš,* taken from Lay. 66:7-8 (cf. *Ann.*, 217-218); cf. note 71. This reading gave rise to the assumption that the words refer to the subjugation of a nomad group, separate from the various groups listed in lines 27-28. Their suggested name was ^{lú}*Bir-'-a-a* (see Rost, p. 36; *ANET,* 283) or ^{lú}Ṣab-'*-a-a* (Albright, *Levi della Vida Festschrift*, 4). An examination of the original copy of Lay. 66 shows, however, nothing but ^{lú}ÉRIN [... *ana* GÌR]^{II} *-ia*,*ú-šak-[niš].* Because of the words 10 LIM ^{lú}ÉRIN^{meš} ... in ND 4301 + 4305 rev. 22, which parallel III R 10,2:27, and the small space they occupy in line 27, there is no reason to look for a new and independent matter in this part of the line. It is preferable to ascribe the words to the end of the former passage on Samsi queen of the Arabs. (In his edition Tadmor suggests that 10 LIM were omitted in Lay. 66, thus explaining Smith's attempt to take ^{lú}ÉRIN.MEŠ as a name of an Arab tribe).

74 Rost, *ibid.* 54 ff.; cf. *AR* I, § 787 ff. On the structure of this document and its character as a historical source, see Olmstead, *Assyrian Historiography,* 33-35; W. Schramm, *Einleitung in die assyrischen Königsinschriften,* II, Leiden-Köln 1973, 133-135; Weippert, *ZDPV* 89 (1973), 52-53.

formula of the inscription, 50 lines have survived, and on the reverse, 35. The passage referring to Arabs consists of five lines at the beginning of the reverse, as follows:

rev., 1': (indecipherable);
2': A passage on Samsi queen of the Arabs,[75] the end of which is indicated by a dividing line;
3'-5': The surrender of various nomad tribes;
6': The assignment of Idibi'ilu to the border of Egypt.
7'-13': Receipt of tribute from various western kings, among them kings of Asia Minor, Phoenicia and Palestine.[76]

A dividing line follows line 13'. The political events mentioned thereafter (the removal of Uassurme of Tabal, who was listed in line 9' above among Tiglath-Pileser's tributaries, and the receipt of tribute from Metenna of Tyre) deviate from the geographical order of the rest of the inscription and are apparently later additions to the original version of the text.[77]

c) **ND 400** (=*ITP,* Summ. 8) — This is a fragment of a clay tablet containing bits from the surviving 27 lines.[78] The document is organized as follows:

75 See note 73.

76 This section (lines 7'-13') is obviously based on the merging of lists of tributaries to Tiglath-Pileser under various circumstances. Thus it is possible to discern that the names in lines 7'-9', even though the final names in each line are missing, were copied from the list of tributaries of 738 B.C. (cf. Rost, *Ann.,* 150-154). On the other hand, lines 10'-12' mention the kings of Arvad, Ammon, Moab, Ashkelon, Judah, Edom, Gaza and of two other places whose names did not survive in the text. These kings, who are not mentioned in the Annals relating to 738 B.C., apparently did not pay tribute before 734 B.C., when Tiglath-Pileser's army first reached Palestine (for the dating of the tribute of Mitinti king of Ashkelon in 734 and perhaps the beginning of 733 B.C., see pp. 83-84.

77 See Olmstead, *Assyrian Historiography,* 34. Also, in ND 4301+4305 discussed below, the Uassurme of Tabal episode comes after the passage about Damascus, Tyre and Palestine as far as its southern border.

78 Published by D.J. Wiseman, *Iraq* 13 (1951), 21-24. Wiseman (p. 21, note 2) points out the similarity between the writing in this tablet and K 3751 and suggests that they may have been written by the same scribe. The document has been re-edited by Tadmor, *Liver Memorial Volume,* 222-230.

lines 1'-9': Military actions against an island city (evidently Tyre whose King Hiram cooperated with Rezin of Damascus),[79] from which tribute was received after its king surrendered. Part of its territory had been annexed to the realm of the governor of the province of Ṣimirra.

10'-13': War against a country whose name has not survived and the retrieval of booty from it. In view of the conventional geographical order in the Summary Inscriptions, it can be assumed that this was the kingdom of Damascus, one of the city-states of Phoenicia, or the kingdom of Israel.

14'-18': Subjecting of Gaza, taking booty and captives from it, and setting up an image of Tiglath-Pileser.

18'-19': Setting up a stele in the town of Naḫal-Muṣur ("town of the Brook-of-Egypt"); the transfer of booty to Assyria. A dividing line follows.

20'-21': The surrender of a king whose name has not survived in the inscription, and whose emissaries (LÚ.MAḪ.MEŠ = ^{lú}*ṣirāni*) were sent to Tiglath-Pileser for the purpose of "doing servitude" while he "did not humble himself nor send messengers to the kings, my predecessors".[80]

22'-23': The surrender(?) of Siruatti the Me'unite "whose (territory) is below Egypt".[81]

24'-27': Samsi queen of the Arabs.

79 Compare ND 4301+4305 rev. 5'-8'.

80 This matter is also discussed in a parallel section in ND 4301+4305 rev. 23'-25'. From both sources it becomes clear that the king discussed was in Palestine or near it. The geographical order in ND 400 makes it possible to locate him near the town of Naḫal-Muṣur and in the area of the Me'unites, i.e. northern Sinai, and to consider him a nomad leader there. On the other hand, the geographical order in ND 4301+4305, where he is mentioned after Samsi queen of the Arabs, whose territory was east of Palestine, makes such a location unlikely. Since it is said that he sent his messenger to Calah to announce his submission to the king of Assyria, his identification as a nomad leader is questionable. Can the reference here be to Ahaz king of Judah (cf. II Kings 16:7-8; II Chron. 28:16)?

81 *ša* KI.TA (=*šapal*) ^{kur}*⌈Mu-uṣ-ri⌉* (for this reading see Tadmor, above, note 78. For the meaning of this expression, see pp. 91, 219-220.

d) **ND 4301 + 4305** (= *ITP*, Summ. 9) — There are two "joins" of a clay tablet inscribed on both sides.[82] On the reverse are 37 fragmentary lines dealing with various events in the western part of the empire during Tiglath-Pileser's reign. The document has a dividing line after every detail listed below:

rev., 1'-2': The inclusion in the territory of Assyria of the provinces of Ḫatarikka and Ṣimirra.[83]

3'-4': The annexation of the kingdom of Damascus (^{kur}*Bīt Ḫaza'ili*) to the territory of Assyria.[84]

5'-8': The subjugation of King Hiram of Tyre.

9'-11': The text is almost completely destroyed and not a single proper name has survived. The words in line 10' — "... I set as king over them..." — and the geographical sequence in the inscription as a whole leads us to conclude that the passage dealt with the kingdom of Israel, and that line 10' refers to the installation of Hoshea instead of Pekah.[85]

12': Taking booty from a place whose name has not been preserved.[86]

13'-16': The subjugation of Gaza.

17'-22': Samsi queen of the Arabs.

23'-25': The surrender of a king (whose name has not been preserved) "who had not submitted to the kings, my predecessors".[87]

82 Published by Wiseman, *Iraq* 18 (1956), 117-129.

83 See K. Kessler, *WO* 8 (1975), 56-63.

84 On this passage see Tadmor, *IEJ* 12 (1962), 114-122.

85 Cf. III R 10,2:17-18.

86 From the list of booty there survive: [1]00 talents of silver. The assumption that this phrase refers to tax from Ahaz king of Judah (Wiseman, *Iraq* 18 [1956], 121) or from the cities of Philistia (E.Vogt, *Biblica* 45 [1964], 351) does not seem likely. The verb *nasāḫu* in this line denotes taking by force (see *AHw*, 750) and accords with taking of booty in a military action, not receiving tribute, usually denoted by the verb *maḫāru*. This line can be compared with ND 400:19: ... *kaspa assuḫamma ana* ^{kur}*Aššur*^{ki}, making it possible to assume that ND 4301+4305 rev. 12' refers to booty taken by Tiglath-Pileser in the region of Naḫal-Muṣur.

87 See note 80.

line 26': A fragment of a tribute list, of which only the words "... 50 talents of gold, 2000 talents of silver..." remain. Since the description of Tiglath-Pileser's activities in that area ends at this point, the large amount of gold and silver may indicate that this was the total tribute (and booty?) which he took from Palestine or perhaps from the entire western part of his empire.

The text from line 27' on (starting with the removal of Uassurme of Tabal) does not follow the geographical order of the document as a whole and was evidently added to the first edition of the text (cf. above, K 3751:14 ff.).

e) **Lay. 66** (=Rost, *Ann.,* 211-228; *ITP,* Summ. 13) — Most of the slab is damaged. The contents divide as follows:

lines 1'-2': (Rost, *Ann.,* 211-212): End of a passage about bringing tribute to Calah.

3'-7': (Rost, *Ann.,* 213-217): Samsi queen of the Arabs.[88]

8'-15': (Rost, *Ann.,* 218-225): The surrender of various nomad tribes and the receipt of tribute from them.

16': (Rost, *Ann.,* 226): The assignment of Idibi'ilu to the Egyptian border.

17'-18': (Rost, *Ann.,* 227-228): What is left of these lines mentions earlier military campaigns of Tiglath-Pileser (*[i]na girrēteya maḫrāte*), taking booty, and sparing Samaria. The continuation probably dealt with a specific action toward the kingdom of Israel, preceded by Tiglath-Pileser's other campaigns and military actions against it.

The passages in Lay. 66 dealing with Samsi queen of the Arabs, with the nomad tribes and with Idibi'ilu are identical with those in Tiglath-Pileser's Summary Inscriptions. Nonetheless, whether this document is of the annalistic or Summary Inscription type — that is, whether the events described were in their proper chronological order — is uncertain. If indeed Lay. 66 is arranged strictly chronologically, one encounters a certain difficulty in reconstructing the sequence of events: Samsi's violation of her allegiance to the Assyrian king, which is treated in Lay. 72b+73a, has been dated by us to 733 B.C. Similary, we have

88 See note 73.

noted above that Tiglath-Pileser's campaign to Galilee described in Lay. 29b was conducted after his campaign against Samsi (i.e. at the end of 733 or in 732 B.C.).[89] However, the reference to *previous campaigns* against the kingdom of Israel in Lay. 66, following a notation on the punitive campaigns against Samsi, compels us to postulate at least two campaigns against Israel *before* the Galilee campaign, a conclusion not in accord with what we know about Tiglath-Pileser's Palestinian campaigns. On the other hand, if Lay. 66 is classified as a Summary Inscription, we face an irregular geographical order: the kingdom of Israel is placed *after* the Arabs (Samsi, the nomad tribes and Idibi'ilu), an order not attested in other Summary Inscriptions of Tigalth-Pileser. Since we have insufficient data for classifying Lay. 66, we shall use it exclusively for textual purposes and refrain from chronological conclusions on the basis of its contents.[90]

f) A comparison of passages from the Summary Inscriptions of Tiglath-Pileser dealing with nomads on the borders of Palestine (as noted above, this includes passages in Lay. 66 as well) makes it clear that they are all based on one *vorlage.* It is therefore permissible to reconstruct a fuller version of the original text by combining the fragments of parallel passages in the various inscriptions. The skeleton for the reconstruction is provided by III R 10, 2, which has preserved the longest text on the nomads. The reconstructed text of the source discussed is as follows:[(1)]

19) [(2)]*ša* [f]*Sa-am-si šar-rat* KUR *A-ri-bi ina* KUR *Sa-qu-ur-ri* KUR-*e*

20) 9 LIM 4 ME *di-ik-ta-[šu-nu a]-duk* 1 LIM x ME UN[meš] 30 LIM ANŠE.A.AB.BA[meš] 20 LIM GU$_4$.NITÁ[meš]

89 For the chronology of the events described in Lay. 29b and Lay. 72b+73a, see above pp. 25-27.

90 In the *Introductory Remarks,* 13, Tadmor assigned Lay. 66 to the Annals category, although with reservations, considering it a single remnant from a special series (Series E). He noted that events are not in actual chronological order in this slab, but believed that it is closer in form and content to the Annals than to the Summary Inscriptions. In his forthcoming edition of the inscriptions of Tiglath-Pileser, however, he has re-classified it, taking the slab as a special, much shorter category of a Summary Inscription.

21) [ ] 5 LIM ŠIM^{ḫá} DÙ.A-*ma x tu-⌈u⌉ né-mat-ti* DINGIR^{meš}*-ni-šá*

22) ^{giš}*til-li* ^{giš}NÍG.PA^{meš} ^{d}*Iš-tar-šá* [NÍG.]GA-*šá e-kim-ši ù ši-i a-na šu-zu-ub* ZI^{meš}-*šá*

23) [. . . . . *ana ma-a]d-ba-ar a-šar ṣu-ma-me* GIM ^{sal}ANŠE.EDIN.NA[2],[3]

24) *taš-ku-na pa-ni-šá si-ta-[at kulta]-ri-šá ḫu-ra-da-at* UN^{meš}-*šá i-na* MÚRU[4] KI.KAL.BAD[5]-*šá*

25) *ina* IZI *áš-ru-[up u* ^{f}*Samsi ša lapān* ^{giš}TUKUL]^{meš}-*ia* KALAG^{meš} *taš-ḫu-tú-ma* ANŠE.A.AB.BA^{meš} $^{\text{sal.anše}}$*a-na-qa-a-te*[6]

26) *a-di* ANŠE *ba-ak-[ka-ri-ši-na ana* KUR *Aš]šur a-[di maḫ]-ri-ia taš-šá-a* ^{lú}*qe-e-pu i-na muḫ-ḫi-šá áš-kun-ma*

27) 10 LIM[7] ^{lú}ERÍN^{meš}[. . . *ana* GÌR]^{II}-*ia ú-šak-[niš* ^{ur}]^{u}*Ma-as-'-a-a* ^{uru}*Te-ma-a-a* ^{lú}*Sa-ba-'-a-a*[8]

28) ^{uru}*Ḫa-a-a-ap-pa-a-a* ^{uru}*Ba-da-na-a-a* ^{uru}*Ḫa-at-te*[9]*-a-a* ^{lú}*I-di-ba-'-il-a-a*

29) [ ] *ša mi-ṣir* KUR.KUR *ša* [10]*šu-lum* ^{d}*šam-ši*[10]

30) *ša mám-ma la i-du-šú-nu-ti-ma a-šar-šú-un ru-ú-qu ta-nit-ti be-lu-ti-ia*

31) *al-[ka-kat qurdiya išmūma uṣallū] be-lu-ti* KÙ.GI KÙ.BABBAR

32) ANŠE.A.AB.BA^{meš} $^{\text{sal.anše}}$*a-na-qa-ti* ŠIM^{ḫá} DÙ.A-*ma ma-da-ta-šú-nu ki-i* DIŠ-*en*

33) *a-di mah-[ri-ia ubilunimma ú-na]-ši-qu* GÌR$^{II.meš}$*-ia*

34) [$^{(11)}$. . . . $^{(11)}$] ^{m}*I-di-bi-'-i-li*$^{(12)}$ *a-na* ^{lú}NI.DUḪ*-ú-ti i-na* UGU KUR *Mu-uṣ-ri ap-qid* $^{(13)}$

NOTES:

1) The various versions are indicated as follows:

A = III R 10, 2 (= *ITP*, Summ. 4): 19-34, and is underlined ————————

B = K 3751 (II R 67) (= *ITP*, Summ. 7) rev., 2'-6', and is underlined – – – –

C = ND 400 (=*ITP*, Summ. 8): 26'-27', and is underlined ....

D = ND 4301+4305 (= *ITP*, Summ. 9), rev., 17'-22', and is underlined —···—···

E = Lay. 66 (= Rost, *Ann.* 211-226; *ITP*, Summ. 13), and is underlined ·—·—·—·

x = indicates any sign which is illegible.

For the reconstruction of the text, Prof. H. Tadmor kindly gave me access to Lay. 66 (in Layard's notebook), G. Smith's rough copies of III R 10, 2 (see above, notes 71 and 73), and relevant passages in *ITP* to use prior to their publication in his *ITP*. The comments of my colleague, Dr. N. Na'aman, during preparation of the final version of the book, helped considerably in reconstructing the text and understanding its bearing upon the problem.

2-2) D varies from A: it has some extra words in line 19, while the description of the booty (A:20-22) has been abbreviated as follows:

D:17 ... *ina* ^{giš}TUKUL *ú-šam-qit-ma gim-ri* KI.[KAL.BAD*-šá-á* ....

18 ... *a-na la ma-ni* DINGIR^{meš}*[-ša* ...

19 ... *a]-šar ṣu-ma-me* GIM ^{sal}ANŠE.EDIN.NA *taš-ku-[na* ...

3) D: <ANŠE> 4) E: <MÚRU> 5) A: <BAD>

6) A: <SAL> ; D: *ti* 7) E: <10 LIM>

8) B: ^{uru}*Sa-ab-'-a-a* 9) E: *ti*

10-10) B: [ ]UTU^{ši}; E: SILIM *šam-ši*

11-11) E: *...di-x-[ni]-šú-nu ...a...*GAL (or: *ma ina) ....ad...*

12) E: *lu*

13) B: *áš-ku-un*

TRANSLATION:

19) As for Samsi queen of the Arabs, at Mt. Saqurri

20) 9400 of (her) warriors I killed. 1000+x hundred people, 30,000 camels, 20,000 cattle,

21) . . . . 5000 (bags) of all kinds of spices, ... pedestals, the resting places of her gods

22) . . . . weapons(?), scepters of her goddess (and) her property I seized. And she for the rescue of her life
23) . . . . to the de]sert, an arid place, like a wild she-ass
24) set her face. The rest of her tents, the might of her people, within her camp
25) I sat on fire. And Samsi, who became terrified of my powerful weapons, brought camels, she-camels
26) together with their young, to Assyria before me. I appointed a *qēpu*-official over her, and
27) 10,000 warriors ... I made bow down to my feet. The people of Massa', Temā, Saba',
28) Ḫayappâ, Badanu, Ḫatte, Idiba'ilu
29) . . . . on the border of the western lands (lit: the countries of the setting sun)
30) of whom no one (of my predecessors) knew and whose place is remote, the praise of my lordship,
31) [my heroic deeds they heard and beseeched] my majesty. Gold, silver,
32) camels, she-camels, all kinds of spices, their tribute as one
33) [they brought] before me (and) kissed my feet.
34) . . . . I appointed Idibi'ilu for the "wardendhip" of (the entrance to) Egypt.

C. INSCRIPTIONS OF SARGON II

1. Annalistic Sources

a) **Annals from Khorsabad, Slab** II, 11 (Lie, *Annals,* 118-130).[91] lines 120-125 deal with Arabs:

lines 120-123: The defeat of the people of Thamūd, Ibadidi, Marsimani and 'Ephah "the distant desert-dwelling Arabs", and the deportation of their survivors to Samaria.

lines 123-125: The receipt of tribute *(maddattu)* from ^{m}*Pir'u* king of Egypt, Samsi queen of the Arabs and Ita'amra the Sabaean.

91 Lie, *Sargon,* 20-22; cf. *AR* II, §17-18.

Line 127 begins a new episode, Sargon's campaign to the region north of his kingdom: "In the eighth year of my reign *(ina VIII palê-ia)* I marched to the land of the Mannaeans and the Medes", indicating that the preceding lines (120-125) apply to Sargon's seventh *palû.*

b) **Prism Fragment from Assur (VA 8424).**[92] This document is arranged in chronological order. Col. ii 6 ff. deals with matters concerning the southwestern border of Palestine:

lines 6-7: Setting exiles on the border of the town of Naḫal-Muṣur ("Brook-of-Egypt") and delivering them to the sheikh of (the town of) Laban (^{lú}*nasīku ša* ^{uru}*La-ba-an*).

8-11: The receipt of 12 big horses, "their like not to be found in Assyria", as a gift *(tāmartu)* from ^{m}*Ši-il-kan-ni* king of Egypt.

Line 12 begins a new section: "In my sixth *palû*", indicating that lines 6-11 apply to Sargon's fifth *palû.*

Because for various reasons the scribes of Sargon's prisms and annals did not adopt a uniform chronological system, there is sometimes a discrepancy of as much as two years in their dating of a specific event.[93] Col. ii of the Assur Prism dates events a year earlier than do the Khorsabad Annals, thus assigning to Sargon's fifth *palû,* i.e. 716 B.C., occurrences attributed in the Annals to the sixth *palû.* There is, however, reason to believe that the scribes of the Khorsabad Annals erred by one year in setting Sargon's activities in southern Palestine (lines 120-125) in his seventh (715 B.C.), when they belong in his sixth *palû* (716 B.C.).[94] Thus the two sources dealing with events on the southern border evidently apply to a single complex of events in 716 B.C.[95]

92 E.F. Weidner, *AfO* 14 (1941), 40-53 (cf. *ANET,* 286). Col. ii 6-11 has a parallel in a damaged fragment of a prism from Nineveh (79-7-8,14), col. i 1-8, published by Winckler, *Sargon,* II, Pl. 45. For a corrected and more complete edition of these two passages see Tadmor, *JCS* 12 (1958), 77-78.

93 For an analysis of the chronological systems in the various historical inscriptions of Sargon and a discussion of the historical conclusions arising from it, see Tadmor, *JCS* 12 (1958), 22-40, 77-100.

94 Tadmor, *ibid.,* 78.

95 On the identification of Šilkanni, mentioned in the Assur Prism, and the question of whether he is the ***Pir'u*** (Pharaoh) king of Egypt, mentioned in the Annals, see note 371.

2. **Documents of the Summary Inscription Type**

Nimrud Prism, Fragment D. Col. iv 25-49 records various activities of Sargon in Palestine and on the Egyptian border:[96]

lines 25-36: Conquest of Samaria and deportation of 27,280 of its inhabitants.

37-41: Rebuilding Samaria, settling exiles there and reorganizing it under the Assyrian provincial system.

42-45: Surrender of the Egyptians and the Arabs (*nišê* ^{kur}⌜*Mu*⌝*-ṣur ù* ^{lú}*A-ra-bi*).

46-49: Opening "the sealed (harbor) of Egypt" and mingling Assyrians and Egyptians for the purpose of encouraging joint commercial activity.

No indication of the time of these events has survived in this fragment. A passage in the Khorsabad Annals (Lie, *Sargon,* 10-18) resembles the present one in the Nimrud Prism (it should be stressed, however, that there is no parallel to lines 42-45 in the prism, which are important to our subject), starting with a time indication: "In the begi[nning of my reign] (*ina rē[š šarru-ti-ia*]) [when I sat on the throne

96 Gadd, *Iraq* 16 (1954), 179.

97 Lie, *op. cit.,* 4-7 (cf. *AR* II, § 4; *ANET,* 284); for comparison of the two sources and interpretation of the date formula, see Tadmor, *op. cit.,* 34 f.

98 Compare, for example, the order of events given in the passage discussed in the Nimrud Prism with their dates in the Khorsabad Annals:

Nimrud Prism, col. iv	**The Subject Matter**	**Khorsabad Annals**
lines 13-24	Deportation of Pisiris of Carchemish and reorganization of his country into a province	Fifth *palû*
lines 25-41	Conquest of Samaria and its reorganization into a province	Accession year (*rēš šarrūti)*
lines 42-45	Surrender of the Egyptians and the Arabs	Missing in this edition
lines 46-49	An action on the Egyptian border	Accession year (*rēš šarrūti*)
lines 50 ff.	War against Kiakki of **Šinuḫtu**	Fourth *palû*

and was crowned with a lordly crown, etc.]"[97] It is nonetheless impossible to deduce the date of the events described in the Nimrud Prism because, despite the similarity in content, the order in the two sources is discrete.[98] Analyzing the substantive and stylistic differences in the descriptions of Sargon's activities in Palestine in the two sources, Tadmor showed that both are abridged versions based on a *Vorlage* which has not been preserved.[99] That source, like the Summary Inscriptions, was arranged in geographical and not chronological order. Parts of it were incorporated in editions of annals and prisms, written later in Sargon's reign to fill gaps in periods not marked by any special military exploits, and present a picture of ostensibly continuous activity. It is therefore possible to separate the various Palestinian events noted in the Nimrud Prism and date the passages regarding the Egyptians and the Arabs later than the conquest of Samaria. On the surface it seems possible that the Nimrud Prism notations on the activities on the Egyptian border refer to 720 B.C., when Samaria was conquered and the Assyrian army defeated the Egyptian forces which came to the assistance of Ḫanun king of Gaza. More probably, however, they apply to 716 B.C., along with the other events in that region reported in the Khorsabad Annals and the Assur Prism.[100]

b) **The "Display Inscription".**[101] This summarizes the first 15 years of Sargon's reign. Following the notation on the conquest of Samaria and its reorganization as an Assyrian province and the defeat of Ḫanun of Gaza and the army which came to his assistance, line 27 mentions the receipt of tribute from ^{m}*Pir'u* king of Egypt, Samsi queen of the Arabs and Ita'amar the Sabaean (cf. Lie, *Sargon,* 123-125).

c) **The Cylinder Inscription.**[102] In line 20 Sargon is described as "the conqueror of the people of Thamūd, Ibadidi, Marsimani and 'Ephah, whose survivors were deported and resettled in the land of Bît Ḫumri" (cf. Lie, *Sargon,* 120-123).

99 Tadmor, *op. cit.,* 34 ff., 77 ff.

100 See note 99.

101 Winckler, *Sargon,* I, 100; cf. *AR* II, § 53 ff.; *ANET,* 284-285.

102 D.J. Lyon, *Keilschrifttexte Sargon's Königs von Assyrien,* Leipzig 1883, 30 ff.; cf. *AR* II, § 117 ff.

D. INSCRIPTIONS OF SENNACHERIB

1. Annals

a) **BM 113203,** a description of Sennacherib's first campaign.[103] Lines 28-29 state that in the course of his war with Merodach-baladan and his allies, he captured, along with ^{m}*Ba-as-qa-nu,*[104] the brother of ^{f}*Ia-ti-'-e* queen of the Arabs and Merodach-baladan's nephew,[105] booty consisting of chariots, wagons, horses, mules, donkeys, dromedaries (ANŠE.A.B.BA^{meš}) and Bactrian camels (^{anše}*udri*). Lines 36-50 give the names of 81 walled towns in western Babylonia which, along with 820 minor settlements within their borders, were conquered and looted by the Assyrian army. The towns are listed according to the territories of Bīt Dakkuri, Bīt Sa'alli, Bīt Amukani and Bīt Yakin. This passage, apparently copied from a geographical list and incorporated into the description of Sennacherib's first campaign,[106] illuminates the

103 S. Smith, *The First Campaign of Sennacherib King of Assyria,* London 1921; Luckenbill, *Sennacherib,* 48-55, 94-98. For a translation only see *AR* II, § 255-267, 363-371. This campaign took place in the second year of Sennacherib's reign, 703 B.C.

104 F.H. Weissbach suggested that the name could be read as ^{m}*Ba-uq-qa-a-nu (ZA* 43 NF 9 [1936], 280), but this does nothing to help clarify its etymology.

105 Smith's and Luckenbill's version (see note 103) ^{m}*A-di-nu* DUMU DAM (*=mār aššat)* ^{md}*Marduk-apla-iddin(na)* calls for the assumption that Merodach baladan's wife was originally married to another. For removal of this difficulty by reading DUMU NIN (*=mār aḫat*) instead of DUMU DAM, thus suggesting that the reference is to the son of Merodach-baladan's sister and not of his wife, see Weissbach, *ibid.,* 280; Brinkman, *Studies presented to A.L Oppenheim,* Chicago 1964, 25, note 140.

106 According to line 50, the total number of walled cities captured was 88, but the text gives the names of only 81. The missing seven were in Bît Dakkuri, where the names of only 26 cities were listed, whereas, according to the summary in line **39,** there were 33 walled cities. Because of the total given in line 50, the scribe cannot have erred in writing the number in line 39. Because the document under discussion and a parallel document (Ki 1902-5-10,1) have, as stated in their colophons, the same number of lines, S. Smith (*ibid.,* 20) rejects the possibility that the scribe skipped a line while copying the original list. Therefore he assumes that in the original the author retained one of a set of identical names which referred in fact to different places, deleting 7 in all. It is more likely, however, that the text from which both documents were taken was not the original geographical list, but a copy from which one line had been accidentally omitted. It is also possible that one of the parallel documents was copied from the other erroneous one.

geography of Babylonia. Among other things, some of the toponyms reflect the Arab connection with the western border region of Babylonia in the Neo-Assyrian period.

The description of the campaign is lengthy because, with only one campaign to write about and a specific space to fill, the scribe inserted the material just outlined. Many of the items in this document, including the Basqanu episode and the above-mentioned geographical listing, were omitted from the editions of Sennacherib's Annals from the second campaign on. This is common to the annalistic literature of the Assyrian kings: As time passed, and faced with a multiplicity of military campaigns and building activities, the scribes shortened the accounts of earlier activities and described only the major details of each event.[107]

b) **An edition of Annals from 694 B.C.** includes in the list of Nineveh's city-gates one called "the Desert Gate (*abul madbari*), through which the gifts of the people of ^{lú}*Te-e-me* and ^{lú}*Su-mu-'*-AN enter".[108] As this is not listed among the gates of Nineveh in the 696 B.C. Annals edition,[109] it was presumably constructed between 696 and 694 B.C.

2. **Other Historical Inscriptions**

a) **VA 3310 (=VS I 77).**[110] Fragment of an alabaster slab inscribed on both sides. Rev. 22-27 preserve a passage about a campaign of Sennacherib's army against the Arabs. The passage records an attack on the camp of [Te'lḫu]nu queen of the Arabs in a place whose name has not survived, after which the Assyrian army pursued her to ^{uru}*Adummatu* in the desert. This records Sennacherib's eighth campaign (691 B.C.)[111] but does not mention the destruction of Babylon (689 B.C.). No edition of Sennacherib's Annals, not even those describing the eighth campaign, mentions the war against the Arabs, which appears on this slab after the eighth campaign. The war must therefore have occurred close to the time the inscription was written.

107 Olmstead, *Assyrian Historiography*, 8.

108 BM 103,000 vii 96—viii 1 (Luckenbill, *Sennacherib*, 113); TM 1931-1932, 2 SH, col. B, 37-38 (R.C. Thompson, *Iraq* 7 [1940], 91); Heidel Prism, viii 8-9 (*Sumer* 9 [1953], 170).

109 See Thompson, *ibid.*, 92.

110 Luckenbill, *Sennacherib*, 89-93; *AR* II, § 353-358. Rev. 22-27, whose subject is the campaign against the Arabs, was first published by V. Scheil, *OLZ* 7 (1904), 69-70.

111 Cf. VA 3310, rev. 1-21 with the Chicago Oriental Institute Prism, v 31 ff.

b) **K 8544.** Fragment of a stone slab from Nineveh inscribed on both sides.[112] The text is quite fragmentary but it is possible to decipher on the reverse (from line 5 on) details dealing with a queen of the Arabs, spices and precious stones. Winckler and others after him identified this slab as an Esarhaddon inscription.[113] R. Borger, however, pointed out the similarity between the extant passages on it observe[114] and the Nebi Yunus Inscription (line 33 ff.), thus proving what G. Smith had already assumed, that this inscription belongs to those of Sennacherib.[115] When the two inscriptions are compared it becomes clear that the eighth campaign was recorded on the obverse of K 8544 and that the reference to the Arabs (rev., 5 ff.) was written after the description of the eighth campaign.

On the rev., line 3, are the name of a town [uru]*Ka-pa-a-nu* and the URU determinative of another town whose name has not survived. Although some suggest that these were also towns conquered in the course of the campaign against the Arabs,[116] the passage extant on the reverse seems not to deal with the war against the Arabs, but rather resembles a description of the construction and the foundation-laying of a temple, whose materials derived from booty, tribute and gifts of various origins, not only the Arabs.[117] Thus [uru]*Ka-pa-a-nu* and the town mentioned next

112 See G. Smith, *History of Sennacherib,* London 1878, 137-138; Winckler, *AOF,* I, 532-534; and *AR* II, § 569-570.

113 In addition to Winckler and Luckenbill (see previous note) see Olmstead, *Assyrian Historiography,* 50.

114 Winckler's erroneous conclusion that this was the reverse is apparent when the inscription is compared with that of Nebi Yunus Inscription (see Borger in the following note).

115 Borger, *Asarhaddon,* 117-118 (§ 91). For G. Smith's assumption, see note 112.

116 Olmstead, *History of Assyria,* 310.

117 Cf. for example, the fragments of the passage discussed with VA 8248 (whose subject is the building of the Temple of the New Year's Festival, the *Bīt Akītu;* see the following note):

K 8544 rev. (collated from photograph)	**VA 8248**
line 2: *man-da-at-ta-šú-nu k[a-bit-tu..]*	lines 41-42: *na-mur-ta/ti-šu-nu* (of the people of Dilmum)
lines 5-7: all kinds of herbs and precious stones from the treasury of the queen of the Arabs.	lines 48-49: choice herbs and precious stones from Karibilu king of Sheba.

K 8544, rev. 12-13, deal with beams of [giš]*šur[meni]* wood and bronze (ZABAR

are apparently among the places which building materials were brought from, and are not connected with the campaign against the Arabs.

c) **VA 8248 (=KAH II, 122).** Foundation inscription from Assur dedicated to the building of the Temple of the New Year's Festival (the *Bīt Akītu*). [118] It was written after the destruction of Babylon (see line 36 ff.), i.e. after 689 B.C. Lines 48-54 state that precious stones and fine spices from the *nāmurtu*-gift of Karibilu king of Saba' were placed in the foundation.

E. INSCRIPTIONS OF ESARHADDON[119]

1. Annals

The Esarhaddon Annals from Nineveh, including episodes relating to Arabs, consist of two main groups written at different times:

The earlier group is represented by the *Heidel Prism* written in Iyyar 676 B.C.[120] There are parallel versions designated as Nin. B^{1-6} by Borger, none of which preserved the date of writing.[121] This edition, from the beginning of the fifth year of Esarhaddon's reign, includes a sizable number of episodes connected with Arabs, among them the return of ᶠ*Ta-bu-u-a* and the image of Arab gods to Dumah, the levy of tribute on Ḫazael, the succession of his son ᵐ*Ia-'-lu-ú* after his death,

=siparru), materials unreasonable to include in booty taken from nomads who lived in the heart of the desert. This confirms the assumption about the relationship of the text to a certain building project.

In line 5, G. Smith and Winckler read .. *[šar]-rat* LÚ *A-ra-bi a-di* DING[IR.MEŠ-*ša*...], which may indicate that the subject of the text is taking booty, including images of gods, from the queen of the Arabs. This makes our foregoing assumption difficult to accept. It should be noted, however, that the photograph of the document (courtesy H. Tadmor) shows no DINGIR sign in line 5.

118 Luckenbill, *Sennacherib*, 135-139; *AR* II, § 434-442.

119 In this study all the historical inscriptions of Esarhaddon are designated according to Borger, *Asarhaddon*.

120 Published by A. Heidel, *Sumer* 12 (1956), 9-37. Borger mentions it in the postscript (*ibid.*, p. 125); see also his additional remarks in *AfO* 18 (1957-1958), 115-116.

121 For details of these parallel versions see Borger, *Asarhaddon*, 37-38. The most important among them is 48-10-31,2 (published by L. Abel—H. Winckler, *Keilschrifttexte zum Gebrauch bei Vorlesungen*, Berlin 1890, 22 ff.), which used to be called Prism A, and in the Borger edition is marked Nin. B. For a transliteration

and the campaign to the land of Bāzu (Heidel Prism ii 46 — iii 36).

The second group, represented by the *Thompson Prism,* written in 673 B.C. (designated Nin. A by Borger),[122] also has numerous parallel versions (designated Nin. A^{2-19} by Borger), two of which have preserved the date of writing, 673 B.C.[123] In addition to the Arab episodes mentioned in the Heidel Prism, this one describes the revolt of ᵐ*Ú-a-bu* against ᵐ*Ia-ta-'* son of Ḫazael, and its suppression with the help of the Assyrian army (Nin. A iv 1-31, 53-77). As compared with Nin. B, Nin. A expands considerably upon such information as the names of the Arab gods returned to Dumah and the names of the kings of the land of Bāzu and their locations, etc.[124] The author of Nin. A must therefore have had access to a different or an additional source from Nin B; this may indicate that Nin. A, although written later than Nin. B, is more significant for events in the early years of Esarhaddon's reign.

The episodes in the two Annals editions are not in identical order,[125] making it impossible to establish from them a definite chronological

and translation see also Borger, *ibid.*, 39-64 (§ 27); for translation only see *AR* II, 525-540.

122 Before Borger it was designated Prism B. For transliteration see R.C. Thompson, *The Prisms of Esarhaddon and Ashurbanipal found at Nineveh, 1927-8*, London 1931, 9-28; Borger, *ibid.*, 40-64 (§ 27). For a translation of the passages of this prism dealing with the Arabs see also *ANET,* 291-292.

123 For a list of the parallels to this edition and their dates see Borger, *ibid.*, 36-37, 64.

124 For the names of the Arab gods cf. Heidel Prism ii 57; Nin. A iv 10-12. On the kings of the land of Bāzu cf. Heidel Prism iii 21; Nin. A iv 62-68; and likewise on the cities of Sidon cf. Heidel Prism i 14-37; Nin. A ii 65 — iii 19.

125 Cf., e.g., the sequence of the following episodes according to each of the main editions of the Annals:

Episode	Heidel Prism	Thompson Prism (Nin. A)
The removal of Nabû-zēr-kitti-lišir after his rebellion and the appointment of his brother	ii 24-33	ii 40-64
The campaign to the land of Bāzu	iii 9-36	iv 53-77
The surrender of Bēl-iqīšâ the Gambulaean	iii 37-52	iii 71-83
The surrender of the Median leaders	iii 53 — iv 20	iv 32-52

sequence. We can use only the dates of the prism as the *terminus post quem* for the events described. All the episodes in both thus preceded Iyyar 676 B.C., and the ^{m}*Ú-a-bu* revolt and its suppression occurred between 676 and 673 B.C.

There is also a considerable difference in the recorded order of events between the Esarhaddon Annals and the Esarhaddon and Babylonian Chronicles.[126] For the implications of this difference, see pp. 52-54, 125-126, 130.

2. **Other Historical Inscriptions**

Other inscriptions of Esarhaddon which include the episodes mentioned above are: Klch. A,[127] Trb. A[128] (both written in 672 B.C., with Klch. A 1-39 and Trb. A 1-21 containing the parallel historical sections); AsBbE;[129] Fragment A[130] (the latter two were written after the

126 Cf. the sequence of episodes in the following sources:

Episode	Date (as per Chronicles)	Heidel Prism	Thompson Prism (Nin. A)
The beheading of Abdi-milkuti king of Sidon and Sanduarri king of Kundu and Sisû	The 5th year of Esarhaddon's reign (676/5 B.C.)	i 38-56	iii 20-38
The conquest of Arṣâ	The 2nd year of Esarhaddon's reign (679/8 B.C.)	i 57-63	iii 39-42
The campaign to the land of Bāzu	The 5th year of Esarhaddon's reign (675 B.C.)	iii 9-36	iv 53-77

127 A cylinder inscription from Nimrud (ND 1126), see Wiseman, *Iraq* 14 (1952), 54-60; Borger, *ibid.*, 33-35 (§ 21). In 1958 four additional cylinder inscriptions were found at Nimrud (ND 7097-7100), mostly paralleling Klch A. Three of them were written in Ab-Elul 676 B.C.; the date of the fourth has not survived, see A.R. Millard, *Iraq* 23 (1961), 176-178.

128 A cylinder inscription from Tarbiṣu, see E. Nassouhi, *MAOG* III, 1-2 (1927), 22-28; Borger, *ibid.*, 71-72 (§ 43).

129 A building inscription on an alabaster tablet from Assur (Assur 3916), see Borger, *ibid.*, 86-89 (§ 57). The best copy of it is in Borger, *ibid.*, Tafel I. For a translation only see *AR* II, § 709-712; *ANET*, 290 (partial translation).

130 A fragment of a historical inscription from Nineveh (K 2671), see Borger, *ibid.*, 110 (§ 71); Winckler, *AOF* I, 522-523; for a translation only see *AR* II, § 543-547; *ANET*, 291 (partial translation).

conquest of Egypt in 671 B.C.); Fragment B[131] (the extant parts of this inscription in the main parallel Nin. A); and an inscription from Til Barsip (Mnm. B).[132] The chief value of these inscriptions for our study lies in the variants of a number of the names connected with Arabs.

Of special importance for our subject are the Fragments F[133] and G,[134] dealing with Esarhaddon's second campaign to Egypt. Here it is stated that the Assyrian army, when crossing the Sinai desert, used the camels of the Arabs to supply water.

F. INSCRIPTIONS OF ASSURBANIPAL

All of the Assurbanipal historical inscriptions which record information about the Arabs were written late in his reign, the earliest of them (Annal Edition B) dating from 649 B.C. The Assurbanipal Annals are arranged according to campaign (*girru*) and not regnal year (*palû*). But since the ordinals for the various campaigns are not identical in the various versions, they cannot establish the date and sequence of the episodes.[135] Evaluation of the information in these inscriptions and determination of the development of events are made possible only by internal evidence and examination of their historiographic development by comparing the episodes and their descriptions in each of the sources.

1. The historical inscriptions of Assurbanipal relative to the Arabs are

131 A fragment of a historical inscription from Nineveh (K 8523), see Borger, *ibid.*, 110-111 (§ 72); Winckler, *AOF* I, 526; for a translation only see *AR* II, § 548-552; *ANET*, 292 (partial translation).

132 See F. Thureau-Dangin - M. Dunand, *Til Barsib*, Paris 1936, 153-155; Borger, *ibid.*, 100-101 (§ 66). Most of the surviving text parallels the Nineveh Annals prisms. This document resembles in form the Senjirli Stele of Esarhaddon, which was written after the conquest of Egypt.

133 Fragments of a historical inscription from Nineveh (K 3082 + K 3086 + Sm 2027), see Borger, *ibid.*, 112-113 (§ 76). For translation only see *AR* II, § 553-559; *ANET*, 292-293.

134 A fragment of a historical inscription from Nineveh (79-7-8,196), see Borger, *ibid.*, 113 (§ 77).

135 To give an example of this fact, we will limit ourselves to the designations of two campaigns in the following prisms:

Event	Rm.	B	F
Campaign against the Mannaeans	col. iv	col. v	col. iii
Campaign against Teumman king of Elam	col. v	col. viii	col. iv

listed below in the order of composition. The episodes are identified by the numbers assigned to each in the account of Assurbanipal's reign, see pp. 142-147.

a) **Prism B.** A group of parallel prisms, complete text edited by A.C. Piepkorn.[136] They were all written within a few months, the earliest in Ab, 649 B.C.[137] The material about the Arabs is in vii 93 — viii 63, at the end of the historical section of the prism, and covers Episodes A and B (in brief), C-J, L, N.

Texts parallel to those in Prism B are:[138] Prism D (parallel in the historical sections but differing in the descriptions of building operations); K 30; and Th. (B_1), viii.

b) **Prism C.** All available copies are fragmentary. One, A.8104 (as yet unpublished), dates from the *limmu* of Nabû-nadin-aḫi.[139] The Arabs are treated at the end of the historical section, in x 27-66 published by Bauer, which includes Episodes G-J, M, N.[140]

Parallel passages are:[141] 81-7-27, 240; and ND 5407 col. ii + 5413 col. i.

136 *Historical Prism Inscriptions of Ashurbanipal,* Chicago 1933, 19-94.

137 For dates of the copies of Prism B see Piepkorn, *ibid.,* 19-20, 88-91.

138 Prism D x 2-16 (=Prism B viii 49-63); see Th. Bauer, *Das Inschriftenwerk Assurbanipals,* Leipzig 1933, 24-26. For the date of this prism see also Millard, *Iraq* 30 (1968), 102-103.
K 30 iii 2-24 (=Prism B vii 93 — viii 16); see Bauer, *ibid.,* 25-26. The text of lines 3-4 is slightly different from the parallel in the Piepkorn edition and similar to that in Streck's Cyl. B.
Th. (B_1), viii 1-45 (=Prism B viii 8-53); see Thompson, *Iraq* 7 (1940), 99, No. 14.

139 Tadmor, *25th Congress,* 240, places this eponym in 646 B.C. M. Falkner's date of 634 B.C. (*AfO* 17 [1954-1956], 113, 118) is unacceptable, if only because of the place of Prism C in the development of historical writing in the Assurbanipal inscriptions.

140 Bauer, *ibid.,* 18.

141 81-7-27, 240 (=Prism C x 32-39); see Bauer, *ibid.,* 65. Since there is no parallel in Prism B for the words ... *it-ti* ^{kur}*Aššur*^{ki} *ik-ki-ru* ... in line 5, the fragment discussed should be related not to that prism (as Bauer believes) but to Prism C. In Prism C the opening of the Ammuladi episode (J) seems to be in its original form, whereas in Prism B (viii 39) the opening merges with the previous episode about the raids of Yauta' in the west (C).
ND 5407 col. ii + 5413 col. i (=Prism C x 27-43); see E.E. Knudsen, *Iraq* 29 (1967), 54.

c) **"Letter to Ishtar" (K 3405).** This tablet deals almost exclusively with the Arabs. The obverse covers events during Sennacherib's reign and the beginning of Esarhaddon's (parallel texts also appear on the obverse of K 3087), the reverse during Assurbanipal's.[142] Comparison of K 3405 rev., 8-12 with Rm. ix 104-110 indicates that the subject is the punishment of Uaite' son of Birdāda for rebelling against Assurbanipal. The episodes treated on this side of the tablet are therefore I and U.

d) **K 2664** + **K 3090.** These are two fragments of a six-column tablet, the end of whose historical section refers to the Arabs (v 1-13).[143] Lines 1-5 deal with the punishment of Uaite' son of Birdāda (cf. Rm. ix 107-111, Episode U). Lines 6-13 compare with Rm. x 4-5 and concern the punishment of Ayammu son of Te'ri and at least one other person (his brother?), and thus constitute, in spite of some stylistic differences, Episode V.

e) **"Letter to Aššur"** (K 2802 + VAT 5600 + Th. 1905-4-9, 97).[144] The text is devoted entirely to the Arabs and late episodes connected with them. The episodes dealt with are A to T, but apparently those from U on, found in the Rassam Cylinder, were originally included in the

142 For K 3405 obv., see Streck, *Assurbanipal,* 222-225; for K 3087 obv., see Streck, *ibid.,* 216-219; for K 3405 rev., see Bauer, *op.cit.,* 45. The combined text of both inscriptions has been newly published, with textual and historical discussion, by M. Cogan, *Imperialism and Religion: Assyria, Judah and Israel in the Eighth and Seventh Centuries B.C.E.,* Missoula, Mont. 1974, 16-20.

143 For K 2664 see Bauer, *ibid.,* 34-35; and for K 3090 see idem, *ibid.,* 20. The joining of these two fragments was first suggested by Borger, *Orientalia* 26 (1957), 1-2. Bauer's column designation should be corrected accordingly.

144 For K 2802 + VAT 5600 see Streck, *ibid.,* 196-207, 376-379. For Th. 1905-4-9,97 (now BM 98591), see Bauer, *ibid.,* 20. Landsberger (in Bauer, *ibid.,* 66 n. 1) was the first to recognize the 'join'; Borger (*ibid.,* 1) was the first to point out that the last fragment belonged to the "Letter to Aššur".
Streck's arrangement of columns in this document should be corrected as follows (Bauer, *ibid.,* 66):

Obverse	**Reverse**
col. i: VAT 5600, i +K 2802, iv	col. iv: K 2802, iii
col. ii: VAT 5600, ii+K 2802, v	col. v: K 2802, ii
col. iii: Th. 1905-4-9,97+VAT 5600, iii+K 2802, vi	col. vi: K 2802, i

The text of the "Letter to Aššur" has been discussed and newly published by Weippert, *WO* 7 (1973), 74-85.

"Letter to Aššur" and did not survive the damage to the document. The text of the "Letter to Aššur" in the episodes shared with the documents above is largely based on the early inscriptions (cf. especially Prism B), with some literary elaboration (cf. especially Episode F), but is here addressed in the second person to Aššur.

f) **K 4687.** A small fragment of a tablet with passages about the Arabs on both sides.[145] Lines 2-6, obverse, contain elements of Episodes D, E, G and H; the reverse, Episodes J to L. Line 1, obverse, of the text can be reconstructed definitely from parallel texts as follows:[146] *[... ia-a-ti ú-maš]-šir-an-ni-m[a it-ti* ^md^*Šamaš-šum-ukin a-ḫi nak-ri iš-ta-kan pi-i-šu].* The subject of this line is therefore Episode I.

The inclusion of Episodes I and K in this document indicates that it is later than Prism B.[147] Stylistic comparison of K 4687 with Prism B and the "Letter to Aššur" shows that only the main facts were cited in K 4687, without literary elaboration. On the other hand, we have seen that in composition K 4687 resembles the "Letter to Aššur" because it includes Episode I, which is missing in Prism B. K 4687 can therefore be considered an abridgment to the "Letter to Aššur". This document, nevertheless, antedates the Rassam Cylinder, since it lacks Episodes II and III.

g) **The Rassam Cylinder.** The longest and latest of the annal editions of Assurbanipal,[148] dated the 15th of Iyyar, *limmu* of Šamaš-da'inanni.[149] The events connected with Arabs, included under "the ninth campaign", appear in vii 82—x 5, 17-19.[150] The episodes covered in this inscription are C to N, Q to W, and I, II, III and IV.

Several of the episodes shared with the "Letter to Aššur" are abridged in the Rassam Cylinder.[151] On the other hand, although the

145 See Bauer, *ibid.,* 64. For the obverse only see also Streck, *ibid.,* 224-225.

146 Cf. Rm. vii 94-101; K 2802 iv 4-7; K 3405 rev. 5.

147 In contrast to Streck, *ibid.,* XXXIX-XL; Bauer, *ibid.,* 64.

148 For its description and parallels see Streck, *ibid.,* XVII-XXI.

149 Tadmor (above, note 140) dates this *limmu* at ca. 643/2 B.C. For dates later than 638 B.C. see Streck, *ibid.,* CDLV, CDLVII, CDLXV; Falkner, *op. cit.,* 116, 118.

150 See Streck, *ibid.,* 65-83; Weippert, *op. cit.,* 39-73 (a translation and a detailed textual and historical discussion).

151 Thus, for example, the episode of the seizure of Ammuladi and Adiya in the Rassam Cylinder was abridged to the minimum (cf. K 2802 v 21-30; Rm. viii 24-

Rassam Cylinder contains purely literary elaborations that add no information to what appears in parallel episodes in earlier inscriptions of Assurbanipal,[152] it does possess historical passages based on sources neither in the "Letter to Aššur" nor in other extant historical inscriptions.[153]

A noteworthy feature is the mechanical nature of the writing in the Rassam Cylinder section on the Arabs, little attention having been paid to proper episodic sequence. Thus the defeat of Abiyate' Ayammu (Episode III) comes after the defeat of Uaite' and his punishment (vii 107 — viii 14), but before the report that Abiyate' replaced Uaite' as king (viii 43 ff.). Similarly, the descriptions of the outcome of the campaign are copied inaccurately, as the parallel passages show:

Prism B	**"Letter to Aššur"**	**Rassam Cylinder**
cf. viii 4-6	K 2802 iv 6-11	vii 100-107
—	—	vii 108-115
viii 7-11	K 2802 iv 12-16	vii 116-122
cf. viii 12-30	K 2802 iv 17-24, VAT 5600 ii 1-20, K 2802 v 1-3	ix 42-74
—	—	ix 75-89 (literary elaboration? see n. 153)
—	—	ix 90 ff. (capture and punishment of Uaite')
viii 30-31	K 2802 v 4-5	vii 123-124

30), and there is no reference to the tribute imposed on Abiyaṭe' by Assurbanipal (cf. K 2802 v 12-14 and parallels).

152 See, for example, Rm. viii 19-22. It is possible that Rm. ix 75-89 is also elaborated. On the other hand, because of the similarity between some of the misfortunes that beset the Arabs and the sanction formulae in ancient treaties (for parallels to the curses in Rm. ix 58-59 [=B viii 25-26], 65-67, see D.R. Hillers, *Treaty Curses and the Old Testament Prophets,* Rome 1964, 61-63), we can assume that Rm. ix 75-89 is based on the text of an Assurbanipal treaty with the Arabs (a fragment of a treaty between Assurbanipal and Yauṭa' king of the Qedarites was published by K. Deller—S. Parpola, *Orientalia* 37 [1968], 464-466) or on a treaty of another Assyrian king (Rm. ix 60 f. [=B viii 27 f.], 72-74 states explicitly that the Arabs were beset because they violated their treaties — *adê, adê rabûti* — thus bringing on themselves the curses listed in them). At the same time it should be noted that the Rassam

h) Inscription from the Ishtar Temple at Nineveh ("The Ištar Slab").[154] One of the later inscriptions of Assurbanipal.[155] Among the political and military achievements (lines 78-162) are events and kings' names unknown from earlier inscriptions of Assurbanipal. As to the Arabs, it includes Episode X, also peculiar to this inscription, as well as Episodes I, J, L, N and W, which are known from the sources cited above. These episodes, with the exception of J, belong to the last chapter of Assurbanipal's relations with the Arabs, and deal with the history of Uaite' (son of Birdāda) and Natnu king of the Nabayateans.[156]

2. The "Letter to Aššur" (K 2802 iv 2-7) and parallel passages[157] mention in the discussion of the revolt of Uaite' (son of Ḫazael) the assistance he gave to Šamaš-šum-ukin. The earlier version (Prism B), however, speaks about a disloyal act of Yauta', which is described as raids in the western part of the Assyrian empire. A chronological examination of the episodes which concern the Arabs in the historical inscriptions of Assurbanipal, taking other sources into account, indicates that the revolt of Yauta' son of Ḫazael and his defeat by the Assyrian army preceded the first hostilities between Assurbanipal and his rebellious brother.[158] Thus this Yauta' (son of Ḫazael) could not

Cylinder varies from the Assyrian vassal-treaties in the sequence of the gods and in the particular sanctions assigned to each (cf., e.g., Esarhaddon's treaty with the princes of Media, Wiseman, *Iraq* 20 [1958], 59-68; see also Hillers, *ibid.*, 12-18).

153 Rm. vii 108-115 (copy of an administrative document?); viii 1-14, 32-42, 48-51, 94-95.

154 R.C. Thompson—M.E.L. Mallowan, *AAA* 20 (1933), 80-98.

155 Tadmor (above, note 139) dates it at ca. 640 B.C.

156 For the determination that the [m]*Ú-a-a-te-' šar* [kur]*Su-mu-*AN who, according to line 113, cooperated with Šamaš-šum-ukin, was Yauṭa' son of Birdāda, and not Uaiṭe' son of Ḫazael, see below, 2. There is no doubt that line 123 and the beginning of line 124 deal with Natnu king of the Nabayateans. Thompson's reconstruction of the rest of line 124: [...*Ia-u-te-' ša a-na* [kur]*N]a-ba-a-a-[ti it-tak-]lu u ta-[mar-ti-šu ik-lu?] ... ad-di(ki?) ina qi-bit* [d]*Aššur* [d]NIN.LIL *etc.* is syntactically questionable and is unsupported in any other source. If we assume correctly that the [m]*Ú-a-a-te-'* discussed in line 113 is Uaiṭe' son of Birdāda, there is no point in searching either this inscription for references to Uaiṭe' son of Ḫazael or Thompson's reconstruction based on Episode G. It appears, therefore, that the subject of lines 124-126 is simply Natnu king of the Nabayateans.

157 K 3405 rev. 3-5; Rm. viii 91-101; K 4687 obv. 1. For reconstruction of this line see above p. 49.

158 For this conclusion see 147-155.

have assisted Šamaš-šum-ukin. On the other hand, the Assurbanipal historical inscriptions composed after 648 B.C., i.e. after his victory over Šamaš-šum-ukin, mention a Uaite' (son of Birdāda) who collaborated with Abiyate' son of Te'ri, who was made king by Assurbanipal in place of Yauta' son of Ḫazael (cf. Episode H). These sources state, in fact, that Abiyate' collaborated with Šamaš-šum-ukin by sending warriors to Babylon (where they arrived with Uaite' himself; Episodes I, III). These were also the leaders — Uaite' son of Birdāda and Abiyate' and Ayammu sons of Te'ri — against whom Assurbanipal's last campaign against the Arabs was conducted (Episodes Q-S, U-W). *The statements about the help given Šamaš-šum-ukin by Uaite' therefore refer to Uaite' son of Birdāda and not to Yauta' son of Ḫazael.*

Proof of this assumption appears in K 3405. The Arab leader treated on the reverse can only be Uaite' son of Birdāda, as is evident from the description of his punishment (cf. K 3405 rev., 8-12; Rm. ix 104-110), and not Yauta' son of Ḫazael (for a description of his punishment cf. Rm. viii 11-14). The primary sources for the passage *ia-a-ti ú-maš-šir-an-ni it-ti* ^{md}*Šá[maš-šum-ukin etc. ...]* certainly referred to Uaite' son of Birdāda. It was included among the lines about Yauta' son of Ḫazael in the "Letter to Aššur" (K 2802 iv 2 ff.) by a scribe who did not distinguish between Yauta' son of Ḫazael and Uaite' son of Birdāda (the fathers' names were mentioned in the passages under discussion). From here on, the confusion was carried over to later inscriptions whose texts were based on the "Letter to Aššur".[159]

2. OTHER AKKADIAN SOURCES

G. BABYLONIAN CHRONICLES

The following passages in the chronicles refer directly to the Arabs:

The Babylonian Chronicle (=Grayson, Chronicle 1) iv 5-6:	Esarhaddon's campaign to the land of Bāzu.[160]
The Esarhaddon Chronicle (=Grayson, Chronicle 14), obv., 7, 8, 13:	Esarhaddon's conquest of the town of Arṣâ and campaign to the land of Bāzu.[161]
BM 21946 (=Grayson, Chronicle 5), rev., 9-10:	The Babylonian army's attack on the Arabs in the Syrian desert during Nebuchadnezzar's sixth regnal year.[162]

The Nabonidus Chronicle (=Grayson, Chronicle 7), i 11 ff. and all col. ii:	Nabonidus' campaign to Tema' and his sojourn there until his 11th regnal year.[163]

Every event in the chronicles is dated and usually includes the month, and sometimes even the day. Consequently, these sources are extremely important, providing as they do a chronological skeleton around which to establish the historical sequence and insert information from other sources which are undated or not in chronological order. The definitive dates in the Babylonian chronicles are used in this study to determine the chronology of Esarhaddon's wars against the Arabs — and thereby the times of contact between them[164] — and to fix dates for the various razzias, mentioned in the inscriptions of Assurbanipal, made by the Arabs on the borders of the Assyrian empire, and their role in the struggle between him and Šamaš-šum-ukin.[165]

The accuracy of the dates in the Babylonian chronicles has until now been unchallenged; they are considered decisive chronological data. From a comparison of the data on various historical episodes reported in both the chronicles and the Esarhaddon Prisms, it appears, however, that the *a priori* preference for the chronological data in the chronicles to those in the royal inscriptions must in some cases be re-examined. To support this view we shall use only data from the material relating to Palestine and its immediate vicinity.

The Heidel Prism of Esarhaddon was written in 22nd Iyyar in the *limmu* of Banbâ (the 5th year of Esarhaddon's reign, cf. ADD 502:13-15, i.e., 676/5 B.C.).[166] Reported, among other matters, are the decapitation of Abdi-milkuti king of Sidon and Sanduarri king of Kundu and Sisû (i 52-56), and the campaign to the land of Bāzu (iii 9-36).

159 See note 157; also cf. the Ištar Slab, line 113.

160 Grayson, *ABC*, 83; cf. Fr. Delitzsch, *Die Babylonische Chronik*, Leipzig 1906, 14; *ANET*, 302.

161 Grayson, *ibid.*, 125-126; cf. Smith, *BHT*, 12; *ANET*, 303.

162 Grayson, *ibid.*, 99; cf. Wiseman, *CCK*, 70-71; *ANET*^{3}, 564.

163 Grayson, *ibid.*, 105-108; cf. Smith, *BHT*, 111-112; *ANET*, 305-306.

164 See below, pp. 125-126.

165 See below, pp. 153-155.

166 Heidel, *Sumer* 12 (1956), 36; Kohler-Ungnad, *ARU*, No. 562; cf. A. Ungnad, *RLA*, II, 426.

These events are mentioned in the Babylonian chronicles as well, the first dated Tishri and Adar respectively, in the 5th year of Esarhaddon's reign (cf. Babylonian Chronicle, iv 6-8; Esarhaddon Chronicle, obv., 14), and the second Tammuz/Tishri of the same year (cf. Babylonian Chronicle, iv 5-6; Esarhaddon Chronicle, obv., 13). Since these events were recorded in the Heidel Prism, we are forced to conclude that there was an error of at least one year in the Babylonian Chronicles.

The error in the date of the campaign to the land of Bāzu raises the question of preferring the accepted data in the Chronicles about the conquest of the town of Arṣâ (in the 2nd year of Esarhaddon's reign)[167] to those in the Esarhaddon Prisms, where this episode immediately follows the description of Abdi-milkuti's and Sanduarri's sad end (which the Chronicles place in Esarhaddon's 5th regnal year):[168] Opting for the relative order of events in the prisms — that is, placing the conquest of Arṣâ closer in time to the conquest of Sidon — reduces the time-span between the conquest of Arṣâ, which was at the southernmost point of Assyrian control in Palestine, and the first campaign to Egypt at the end of the 7th year of Esarhaddon's reign (673 B.C.); this may help to explain the significance of the conquest of Arṣâ as preparation for the campaign to Egypt.

Another error, involving 3-4 months, occurs in the date of Nabonidus' departure on his campaign to Mt. Ammananu in the 3rd year of his reign, which the Nabonidus Chronicle dates in the month of Ab (i 11) and BM 34167 + puts in Iyyar (iv 57-58).[169]

H. ASSURBANIPAL'S TREATY WITH THE QEDARITES; LETTERS AND ADMINISTRATIVE DOCUMENTS

1. It was known from the annals of Assurbanipal that he had made a treaty with the Qedarites; it can also be inferred from a letter of Nabû-šum-lišir (ABL 350).[170] Some years ago a fragment of such a treaty from

167 H. Hirschberg, *Studien zur Geschichte Esarhaddons, Königs von Assyrien,* Ohlau 1932, 42-45; Tadmor, "Mesopotamia", *Enc. Miqr.,* V., 107.

168 See note 126.

169 Cf. Smith, *BHT,* 111, 115; W.G. Lambert, *AfO* 22 (1968-1969), 5, 7.

170 See Cyl. B (Streck), vii 87-94; Rm. vii 83-86; cf. also ABL 350 rev. 4-7: *adê šá šarri bēliya kî ikšudušunuti šá lapan paṭar parzilli ušēzibu ina bubūtu imāti,* "as soon as

the Kuyunjik Collection in the British Museum (Bu 91-5-9, 178) was published by K. Deller and S. Parpola.[171] It contains 16 lines on the obverse and 10 on the reverse, in which Assurbanipal addresses the Qedarite leaders in the present tense.[172] Their chief, whose name appears in the treaty, is ^{m}*Ia-ú-ta-'*, that is Yauṭa' son of Ḫazael, who enjoyed the favor of Esarhaddon and Assurbanipal. Extant are certain of the sanctions to be imposed on the Qedarites for breach of treaty with Assurbanipal, definition of the position of Yauta', and the statement that the treaty is valid for future generations. By virtue of the correspondence of events with other Assurbanipal documents, the treaty can be dated prior to 652 B.C. (see pp. 147-155).

2. **Letters.** Most of the letters concerning the Arabs are in groups that can be dated:

a. The Nimrud Letters were discovered in the Nimrud (Calah) excavations in 1952 and published by Saggs, beginning in 1955.[173] We are concerned with letters XIV (=ND 2773), XVI (=ND 2765), XIX (=ND 2381), XX (=ND 2437) and XXIII (=ND 2644). The first four deal with the Assyrian administration in the Valley of Lebanon and in the desert border regions east of the Anti-Lebanon; the last with tribute or gifts from vassal kingdoms in southern Palestine and Transjordan.[174] The letters, therefore, do not antedate the conquest of Damascus by Tiglath-Pileser III (732 B.C.) and the integration of its territory into the Assyrian provincial system. The *terminus ad quem* for the letters, and for the entire Nimrud archive, is the transfer of the Assyrian capital from Calah (Nimrud) to Dūr-Šarrukīn (Khorsabad) during Sargon's reign (about 705 B.C.). Existing evidence allows no more precise dating. The historical relevance of these letters is discussed in Chapter IV.

Since in subject matter and one proper name the letters are similar to

the king's oath overtakes them, any who has saved (his life) from the sword will die of hunger".

171 *Orientalia* 37 (1968), 464-466.

172 Assurbanipal's name appears on obv. 8: [*Aššur*]-⌜DÙ⌝-A. Obv. 2 mentions the gods of both parties: *[ilāni*^{kur}*] Aš+šur* ^{kur}*Qi-id-[ri...]*.

173 On the discovery and classification of the Archive see H.W.F. Saggs, *Iraq* 17 (1955), 21-22. For the letters dealing with the western part of the Assyrian empire, including those discussed here, and a discussion of their historical background, see Saggs, *ibid.*, 126-154.

174 For the contents of the letters see pp. 94-98; and also note 342.

ABL 414 (=Rm. 77), it too should be considered part of the Nimrud correspondence.[175]

b. The Harper Letters include some Neo-Babylonian letters regarding Arabs sent to the king of Assyria by Nabû-šum-lišir:

ABL 260 reports that ^{md}*A-a-ka-ba/ma-ru* son of ^{m}*Am-me-'-ta-'* of Massa' (rev., 3-4) attacked a caravan (*alaktu*), which left the territory of the Nabayateans (^{lú}*Ni-ba-'-a-ti*); only one of its members escaped and reached a fortified outpost of the king.[176]

ABL 262 is an account of the losses suffered by Assyrian soldiers as a result of an assault by Arabs (^{lú}*A-ra-bu*) in the vicinity of the town of ^{uru}*Bi-maš-maš;* and of Nabû-šum-lišir's attack (on the Arabs?).[177]

ABL 350 recounts Nabû-šum-lišir's defeat of the Qedarites (^{lú}*Qí-dar-a-a*) and the troubles that would beset them (because they violated their treaty with the king of Assyria).[178]

ABL 1117 tells of contacts between the king of Babylonia and Natnu the Nabayatean (^{m}*Na-at-nu* ^{lú}*Na-ba-a-tu-ú-a*), who was given Assyrian and other prisoners taken at Sippar.[179]

Other Harper Letters sent to the king of Assyria by Nabû-šum-lišir alone or with Aqar-Bēl-lumur are ABL 259, 261, 264, 265, 811 and 1128.

L. Waterman attributed the letters to two people named Nabû-šum-lišir and assigned them as follows:[180]

I. ABL 259, 1117, 1128

II. ABL 260-262, 264-265, 350, 811, 1101.

The name of the Assyrian king does not, of course, appear in the salutation of any of these letters. By means of the titles of the letters in his book, Waterman indicates that 259, 811, 1117 and 1128 were written to Assurbanipal, whereas 260-262, 264-265, 350, and 1101 are entitled by him "to the king" and are not identified further.[181]

175 See Waterman, *RCAE,* I, 288-289; Pfeiffer, *SLA,* No. 90. On the contents and date of ABL 414 see below, pp. 95-97.

176 See Waterman, *ibid.,* I, No. 260; Pfeiffer, *ibid.,* No. 91. For translation only see A.L. Oppenheim, *Letters from Mesopotamia,* Chicago 1967, No. 118.

177 See Waterman, *ibid.,* I, No. 262.

178 See Waterman, *ibid.,* I, No. 350; Pfeiffer, *ibid.,* No. 24.

179 See Waterman, *ibid.,* II, No. 1117; Pfeiffer, *ibid.,* No. 63.

180 Waterman, *ibid.,* IV, 131.

We agree that these letters were written by two people with the same name, but classify them otherwise, according to period:

I. ABL 261, 264, 265 — the Sennacherib period (not later than 700 B.C.)

II. ABL 259, 260, 262, 350, 811, 1117, 1128 — the Assurbanipal period.

The following considerations govern our classification:[182]

(i) All the letters in Group II have a uniform salutation (somewhat shortened in ABL 259), with blessings to the king in the name of Nabû and Marduk, who are enjoined to prolong the king's life and grant him a just scepter and a permanent throne.[183] The king's epithet is *šar mātāti* ("king of all countries"), which was very common in Assurbanipal's time.[184]

(ii) ABL 261 and 264 were composed jointly by Nabû-šum-lišir and Aqar-Bēl-lumur, and have a uniform salutation.[185] Although ABL 265 is damaged and was composed by Nabû-šum-lišir alone, its salutation places it in Group I. Other letters to the king composed only by Aqar-Bēl-lumur (ABL 852, 853, 856, 857, 1259), also definitely belong in Group I. M. Dietrich has reported 11 additional letters in the British Museum, composed either by Nabû-šum-lišir or Aqar-bēl-lumur or

181 In order to flesh out the picture, it should be noted that Olmstead (*History of Assyria,* 427-428, 470) sets ABL 260-262, 350 in Assurbanipal's period, and S.S. Ahmed (*Southern Mesopotamia in the Time of Ashurbanipal,* Hague-Paris, 1968, 37, 94) puts ABL 259, 260, 1117 in the days of the war with Šamaš-šum-ukin.

182 Because the ensuing criteria do not apply to ABL 1101, we cannot determine its date. At any rate, it should probably not be included in either of the two groups as we have classified them.

183 *ana šar mātāti bēliya arduka* [md]*Nabû-šum-lišir* [d]*Nabû u* [d]*Marduk ūmē*[meš] *arkūti*[meš] *šanāti*[meš] *darāti*[meš] [giš]*ḫaṭṭu išartu* [giš]*kussu darû ana šar mātāti bēliya liddinu* ("To my lord, the king of all countries, your servant Nabû-šum-lišir: May Nabû and Marduk grant my lord, the king of all countries, a life lasting through many days and years, a just scepter and a permanent throne").

184 Nevertheless it should be pointed out that this epithet also occurs in a few letters from the time of Sargon and Esarhaddon, see M.-J. Seux, *Épithètes royales akkadiennes et sumériennes,* Paris 1967, 315, note 262.

185 An identical salutation is found in ABL 1335. The text is damaged and only the name of Aqar-bēl-lumur remains, but from the contents it is clear that the letter was sent by two signatories, of whom the second was undoubtedly Nabû-šum-lišir.

both.[186] All the letters, including Dietrich's, belong to one complex. Eight of them (including ABL 261 and 264) refer to *mār Yakin* and his whereabouts. Since Dietrich's opinion that *mār Yakin* signifies Merodach-baladan seems plausible,[187] the *terminus ad quem* for these letters is 700 B.C., when Merodach-baladan fled his homeland Bīt Yakin to escape Sennacherib's army (in the fourth campaign of that Assyrian king).

(iii) The letters of Group II, in contrast, designate the king's adversary as *šar Babili*^{ki} (ABL 259, 1117), the title applied to Šamaš-šum-ukin. The *terminus ad quem* for these two letters is therefore 648 B.C. when Šamaš-šum-ukin lost the war and died.[188]

The spelling ^{lú}*Ni-ba-'-a-ti* in ABL 260 is different from the spelling in the Assyrian documents for the people of Nebaioth (cf. Appendix A, 10). It seems especially strange when compared with the name of their chieftain ^{m}*Na-at-nu* ^{lú}*Na-ba-a-tu-ú-a* in ABL 1117:7, because both letters were undoubtedly sent by the same person. Another example in ABL 260 of the use of *-'a* instead of the usual *-a-a* or *-ia* after the vowel *i* or *a* appears in ^{m}*Am-me-'-ta-'* (rev., 3), which is simply *'myṯ'*, a common personal name in Old Arabic inscriptions.[189] For this spelling practice compare ^{íd}*Ba-di-ia-a-tum* (BE IX 29:3), ^{íd}*Ba-di-'-tum* (BE IX 29:17), ^{íd}*Ba-di-'-tum* (TMH II/III 147:2, 11), בדיתא (Bab. Talmud, *Mo'ed Qaṭan* 11:1); ^{m}*Da-ri-'-a-šu,* ^{m}*Da-ri-'-mu-šu,* ^{m}*Da-ri-'-us.*[190]

The salutations, which are identical and in a style peculiar to them alone, contrast with the varied spelling of proper names and indicate that they underwent no change despite their having been written by different scribes. The letters seem therefore to have been dictated by Nabû-šum-lišir himself (and not composed by scribes who were given the general contents), or written by scribes

186 M. Dietrich, *WO* 4 (1968), 193-201. The full text of the letters has not yet been published, but in Dietrich's announcement of their contents salutations and special expressions were given.

187 Dietrich, *ibid.*, 193 f., with additional arguments for dating the letters to the period of struggle between Sennacherib and Merodach-baladan.

188 For a more precise dating of ABL 1117 see pp. 153-154.

189 Cf. *RNP*, II, 108.

190 *NBN*, 53-54.

employed by Nabû-šum-lišir, each of whom used the salutation decided on by the first one.

c. ABL 547 is a Neo-Assyrian letter to the king about the transgression of Arabs from their allotted grazing land and the razzias they made in the Middle Euphrates region (^{kur}*Ḫi-in-za-ni* and ^{kur}*Su-ḫi* are mentioned in it). It opens with a blessing in the name of Aššur and Ninlil. Of the signatory's name only ^{m}*Ṭab(?)-...* survives. A comparison of the salutations in ABL 87-91, 93-98, 396, 398, 480-483 supports Waterman's opinion that the signatory is Ṭab-ṣil-Ešarra of the period of Sargon.[191]

Another letter from Ṭab-ṣil-Ešarra (ABL 88) quotes the king's order (*abit šarri*) to Nabû-bēl-šumāte, whose title was ^{lú}*qēpu ša* ^{uru}*Bi-ra[t]*, with the accusing question: *ma-a a-ta-a* ^{kur}*Aŕ-bá-a-a ḫu-ub-tu ša* ^{uru}*Si-par iḫ-bu-tú-ni,* "why did the Arabs plunder Sippar?" (rev., 3-5).[192] Waterman and Pfeiffer misread it as ^{kur}*Up-pa-a-a* (instead of ^{kur}*Aŕ-bá-a-a*) and had difficulty identifying it. Although ^{kur}*Up-pa-a-a* might seem to refer to the people of Upê (=Opis), a town on the Tigris dozens of miles from Sippar, ABL 547, which refers to ^{kur}*Ar-bá-a-a* (rev. 10), was sent by the same signatory and deals with a similar situation. The name in ABL 88 should therefore be read ^{kur}*Aŕ-bá-a-a.*[193]

d. The non-historical sources also include administrative and economic documents, such as receipts, payment orders, instructions as to the distribution of various commodities. Each bears the date of writing and illuminates the relations of northern Arabia and Babylonia, mainly during the Neo-Babylonian and Persian periods. These documents and their contents are listed in pp. 188-191.

191 Waterman, *RCAE,* I, 388-389. On lines 3-5 see Deller, *Orientalia* 30 (1961), 350.

192 Waterman, *op. cit.,* I, No. 88; Pfeiffer, *SLA,* No. 154.

193 See Deller, *Orientalia* 31 (1962), 187-188.

Chapter II

THE BIBLICAL SOURCES

A. CLASSIFICATION

There are numerous references in various books of the Bible to nomads in the border regions of Palestine and in the desert to the east and south. In the historical and prophetic books, these references span the entire biblical period from the Patriarchs and the desert wanderings to the time of Nehemiah; they occur in the poetical and wisdom books as well. For purposes of our study they will be classified as historical or literary sources. (The genealogical lists constitute a category unique to itself, but since the information from extra-biblical sources must precede the study of the nomad groups included there, this material will be discussed in Appendices A and B). We shall also distinguish chronologically between the period to the end of David's reign, i.e. to about the mid-10th century B.C., and the period subsequent to it. These criteria bring us to the following classifications:

Historical Sources, including the Pentateuch and Chronicles (except the genealogical lists), Joshua-Kings and Nehemiah	Literary Sources, including prophetic, poetical and wisdom books
i. Sources for the period to the end of David's reign (mid-10th century B.C.)	
Amalek(ites) Gen. 14:7; Ex. 17:8-16; Num. 13:29;14:25, 43, 45; 24:20; Deut. 25:17-19; Judg. 3:13; 5:14; 6:3, 33; 7:12; 10:12; 12:15; I Sam. 14:48; chap 15; 27:8; 28:18; 30:1, 13, 18; II Sam. 1:1, 8, 13; 8:12; I Chron. 18:11	Ps. 83:8

Historical Sources (cont'd)	**Literary Sources** (cont'd)
Hagarites I Chron. 5:10, 19-20; 27:31	Ps. 83:7[194]
Ishmaelites Gen. 37:25-28; 39:1; Judg. 8:24; I Chron. 2:17; 27:30 (see also Gen. chaps. 16-17 on Ishmael)	Ps. 83:7
Jetur I Chron. 5:19[195]	
Ma'on (מעון) Judg. 10:12[196]	
Midian(ites) Gen. 36:35 (= I Chron. 1:46); 37:28, 36;[197] Ex. 2:15-16; 3:1;	Ps. 83:10; cf. Isa. 9:3; 10:26

194 For determination of the historical background of Psalm 83 in the period of the Judges, see B. Maisler (Mazar), *BJPES* 4 (1937), 47-51; S.I. Feigin, *Missitrei Heavar,* Biblical and Historical Studies, New York 1943, 31-33 (Hebrew). There are other approaches which rely mainly on the reference to Ashur (אשור) in verse 9 and therefore date the psalm to the period of the height of the Assyrian empire (see e.g., commentaries on the book of Psalms: H. Schmidt, 83; A. Weiser, 1950, 369-370; M.J. Dahood, 273), or the Restoration (e.g., Ch. and E.G. Briggs, 217-223), and even Hasmonaean times (for a summary of this approach see the argument against it in W.H. Barnes, 399). Along with Mazar's suggestion connecting *Ashur* in this verse with the campaign of Tiglath-Pileser I to the Lebanon there is another way to eliminate the difficulty, by assuming that the term *Ashur* refers not to the Assyrian empire but to nomads in the Arabian desert mentioned among the descendants of Dedan (Gen. 25:3), and perhaps also in Num. 24:22,24; see H. Gunkel, *Die Psalmen,* Göttingen 1926, 365; Albright, *Alt Festschrift,* 9-11.

195 We can include I Chron. 5:19 in the list of sources to the end of the Davidic period if we connect the contents of I Chron. 5:18-22 with what is said in 5:10 about the war against the Hagarites in the time of Saul. However, the inclusion of Jetur and Naphish in the list of the "Sons of Ishmael" (Gen. 25:13-15; I Chron. 1:29-31) makes it possible for the names listed in verse 19, in addition to the Hagarites, to point to a later ethno-geographic situation in northern Transjordan (about this see below, p. 67; and also Appendix B). Under such circumstances, the people of Jetur and Naphish must be removed from their place in the table and included in the group of later sources (listing Nodab here, which is nowhere again mentioned, is hypothetical and based only on its reference to Jetur and Naphish in I Chron. 5:19).

196 According to the Septuagint, A,B, Μαδιαμ, it appears that here it should be Midian (מדין); see J. Liver, "Ma'on, Me'unites", *Enc. Miqr.,* V, 188.

197 The name Medanites (מְדָנִים) possibly refers to the people of Medan (מְדָן), who are included with Midian in the list of the "Sons of Qeturah" (Gen. 25:2; I Chron. 1:32). This, however, may be an erroneous version of the Midianites (מִדְיָנִים) mentioned in Gen. 37:28. Earlier translations give Midianites (מִדְיָנִים) in both places.

Historical Sources (cont'd)	**Literary Sources** (cont'd)
Midian(ites) (cont'd) 4:19; 18:1; Num. 10:29; 22:4, 7; 25:6-18; 31:1-9; Josh. 13:21; Judg. chaps. 6-8; 9:17; I Kings 11:18	
Naphish I Chron. 5:19[195]	
Nodab I Chron. 5:19[195]	
People of the East (בני קדם) Gen. 29:1; Judg. 6:3, 33; 7:12; 8:10.	

ii. Sources after the reign of David (from mid-10th century B.C. on)

"The remnants of the Amalekites that had escaped" I Chron. 4:43	
Arab(s) (ערב(ים)) Neh. 2:19; 4:1; 6:1; II Chron. 9:14 (I Kings 10:15 has הָעֶרֶב); 17:11; 21:16; 22:1; 26:7	עֲרָב: Isa. 13:20; 21:13; Jer. 3:2; 25:24; Ezek. 27:21 הָעֶרֶב: Jer. 25:20, 24
Buz	Jer. 25:23; cf. Job 32:2,6
Dedan	Isa. 21:13; Jer. 25:23; 49:8; Ezek. 25:13; 27:15[198], 20; 38:13
Dumah	Isa. 21:11
'Ephah	Isa. 60:6
Massa'	Prov. 30:1; 31:1
Me'unites I Chron. 4:41; II Chron. 26:7	
Midian	Isa. 60:6; Hab. 3:7[199]
Nebaioth	Isa. 60:7
People of the East (בני קדם) I Kings 5:10 (RSV 4:30)	Isa. 11:14; Jer. 49:28; Ezek. 25: 4, 10; Job. 1:3
Qedar	Isa. 21:16-17; 42:11; 60:7; Jer. 2:10; 49:28; Ezek. 27:21; Ps. 120:5; Cant. 1:5

198 The Septuagint B has υἱοὶ Ῥοδίων. This translation, and the reference to the "men of Dedan" (דדן) in Ezek. 27:15 close to the reference to Tarshish, Javan, Tubal, Meshech and Beth-togarmah in verses 12-14, suggest that the more probable reading of the text is "the men of Rodan" (=Rhodes, רֹדָן). Cf. the proximity of these nations in the list of the "Sons of Japheth" in Gen. 10:2-4; I Chron. 1:5-7. For the substitution of ד for ר, cf. דֹּדָנִים Gen. 10:4 - רֹדָנִים I Chron. 1:7.

Historical Sources (cont'd)		Literary Sources (cont'd)
Sheba	I Kings 10:1-13 (=II Chron. 9:1-9,12)	Isa. 60:6; Jer. 6:20; Ezek. 27:22-23; 38:13; Ps. 72:10,15; Job. 1:15; 6:19
Tema'		Isa. 21:14; Jer. 25:23; Job. 6:19

For **Jetur, Naphish** and **Nodab,** see note 195.

This table reveals that in the historical and literary parts of the Bible there are radical changes in names of the nomad groups, the turning-point occurring in the mid-10th century B.C.: thereafter Hagarites, Ishmaelites, Midianities and Amalekites do not appear (nor, it should be noted, do they figure in extra-biblical sources, either of the period of this study or prior to it). Instead, the collective noun "Arab(s)" begins to be used, and various groups (Buz, Dedan, Dumah, 'Ephah, Massa', Nebaioth, Qedar, Sheba and Tema') not in the sources for the earlier period are referred to. Only the designation "People of the East" (בני קדם) spans both periods.

It must therefore be asked whether a connection exists between the various groups mentioned in sources for the periods before and after the 10th century B.C.; if there is none, was there a change in the ethnic outline of the nomad population in the border regions of Palestine at approximately the time of David? We can apply ourselves to this question only after examining the extra-biblical sources which clarify the historico-ethnic picture of the time; this is done in Appendix B. Since this study deals only with the nomad groups listed for the later period, we shall concentrate on evaluating the sources concerning them.

B. HISTORICAL SOURCES

1. I Kings 10:1-10,13 (= II Chron. 9:1-9,12), an account of the Queen of Sheba's visit to Solomon, is part of the Wisdom Literature devoted to Solomon and his wisdom that surpassed that of all other peoples.[200]

199 Midian in these two references has a geographical rather than an actual ethnological meaning, see O. Eissfeldt, *JBL*, 87 (1968), 383 ff., esp. 392-393.

200 For an analysis of the literary and linguistic characteristics of this kind of narrative source, see R.B.Y. Scott, *SVT* 3 (1955), 264-272 (on stories connected with the wisdom of Solomon, see also J.A. Montgomery-H.S. Gehmann, *Kings*, Edinburgh 1951, 129-131). The passages contain verbal features typical of post-exilic literature.

Most scholars, assuming that this account has a kernel of authenticity, locate the homeland of Solomon's royal visitor in northern Arabia, and connect her with the Sabaeans known from the inscriptions of Tiglath-Pileser III and from Job 1:15.[201] However, recent archaeological research has uncovered evidence of sedentary populations organized as kingdoms in southern Arabia at the beginning of the first millennium B.C., suggesting that the spice trade operated from there at that time. It is therefore highly probable that the queen mentioned in I Kings chap. 10 came to Jerusalem from Sheba in southern Arabia to settle questions of the spice trade with king Solomon, who dominated all the Palestinian trade routes from the Mediterranean and the Gulf of Elath to the desert border regions.[202] Although dozens of rulers are known from the Sabaean inscriptions, not one is a woman, but it should be remembered that these inscriptions do not antedate the 8th century B.C. (even according to their earliest dating which is controversial, see Appendix A, note 46) and that, actually, we know nothing about the earlier leaders of the South-Arabian kingdoms.

2. II Chron. 9:14 records Solomon's revenue from the taxation of merchants and "all the kings of the Arabs (מלכי עֲרָב; the parallel passage in I kings 10:15 has מלכי הָעֶרֶב) and governors of the land". The term פחות הארץ, "governors of the land", which originated in the Mesopotamian administrative structure, points out that such an expression could not have been used in Israelite sources before the Assyrian empire expanded westward. Consequently we may ask whether the reference here to the "kings of the Arabs" reflects the ethnic situation in the Solomonic period, and whether this is also a late term designating parties connected to Arabian trade and known from Assyrian sources.[203]

201 For a summary of this approach see Montgomery, *Arabia and the Bible*, 180-181; idem, *Kings*, 215-216.

202 Albright, *Eretz-Israel* 5 (1958), 1*-9*. Mazar (*Western Galilee and the Coast of Galilee*, The Israel Exploration Society XIXth Archaeological Convention, Jerusalem 1965, 15, Hebrew) drew attention to Ps. 72:10, which also refers to the relations of Israel with Sheba in South Arabia during Solomon's time.

203 In any case, we should not connect the term "Arab(s)" in the biblical and Assyrian sources with the southern part of the peninsula and its population. This term originated in the northern part of the peninsula, and was applied to the south at

3. The following passages from Chronicles, relating to various nomad groups and their contacts with Israel during the period of the monarchy, have no parallel in Kings: I Chron. 4:38-43; 5:10, 18-22; II Chron. 17:10-11; 20:1 ff.; 21:16-17; 22:1; 26:7-8. Although it is no longer possible to accept the view enunciated by J. Wellhausen — that all the passages in Chronicles which are without parallel in the books of Samuel and Kings were written later and have no historical validity — it is clear that Chronicles does include many late legendary and midrashic elements.[204] Before citing such a passage for our study it must be evaluated as a historical source, although it is usually impossible to check these data against extra-biblical sources, which in any case are all but non-existent. Such an examination must therefore be based mainly on literary characteristics, bias and historiosophical concepts, noting the terminology and technicalities that occur in the sources. Most passages bear the linguistic stamp of the Chronicler and reflect a later stage of biblical language. The crucial question, then, is whether the later linguistic, stylistic and conceptual features of the passages are sufficient to invalidate them as sources for the history of a period which preceded the writing of the later parts of Chronicles by hundreds of years, or whether they are derived from a kernel of history afterwards reworded in Chronicles. No unequivocal answer can be given, nor are the other criteria for dating the passages absolute.

I Chron. 4:38-43 mentions the expansion of the Simeonites as far as the entrance to Gedor (למבוא גדר; following the Septuagint's ἕως τοῦ ἐλθεῖν Γεραρα, this is commonly read "Gerar", גרר; the correct version is important in connection with the location of the Me'unites in the 8th century B.C.) and Mount Seir: (41) "These, registered by name, came in the days of Hezekiah king of Judah, and destroyed their tents and the

approximately the beginning of the Christian era, see Eph'al, *JNES* 35 (1976), 233-235.

204 See, *inter alia,* Eissfeldt, *The Old Testament: An Introduction,* Oxford 1965, 531-540, and the studies listed there; also S. Japhet, *The Ideology of the Book of Chronicles and its Place in Biblical Thought,* Jerusalem 1977, 7-15, 111-121, 132-154, 166-172, 361-370, and *passim* (Hebrew). Relevant to the war episodes peculiar to the book of Chronicles — including references to other scholars — is P. Welten's *Geschichte und Geschichtsdarstellung in den Chronikbücher,* Neukirchen-Vluyn 1973. The author, who believes that all these descriptions accord with common *topoi,* dates

Meunim (= Me'unites) who were found there, and exterminated them to this day ... (42) And some of them, five hundred men of the Simeonites, went to Mount Seir ... (43) And they destroyed the remnant of the Amalekites that had escaped, and they have dwelt there to this day." The expression "to this day" at the end of verses 41 and 43 suggests that they were copied with no great change from a source written at a time when the Simeonites were still settled in the border region west and south of Judah, i.e. during the period of the monarchy. It is, however, difficult to determine more precisely the time of the events described: From the syntactic point of view, it is impossible to say whether the expression "in the days of Hezekiah king of Judah" in verse 41 applies to the census of the Simeonites (for censuses during the monarchy, cf. I Chron. 5:17) or to their war against the Me'unites (or perhaps even to the five hundred who went to Mount Seir). From the point of view of content, what is said about the expansion of the Simeonites towards Philistia and the area west of the Arabah[205] and their relatively long stay there (indicated by the phrase "to this day") accords with periods during which the kingdom of Judah strengthened and solidified its control of these regions, as in the days of Jehoshaphat[206] and Uzziah.[207] It is difficult to set such events in the reign of Hezekiah, when the territory of the kingdom of Judah was diminished in southern Palestine (after Sennacherib's campaign in 701 B.C.).[208] It may be that verses 39-43 recount two Simeonite expansion activities.

their composition and the historical background of most of them to the later part ot the Restoration period. Many of Welten's historical conclusions, however, are for us unacceptable.

205 There is no doubt that the name "Mount Seir" refers here not to Edom but to an area west of the Arabah (cf. Deut. 1:2, 44; 33:2; Josh. 11:17; 12:7), contradicting Musil, *Arabia Deserta,* 492; W. Rudolph, *Chronikbücher,* Tübingen 1955, 42. Judah's hegemony over Edom ceased in the time of Jehoram son of Jehoshaphat (II Kings 8:20-22; II Chron. 21:8-10).

206 See I Kings 22:48-49; II Kings 3:9 ff.; II Chron. 17:11. For the limits of the kingdom of Judah and its expansion during the reign of Jehoshaphat, see Mazar, "Jehoshaphat", *Enc. Miqr.,* III, 466-470.

207 See II Chron. 26:6-8. In that time the kingdom of Judah still controlled the south as far as Elath. II Kings 16:6 and II Chron. 28:18 indicate appreciable shrinkage in Judah's territory on the border of Philistia and in the south, close to the campaign of Tiglath-Pileser III to Palestine, i.e., some time before Uzziah's death. See note 210 below.

208 Luckenbill, *Sennacherib,* 33:30-34; 70:29-30.

I Chron. 5:10 tells of the war of the Reubenites against the Hagarites in the days of Saul, and verses 18-22 report a war of the Reubenites, the Gadites and the half-tribe of Manasseh against "the Hagarites, Jetur, Naphish and Nodab" without specifying when. The Hagarites are mentioned in the Bible in connection with the period of the Judges and the early Monarchy, and are never referred to in later periods.[209] Their appearance in a single verse, together with the people of Jetur, Naphish and Nodab, might be taken to indicate that the latter lived in the area at the same time. On the other hand, some importance must be ascribed to the inclusion of Jetur and Naphish in the list of the Sons of Ishmael (Gen. 25:13-15; I Chron. 1:29-31), most of whose other components are known only from a period not earlier than the 9th century B.C. (see pp. , and also Appendix B.). Verses 18-22 show the characteristic features of the Chronicler's narrative technique and his usual style in describing the wars of Israel (such as quantitative exaggeration as regards warriors, prisoners and booty, faith in God and praying during battle). This leads us to suggest that the description in verses 18-22 of the enmity between the Transjordanian Israelites and the people of Jetur, Naphish and Nodab reflects a situation which obtained hundreds of years after Saul. Thus the inclusion of these groups in the biblical report of the war against the Hagarites is nothing but a later addition about a war which may never actually have taken place.

II Chron. chap. 17 describes Jehoshaphat's operations in purifying the ritual, disseminating the Book of the Law of the Lord, organizing the civil administration, organizing and extending the army and fortifying the kingdom. The technical terms and the names of the officials, priests and Levites involved in these organizational activities (see especially verses 2, 7-9, 14-19) give weight to the reliability of the descriptions,[210]

209 The other references to the Hagarites are in Ps. 83:7 and I Chron. 27:31. For an ascription of Ps. 83 to the period near Saul's ascension to the throne, assuming that the psalm lists the enemies of Israel during the period of the Judges, see Maisler (Mazar), *BJPES* 4 (1937), 47-51.

210 For the chapter as a whole, see Rudolph, *op. cit.*, 249 ff. For the reliability of what is said about Jehoshaphat's reform and the dissemination of the Book of the Law in Judah (verses 7-9), also see Albright (although most of his arguments here seem irrelevant), *Marx Jubilee Volume*, 74-82; A. Demsky, *Literacy in Israel and among Neighboring Peoples in the Biblical Period*, unpublished Ph.D. dissertation, Hebrew University, Jerusalem 1976, 107-113.

even though verses 14-19 show signs of the numerical exaggeration typical of Chronicles material of late composition. After noting the strengthening of the kingdom of Judah and its neighbors' fears (verse 10), the text states (verse 11) that the Philistines brought Jehoshaphat presents and silver for tribute "and the Arabs (הערביאים) also brought him seven thousand seven hundred rams, and seven thousands seven hundred he-goats". The arrangement of this chapter suggests that the two verses describe Jehoshaphat's reward for his religious activities, but it seems possible to separate them: the spirit and language of verse 10 belong to the later stage of Chronicles, perhaps extending the general statements of verse 5. On the other hand, the details of verse 11 suggest that it is based on a reliable source and fits the historical information in the chapter, and was inserted in its present place in accordance with the Chronicler's conceptions.

II Chron. 26:6-15, the main scriptural source for Uzziah's reign, is detailed about the military and political flourishing of the kingdom of Judah of the time. Despite its many late linguistic features, its details are generally considered reliable, since they are factually written and not ideologically burdened (also II Kings 16:6 and II Chron. 28:18 referring to the loss of Judah's territories during the reign of Ahaz — i.e. during Uzziah's lifetime — may be taken as supporting the ascription of reliability to the narrative in II Chron. 26 about Uzziah's military achievements.[211] Such an estimate applies as well to the information in verses 6-8 about Uzziah's military operations in Philistia and his superiority over "the Arabs that dwelt in Gurbaal and the Me'unites". According to the Septuagint οἱ Μιναῖοι, verse 8 should apparently

211 The common concept about the greatness and power of the kingdom of Judah during the reign of Uzziah — with a military and political dominance extending to northern Syria — emerged from the belief that Uzziah/Azariah king of Judah was referred to in the inscriptions of Tiglath-Pileser (for the latest extensive discussion supporting this opinion see Tadmor, *Scripta Hierosolymitana* 8 [1961], 232-271). N. Na'aman had recently challenged this opinion, proving that one of the fragments (K 6205=III R 9, 2) refers to ^{m}*Ḫazaqiyau* = Hezekiah king of Judah and in fact belongs to the inscriptions of Sennacherib and not Tiglath-Pileser III (*BASOR* 214 [1974], 25-39). The remaining text (III R 9,3), however, still explicitly mentions an Azriyau of a country whose name has not survived (Rost, *Ann.*, 123, 131). Whether he was a king of Judah (as Tadmor has suggested) or of a North Syrian state (as Na'aman now proposes) is an open question which cannot be resolved without further evidence.

read "Me'unites" (מעונים) instead of "Ammonites" (עמונים).[212] From the geographical context this reading seems preferable (see also note 213).

II Chron. chap. 20 tells of the rise of "the Moabites (בני מואב, lit. "children of Moab") and the Ammonites (בני עמון, lit. "children of Ammon") and with them some of the Ammonites (עמונים)... against Jehoshaphat for battle" (verse 1). It is hard to explain the juxtaposition of "the children of Ammon" and "some of the Ammonites" which latter, following the Septuagint ἐκ τῶν Μιναίων, can be plausibly read as Me'unites (מעונים).[213] Jehoshaphat's victory over the raiders is here characterized, in midrashic style, as a true miracle and salvation from on high: verses 15-17 specify that Jehoshaphat and the people of Judah did not fight, but concentrated on prayer, praise of god, and thanksgiving. This concept undoubtedly reflects a later period, closer to the time Chronicles was composed,[214] for which reason many reject the validity of II Chron. 20:1-30 as a source for the reign of Jehoshaphat.[215] On the other hand, it may well be that though its present form is late, its background, of an incursion into Judah from Transjordan in the last years of Jehoshaphat's reign, after Moab was freed of Israelite control, is historical fact.[216] But in that case the incursion was much more

212 E.g., E.L. Curtis-A.A. Madsen, *The Book of Chronicles,* Edinburgh 1910, 449-450; Rudolph, *op. cit.,* 282.

213 E.g., Curtis, *ibid.,* 406; Rudolph, *op. cit.,* 258. It is noteworthy that the name עמונים occurs in the book of Chronicles only in II Chron. 20:1 and 26:8, the common name for the Ammonites in this book being בני עמון. In both verses the Septuagint reads οἱ Μιναῖοι = Me'unites, instead of οἱ 'Αμμανῖται = the Ammonites.

214 On these historiosophical features see Japhet, *The Ideology of the Book of Chronicles,* 65, 112-117, 218-220.

215 For the opinion of those who completely dismiss the value of the story as a historical source, see Curtis, *ibid.,* 404-405. M. Noth, *ZDPV* 67 (1945), 45-71, differs, assuming that at the basis of the story lies a local tradition about a historical event originating in southern Judea. However, in his view, this event is late and merely refers to a Nabataean incursion into southern Judea around 300 B.C. This approach is based on groundless assumptions, such as that the name of the Nabataeans, residents of Edom (Mt. Seir) in the 4th century B.C., is here represented by the Me'unites, and that mention of the Moabites and Ammonites is only a later unimportant addition influenced by II King chap. 3. See also Welten, *op. cit.,* 140-153.

216 See Rudolph, *op. cit.,* 258-260. For a view that there is a historical basis for various events peculiar to Chronicles, among them the story here discussed, see also Eissfeldt, *The Old Testament,* 536 f., 539 f.

limited in scale and effect than this chapter indicates. Nor is it possible, from the present form of the story, to determine what part, if any, was played in the raid by the Ammonites and the Me'unites. At any rate, from what we know of the Me'unites and the Edomites in the course of two hundred years from the middle of the 9th century B.C. on, the identification of Me'unites as inhabitants of Mount Seir (as emerges from the comparison of verse 1 with verses 10, 22, 23) does not fit the Jehoshaphat period.[217]

II Chron. 21:12-19 is a prophetic story of Elijah's epistle to Jehoram king of Judah. As the story progresses the punishments promised in the letter materialize, among them the raid of "the Philistines and of the Arabs who are near the Ethiopians (כושים)" into Judah, who captured "all the possessions they found that belonged to the king's house, and also his sons and his wives, so that no son was left to him except Jehoahaz, the youngest son" (verses 16-17; according to II Chron. 22:1 which is based on 21:17, all of Jehoram's older sons were in fact killed). This passage provides information about Jehoram's reign which is given nowhere else in the Bible. Despite the legendary character of the story, and certain difficulties in coordinating this affair with the story of Jehu's murder of the brothers of Ahaziah king of Judah (II Kings 10:13-14), and of Athaliah's seizure of the throne and her destruction of all the royal family (II Kings 11:1; II Chron. 22:10), there is no reason to doubt the basic facts of the tale. However, though the raid into Judah in Jehoram's day can be considered historically true, its effects were surely grossly exaggerated in the prophetic story.[218]

217 Welten assumes — trying to remove the difficulty raised by this identification — that it could have been true only when the territories of the Me'unites, "the inhabitants of Mount Seir", and "Edom" (cf. verse 2) overlapped, i.e. during the existence of Idumaea, which was south of Judea. For the location of the Me'unites in the 8th century B.C. see pp. 79-80, 91.

218 Maisler (Mazar), *Tarbiz* 19 (1949), 123-124, proposed that the Philistines and Arabs were able to attack because of the absence from Judah of Jehoram and his army, who had gone to war against Shalmaneser III in 845 B.C. That view is based on the assumption that the very same league of "the twelve kings of the land of Ḫatti and the seashore" which fought at Qarqar in 853 B.C. also fought against Shalmaneser III in 845 B.C. Yet we should note that "the twelve kings ..." is a stereotypical — not a literal — expression used for each one of his campaigns in that region (for his 6th regnal year [853 B.C.] see *AR* I, § 563, 610, 647; F. Safar, *Sumer* 7 [1951], 7 [=E. Michel, *WO* 2 (1954), 32]; for the 10th [849 B.C.] see *AR* I,

Thus it is clear how subjective is any evaluation of those passages in Chronicles which have no parallels in other books of the Bible that deal with the period of tne Monarchy, among them those relating to the Arabs and the Me'unites. Because the validity of such passages cannot be established by analyzing only biblical sources, difficulties arise over the historicity of Arab-Philistine contiguousness, which Chronicles alone mentions (II 21:16-17; 26:6-8), and over the location of the Me'unites, giving data insufficiently complete (I 4:41; II 26:6-8). A fundamental problem, strongly used in argument by those who postdate the topological background of the discussed references in the book of Chronicles, is the phenomenon that names of nomad groups mentioned there — such as the Hagerites, the Me'unites and the Arabs — do not occur even once in the books of Samuel and Kings, which also cover the age of the Monarchy, thus diminishing (or even canceling out) their value as historical sources for that period. In regard to all these questions, the Assyrian sources of the 8th century B.C. offer crucial evidence for the various nomad groups on the borders of Palestine and Egypt, without which no evaluation of the statements in Chronicles can be made. Such an evaluation will disclose that various scholarly approaches to the question, based mainly on classical historiographic works and the Septuagint, which reflect ethno-geographical conditions of a relatively late period (the 5th century B.C. and later), are mistaken and lead to erroneous conclusions.[219]

C. LITERARY SOURCES

The literary sources in the Bible offer typological details about nomads and their groups, their way of life and the nature of their contacts with

§ 652; for the 11th [848 B.C.] see *AR* I, § 568, 654; Safar, *ibid.*, 9 [=Michel, *ibid.*, 36]. For the 14th [845 B.C.] see *AR* I, § 571, 659; Safar, *ibid.*, 9 [=Michel, *ibid.*, 36]; see also descriptions of campaigns in two inscriptions in which the year they refer to is not clear: Michel, *WO* 1 [1947], 57; 3 [1964], 154 [=*AR* I, § 691]. Regarding the question of the "twelve kings" in the Monolith Inscription from Kurkh, see also Michel, *ibid.*, 1 [1947] 70, n. 13). Mazar's view, furthermore, presumes, with no corroborative evidence, constant shifts from conflict to cooperation in Israel's relations with Damascus after Ahab's death in the war against Aram in 852 B.C. The presence of Jehoram king of Judah in Syria in 845 B.C. thus is unproven, and the circumstances of the invasion of Judah during his reign remain clouded.

219 See more details on this below in pp. 77-80; and also pp. 89-90.

the sedentary population. Since clear chronological data is lacking, they present very little information that can be related to specific historical events. Therefore opinion differs as to the chronological and literary framework of various oracles referring to nomads, and their attribution to the prophets in whose books they appear; opinions about the dating and historical background of the oracles may vary by hundreds of years.[220] Thus, for example, Procksch believes that Isa. 21:11 ff. (including "the oracle concerning Arabia" and a short oracle on Qedar) refers to Sargon's campaign against the Arabs,[221] whereas others would place these oracles in the days of Nabonidus or even after the fall of Babylon in 539 B.C.[222] An exception is Jeremiah's oracle on Nebuchadnezzar's smiting of Qedar (49:28-33), the historical background for which is clarfied by the Babylonian Chronicle's testimony about the Babylonian army's raid against the Arabs in the desert in Nebuchadnezzar's sixth regnal year (599/8 B.C.).[223]

220 For a full summary of the approaches to the historical background of the oracles about the nations in the books of Isaiah, Jeremiah and Ezekiel, including those connected with the nomads, see Eissfeldt, *The Old Testament*, 321-322, 362-364, 377-378 (which also includes a detailed bibliography).

221 O. Procksch, *ZDMG* 84 (1930), *78*; idem, *Jesaja Ch. I-XXXIX*, Leipzig 1930, 271-275.

222 See, e.g., K. Galling, *Tradition und Situation (A. Weiser Festschrift)*, Göttingen 1963, 49-62; G. Fohrer, *Studien zur alttestamentliche Prophetie*, Berlin 1967, 132 ff.

223 See pp. 171-176.

PART TWO
HISTORICAL SURVEY

Historical Survey

The available sources enable us to follow sequentially the relations between the nomads and the sedentary populations in Palestine and its environs, as well as the imperial bodies which ruled the area beginning with the reign of Tiglath-Pileser III. Still, it seems advisable to begin the historical survey from the mid-9th to the second half of the 8th century B.C. Though information is scanty, it does enlighten us somewhat regarding the nature of the relations between the nomads and local political entities before the Assyrian period; it also contributes to an understanding of settlement and ethnographic conditions during the period of Assyrian rule — the main part of this survey.

Chapter III

FROM MID-9TH CENTURY B.C. TO ASSYRIAN IMPERIAL EXPANSION TO PALESTINE

The presence of nomads in two of the border regions of Syro-Palestine is documented as follows: 1) The Monolith Inscription of Shalmaneser III from Kurkh,[224] the oldest document mentioning Arabs, lists ^{m}*Gi-in-di-bu-'* ^{kur}*Ar-ba-a-a*[225] among the leaders of the coalition which opposed the Assyrian army at Qarqar in 853 B.C. It will be seen later that the territory of Gindibu' was in the northern part of the Syro-Arabian desert; 2) the book of Chronicles mentions various nomad groups in the western and southern border regions of the kingdom of Judah. In addition to the general term "Arabs", it gives the names of individual groups, like the Me'unites and "the remnant of the Amalekites".

224 *AR* I, § 610; *ANET,* 278-279.

225 For ^{m}*Gi-in-di-bu-'* cf. *jindub,* in Arabic a kind of locust, a word found as a proper name in early Arabic sources (e.g. Ibn Hishām, *The Life of Muhammad,* 974; Al-Hamdāni, *Iklīl,* I, 349, 353; II, 24, 291, etc.). The suffix *-'u* in the Assyrian transliteration of the name signifies a lengthened last vowel, i.e. Gindibû, and not a constant Aleph at the end of the name (cf. ^{m}*Ab-du-'* ^{ld}*Ar-ba-a(-a),* CT XXII, 86:7, which is merely Abdû; and see p. 211 regarding this spelling). There is no basis for the suggestion (by K. Petráček, *ArOr* 27 [1959], 44-53) of a Safaitic origin, like *ka-nadību-hu.* For Hebrew names similar in meaning to Gindibu', compare חגב, חגבא, חגבה (Ezra 2:45, 46; Neh. 7:48; Lachish Letter 1:3); and also the seal לעזרי/ו הגבה ("belonging to Azaryau [son of] *hgbh*"), on the bottom of which is the image of a locust. The affinity of the image to the inscription makes it likely that *gbh* is a variant of *gobai* (גו[ו]בי, locust), apparently the family name of the owner of the seal (see N. Avigad, *IEJ* 16 [1966],50-53). Cf. also the name גַּזָּם (locust, usually גָּזָם) Ezra 2:48; Neh. 7:51.

a. The Arabs are mentioned neither in the inscriptions of Shalmaneser III about his 841 B.C. campaign to Damascus and Mount Hauran,[226] nor among those who paid tribute to Adad-nirari III after he subdued Barhadad III (m*Ma-ri-'*) king of Damascus in about 805 B.C., although rulers paying tribute from such distant territories as Philistia, Edom and Israel are included.[227] This seems to indicate that the territory of the Arabs led by Gindibu' was far from the campaign routes of the Assyrian kings in the second half of the 9th century B.C., and was not under the hegemony of Damascus.[228] The distance from the battlefied at Qarqar reduces the likelihood that Gindibu' came from northern Arabia, and it seems more reasonable to set him in the Syrian desert in the vicinity of Wadi Sirḥān. It is possible that Gindibu' participated in the battle of Qarqar because he was afraid that his interests would be threatened by Shalmaneser III's victory. In view of his remoteness from the campaign route, there was probably danger not of physical harm but of Assyrian interference with transport along the desert and border routes where the Arabs had economic interests.[229] It may be assumed that these interests, and the contacts with the border regions of Damascus and Israel — both of which had achieved considerable power at the time — led Gindibu' to opt for normal relations and alliance with Barhadad and Ahab. The Monolith Inscription states that the army of Gindibu' numbered 1000 camels,[230] a

226 E. Michel, *WO* 1 (1949), 265-268 (=*AR* I, § 672; *ANET*, 280); and also F. Safar, *Sumer* 7 (1951), 3-21 (=Michel, *WO* 2 [1954], 27-45).

227 On the subjugation of Mari' of Damascus see Calah Slab, lines 14-21; Saba'a Stele, lines 18-20; and Tell al-Rimah Stele, lines 6-7. For the list of the western territories whose rulers paid tribute to the Assyrian king, see Tell al-Rimah Stele, lines 8-9, and Calah Slab, lines 11-14. An improved transliteration of these three inscriptions is provided by H. Tadmor in *Iraq* 35 (1973), 141-150.

228 For the assumption that the kingdoms in Palestine and Transjordan mentioned in the Adad-nirari III inscriptions were dependencies of Damascus, see B. Mazar, *BA* 25 (1962), 114 and also 103 n. 10; Tadmor, *Scripta Hierosolymitana* 8 (1961), 241-243.

229 For trade and economic interests among the members of the coalition which opposed Shalmaneser III at Qarqar, and for the position of Gindibu' the Arab within this framework, see S.M. Batsieva, *VDI* 2 (44) (1953), 17-26; Tadmor, *ibid.*, 245-246.

230 So large a number of camels implies that they were brought to Qarqar as a fighting force and not as pack animals, the earliest evidence of their participation in battles

figure which, although possibly exaggerated, reflects the exalted position of Gindibu' even if all the camels did not belong to his own subjects.

b. Most of our information on nomads in the border regions of Palestine in the 9th century B.C. and the first half of the 8th comes from the book of Chronicles. Some passages dealing with Arabs and Me'unites are pre-exilic, but the data are insufficient to date each source accurately.[231] In considering the territory and condition of the various nomad groups, we shall therefore treat the pre-exilic sources for the period under discussion as one entity, without regard for intermediate developments.

In II Chron. 21:16-17 and 26:6-8 the Arabs are mentioned jointly with the inhabitants of Philistia — a proximity referred to only in Chronicles. Within these references there is further information about where these Arabs lived: (a) II Chron. 26:7 lists "the Arabs that dwelt in Gurbaal" among the peoples subdued by Uzziah. Gurbaal is otherwise unknown, and the question of its location has been argued since ancient times.[232] But the proximity of the Philistines and "the Arabs that dwelt

involving mainly infantry and chariots. They were probably used for flank-securing and pursuit. In countries far from the Syro-Arabian desert, camels were not used in battle until some centuries later, which is probably the reason why the horses recoiled from the smell of the camels taking part in Xerxes' campaign in Greece in 480 B.C. as described in Herodotus VII, 87. For the use of camels in warfare in western Asia Minor and Greece, see also Herodotus I, 80; VII, 125, where, however, the camels referred to were used as pack and not cavalry animals, and seem to have been of the Bactrian type.

231 On the value as historical sources of the passages discussed below, as well as other relevant passages in Chronicles not cited here, also mentioning nomads, see pp. 65-71.

232 LXX, II Chron. 26:7: καὶ κατίσχυσεν αὐτὸν κύριος ἐπὶ τοὺς ἀλλοφύλους καὶ ἐπὶ τοὺς Ἄραβας τοὺς κατοικοῦντας ἐπὶ τῆς πέτρας καὶ ἐπὶ τοὺς Μιναίους. Gurbaal is here identified with Petra (the Septuagint likewise identifies Sela - סלע, Heb. rock — in II Kings 14:7 with Petra) and the Me'unites with the people of the kingdom of Ma'în (in classical sources οἱ Μ(ε)ιναῖοι who from the 5th century B.C. on participated heavily in North Arabian trade (see F.V. Winnett, *BASOR*, 73 [1939], 3-9; some set the start of their activity in North Arabia in the 4th century B.C., see J. Ryckmans, *JEOL* 15 [1957-1958], 242). The identifications in the Septuagint reflecting the economic and socio-geographic reality of the translators' times certainly do not fit the time of Uzziah. On the other hand, Josephus (*Ant.* IX, x, 3) says that after Uzziah's war in Philistia, in which he conquered Gath (Γιττα) and Yabneh (Ἰαμνεια) (cf. II Chron. 26:6), he assailed "the Arabs living on the borders of Egypt".

in Gurbaal" and the continuation "and his fame spread even to the border of Egypt" (v. 8), the result of Uzziah's military activities, indicate that Gurbaal should be located in the southwestern part of the kingdom of Judah;[233] (b) the reference to "the Arabs who are near the Ethiopians (כושים)"(II Chron. 21:16) relating to the invasion of Judah by Philistines and Arabs during Jehoram's reign points to the same direction, if we identify these Ethiopians with those in II Chron. 14. The description of Asa's pursuit of Zerah "the Ethiopian" and his host reads: "Asa and the people that were with him pursued them as far as Gerar... And they smote all the cities round about Gerar... They plundered all the cities... They smote the tents of those who had cattle, and carried away sheep in abundance and camels" (II Chron. 14:12-14).[234] Placing the "Ethiopians" (Cushites) in that region seems implicit also in the remark in I Chron. 4:39-40 about the ethnic origin of the inhabitants of the "entrance of Gedor" (מבוא גדוֹר)[235] in the days of Hezekiah: "for the former inhabitants there belonged to Ham", forebear of Cush (cf. Gen. 10:6; I Chron. 1:8). These data suggest therefore that in the 9th and 8th centuries B.C. Arab tribes inhabited the Naḥal Gerar (Wadi esh-Shari'ah) region and southwards, even "to the entrance of Egypt". This conclusion accords with the information in inscriptions of Tiglath-Pileser and Sargon about the border area between Palestine and Egypt.

233 Accordingly, we must reject Alt's suggestion (*Kleine Schriften*, III, 404-405, 433) of identifying Gurbaal with Jagur, near Arad, mentioned in Josh. 15:21 in the list of towns in the extreme south of the territory of Judah.

234 The problem of identifying these Cushites still exists. Some believe they were nomadic or semi-nomadic descendants of the Cushu tribes (biblical Cushan), mentioned in Middle Kingdom Egyptian documents, who lived on the southeastern border of Palestine and were absorbed by the Midianites; see J. Liver, "Cush III", *Enc. Miqr.*, IV, 69; Mazar, "Cushan", *ibid.*, 70-71. This suggestion presents some difficulty, in view of the references to Cushites in connection with the western border of the kingdom of Judah in the 9th and 8th centuries B.C. Or can we assume that they were descendants of the troops garrisoned in Philistia by the Egyptian kings of the 10th century B.C., Siamūn or Shishak (on these garrisons, see A. Malamat, *JNES* 22 [1963], 12); cf. also "Zerah the Cushite", *Enc. Miqr.*, II, 943.

235 Apparently "to the entrance of Gerar" (למבוא גרר) according to the Septuagint: ἕως τοῦ ἐλθεῖν Γεραρα. On the region as a buffer between the settled land and the grazing areas of the nomads, see Y. Aharoni, *IEJ* 6 (1956), 26-32.

The list of Uzziah's tributaries includes the Me'unites along with the Philistines and "the Arabs that dwelt in Gurbaal" (II Chron. 26:7).[236] In the context of the expansion of the sons of Simeon, at or about the time of Hezekiah, the Me'unites appear in the area of the "entrance to Gedor" (I Chron. 4:39-41). Until a few years ago the Me'unites were identified solely on the basis of the instances of οἱ Μιναῖοι in the Septuagint and in classical historiographers of the 3rd century B.C. on,[237] thus giving rise to the suggestion that the Me'unites in the book of Chronicles are identical with the people of Ma'īn (מע[י]ן), a South Arabian kingdom known from Old Arabic inscriptions and classical sources. The 9th and 8th century B.C. Me'unites, mentioned in the book of Chronicles as in contact with the kingdom of Judah, were considered to have inhabited mercantile colonies founded by the people of Ma'īn in the Dedan (al-'Ulā) region in northern Arabia,[238] or in the Ma'ān region in southeast Edom.[239] This interpretation, however, was undermined when modern research based on the study of Arabian inscriptions revealed that commercial activity and colonization of the kingdom of Ma'īn in North Arabia could not be set earlier than the Achaemenid period.[240] A decisive source for the location of the Me'unites is ND 400, describing Tiglath-Pileser's activities on the border of Palestine and mentioning the clear connection of the Me'unites

236 In verse 8 the reading should also be Me'unites (המעונים) instead of Ammonites (העמונים), following the Septuagint on this passage; see above note 213.

237 For the classical sources on οἱ Μιναῖοι see Winnett, *BASOR* 73 (1939), 3-9; A. Grohmann, "Minaioi", *PW* Supplementband 6, 461 ff. All these sources, however, reflect a social geography later than that in Chronicles.

238 J.A. Montgomery, *Arabia and the Bible,* Philadelphia 1934, 182-184.

239 Musil, *Northern Ḥeǧâz,* 243-247.

240 Winnett, *op. cit.;* J. Pirenne, *Paléographie des inscriptions sud-arabes, I: Des origines jusqu'à l'époque himyarite,* Brussels 1956, 181-183; Ryckmans, *JEOL* 15 (1957-1958), 242. The removal of the 8th century B.C. Me'unites from the Ma'ān region resolves questions raised by locating them there, among them: 1) How could nomads have installed themselves in so important a military and economic area at a time when the governmental stability of South Edom is emphasized by Edomite control of Elath (II Kings 16:6), by the findings of Tell el-Kheleifeh stratum IV (see N. Glueck, *BA* 28 [1965], 86) and by the excavations at Umm al-Biyara (see C.M. Bennett, *RB* 73 [1966], 372-403) and Tawilan (see Bennett, *Levant* 3 [1971], v-vi)? 2) How could the sons of Simeon have been in the Ma'ān region, in the heart of Edom, during the reign of Hezekiah (cf. I Chron. 4:41)?

(^{kur}*Mu-'-na-a-a*) with Egyptian territory.[241] This extra-biblical source, as well as I Chron. 4:39-41, indicates that the Me'unites referred to in Chronicles can be located southwest of the kingdom of Judah. Their territory thus falls within the area designated above as belonging to the "Arabs" mentioned in Chronicles, i.e., from Naḥal Gerar (Wadi esh-Shari'ah) to the Brook-of-Egypt (נחל מצרים; Wadi el-Arish), and perhaps even farther in the direction of northern Sinai.

The common concept that Jehosophat and Uzziah based their control in southern Palestine on a network of small settlements and fortresses at key points along the principal routes,[242] turns out to be wrong. It seems today that this system, whose existence did not last more than some generations, should be dated earlier (to the 10th and perhaps even to the 11th centuries, B.C.)[243] Our only reference to the population in or of the Negeb hills in the 9th and 8th centuries, B.C. is the statement about "the remnant of the Amalekites" in Mount Seir,[244] who were smitten by Simeonite families, apparently in the days of Hezekiah (I Chron. 4:42-43). Probably other nomad groups, including those discussed and possibly some Simeonite families, inhabited the region (certainly in the water-rich Kadesh-barnea neighborhood), living by grazing and perhaps by contacts with trade caravans.

241 For the location of the Me'unites mentioned in ND 400 see p. 91.

242 See Y. Aharoni, *IEJ* 17 (1967), 1-7; cf. also B. Rothenberg, *Negev,* Tel Aviv 1967, 89, 98 ff. (Hebrew).

243 Z. Meshel, *History of the Negev in the Kings of Judah,* Unpublished Ph. D. disseration, Tel Aviv University 1974; R. Cohen *Qadmoniot* 12 (1979), 38-50.

244 The toponym "Mount Seir" applies here also to the area west of the Arabah; see above, n. 205

Chapter IV
FROM TIGLATH-PILESER III TO SARGON II

The inscriptions of the Assyrian kings dealing with campaigns to Syria from the mid-9th century to 738 B.C. do not mention Arabs.[245] The military and political contacts of the Assyrian kings with the nomads of the Syro-Arabian desert, and certainly with those of Sinai and North Arabia, only began when the Assyrian armies reached the western end of the Fertile Crescent in an attempt to annex that area to the empire, i.e. in the days of Tiglath-Pileser III. From that time on, references to nomads in the border regions of Palestine and in the desert within the Fertile Crescent increase.

The chronological framework of this chapter, covering the reigns of Tiglath-Pileser and Sargon, was determined by the following considerations: The discussion of demographic and administrative patterns connected with the nomads is largely based on information contained in the Nimrud Letters. So far as chronology is concerned, only the dates 732–705 B.C. can be established for the general period of the relevant letters, which are impossible to date individually.[246] These documents and the inscriptions of Tiglath-Pileser and Sargon (which date the events more precisely than do the letters) indicate that in fact we are dealing with various aspects of a single stage in the history of the Assyrian empire, when Assyria established itself at the western end of

245 For details of the campaigns of the Assyrian kings Shalmaneser III, Adad-nirari III, Shalmaneser IV, Aššur-nirari V and Tiglath-Pileser III to Syria and Palestine, see Tadmor, "Mesopotamia", *Enc. Miqr.*, V, 107.

246 See above p. 55.

the Fertile Crescent. This process continued uninterruptedly from the days of Tiglath-Pileser till the end of Sargon's reign, and it is therefore advisable to consider the aspects relative to the Arabs in a single framework.

The present framework was determined also by the contents of the available sources: Most of the source material on Arabs until the end of Sargon's reign refers to the southern Syria and Palestine environs. Later material from the time of Sennacherib to the end of the Assyrian period, however, refers mainly to more easterly regions, with only a few references to the western part of the Fertile Crescent.

A. ETHNOGRAPHIC-HISTORICAL SURVEY

1. The Annals of Tiglath-Pileser III list Zabibe[247] queen of the Arabs as one of the leaders who, with Rezin of Damascus, Menahem of Samaria, Hiram of Tyre and other kings in southern Anatolia, Syria and Phoenicia, paid tribute to the Assyrian king in 738 B.C.[248] The tribute episode also appears in the upper section of the Tiglath-Pileser stele found in Iran, as follows: col. ii (1) *šarrāni šá* ^{kur}*Ḫat-ti* ^{kur}*A-ri-me šá šiddi tam-ti[m]* (2) *šá šulum* ^{d}*Šam-ši* ^{kur}*Qid-ri* ^{kur}*A-ri-⌈bi⌉* ("the kings of Ḫatti, the Aramaeans on the shore of the western sea, ^{kur}*Qidri*, ^{kur}*Aribi...*"). Thereafter, beginning with line 3, the kings listed are essentially identical with the tribute payers listed in the Annals.[249]

The version in the stele presents a serious problem, implying as it does that the Qedarites and the Arabs were separate socio-ethnic units. This contradicts what emerges from the sources dated to the reign of Assurbanipal and later, according to which $^{\text{kur/lú}}$*Aribi* is undoubtedly a collective name for all the nomads in the Syrian desert, while $^{\text{kur/lú}}$*Qidri*

247 For ancient Arabic examples of this name cf. *Zbbt* (Van den Branden, *IT*, 161); *Zabībah* (E. Gratzl, *Die altarabischen Frauennamen*, Leipzig 1906, 30). The name can be explained as deriving from Arabic *zabīb*, raisin. Comparison of the ending of the name ^{f}*Za-bi-bi-e* with the ending of ^{m}*Me-na-si-e, Mi-in-si-e* for the name of Manasseh king of Judah as written in the inscriptions of Esarhaddon and Assurbanipal (see *APN*, 136), and also the Arabic forms noted here, show that the queen's name was pronounced Zabibeh and not Zabibiyeh.

248 Rost, *Ann.*, 150-157.

249 L.D. Levine, *Two Neo-Assyrian Stelae from Iran*, Toronto 1972, 18-20; cf. idem, *BASOR* 206 (1972), 40-42; M. Weippert, *ZDPV* 89, (1973), 29, 31.

is the name of a single unit in the general category of "Arabs".[250] The final vowels in ^{kur}*Qidri* ^{kur}*Aribi* as well the style of the sentence negate the assumption that this is a compound name like Amnān-Yaḫruru or ^{kur}*Aḫlamê* ^{kur}*Armaya*^{meš}; at present we are in no position to suggest a syntactical solution to the problem. Despite the difficulty described, the unavoidable conclusion emerging from the inscriptions of Assurbanipal is that here too the expression ^{kur}*Qidri* ^{kur}*Aribi* refers to the same unit. Accordingly, Zabibe's actual title would be "queen of the Qedarites", while the appellation "queen of the Arabs" is the general title applied by Assyrian scribes to nomad leaders until the time of Assurbanipal. Some support for this assumption is provided by the fact that the list of tributaries which follows the text contains not the name of a Qedarite king but only Zabibe's.

In 738 B.C. the Assyrian army had not yet reached Transjordan and southern Palestine and was not in direct control of its rulers. Thus, Zabibe's payment of tribute to Tiglath-Pileser in that year is, at first glance, an enigma. Her behavior, however, can be explained by considering the Arabian trade in the Syro-Arabian desert, in which nomad leaders took significant part. This trade was conducted primarily along the King's Highway, whose principal outlets were Damascus and Tyre (the western bifurcation which branched off to Tyre from the King's Highway passed through the territory of the kingdom of Israel). Consequently, when the rulers of these two trade centers became subordinate to the Assyrian king (even Menahem king of Israel paid tribute), Zabibe too was obliged to join the tributaries to avert a possible disruption of the Arabian trade and her income from it.

2. Real contact between the nomads in the border areas of Palestine and the Assyrian authorities started when Tiglath-Pileser reached southern Philistia and Transjordan. A passage in the fragmentary Annals of Tiglath-Pileser, Lay 72b + 73a, last line, relating to the events of 733 B.C.,[251] mentions "Samsi queen of the Arabs who violated the oath (sworn) by Shamash..." (^{f}*Sa-am-si šar-rat* ^{kur}*A-ri-bi ša ma-mit* ^{d}*Šá-*

250 See pp. 165-166; likewise compare the designation of the nomads in the Syrian desert — Qedarites — in Jeremiah, and ^{lú}*Arabi* in the Babylonian Chronicle, pp. 171-172, below.

251 Rost, *Ann.*, 210. For the dating of events described on this slab see pp. 25-27.

maš te-ti-qu-ma).[252] It appears that Samsi took an oath of allegiance sometime before 733, evidently in the course of Tiglath-Pileser's campaign to Palestine in 734 B.C. (it could hardly have taken place between 737 and 735 B.C., the years when Tiglath-Pileser campaigned in the northern and eastern parts of the empire). The change in Samsi's attitude to Assyria must be considered against the background of general political developments in Palestine and southern Syria: a) According to the Annals of Tiglath-Pileser, Mitinti of Ashkelon's violation of his oath to the Assyrian king was linked with the political and military activity of Rezin king of Damascus.[253] Since Mitinti not only did not oppose Tiglath-Pileser's campaign to Philistia in 734 B.C. but even paid tribute,[254] his rebellion, like Samsi's, can be set *after* payment of tribute in 734 B.C. and before the final downfall of Rezin and the conquest of Damascus in 732 B.C. b) From the reference in the Eponym Chronicle to Philistia as Assyria's main destination in 734 B.C., as well as from the inscriptions of Tiglath-Pileser, it appears that military activity that year was limited (to Gaza and perhaps the border area near the "Brook-of-Egypt"). Apparently this activity was insufficiently impressive to deter the leaders of the region from breaking their formal allegiance to the Assyrian king. More extensive military operations, in the course of which Damascus and parts of the kingdom of Israel were conquered, and many people exiled, took place in 733-732 B.C. c) Examination of the data on the war of Pekah king of Israel and Rezin king of Damascus against Ahaz (and apparently also of the hostile actions against Judah by her neighbors which were connected with that war, II Kings 16:6; II Chron. 28:17-18) makes it possible to date this war after Tiglath-Pileser's campaign to Philistia in 734 B.C.[255] Samsi's violation of the oath is thus one instance of the extensive anti-Assyrian activity of the kings of Damascus, Israel and Tyre throughout the area.[256]

252 So far as we know, Shamash did not appear first among the gods in the concluding sections of the Assyrian vassal treaties listing curses. Here we seem to have word-play: ᶠ*Samsi* - ᵈ*Šamaš*. For *māmītu etēqu,* which means breaking a vassal oath of allegiance, see *AHw,* 599b; *CAD,* E 389, *etēqu* 2,c.

253 Lay. 29b: 8'-9'; Rost, *Ann.* 235-236: [ᵐ*Mitinti* ᵏᵘʳ]*As-qa-lu-na-a-a ina a-di[-ia iḫṭima ...dabdê ša* ᵐ*Ra]-ḫi-a-ni e-mur-ma ina mi-qit...,* "[Mitinti of] Ashkelon [violated the] oath [sworn to me]... [the defeat of Re]zin he saw and in an attack of [...he died?]

254 K 3751, rev. 11. On the complicated nature of the list of tribute payers in this document, rev. 7-12, see p. 29.

255 For a detailed discussion see Eph'al, *WHJP,* IV/1, 182-186.

The war against Samsi and her surrender are treated in several of the Summary Inscriptions of Tiglath-Pileser,[257] but all these texts are badly damaged, and although parts are identical and overlaping and the *Vorlage* from which they were copied can be partially reconstructed by joining the extant fragments,[258] much is still missing. We can therefore establish only the general outline of the episode: Tiglath-Pileser defeated Samsi in the neighborhood of Mount *Sa-qu-ur-ri,* killed many of her men, and took a great deal of booty, including captives, camels, sheep, and many spices[259] (and possibly also images).[260] Samsi fled for her life "like a wild she-ass" to the desert. At this point she apparently decided to surrender to Tiglath-Pileser, and paid tribute of camels, she-camels and their young, and probably also spices, sheep and the like, notation of which has not been preserved in the fragmented text.[261]

The statement that Samsi fled from the Mount Saqurri region (unknown in any other source) to the desert suggests that the mountain was adjacent to, not in, the desert, possibly on the border of the Hauran region (Jebel a-Drūz).[262] It stands to reason that she fled to Wadi Sirḥān.

256 The anti-Assyrian stance of Hiram king of Tyre and his alliance with Rezin are alluded to in ND 4301+4305, rev. 5'-8'; ND 400:1-7. For the contents of these passages see pp. 29-32.

257 III R 10, 2:19-26; ND 4301+4305, rev. 17'-22'; ND 400:24'-27'; K 3751, rev. (1'-)2'; Lay. 66:3'-7'.

258 See above, pp. 33-35.

259 The considerable power of Samsi is attested by the large number of dead (9400), preserved only in ND 400. The list of booty in III R 10, 2:20-21 includes 1000 and several hundreds more captives, 30,000 camels, 20,000 sheep, and 5,000 (measures of) spices of all sorts. For the containers in which the spices were measured see note 447.

260 See ND 4301+4305, rev. 18'.

261 The war against Samsi is also depicted in a group of reliefs from the Central Palace in Nimrud (R.D.Barnett-M. Falkner, *The Sculptures of Tiglath-Pileser III,* London 1962, Pls. XIII-XX, XXIII-XXX; see discussion of slabs, pp. 8-12, and bibliography). These reliefs show the pursuit of Arab camel riders by Assyrian cavalry and Tiglath-Pileser in his chariot, as well as the transfer of captives, booty and tribute, including camels, sheep, goats and cattle. The cattle as booty (Pls. XXVII-XXVIII) is of some help in locating Samsi, for these were raised close to settled areas and not in the desert. Pls. XXV-XXVI show a woman — possibly Samsi — her left hand to her forehead (a sign of submission?), leading four camels.

262 A comparison of the biblical and Assyrian sources dealing with the wars of Tiglath-

Samsi remained queen after surrendering to Tiglath-Pileser, but a ^{lú}*qēpu* was appointed over her by the king of Assyria.[263] The status and functions of the ^{lú}*qēpu* in the Assyrian administrative system have not yet been satisfactorily defined. The title was generally given to Assyrian officials of various ranks who supervised the policy and administration in vassal states.[264] Tiglath-Pileser may have appointed this sort of "overseer" to prevent Samsi from extending aid to Damascus before its final collapse, or primarily to supervise Samsi's commercial activities and ensure revenue to the royal treasury. Testimony to Samsi's lofty status in the subsequent period appears in the inscriptions of Sargon, which tell of the gift the Assyrian king received from Samsi queen of the Arabs, Pir'u king of Egypt and It'amara the Sabaean, in about 716 B.C.[265] The list of booty Tiglath-Pileser took from her, her share of the gift to Sargon, and also ABL 631 which mentions a ^{f}*Sam-si,* identifiable as this same queen,[266] indicate that her wealth included camels, sheep, spices, and apparently gold as well. It would seem, then, that besides desert pasturage, Samsi shared considerably in the Arabian trade, which explains why her policy toward Assyria, like that of Gindibu' and Zabibe, followed the kingdoms of Damascus and Israel. The fact that the nomads were in no direct military danger from Assyria in the days of these three leaders indicates that their Assyrian policy was motivated not by military considerations but rather by their relationship with the kingdoms of Damascus and Israel, which controlled important sections of the Arabian trade routes and pasture and water sources in the desert

Pileser in Palestine indicates that there is no connection between his campaigns in Galilee and Transjordan (Tadmor, in *All the Land of Naphtali,* 62 ff., especially p. 66). The wars in Transjordan, in the course of which Ashtaroth was conquered (as depicted on slab BM 118908 from the Southwest Palace in Nimrud; see Barnett-Falkner, *ibid.,* Pls. LXIX-LXX. p. 30, with additional bibliography) and the tribes of Reuben, Gad and the half-tribe of Manasseh were exiled from Gilead (I Chron. 5:6, 26), are almost certainly connected with Tiglath-Pileser's campaign against Samsi in the desert border area. One may further suggest that this campaign started at Damascus and took place along the main route southward to Gilead.

263 III R 10, 2:26. Cf. also ND 4301+4305 rev. 22'; Lay. 66:7 (Rost, *Ann.* 217); K 3751 rev. 2.

264 D. Opitz, *RLA,* I, 463; Postgate, *Taxation,* 194-195.

265 About this gift and the circumstances, see pp. 108-111.

266 About this letter, see further pp. 98-99.

border areas which were vitally important, especially in drought years. (The disintegration of Aram-damascus and Israel had an immediate effect on nomad penetration of pasture land within the settled areas, and on the improvement of the nomad position in Arabian trade; see pp. 94-100). The fact that Tiglath-Pileser did not displace Samsi, but accepted her repeated surrender and assigned her a supervisor, seems to have stemmed from his desire to avoid disturbing the governmental framework and social organization in the border regions of his realm, whose inhabitants were a vital mediating link in international trade, and the orderly conduct of an activity essential to the imperial economy.[267]

3. The inscriptions of Tiglath-Pileser III and Sargon II contain two lists of nomad groups in the border region of Palestine and North Arabia:

List A. Tiglath-Pileser[268]	**List B. Sargon**[269]
[ ][270]*Ma-as-'-a-a*	
^{uru}*Te-ma-a-a*	
$^{uru/lú}$*Sa-ab/ba-'-a-a*	
^{uru}*Ḫa-a-a-ap-pa-a-a*	^{lú}*Ḫa-ia-pa-a*
^{uru}*Ba-da-na-a-a*	
^{uru}*Ḫa-at-te/ti-a-a*	
^{uru}*I-di-ba-'-il-a-a*	
	^{lú}*Ta-mu-di*
	^{lú}*I-ba-(a)-di-di*
	^{lú}*Mar-si-(i)-ma-ni*

267 Similar considerations weighed with Tigalth-Pileser and most of the Assyrian kings who followed in determining their attitude to the inhabitants of Philistia (regarding Sargon's special political and economic approach see pp. 101-108. By means of the intermediary trade through Philistia, the Assyrian kings obtained valuable goods from Egypt. On receipt of horses from Philistia see ND 2765 (H.W.F. Saggs, *Iraq* 17 [1955], 134-135); ND 2672:6 (B. Parker, *Iraq* 23 [1961], 42); on receipt of elephant hides, rolls of papyrus (*kirki niāri*) and garments made of byssus from Ashdod and from another kingdom lying on the seacoast, probably Gaza or Ashkelon, see ABL 568. (On this document and the goods listed there see W.J. Martin, *Tribut und Tribtleistugen bei den Assyrern,* Helsinki 1936, 40-49; Postgate, *op. cit.*, 283-284; M. Elat, *Economic Relations in the Lands of the Bible,* Jerusalem 1977, 135-138, Hebrew).

268 III R 10, 2:27 ff.; K 3751, rev. 3' ff.; Lay. 66:9' (=Rost, *Ann.* 219). See the reconstruction of the list in p. 34.

269 Khorsabad Annals, line 120 ff.; Cylinder Inscription, line 20.

270 The determinative is not preserved.

Most of the names in List A can be identified:[271] The people of Massa', Tema' and Adbeel, listed among the Sons of Ishmael (Gen. 25:13-15; I Chron. 1:29-30), inhabited North Arabia and North Sinai. The people of 'Ephah (^{uru}*Ḫa-a-a-ap-pa-a-a,* ^{lú}*Ḫa-ia-pa-a*), included in the Sons of Qeturah list (Gen. 25:4; I Chron. 1:33), dwelt in North Arabia along the route followed by caravans heading for Palestine.

As to the Sabaeans ($^{\text{lú/uru}}$*Sa-ab/ba-'-a-a*), recent research on South Arabia has removed all doubt about the existence there of the kingdom of Sheba in the 8th century B.C. Nonetheless, it is unreasonable to connect the Sabaeans in the Tiglath-Pileser list with the kingdom of Sheba in South Arabia, since the other groups mentioned can be found in North Arabia and North Sinai.[272] The determinative LÚ for the Sabaeans in III R 10, 2:27 possibly stresses their nomadic character and contrasts with the determinative URU for the other groups, an impression supported by the description of the Sabaean attack on Job's cattle and asses in the land of Uz (Job 1:15). [273] And although scholars disagree about the location of the land of Uz and about the cultural and historical background of the narrative framework in the book of Job, the reference is undoubtedly not to South Arabia but to a region near the western end of the Fertile Crescent. It thus appears that besides the sedentary Sabaean population in South Arabia there were nomads in the 8th century B.C. (and possibly later as well[274]) known as Sabaeans in North Arabia or the extended border region of Palestine. That Ita'amara the Sabaean (obviously a South Arabian ruler; see Appendix A, 12) participated in gifts to Sargon indicates that the kingdom of

271 Only the main points needed for the ethnological-geographical conclusions arising from the Tiglath-Pileser and Sargon lists are given here. For a detailed discussion of the data and problems connected with the identification and location of each of the groups mentioned here, see Appendix A.

272 It should be noted that more than 1,000 kilometers separate Sheba in South Arabia from Tema', one of the most southernly references in the Tiglath-Pileser list.

273 This characteristic of the Sabaeans in Job. 1:15 does not depend on the location of the land of Uz or on the historical-cultural background reflected in the narrative portion of the book of Job, about which scholars differ (see note 274).

274 This depends on the time and background of the narrative framework of the book of Job. See, in addition to commentaries on the book of Job, Maisler (Mazar), *Zion* 11 (1946), 1-16; A. Guillaume, *Promise and Fulfilment,* Essays presented to S.H.Hooke, Edinburgh 1963, 106-127.

Sheba had economic interests in North Arabia.[275] It is not impossible that the name uru*Saba'aya* in List A refers to the inhabitants of a Sabaean trading colony in North Arabia (or perhaps to the most important of several).

There are no clear data from the biblical period or from classical sources to help identify uru*Ḫa-at-te/ti-a-a* and uru*Ba-da-na-a-a,*[276] the latter of whom may be related to the tribe of *Bdn* cited in a Thamudic inscription from Sakākah and in Safaitic inscriptions.[277] In any case, since in List A these two groups appear along with the others identified above, they should presumably be sought in North Arabia or northern Sinai.

Because five of the seven groups in List A have been identified, their territories can be located in North Arabia, in the Syro-Arabian desert and in northern Sinai. List B is another matter, even though the lú*Ta-mu-di* are undoubtedly the people of Thamūd mentioned in classical sources, in the Koran, in Arabic geographical and historical works and in inscriptions found in North Arabia,[278] and the lú*Mar-si-ma-ni* seem to correspond to the Μαισαιμανεῖς mentioned by Ptolemy (*Geographia* VI, 7,21)[279] (the proposed identification of the lú*I-ba-di-di*[280] is not acceptable). However, all the classical and Arabic sources for the nomad groups were written much later than the period under discussion and their socio-geographic configuration reflects a time close to their composition. It is essential to state that in view of the changes during the centuries in territories of various socio-ethnic groups, particularly vis-à-vis the nomads, these later sources can be utilized solely for the more

275 On this gift and the extent of commercial activity on the Palestine border in the days of Sargon, see pp. 101-111.

276 Therefore the suggestions made heretofore as to their identification cannot be accepted (regarding uru*Ḫa-at-ti-a-a* see Glaser, *Skizze,* 263; Musil, *Northern Ḥeǧâz,* 290-291; regarding uru*Ba-da-na-a-a* see Glaser, *ibid,* 261; Musil, *ibid.,* 290). These suggestions are based on homophones alone, without reference to geographical logic, or arbitrary alterations in the spelling of toponyms.

277 F.V. Winnett, *Safaitic Inscriptions from Jordan,* Toronto 1957, Nos. 87, 237; idem, *AR,* p. 79, No. 18.

278 For details of these sources see A. Van den Branden, *Histoire de Thamoud,* Beyrouth 1960, 1-20.

279 Delitzsch, *Paradies,* 304; Glaser, *op. cit.,* 262; Hommel, *EGAO,* 598-599.

280 Glaser, *op. cit.,* 259; Hommel, *op. cit.,* 600; Musil, *op. cit.,* 292.

ancient periods for ethnographic identification; only with the greatest reservations can nomadic groups be located according to the geographic data in such late sources. The nomad groups in the Sargon list, therefore, should be assigned by means of more or less contemporary sources. The absence of most of the groups in the list (with the exception of 'Ephah) from the purview of the biblical period up to the 5th century B.C., and the description of the nomad tribes as "remote Arabs who live in the desert, who knew neither overseers nor officials, who had not brought their tribute (*bilassunu*) to any king",[281] indicate that their territory extended farther than that of the nomad groups in Tiglath-Pileser's list. In a general way, therefore, Lists A and B may be said to represent two territorial-tribal divisions, the one in Sargon's list being the more remote. Nevertheless, because of the Bedouin custom of traversing a course often hundreds of miles long which sometimes crosses that of other groups, the two territories probably overlapped sometimes.[282]

Nowhere do the Annals of Tiglath-Pileser mention battle with the groups listed, merely that they surrendered and brought tribute upon hearing of the might of the king of Assyria, a well-known *topos* in Assyrian historical writing.[283] The southernmost point of Palestine or Transjordan, the farthest place that Tiglath-Pileser's army can be shown to have reached, is about 500 arid kilometers from Tema', with principal oases generally several dozen kilometers apart.[284] It therefore seems unlikely that Tiglath-Pileser's army operated in this difficult region to subdue the population of the oases and their vicinity, especially since the sources never suggest that it did so. (It is even doubtful whether the Assyrian army was capable of conducting such a

281 Khorsabad Annals, lines 120-122.

282 The inclusion of the people of 'Ephah (*Ḫayapâ*) in both listings indicates partial overlapping of the two divisions (which Glaser, *op. cit.*, 262 ff. has pointed out). For an example of the length of the circuit of a nomad tribe see pp. 218-219. For the crossing of the course of various groups in North Arabia and overlapping of their areas see Great Britain Admiralty, Naval Intelligence Division, *Western Arabia and the Red Sea*, 1946, 398 fig. 38; E. Wirth, *Syrien*, Darmstadt 1971, Karte 11.

283 III R 10, 2:27-33. See also parallels to this passage in pp. 33-35.

284 For a general geographic description of the region see Great Britain Admiralty, *op. cit.*, 37 ff.; and descriptions of travels in North Arabia (especially Musil, *Northern Ḥeǧâz).*

desert campaign, given its organization and equipment.) The tribute included gold, silver and spices, indicating that the nomads lived along the Arabian trade routes and profited thereby. Since Arabian trade was confined to established routes, it would have been sufficient for Tiglath-Pileser to control the northern termini in order to affect their use as commercial arteries even in the remotest sections. No wonder that even far-away Arabs, remote from the scene of Tiglath-Pileser's activity, paid to protect their interests in the regular conduct of the Arabian trade within their territory.[285]

Another people in the inscriptions of Tiglath-Pileser separated from those who surrendered are the Me'unites. The surrender of a Me'unite leader is mentioned in ND 400:22-23, but the territorial statement there — $^{\ulcorner m \urcorner}$*Si-ru-at-ti* ^{kur}*Mu-'u-na-a-a šá šapal*(KI.TA) ^{kur}*⌜Mu⌝-⌜uṣ⌝-[ri šit-ku-nu šu-bat-su ...],* i.e. "Siruatti the Me'unite whose (territory is) south (lit. below) of Egypt..."[286] — is not sufficiently clear. Whatever its exact meaning, however, it does indicate a geographical link between the Me'unites and Egyptian territory which in the days of Tiglath-Pileser extended to "the Brook-of-Egypt", conventionally identified with Wadi el-Arish.[287] Tiglath-Pileser's action against the Me'unites can thus be set in northern Sinai, which agrees with what is said of them in Chronicles in connection with various events during the 8th century B.C.[288]

The inscriptions of Sargon include other references to nomads in southern Palestine and northern Sinai: "the sheikh (of the city of) Laban", leader of one of those nomad groups, was, in the name of the

285 The inclusion among these groups of the people of Adbeel, whose territory was on the frontier of the Negeb and in northern Sinai, may indicate that a western branch of Arabian trade toward northern Sinai existed in the 8th century B.C. If so, Uzziah's wars in Philistia and the southwestern part of his kingdom (II Chron. 26:6-8) were probably economically motivated for control of sections of roads along which international trade was conducted.

286 D.J. Wiseman (*Iraq* 13 [1951], 24), who published the document, erroneously believed that it referred to the Euphrates region in northern Syria. For the conclusion that it referred to the Me'unites near Egypt see Tadmor, *BA* 29 (1966), 89; and in more detail, idem, in *Liver Memorial Volume,* 222-230.

287 For this identification see Alt, *Kleine Schriften,* II, 227 f.; Y.M. Grintz, *Y. Kaufmann Jubilee Volume,* Jerusalem 1960, יד-טו (Hebrew).

288 See further pp. 68-71, 219-220.

king of Assyria, put in charge of the people brought to the region of "the City of the Brook-of-Egypt (URU *Na-ḫal Mu-ṣur*)".[289] In a passage immediately preceding the report of the opening of "the sealed-off harbor(?) of Egypt",[290] the Nimrud Prism also describes the terror of Egyptians and Arabs (*nišê* [kur]*Mu-ṣur u* [lú]*A-ra-bi*) when they heard of his mighty deeds suggesting that these Arabs inhabited northern Sinai.[291]

There are no extant sources by means of which 8th century B.C. nomad groups can be identified and located on the eastern border of the Transjordan kingdoms. Nimrud Letter XIV (ND 2773), evidently from the reign of Tiglath-Pileser, speaks of [kur]*Gi-di-ra-a-a,* who invaded the land of Moab and killed the inhabitants of one of its cities.[292] On both graphic and phonetic grounds, it is difficult to identify the aggressors as Qedarites.[293] There is no evidence that the GI sign, which in Old Babylonian also represented *qì* and *qè,* did so in the Neo-Assyrian period as well,[294] nor are there any examples of the *q* >*g* shift in names transcribed from West Semitic to Akkadian.[295]

289 VA 8424 ii 6-7. Regarding his status and geographical location, see pp. 93-94.

290 Nimrud Prism, Fragment D, col. iv, 42-46. The determinative LÚ prefixed to the Arabs suggests that they were nomads, in contrast to KUR for the Egyptians.

291 Various sources include the nomads of North Sinai along with one of the two politico-military bodies on either side of the desert (cf., for example, the title of Sennacherib as "king of the Arabs and Assyrians", Herodotus II, 141), reflecting the geopolitical situation in this area and the importance of the nomads as a military-logistic factor; see pp. 137-142.

292 Saggs, *Iraq* 17 (1955), 131-133; W.F. Albright, *BASOR* 140 (1955), 34; H. Donner, *MIO* 5 (1957), 156-159.

293 This possibility, with certain reservations, was raised by Saggs (*ibid.,* 133) at the time the document was published. For the reasons for rejecting it, see Donner, *ibid.,* 172-178. Donner suggested that the name derived from גדרה (Arabic *jadīrah*), that is, "a sheep-fold", (cf. Num. 32:16-36; I Sam. 24:3; Zeph. 2:6), and that the name [kur]*Gi-di-ra-a-a* applied to semi-nomads in the border area of Moab. For other suggestions that the invaders discussed in this document were a sedentary population in eastern or western Palestine, see Albright, *ibid.,* 34-35; Mazar, *IEJ* 7 (1957), 237-238; S. Mittmann, *ZDPV* 89 (1973), 15-25.

294 Cf. W. von Soden-W. Röllig, *Das akkadische Syllabar*[2], Roma 1967, 12, No. 60.

295 Until the discovery in Iran of the stele of Tiglath-Pileser III on which reference to the Qedarites is made (see above, p. 82), Isa. 21: 16-17 was the only 8th century

B. THE INTEGRATION OF NOMADS INTO THE ASSYRIAN ADMINISTRATIVE SYSTEM DURING THE REIGNS OF TIGLATH-PILESER AND SARGON

The inscriptions of Tiglath-Pileser and Sargon clarify the method used to acquire control over the southwestern border region of Palestine. We have already seen that Idibi'ilu was assigned to the border of Egypt by Tiglath-Pileser.[296] The term "wardenship" (LÚ NI.DUḪ-*ú-tu*= ^{lú}*atûtu*) for his assignment certainly implies duties of supervision and checking and possibly the remuneration attached to them.[297] Supervision seems to have been undertaken by Idibi'ilu's tribesmen,[298] whose leader meanwhile acquired an official position under the king of Assyria and doubtless enjoyed the benefits of supervising the traffic through the important border area with Egypt.

Another notable in the region was the sheikh of the city of Laban (^{lú}*nasīku ša* ^{uru}*La-ba-an*), whom Sargon put in charge of the deportees settled on the "border of the City of the Brook-of-Egypt".[299] His title indicates that he was a nomad leader[300] who as we shall see below, dwelt in the area between Raphia and el-Arish.[301] His appointment over the

B.C. source for such a reference. Although certain scholars dispute the chronology of the oracle (see Smith, *Isaiah Chapters XL-LV,* 150-151; Eissfeldt, *The Old Testament,* 321-322), this stele resolves the difficulty. It still does not verify, however, the existence of Qedarites on the Transjordanian border.

296 See III R 10, 2:34 and parallel sources p. 35.

297 This is an abstract form, frequent in Neo-Babylonian but rare in Assyrian, of the title LÚ.NI.DUḪ = ^{lú}*atû,* "gatekeeper, warden" (see *AHw,* 88; *CAD,* A/II, 522). The meaning of ^{lú}*atûtu* in Neo-Babylonian is revenue of the "wardenship"; it seems, however, that in the inscriptions of Tiglath-Pileser it primarily describes the nature of this appointment.

298 On the question of the identity of this Idibi'ilu and his connection with the people of Adbeel in northern Sinai, see Appendix A, 1.

299 VA 8424 ii, 1-7 (see Tadmor, *JCS* 12 [1958], 77-78). On the origin of these people and the purpose of their settlement in the "Brook-of-Egypt" area, see pp. 106-108.

300 *AHw,* 754a translates ^{lú}*nasīku* as *"Aramäerscheich,-fürst",* since most of the Akkadian sources in which this title is found refer to Aramaeans. But in fact the title means leaders of West Semitic nomads in general; cf. ADD 1110+ B ii 4'-5': ^{m}*Ilu-anasaka n[a?-si-]ku Ar-ba-a-a* (Postgate, *Taxation,* 340); Ps. 83:12 (שיתמו נדיבמו כערב וכזאב, וכזבח וצלמנע כל נסיכמו), and Josh. 13:21 (נשיאי מדין... נסיכי סיחון).

301 On the location of the city of Laban see pp. 103-105.

new inhabitants was made in the context of the Sargon-initiated administrative-economic activity in southern Palestine, and probably gave him status in the Assyrian governmental system. If it is not an isolated case, it is possible that, under both Tiglath-Pileser and Sargon, control of the Egyptian border was entrusted to local nomad chiefs, who were absorbed into the Assyrian administrative system.

A group of Nimrud Letters referring to Arabs or nomad matters points to a similar policy on the border of the Syrian desert during the last third of the 8th century B.C. As these documents are of special significance to our study, we shall discuss them in detail, translating the relevant passages:

a. **ND 2644 (Nimrud Letter XXIII):**[302] A draft of a "king's order" (*abat [ša]rri*) to an official whose name has not survived in its entirety (^{md}*X-bēl-uṣur*). The poor condition of the text permits only a general outline: (lines 3-5): "The camels, as many as the ^{lú}***turtānu*** has delivered to you, get ready and look (them) over.[303] (lines 6-8): Give ^{m}*Ba-di-'-ilu* (or ^{m}*Su-di-'-ilu*)[304] an appointment before you and let him pasture in the midst of the land.[305] (lines 9-12): Now, these Arabs... the ^{lú}*turtānu...* your checkpoints in the desert as before."[306] In lines 14-17 permission is given (most certainly to Arabs, see ABL 414 below) to graze their flocks in the land.[307] Lines 18-20 are not sufficiently clear. Lines 21-24 mention four command posts (*birāti*)[308] but the names of only two — ^{uru}*Ni-u*[309] and ^{uru}*[Qi]-di-si*[310] — have been preserved. Lines 25-29 deal with tending of sown-land and going to Damascus.[311]

302 Saggs, *Iraq* 17 (1955), 142-143.

303 See von Soden, *Orientalia* 35 (1966), 20.

304 For the Old Arabic name *Bd'l* see Harding, *Pre-Islamic Names,* 97; for *Šd'l, ibid.,* 343.

305 PN *ina pa-ni-ka pi-iq-da-šú lìb-bi māti li-ir-'-ú.*

306 *an-nu-rig* ^{lú}*Aŕ-ba-a-a an-nu-ti* ^{lú}*tar-ta-nu....*EN.NUN-*ku-nu ki-i ti-ma-li šal-ši* u_4*-me mu-da-bi-ri ⸢lu-ú⸣...* . The exact meaning of the passage is not clear, since the verb has not been preserved. For the reading ^{kur}*mu-da-bi-ri* in lines 12, 15 see *AHw,* 572a; B. Oded, *IEJ* 14 (1964), 273, n. 11.

307 ⸢UDU.NITA⸣. MEŠ-*šu-nu [i-na?]* KUR *m[u]-da-bi-ri [i-na?] lìb-bi ma-a-ti ⸢a⸣-⸢šu⸣-ra li-ir-i-u.*

308 For the meaning of *birtu* see Weippert, *ZDPV* 89 (1973), 38 n. 43.

309 Oded's proposed identification of ^{uru}*Ni-u* with Neia, known from *Notitia dignitatum* as part of the Phoinike Libanesia province, *ibid.,* n. 13, seems acceptable. For the

b. **ND 2381 (Nimrud Letter XIX):**[312] This is a letter from ^{m}*Addu-ḫa-ti*[313] to the king. The text is badly damaged but seems to concern the dispatch of a caravan from Damascus (^{uru}*[Di]-maš-qa*). It mentions, *inter alia,* more than 1500 donkeys, as well as preparing of 300 she-camels for a journey.[314]

c. **ND 2437 (Nimrud Letter XX):**[315] A letter from Addu-ḫati to the king, discussing, *inter alia,* the sown-land of various cities, of whose names only that of ^{uru}*La-ba-'-u* (biblical Lebo'-[hamath]) remains. It refers to ten fortified villages in the desert (line 37: *10 alāni*^{meš} *bīt dūrāni ina mad-bar*),[316] as well as sentry-posts (*maṣṣarāte,* line 41). The meaning of lines 31-33 is uncertain, because the verb is missing and some signs at the beginning of line 31 are damaged. Still, it is clear enough that the subject is a shortage(?) of Assyrian manpower in the city of Ṣupite.[317]

d. **Rm. 77 (ABL 414):**[318] "To the king, my lord, your servant Bēl-liqbi. May it be well with the king my lord. The city of Ḫēsa is (only) a road station (*bīt mardīte*). No *nīš bīti* personnel are stationed there, and post station and escort officers (^{lú}*rab kallê* ^{lú}*rab raksi*)[319] are not on watch

suggested location of Neia along one of the routes connecting Palmyra with Damascus or Ḥoms see E. Honigmann, "Neia", *PW,* XVI, 2182.

310 For this reconstruction see Oded, *ibid.,* 273.

311 Regarding the special form of this document and the question of whether lines 25-29 belong to the original "king's order" see Saggs, *Iraq* 17 (1955), 143.

312 Saggs, *ibid.,* 138.

313 For the name Addu-ḫati, instead of its former reading Uḫati, see Postgate, *Taxation,* 382.

314 For the reading of lines 4-6 and an explanation of the reference to she-camels, see K. Deller, *Orientalia* 31 (1962), 460.

315 Saggs, *op. cit.,* 139-140.

316 For this reading see Postgate, *op. cit.,* 382.

317 J.V. Kinnier Wilson, *The Nimrud Wine Lists,* London 1972, 9, suggested reading of lines 31-33 is: *la-a* ^{lú}*šá muḫḫi āli la-a* ^{lú}*petiūte* (LÚ.NI.DUḪ.MEŠ) ⌜kur⌝*Aššur-aya i-na* ^{uru}*Ṣu-pi-te* <*ú-si-ri-bu*>, "Neither the *ša muḫḫi āli* nor the gatekeepers are allowing Assyrians to enter Ṣūpatu". On the location and extent of the Assyrian province of Ṣupite, which included the Anti-Lebanon, see Forrer, *Provinzeinteilung,* 62 f., 69, and Malamat, "Aram Zobah", *Enc. Miqr.,* I, 582-583; cf. also the bibliographical list there.

318 See Waterman, *RCAE* I, 288-289; Pfeiffer, *SLA,* 76-77. For translation only and discussion of the contents of the document see A. Alt, *ZDPV* 67 (1945), 153-159.

319 These were titles for two kinds of officials in charge of transferring letters and

there.[320] Now, I would like to have 30 houses built there. There was no engineer ([lú]*mār ki-it-ki-te-e*) (there) during the days of Nabû-ṣalla the [lú]*šaknu.* They should bring out every soldier staying in Ḫ̌ēsa, settle them in the city of Argite and give them houses and gardens. If it be acceptable to the king, let them write a letter to Nabû-ṣalla the [lú]*šaknu.* Ya'iru, the deputy of the ruler of the city of Šibte I would appoint therein,[321] and Sin-iddina, the 'house overseer' ([lú]*rab bīti*) of Addu-ḫ̌ati, I would appoint in the city of Sazana. They will keep watch over these road stations... they will serve the king. The Arabs, as formerly, go in and out (*a-ki šá ti-ma-li ša-šú-me e-ru-bu ú-ṣu-u*), it is well indeed. Amili'ti son of Ameri came to me in the city of Ṣupite, (and) I asked him for reports. It is well indeed. From/Concerning the son of Ašapi, who had been taken to the land of Masa', so far we have heard nothing".[322]

ABL 414 was previously assigned to the period of Assurbanipal, on the basis of the similarity between the name Ašapi mentioned in it and the name Ašipa in other letters from the reign of this king.[323] The same period was consequently assigned to ABL 224-225, sent by Addu-ḫ̌ati (whose name figured above in ABL 414, rev. 3) and dealing with Syria. However, the discovery of ND 2381 and ND 2437, sent by Addu-ḫ̌ati

cargoes, part of the communication and control system of the Assyrian empire, which was based on stations along the main roads, see Kinnier Wilson, *op. cit.*, 57-62; Martin, *Tribut und Tributleistungen*, 32-34; A. Salonen, *Hippologica Accadica*, Helsinki 1956, 230; *CAD*, K, 84 *kalliu.* On the existence of such a network in Syria and Palestine as early as the second half of the 8th century B.C. see Alt, *ibid.*, 147-159, some of whose identifications are, however, incorrect.

320 For this translation of lines 4-7 cf. Kinnier Wilson, *op. cit.*, 59.

321 [m]*Ia-'-i-ru* [lú]*šanû*[nu] *a-na* [lú]*rab* [uru] *Šib/Me-te ina lib-bi la-ap-qid.* The position of the word *ana* demands the translation "Ya'iru the deputy I will appoint as overseer of the city of Šibte". This, however, removes the sentence from the general context of the document.

322 Rev. 13-15: *mār* [m]*A-šá-pi a-na* [kur]*Ma-sa-' ša il-qú-u-ni ú-di-ni ṭè-en-šú la-a ni-šá-me.* Waterman's and Pfeiffer's version (also reflected in Alt, see note 318), *a-na* [kur]*Ma-ni-'-ša il-ku/qú-u-ni,* presents two difficulties: the form of the verb *il-ku/qú-u-ni* is not clear, and the country named [kur]*Ma-ni-'-ša* is unknown from any other source. Our version is based on the similarity of the *ni* and *sa* signs and on the assumption that the passage discussed is an indirect statement (i.e. the verb is in the subjunctive mood).

323 Olmstead, *History of Assyria,* 428; Waterman, *RCAE* III, 92, 155; Pfeiffer, *SLA,* 265.

and concerned with southern Syria, reinforces Saggs' view that all the above (including ABL 414) belong to the period between the conquest of Damascus by Tiglath-Pileser (732 B.C.) and the transfer of the Assyrian capital from Calah (Nimrud) to Dūr-Šarrukīn (705 B.C.).[324]

The common chronological and geographical background of these four letters favors locating the caravanserais, whose maintenance is discussed in ABL 414, in the region of Damascus and the Anti-Lebanon. The town of ^uru^*Ḫe-e-sa* can be identified as present-day Ḥasiyyeh, a village some 40 kms south of Ḥoms at the northern extremity of the Anti-Lebanon.[325] Ḥasiyyeh lies on the Damascus-Ḥoms route and is the most southerly crossroad between Qaryatein and Quṣṣeir, which is in the northern part of the Valley of Lebanon; there the remains of a Mameluke khan are still visible. ^uru^*Ar-gi-te* seems to be identical with the ^uru^*Ḫa-ar-gi-e* near the Ṣupite region in Assurbanipal, Rm. vii, 113-114.[326] ^uru^*Sa-za-na* is ^uru^*Ša-za-e-na,* referred to in letter Kl. 69:279 from Kāmid el-Lōz in the Valley of Lebanon. The contents of this letter as well as of ABL 414, and the geographical and archaelogical considerations, lead us to locate this city on the highway north of Kāmid el-Lōz, probably near the junction of the Beqa' route and the Beirut-Damascus route.[327]

The documents described above illustrate the Assyrian control system over south Syrian routes (the Ḥoms-Damascus road along the fringe of the desert, the Ḥoms-Ṣupite road along the Valley of Lebanon, and apparently also the roads from Ḥoms and Damascus to Palmyra), a network of sentry stations, and check-posts (*maṣṣarāti*) at key points, along with fortresses (*birāti*) and centers of government and

324 Saggs, *Iraq* 17 (1955), 139, 153-154. We can conclude that ABL 414 (=Rm. 77) actually came from Nimrud. The letters, marked Rm. sent by Rassam to the British Museum, came from both Calah (Nimrud) and Nineveh (Kuyunjik). For the attribution of three other documents from the K(uyunjik) Collection to the Nimrud documents (K 296, 382, 418) see Deller, *Orientalia* 35 (1966), 190-192.

325 This identification has already been proposed by Alt, *ZDPV* 67 (1945), 157 ff. The Nimrud Letters discussed here, discovered after Alt's article was published, offer some support for his suggestion. In Lettter XX (=ND 2437):25 the toponym preserved is ^uru^*Ḫi-[e?...].* The affinity of this letter to ABL 414 caused Saggs (*ibid.,* 140) to consider reconstructing it as ^uru^*Ḫi-[e(?)-sa(?)]* here as well.

326 As already pointed out by Hommel, *EGAO,* 585 no. 5.

327 See Eph'al, *IEJ* 21 (1971), 155-157.

administration in the cities.[328] In order to control the region, the Assyrian authorities were clearly inclined to allow the nomads to graze their flocks within the settled areas, as is explicitly shown in the "king's order" (ND 2644:16-17) and in Bēl-liqbi's confirmation that this policy was actually carried out (ABL 414, rev. 7-9).[329]

The passage in the "king's order" about the appointment of Badi'ilu and permission for him to graze "within the country" (ND 2644:6-8) is of paramount importance. Unless Badi'ilu was a nomad chief and not a permanent resident of the area, it is difficult to understand why he would need a special grazing permit. The order appointing him indicates that, besides his honored postition within his tribe, he was awarded official status by the Assyrian authorities. Although the document does not mention the functions assigned to him, since the nomads grazed outside the settlements proper, he was presumably connected with the Assyrian supervisory system involving key points in the areas bordering the desert.

Another document related to the problem of the official status held by Arabs vis-à-vis the Assyrian authorities is ABL 631 (=K 1265), contemporary with the letters discussed.[330] It acknowledges the receipt of 125 white camels from the Arabs (^{kur}*Ar-ba-a-a*) and mentions five people. One of them, ^{f}*Sam-si,* can reasonably be identified with the queen of the Arabs in the inscriptions of Tiglath-Pileser and Sargon. ^{m}*Ḫa-sil-a-nu*[331] and ^{m}*Ia-ra-pa* are designated $^{l\acute{u}}$*rab kiṣir,* and the last two are ^{m}*Ta-am-ra-a-nu* and ^{m}*Ga-na-bu.* These are not Akkadian names and

328 This group of documents also includes Nimrud Letter LXX (=ND 2766, see Saggs, *Iraq* 25 [1963], 79), indicating the existence of a *birtu* and a *maṣṣartu* in the city of ^{uru}*Ra-ab-le-e* (biblical Riblah). Line 11 refers to Qadesh (for the reading ^{uru}*Qi-di-si* here see Oded, *IEJ* 14[1964], 272). The word *mu-da-bi-ru* in this letter has its usual meaning of the grazing area on the desert edge and relates to nomads.

329 As we saw, ND 2644 was not addressed to Bēl-liqbi but to another official, ^{md}*x-bēl(?)-uṣur.* Since Bēl-liqbi's letter shows that he received a similar order, it can be assumed that such orders went as a general policy to various Assyrian officials in the area. Allotment of grazing lands to Arabs and supervision by Assyrian authorities to prevent their violating the borders of the settled land (in the Middle Euphrates region) is also pointed out in ABL 547 from the reign of Sargon, see Deller, *Orientalia* 30 (1961), 350.

330 Cf. *ADD* 759. For transliteration and translation see *ADD,* III, pp. 538-539; Waterman, *RCAE* II, 440-441.

might, at least in part, be Arabic.[332] The involvement of these people with the delivery of camels indicates that they came either from camel-grazing areas or the routes along which camels were sold. The title [lú]*rab kiṣir,* however, bestowed upon two of the people, designates commanders of small military units.[333] The obvious assumption is that they were in charge of key points on the fringes of the desert where water was available and roads intersected.

It can be concluded, therefore, that, in the time of Tiglath-Pileser and Sargon, the Assyrian authorities clearly tended to integrate various nomad groups into their control system in the border regions of Palestine and Syria.[334] This was important as insurance for the loyalty of the nomads and as a barrier against the penetration of other nomads from the desert into the settled areas, making it unnecessary to assign to the border region Assyrian military units at a time when they were needed for the frequent wars throughout the empire and on its frontiers.[335] While they were being integrated into the system, the nomads penetrated the settled regions up to the Valley of Lebanon. This was essentially because of the dissolution of the national-political bodies in the region (the kingdoms of Israel and Damascus) and the consequent violation of their eastern frontiers, the Assyrian imperialist

331 The above-mentioned editions give this name as [m]*Ḫa-tar-a-nu,* but it is preferable to read [m]*Ḫa-sil-a-nu;* cf. *Ḥsl, Ḥsln, RNP,* I, 96; Harding, *Pre-Islamic Names,* 189.

332 For the name [m]*Ia-ra-pa* cf. *Yrf'* (*RNP,* I,202; Harding, *ibid.,* 667) and *Yrf'l* (Van den Branden, *IT,* 287, 300; Harding, *ibid.,* 668). For [m]*Ga-na-bu* cf. *Gnb (RNP,* I, 62; Harding, *ibid.,* 169), and also *Gnb'* in a Palmyrene inscription (S.A. Cook, *A Glossary of Aramaic Inscriptions,* Cambridge 1898, 37). For [m]*Ta-am-ra-a-nu* cf. *Tmrw (RNP,* I, 271, 406); *Ṯmr, Hṯmr* (Van den Branden, *TTP,* I, 131; II, 107, 126; Harding, *ibid.,* 148).

333 This title applied initially to military organization but eventually to those who filled various positions in the Assyrian administrative system, which was militarily based. Concerning this title see W. Manitius, *ZA* 24 (1910), 212-218; B. Meissner, *Babylonien und Assyrien,* I, Heidelberg 1920, 103-104; Forrer, *Provinzeinteilung,* 51.

334 The general chronological framework of the letters discussed in this chapter is 732-705 B.C., but we lack the information to pinpoint the date of each letter. We can, therefore, use them as a single chronological entity, not distinguishing the policy of Tiglath-Pileser from that of Sargon.

335 Nomad groups native to the region were used for guarding the borders beginning with the introduction of Assyrian rule in Palestine and Syria and continuing until

policy cited above, and the overriding Assyrian interest in regular traffic along the King's Highway, making what happened to the sedentary populations to the west of secondary importance.[336,337]

the Ottoman period. The nomad groups' responsibility for order in areas traversed by major roads or otherwise important to the empire was ensured by the official status granted their leaders and by such privileges as grazing rights, tax exemptions or access to other income. Thus, for example, the southern border of Palestine at the end of the Byzantine period was secured by Arab tribes who received fixed annual payments from the authorities (Ph. Mayerson, *Transactions and Proceedings of the American Philological Association* 95 [1964], 155 ff.; 185 f.; 192 f.); in the days of Justinian, the heads of Ghassānian and Saracen tribes were put in charge of the borders of Syria and North Arabia and given the status of phylarchs (*ibid.,* 188-190). Similarly, in the Ottoman period, actual control over the border areas of South Syria and Transjordan belonged to the Bedouin tribes, and the sheikhs were assured to revenue in return for taking responsibility for safe communications along the roads within their area of authority; see U. Heyd, *Ottoman Documents on Palestine 1552-1615,* Oxford 1960, 41, 91.

336 There are also certain indications of this in southwest Philistia: the enhanced status of the sheikh of Laban (regarding the location of Laban near Raphia, see n. 347) and perhaps the penetration and spread of the nomads in that region seem linked with the destruction of Raphia and the deportation of its inhabitants by Sargon in 720 B.C.

337 These conclusions touch on a troublesome question: I Chron. 5:10, 18-22 describe the struggle between the Israelite tribes in Transjordan and the Hagarites, the people of Jetur, of Naphish and of Nodab, in which the nomads were driven east of Gilead. According to verse 10, the sons of Reuben had fought the Hagarites during Saul's reign (echoes of a struggle with the Hagarites at about that time are sounded in Ps. 83:7; see note 209). The nomads are again referred to in the report of the war of Alexander the Great against "Arabs" in the Anti-Lebanon in 332 B.C. (Arrian, *Anabasis* II, 20, 4; Plutarch, *Alexander,* 24; cf. Curtius Rufus, *Alexander,* IV, ii, 24. The name "Arabs" as used here is too general a designation for the exact identity of the nomads mentioned to be determined). Greek epigraphic and literary sources also offer much evidence of the Ituraeans in the region of the Valley of Lebanon from the 2nd century B.C. on. Until now, it has been difficult to bridge the gap in time and space between the various references to nomads, especially the Ituraeans in Gilead, northern Transjordan and southern Syria, and to determine when and under what circumstances they made their way to the Valley of Lebanon. (The most exhaustive discussion in historical and epigraphic sources of the Ituraeans is still E. Schürer, *Geschichte des jüdischen Volkes etc.*[4], I, Leipzig 1901, 707-725. See also Liver, "Jetur", *Enc. Miqr.,* III, 673-674; R. Dussaud, *La pénétration des Arabes*

C. SARGON'S ECONOMIC POLICY AND ITS EFFECT UPON THE NOMADS

The reign of Sargon II (722-705 B.C.) was marked by a drive to strengthen Assyrian rule and establish it solidly in Palestine. This was accomplished by vigorous campaigns to suppress rebellion, followed by such punitive measures as reorganizing various territories into Assyrian provinces (Samaria and Ashdod) and transferring populations. It involved, as well, economic and settlement projects initiated by the Assyrian authorities, especially in the border regions.[338] All of this affected the nomads of the area as well as those farther afield.

The inscriptions of Sargon state that he opened "the sealed-off harbor (*kāru*) of Egypt", mingled Assyrians with Egyptians, and encouraged mutual trade.[339] Although the expression "to open the sealed-off harbor of GN" (*kāri* GN *kangu petû*) is unique to Assyrian and insufficiently explicit, the meaning seems generally understandable: The place under discussion was a commercial center[340] for Assyrians and Egyptians, and was linked with Egypt (as reflected by its designation *kāri* ^{kur}*Muṣur*).

en Syrie avant l'Islam, Paris 1955, 177-178). The gap may narrow when the Assyrian documents concerning the nomads penetration of South Syria during the Assyrian period are integrated with the sources for the nomads in that region. It is quite possible, on the other hand, that the reference to the people of Jetur, Naphish and Nodab in I Chron. 5:19 depicts not the demographic situation of ca. 11th century B.C., but of a later period, perhaps when the book of Chronicles was edited (see pp. 67, 238-239). This alternative reduces the time-space gap between biblical and Greek reference to the Ituraeans. Even so, the reference to the Ituraeans in I Chron. 5:19 antedates by several centuries those in extra-biblical sources. The inclusion of the people of Jetur and Naphish in the list of the "Sons of Ishmael" (Gen. 25:13-15; I Chron. 1:29-31), most of them known from the 8th century B.C. on (see Appendix B), indicates that the "Arabs" whose penetration of southern Syria is reflected in the Nimrud Letters may be the ancestors of the people of Jetur and Naphish.

338 Regarding Assyrian activity in Palestine and its vicinity, particularly in 720, 716 and 713-712 B.C., see Eph'al, "Sargon", *Enc. Miqr.,* V, 1124-1125, and the bibliography listed there.

339 Khorsabad Annals, lines 17-18; the Nimrud Prism, Fragment D, col. iv, 46-48. For reconstruction of the texts, see Tadmor, *JCS* 12 (1958), 34. Tadmor read here: *[ka]r-ri* ^{kur}*Mu-ṣur kan-gu ap-te-e-ma,* "I opened the sealed [harbo]r of Egypt". On this point he has offered the following observations: "The passage in question has not been fully preserved in the historical inscriptions of Sargon. Gadd's copy of the Nimrud Prism (Fragment D, col. iv, 46) reads *⸢x⸣-ri.* This could be restored as *⸢kar⸣-ri* or *[ka]-⸢a⸣-ri.* The first possibility is not entirely excluded, though seems to

This points to an emporium near the border between the Assyrian Empire and Egypt, evidently close to the sea. It is reasonable to assume that such a trading station in northern Sinai would be easily accessible by land or sea and would offer decent living conditions. Since these two requisites do not obtain in the region between el-Arish and Pelusium, the "harbor of Egypt" cannot be set there. As there is not the slightest hint of Assyrian authority having acquired a foothold west of the North Sinai buffer area — the area near Egypt — it is more reasonable to seek the "sealed-off harbor of Egypt" to the east, in the el-Arish area.[341] This

be less likely. (The spelling *karru* for *kāru* in the prism, although unusual, is not unprecedented, e.g. *me-e kar-ri el-lim,* PBS 1/2 122:35 f.; *bīt kar-ri,* see *CAD,* K 238b and 239a sub 3; and [lú]*rab kar-ri, ibid.* 239b, common in the Neo-Babylonian texts. Cf. also the Assyrian plural *kar-ra-ni* as against *ka-ra-a-ni, CAD,* K 238, sub 2). The latter possibility is now supported by the parallel passage of the Annals in Abel's copy (Saal II, Winckler, Plate 2, line 4) *⸢ka⸣*(!), which can only be restored as *⸢ka⸣-[a-ri].* In any event, the word in question in the Nimrud Prism cannot be reconstructed *[mi]-⸢iṣ⸣ri* = "border(?)", as suggested in *CAD,* K 153a".

340 The word *kāru(m)* in Akkadian designates, beside a quay or harbor, a center of commercial activity (not necessarily on a sea or river, see *CAD,* K, 231 ff., esp. 234-237; *AHw,* 451-452). The same semantic inclusiveness occurred in West Semitic and Greek, certainly as a result of similar processes of settlement and economic development: מחוז(א) means *harbor* (cf., for example, Ps. 107:30; Targum on Gen. 49:13 and Ezek. 27:3). For מחוז(א) meaning *market, trading place,* see Aramaic Targums of חוץ (Num. 22:39; Lam. 5:10; Job 2:19; 4:2), the Palmyrene inscriptions (J. Cantineau, *Inscriptions palmyréniennes,* Damas 1930, p. 8, No. 6; idem, *Syria* 12 [1931], 124), and the equation מחוז = *forum* in a bilingual (Punic and Latin) inscription from Leptis Magna, Donner-Röllig, *KAI,* 124:2. Similarly, λιμήν, usually *harbor,* sometimes is synonymous with ἀγορά, which designates *market* (see H.G. Liddell-R.D.D. Scott, *A Greek-English Lexicon,* Oxford 1925, 1050 b). For *custom-house,* a meaning eventually appended, see Tariff of Palmyra (*CIS* II 3913 = G.A. Cook, *North Semitic Inscriptions,* Oxford 1903, No. 147), col. ii, 1 למנא די הדרינא תדמר, "the custom-house of Hadriana Tadmor". A lexicographical list from Ugarit offers decisive proof of the parallel meaning of *kāru(m)* and מחוז(א): the Akkadian *ka-a-ru* is translated by the Ugaritic *ma-aḫ-ḫa-[zu]* (RS 137 ii 21', J. Nougayrol, *Ugaritica,* V, 1968, 242-243). For a detailed discussion of the uses of these two terms and their development see E.Y. Kutscher, *Lešonénu* 34 (1969), 5-18.

341 Tadmor's various suggestions illustrate our uncertainty about the location of "the sealed-off harbor of Egypt": a. in el-Arish (in *Military History,* 272); b. on the bay of Sabkhat Bardawil (*JCS* 12 [1958], 78, n. 197); c. in Pelusium or Sile (*BA* 29 [1966], 92). In view of the geographical conditions in North Sinai and our

mercantile colony seems to have been a connecting and intermediary link in the Palestine-Egypt trade.[342] The settlement of Assyrian merchants beside Egyptian tradesmen there and the encouragement by the authorities of trade between the two groups reinforced the Assyrian hold in southern Palestine and increased Assyrian influence on economic activity in the region.

The location of the "sealed-off harbor of Egypt" according to the above considerations and the statements in the inscriptions of Sargon about settling people "on the border of the Brook-of-Egypt"[343] constitute the limits of Assyrian control in southwestern Palestine in the days of Sargon, suggesting that this area apparently extended no farther west than the "Brook-of-Egypt", which is Wadi el-Arish,[344] and did not include northern Sinai.[345] The documents from Sargon's period regarding the nomads must be evaluated in light of this.

Assuming that the limit of Assyrian dominion was the area of Wadi el-Arish, it must follow that before the conquest of Egypt by Esarhaddon (671 B.C.) the places included — among them "the

information about Sargon's military activity, the latter two alternatives are improbable. Another suggestion, archaeologically oriented, locating the "sealed-off harbor of Egypt" in Sheikh Zuweid, appears in R. Reich, *Eretz-Israel* 15 (Y. Aharoni Memorial Volume) (forthcoming).

342 Nimrud Letter XVI (=ND 2765) tells of horses brought to Calah by emissaries (LÚ.MAḪ.MEŠ= [lú]*ṣirāni*) from Egypt, Gaza, Judah and other countries in Transjordan and Philistia (see Saggs, *Iraq* 17 [1955], 134-135; Donner, *MIO* 5 [1957], 159-161; Postgate, *Taxation,* 117-118). The reason Egyptian representatives are included among the tax- (or gift-) bearers of Palestinian vassals is not sufficiently clear, for Egypt was not under the control of Tiglath-Pileser or Sargon (contemporaries of the Nimrud Letters). The difficulty is eliminated if we assume that the Egyptians in the letter under discussion were not residents of Egypt proper but representatives of the "sealed-off harbor of Egypt", which was actually in the area of control of the Assyrian kings, in the vicinity of Gaza and the other kingdoms of Philistia mentioned here. For another view of the reasons for including the Egyptians in the letter, see Donner, *ibid.,* 178-184 and n. 371 below.

343 VA 8424:6-7.

344 See above, n. 287.

345 During the reign of Tiglath-Pileser actual Assyrian control was weak even in the Naḫal-Muṣur region itself, and was strengthened only by Sargon: He put down the rebellion of Ḫanūn of Gaza, who was aided by an Egyptian expeditionary force, and destroyed Raphia and deported its inhabitants in 720 B.C. His prisms report that in ca. 716 B.C. he brought Assyrian merchants to the "sealed-off harbor of

sealed-off harbor of Egypt", "the town of the Brook-of-Egypt", and the towns of Laban and Arṣâ — could not have been west of the Wadi el-Arish region. "The town of the Brook-of-Egypt" (*āl Naḫal Muṣur*) can presumably be located in el-Arish and identified with the Rhinocorura of the Greek sources.[346] The others were undoubtedly between Raphia and el-Arish; various proposals for locating them more exactly have been made: Alt's proposed identification of ^uru^*La-ba-an* in the inscriptions of Sargon with the *L/Rbn* near Raphia in Shishak's geographical list seems acceptable.[347] The identification of ^uru^*Ar-ṣa-a,* according to the inscriptions of Esarhaddon, as "near the Brook-of-Egypt",[348] may not be as precise as it sounds, since Raphia, which is similarly described in these inscriptions as "close to the Brook-of-Egypt"[349] is about 45 kilometers from el-Arish. Mazar suggests that ^uru^*Arṣâ* is ^uru^*Iu-ur-ṣa*^ki^ of the Amarna Letters (nos. 314-315) and of the geographical lists of Thutmose III and Shishak (as nos. 60 and 133

Egypt" and nomad groups to the Naḫal Muṣur area, probably to develop commerce under Assyrian supervision (On the conclusion that the reference here is to nomads see pp. 107-108). It is, however, unnecessary to accept Alt's opinion (*Kleine Schriften* II, 224 ff., 234-240) that Sargon organized the border area with Egypt, including Raphia, into the Assyrian military-administrative framework: the Assyrian documents state specifically that exiles were brought from the east of the Assyrian empire and settled in the cities of the territory of Ashdod, now established as a province by Sargon after the revolt of Yamani in 712 B.C. (Khorsabad Annals, 256-262; Prism fragment from Nineveh 81-7-27, 3, in E.F. Weidner, *AfO* 14 [1941], 49). But nothing is said about settling these exiles in Raphia and Naḫal-Muṣur or appointing an Assyrian official over the region.

346 Cf. F.-M. Abel, *RB* 48 (1939), 537 ff.; Alt, *ibid.,* 227 ff. The paucity of Iron Age II finds at el-Arish does not support the reservation to this identification (as made by Aharoni, *'Atiqot* [Hebrew Series] 7 [1974], 88-90), because the archaeological survey there was not followed by excavation. Thus, for example, although no finds earlier than the Hellenistic period were discovered at Tell Rafaḥ (Raphia) (Aharoni, *ibid.,* 88), its existence in the 8th century B.C. is verified by the inscriptions of Sargon and Esarhaddon.

347 Alt, *ibid.,* 230-231. Cf. J. Simons, *Handbook for the Study of Egyptian Topographical Lists relating to Western Asia,* Leiden 1937, 186.

348 Borger, *Asarhaddon,* Klch. A 16; Nin. A iii 39: ^uru^*Ar-ṣa-a šа i-te-e/pa-a-ṭi Na-ḫal* ^kur^*Mu-uṣ-ri/Mu-ṣur.*

349 Cf. Frt. F, obv. 16-17: *ultu* ^uru^*Apqu šá pāṭi* ^kur^*Sa-me-n[a x?] adi* ^uru^*Rapiḫi ana itê Naḫal* ^kur^*Muṣur,* "from the town of Apqu (Aphek) which is in the region of

respectively), and situated in Tell Jemmeh, near the Besor Brook (Wadi Ghazzeh),[350] where 7th century B.C. Assyrian buildings and a fortress were recently discovered.[351] The name of Arṣâ may have survived in 'Αρίζα, which in the Byzantine period was one of the cities of Palestina Prima.[352] If we accept literally, however, the description of Arṣâ as "close to the Brook-of-Egypt", we have to look for it in the vicinity of el-Arish and dissociate it from Yurṣa, which is at least 25 kilometers away.[353]

Sargon records the suppression of the people of 'Ephah (lú*Ḫa-ia-pa-a*), Thamūd, Marsimani and Ibadidi, "the distant Arabs dwelling in the desert who knew neither overseers nor officials and had not brought their tribute to any king".[354] We have already seen that these tribes were part of a territorial bloc most of whose components were not in the purview of the Bible, and some of whom are not known even from later sources.[355] This ethnological complex must be located south of Tema' and of the area inhabited by the Sabaeans in North Arabia to whom the inscriptions of Tiglath-Pileser refer. If we accept the literal description of Sargon as the conqueror of these tribes, we must assume a wearisome military campaign, one of the longest undertaken by Sargon's army. The short and relatively restrained accounts in Assyrian inscriptions make such a campaign unlikely. Furthermore, the inscriptions of Sargon never refer to taking booty from these nomad tribes, a detail generally not omitted if it took place, especially after a long, hard campaign. Likewise, what is said about the deportation of the tribal remnants to Samaria[356] (or to "the land of Bīt Ḫumri" in general[357]) is

Samerīna (?) as far as the town of Raphia (in) the region close to the Brook-of-Egypt".

350 Maisler (Mazar), *PEQ* 1952, 48-51; idem, *SVT* 4 (1957), 65. Cf. note 353.

351 On these excavations see G.W. Van Beek, *IEJ* 22 (1972), 245-246; 24 (1974), 138-139, 274-275.

352 For further identifying considerations, see Aharoni, *ibid.*, 90; and the next note.

353 In another approach, N. Na'aman suggests that Naḫal-Muṣur="The Brook-of-Egypt" should be identified not with Wadi el-Arish but with the Besor Brook (Wadi Ghazzeh), thus identifying Arṣâ with Yurṣa and with Tell Jemme, *Tel Aviv* 6 (1979), 68-90.

354 Khorsabad Annals, 120 ff.; Cylinder Inscription, 20.

355 See above, pp. 87-91.

356 Khorsabad Annals, 122-123.

357 Cylinder Inscription, 20.

not literally acceptable, since it runs counter to the usual Assyrian practice of putting considerable distance between uprooted populations and their homeland. Moreover, the transfer of *nomads* to Samaria or "the land of Bît Ḫumri", a clearly agricultural area, does not accord with the organized Assyrian deportation system. It was a system based on transferring populations in both directions in order to resettle regions depleted by wars or deportations, thus preventing their desolation and impoverishment.[358] On the other hand, the transfer of Arabs to Samaria, especially when it was burgeoning under Sargon,[359] is reasonable only if their special *nomadic* characteristics were utilized. Settling them in Samaria would probably divert to that area some of the Arabian trade in which the nomads played an important role.[360]

Sargon's court historians therefore seem to have exaggerated when they wrote about the conquest of North Arabian tribes and the deportation of their "remnants" to Palestine.[361] The "deportation"

358 On the system of organized deportation in the Assyrian empire, see B. Oded, *Mass Deportation and Deportees in the Neo-Assyrian Empire,* Wiesbaden 1979, esp. chapter IV.

359 For the rehabilitation of Samaria and its establishment as the capital of the Assyrian province Samerîna, see Sargon, *Lie,* lines 16-17; Nimrud Prism, Fragment D, col. iv, 37-41 (Gadd, *Iraq* 16 [1954], 179).

360 The importance of the nomads in Arabian trade is apparent from the taxes and booty taken by the Assyrian kings from Arab tribes:

	Tiglath-Pileser	**Sargon**	**Sennacherib**	**Esarhaddon**
Gold	III R 10, 2:31	Lie, line 124		Nin. A iv 20
Precious Stones		Lie, line 124	K 8544 rev. 6; cf. VA 8424:49	1000 choice gems, Nin. A iv 20
Spices	5000 bags, III R 10,2:21; K 3751 rev. 5	Lie, line 124	K 8544 rev. 7; cf. VA 8424:49	100 (Heidel Prism: 1000) *kunzi riqqē,* Nin. A iv 21; Heidel iii 7
Camels	III R 10,2:20, 25; K 3751 rev. 5	Lie, line 125; cf. ABL 631		Nin. A iv 17,21

The Bedouin possessed luxury goods only by reason of their Arabian trade.

361 Such exaggeration can be found elsewhere in his inscriptions, see for example, below, pp. 108-111 on the "tribute" to Sargon from the three "kings of the

seems only to have grown out of an arrangement between Sargon and the nomad groups in the land of Midian, who were connected with the Arab trade. The members of these tribes were to be settled in Samaria to carry out special economic activities useful to both parties.[362] The diversion of some Arab trade, most of it presumably to Tyre, from routes in the desert border regions farther inland increased Assyrian control and augmented imperial profits.[363]

We have noted that in southern Palestine Sargon settled people "on the border of the Brook-of-Egypt" under the supervision of the sheikh ([lú]*nasīku*) of the town of Laban.[364] The name of the country of origin of

seashore and the desert", or the victory claimed in the battle of Dēr, see Grayson, *Studies Landsberger,* 340-342; cf. also J.A. Brinkman, *Studies presented to A.L. Oppenheim,* Chicago 1964, 14-15.

362 We have no additional sources for the history of the Arabs settled in Samaria. Among the finds of the Samaria excavations was an Assyrian clay tablet, undoubtedly written after the conquest of Samaria, as indicated by its reference to two Assyrian officials, one named [m]*Nergal-šal-lim,* the other, whose name has not survived, titled [lú]*rab ālāni* (the tablet was published by G.A. Reisner, C.S. Fisher, D.G. Lyon, *Harvard Excavations at Samaria,* I, Cambridge, Mass. 1924, 247; for corrections of the text and names see S. Langdon, *JRAS* 1936, 501-502). Mentioned also is A.A.PAP.ME = *Aya-aḫḫē,* possibly the name of an Arab. For Arab names beginning with *Aya-* (=A.A) cf. [m]*A-a-ka-ba/ma-ru* (ABL 260, rev. 2), [m]*A-a-mu* (Rm. vii 97; viii 31; *passim;* this may be an abbreviated from of [m]*Aya-'ammu*); perhaps [m]*A-a-nu-ri* (ND 2773 = Nimrud Letter XIV:4) also is Arab.

The introductory element *Aya-* (A.A) is certainly not related to the goddess [d]*Aya,* consort of Šamaš of Larsa and Sippar (on *Aya-* as other than a theophorous element see R. Zadok, *WO* 9 [1976], 44-53; cf. also W.F. Albright, *JAOS* 74 [1954], 226). Although it is evident from the Assyrian documents that various nomads in the Syrian desert in the 8th and 7th centuries B.C. as well possessed the element *Aya-* in their names (cf. Maisler [Mazar], *Lešonenu* 15 [1947], 39-40, who combines [md]*A-a-ram-mu* king of Edom, in the Annals of Sennacherib, with עירם in the list of Esau's chiefs, Gen. 36:43; I Chron. 1:54), very few names beginning with *'y-* or *'y-* have been found in early Arabic inscriptions.

363 The results of this economic-administrative activity of Sargon seem to have occured to the benefit of the kingdom of Judah in the time of Hezekiah, since it was a transit area for Arabian trade to Samaria (see Mazar, *Jerusalem Through the Ages,* XXVth Archaeological Convention, Israel Exploration Society, Jerusalem 1968, 8-9, Hebrew). The inclusion of spices in the treasures of Hezekiah (II Kings 20:13 = Isa. 39:2; II Chron. 32:27) connects him with the Arabian trade.

364 VA 8424 col. ii, 1-7; cf. also 79-7-8, 14 col. ii, 1-2. The two texts are fragmentary

the new inhabitants is not preserved because of defective documentation. At the same time, the words "... together with ...... sheep ... ... from [the land of ... I deported]", which begin the passage about this episode, help to ascertain their point of origin. For though people were commonly transported over long distances in the Assyrian Empire,[365] there would have been no sense in (and perhaps no real possibility of) such lengthy transportation of flocks. Moreover, the appointment of a nomad chieftain like the sheikh of Laban over a sedentary population in a border area is an exception to the usual Assyrian practice of appointing Assyrian officers (lú*šu-ut rešē*) over the deportees.[366] Our doubts will disolve, however, if we assume that the inhabitants Sargon brought to the area of Wadi el-Arish were also nomads from North Arabia, and were removed for the same reasons as were the Arabs in Samaria.

The transfer of nomads to Samaria and the southern border region of Palestine, the opening of "the sealed-off harbor of Egypt" and the concomitant encouragement of trade between Egyptians and Assyrians were threads in the web of Assyrian activity in Palestine and its border regions, reflecting a policy peculiar to Sargon and not to his successors. Some of this policy's underlying principles were exploitation of the political and economic possibilities arising from Assyrian control of an area whose edges were traversed by international trade routes; deepening influence and control by settling Assyrians and members of nomad tribes at key-points of the international trade, and lessening dependence on the economic activity of the native population of southern Philistia;[367] the avoidance of the considerable military effort of extending borders and conducting military campaigns toward Egypt.

Sargon's policy is reflected in the behavior towards him of the chief participants in international trade in the western part of the Assyrian

and have been considerably reconstructed, see Tadmor, *JCS* 12 (1958), 77-78; cf. Weidner, *AfO* 14 (1941), 43.

365 See above n. 358.

366 This, for example, was Sargon's practice in Samaria and Ashdod (Lie, lines 260-261; Tadmor, *op. cit.*, 34).

367 Sargon destroyed the effectiveness of the local population near the border by laying Raphia waste and deporting its inhabitants. This was also true of the cities of the kingdom of Ashdod to which he brought exiles after suppressing a revolt. Among the Assyrian kings, only Sargon's inscriptions record such an action.

empire. His inscriptions report receipt of gold, precious stones, ivory, willow seeds, all kinds of aromatic substances, horses and camels from ᵐ*Pir'u* king of Egypt,[368] Samsi queen of the Arabs, and It'amara the Sabaean, "the kings of the seashore and the desert".[369] Though the documents state that Sargon received tribute (*maddattu*) from these rulers, it is hard to take the term literally, at least so far as two of them are concerned: even if It'amara had lived in a North Arabian Sabaean colony, he would not have been under Sargon's direct control; living in South Arabia, he could not have been.[370] The same applies to ᵐ*Pir'u* king of Egypt, who was surely one of the Delta rulers, though his exact identity is unclear.[371] Although, in view of the Nubian threat to his country, the Egyptian king's interest in developing normal relations with Assyria in ca. 716 B.C. is understandable, nothing indicates Assyrian control of or threat to Egypt at that time. Evidently then, the

368 Fomenting a lengthy debate, H. Winckler sought to prove that ^{kur}*Muṣur* in Neo-Assyrian inscriptions, including those of Sargon, sometimes refer to a North-Arabian region rather than to Egypt. He was followed by several scholars, including Hommel, *EGAO*, 580, 661 n. 2; T.W. Rosmarin, *JSOR* 16 (1932), 4; G. Ryckmans, *AfO* 14 (1941), 54-56; and even Gadd, *Iraq* 16 (1954), 182. These postulations, however, have long since been disproved by A.T. Olmstead, *Western Asia in the Days of Sargon of Assyria*, New York 1908, 56-71; and more recently by Tadmor, *IEJ* 11 (1961), 143-150; and P. Garelli, "Muṣur", *Supplément au Dictionnaire de la Bible*, V, Paris 1957, 1468-1474; idem, *Hommages à A. Dupont-Sommer*, Paris 1971, 37-48. There is no further need to expatiate on the fact that ᵐ*Pir'u šar* ^{kur}*Muṣur* was a king of Egypt (on the question of his specific identification see n. 371).

369 Khorsabad Annals, 123-125; cf. Display Inscription, 27.

370 On the location of the Sabaeans in the second half of the 8th century B.C. and the identification of It'amara, see Appendix A, 12.

371 The history of Egypt in Sargon's time is not lucid enough for us to identify the *Pir'u* (Pharaoh) discussed here or why he appears among the senders of gifts to Sargon. The rulers of Egypt possibly to be identified with him are:
A. **Osorkon IV**, the last king of the XXIInd Dynasty. He ruled in Tanis and Bubastis in the eastern delta when the rulers of Lower Egypt, led by Tefnakhte, fought against Pi'ankhy, the invading Nubian king. He should be identified with ᵐ*Ši-il-kan-ni* king of Egypt, of whom it is said in VA 8424:8-11, that he gave Sargon a gift (*tāmartu*) of 12 great horses whose like did not exist in Assyria (von Bissing, in Weidner, *AfO* 14 [1941], 44-45; Albright, *BASOR* 141 [1956], 23-26; K.A. Kitchen, *The Third Intermediate Period of Egypt (1100-650 B.C.)*, Warminster 1973, 376; A. Spalinger, *JARCE* 10 [1973], 96-97).

inscriptions of Sargon refer not to real tribute but to a gesture made by the three rulers, a more fitting term for which would be *tāmartu*, "gift in honor of a special event", applied to the horses received from ^{m}*Ši-il-kan-ni* king of Egypt.[372] Such a gesture probably served to maintain and

B. **Tefnakhte,** the founder of the XXIVth Dynasty and Egypt's leader in the war against Pi'ankhy. Identifying him with the *Pir'u* under discussion should be weighed in the light of the following facts:

1) If the suggested identification of So in II Kings 17:4 with Sais is correct, then there is no doubt that he is the Egyptian king to whom Hoshea king of Israel, when he rebelled against the king of Assyria, sent emissaries in 724 B.C. (H. Goedicke, *BASOR* 171 [1963], 64-66); he is apparently also the Egyptian king who sent an expeditionary force to assist Ḫanūn of Gaza who rebelled in 720 B.C. (for his political status and the chronology of his rule see also H. von Zeissl, *Äthiopen und Assyrer in Ägypten,* Glückstadt-Hamburg 1944, 18-20; E. Drioten-J. Vandier, *L'Egypte*[4], Paris 1962, 539-544). For the possibility that biblical So does not mean Sais, and the assumption that Hoshea's emissaries were sent to Osorkon IV, see Kitchen, *ibid.,* 182, 372-374.

2) Opinion differs about when Tefnakhte's rule ended: according to Drioton-Vandier (*ibid.,* 544), in 720 B.C. (see also A.H. Gardiner, *Egypt of the Pharaohs,* Oxford 1961, 449-450), according to Albright (*ibid.,* 25), in the winter of 716/5 B.C. This poses the question of whether Tefnakhte or his son Bocchoris was king in 716 B.C. at the time of Sargon's activity on the border of Palestine (on the chronology of Tefnakhte see also Kitchen, *ibid.,* 138-147, 179).

C. **Bocchoris** son of Tefnakhte. His reign lasted for six years and ended with the capture of Egypt by Shabako (for possible identification with the *Pir'u* under discussion see Alt, *Kleine Schriften,* II, 233 f.); he was presumably interested in good relations with Assyria and keeping Egypt's border with Asia secure, in order to concentrate all his efforts against the Nubians.

The inscriptions of Sargon also refer to "*Pir'u* king of Egypt", for whom Yamani of Ashdod sent when he rebelled against Assyria in 712 B.C. For considerations of the identification of this *Pir'u* — who is not directly relevant to our discussion — see Kitchen, *ibid.,* 143-144. It should be noted that the Assyrian data on which Kitchen established his chronological reckoning for the history of Egypt during the reign of Sargon are insufficiently clear.

372 VA 8424:8-11.

expand the trade relations between the three rulers and the political and economic bodies in the western border regions of the Assyrian empire, and was necessitated by Sargon's economic and administrative activity in the area. From this trade conditions developed, as well as a broad geographic complex of economic interests, in which It'amara, Samsi and perhaps the king of Egypt played decisive roles. The expression, "the kings of the seashore and the desert", possibly refers not to the actual territory of the kings, but to the extent of their influence along the trade routes in North Arabia, the Syro-Arabian desert, and northern Sinai. It is also possible that the account of the "tribute" of these three rulers is a combined list of gifts that Sargon received on separate occasions under different circumstances (cf.,e.g., the list of tribute received by Tiglath-Pileser, Rost, *Ann.* 150-157). It'amara and Samsi obviously had an economic motive; that of the king of Egypt, since there is no solid evidence of economic motivation, appears to have been essentially politico-military.

Chapter V

FROM SENNACHERIB TO ASSURBANIPAL

Most of the material about the nomads during ca. 703-644 B.C., at the time of Sennacherib, Esarhaddon and Assurbanipal, concerns the southwestern border region of Mesopotamia; only at the end of this period do we learn more about the immediate border regions of Palestine and southern Syria. Some of the nomad groups in the eastern part of the cup of the Fertile Crescent at this time are found during the Chaldaean and Achaemenid periods on the border region of Palestine.

A. THE REIGN OF SENNACHERIB (705-681 B.C.)

The reign of Sennacherib is marked by bitter struggle between Assyria and Babylonia and repeated Assyrian military campaigns, culminating in the total destruction of Babylon in 689 B.C. During this time Sennacherib obviously sought control of the nomads in the western frontier of Babylonia and of the principal routes crossing the northeastern part of the Syro-Arabian desert to southern Mesopotamia. He was apparently the first Assyrian king to try to subjugate nomads in this area. We shall investigate the causes and circumstances of this development, its politico-military aspects and its economic consequences.

1. Politico-Military Survey:

a. The first campaign of Sennacherib (703 B.C.) was conducted against the Chaldaeans, led by Merodach-baladan II and supported by an army from Elam. The full account of this campaign, in the first edition of the Annals of Sennacherib (BM 113203), is an important source which has not been sufficiently used for the study of the ethnological structure and the demography of southwestern Babylonia in the 8th century B.C.[373] Among the enemy chieftains captured in that campaign was ^{m}*Ba-as-qa-nu,* the brother of ^{f}*Ia-ti-'-e* queen of the Arabs (line 28); this is the earliest occurrence in Assyrian documents of the Arabs as an ethnic element in Babylonia. This document gives the title ^{lú}*A-ri-bi* for the Arabs, usual in Assyrian royal inscriptions, whereas the letters, written in the Assyrian and Babylonian dialects, generally use ^{lú}*Ar-ba-a-a.*[374] ^{lú}*Aribi* has nothing to do with ^{lú}*urbi,* which, as several scholars have suggested, is neither a variant name for Arabs in Assyrian sources nor has any etymological connection with the term "Arab", but is a designation for a specific kind of warrior.[375]

Lines 36-50 give the names of 81 walled towns (*ālāni*^{meš} *dannūti bīt dūrāni*$^{meš.ni}$)[376] and mention 820 minor settlements nearby (*ālāni*^{meš} *ṣiḫrūti*^{meš} *šá limētišunu*) that were conquered and looted in southern Babylonia by the Assyrian army. A few of these toponyms indicate the ethnic origin of the inhabitants: ^{uru}*Dūr-*^{m}*A-bi-ia-ta-'* (line 37) in the territory of Bīt Dakkuri; and ^{uru}*Dūr-*^{m}*Ú-a-a-it* (line 44) and ^{uru}*Dūr-*^{m}*Bir-da-da* (line 43) in the territory of Bīt Amukani.

The components of Abiyata' and Uait/Uaite' are known from the personal names of later Arab chieftains in the inscriptions of Assurbanipal (see in detail pp. 147-169): (1) ^{m}*A-bi-ia-te-' mār* ^{m}*Te-'-ri* ^{kur}*Qid-ra-a-a* (B viii 32-35; K 2802 iii 18-20; Rm. viii 31, ix 16-17). (2) ^{m}*Ú-a-a-te-'*, the designation for both **son of Birdāda,** as *šar* ^{kur}*A-ri-bi* (K 2802 ii 3; Rm. viii 2; ix 2) and as *šar* ^{kur}*Su-mu-*AN (*AAA* 20 [1933], p. 86:113); and the **son of Ḫazael** (VAT 5600 i 3; Rm. viii 1, 46), called ^{m}*Ú-a-a-te-' šar* ^{kur}*A-ri-bi* (Rm. vii 83), ^{m}*Ia-u-ta-' šar* ^{kur}*Qi-id-ri/Qa-da-ri* (Cyl. B [Streck] vii 88; B [Piepkorn] vii 94; cf. also ^{m}*Ia-ú-ta-'* in the treaty between Assurbanipal and the Qedarites, obv. 4', 12' (*Orientalia*

373 On this document see pp. 40-41.

374 See above, p. 6.

375 For the assumption that ^{lú}*urbi* has an ethnic meaning see Delitzsch, *Paradies,* 305 f.; Streck, *Assurbanipal,* 28, n. 3; Dougherty, *The Sealand of Ancient Arabia,* 60-61; Rosmarin, *JSOR* 16 (1932), 32-33; and D. Neiman, *JQR* 60 (1969), 237-258. For detailed arguments against such an assumption see Winckler, *OLZ* 9 (1906), 333-334; Th. Bauer, *Das Inschriftenwerk Assurbanipals,* Leipzig 1933, II, 1; Eph'al, *JAOS* 94 (1974), 110, note 16.

376 On the total number of the conquered walled cities see note 106.

37 [1968], 464). In later inscriptions of Assurbanipal the names ^{m}*Ia-u-ta-'* and ^{m}*Ú-a-a-te-'* were confused, and both were written ^{m}*Ú-a-a-te-'*.[377]

The component *Wa/Ia-[a-a]-ta/ti-'* in such names as ^{m}*A-bi-ia-te-'* and ^{m}*Ú-a-a-te-'* derives from *yṯ'-wṯ'*,[378] a root known only in South Arabic and common in personal names like *Yṯ''l, 'lyṯ', Whbyṯ', Yd'yṯ', 'bdyṯ', 'myṯ', R'nyṯ', Ywṯ'* and *Mwṯ'*.[379] The theophorous character of some of these names suggests that *yṯ'* is not only a verb but a divine attribute.[380] On the transcription of Arabic *ṯ* in proper names to Akkadian *t*, cf. *Yṯrb* = ^{uru}*Ia-at-ri-bu* (Nabonidus H_2 col. i 25).

Usually *yṯ'* is connected etymologically with *yš'* in Hebrew and Moabite, and with *yšḫ̬* in the Amorite personal names in the Mari texts.[381] This etymological relationship cannot be taken for granted, since South Arabic *yš'*[382] and *ws'*[383] approximate the meaning of Northwest Semitic *yš'-yšḫ̬* but are distinct from *yṯ'* (none of these West Semitic roots occurs in Aramaic).

The name Birdāda, father of ^{m}*Ú-a-a-te-'*, appears thus in the Assyrian inscriptions: ^{m}*Bir-da-da* (BM 113203:43), ^{m}*Bir-da-ad-da* (K 2802 iii 3), ^{m}*Bir*-DINGIR.IM (Rm. viii 2; ix 2). The element *dd* is a theophorous component in Sabaean, Thamudic and Lihyanite proper names,[384] and appears separately as a divine attribute in Thamudic votive inscriptions.[385]

377 Discussed in detail in pp. 51-52, 146-147, 165-168.

378 Cf. names of other Arab leaders: ^{f}*Ia-ti-'-e šarrat* ^{kur}*A-ri-bi;* ^{m}*Ia-u-ta-'* (var.: *Ia-u-ti-', Ia-u-te-', Ia-ta-'*) *mār* ^{m}*Ḫa-za-ilu;* ^{m}*It-'-am-ra* ^{kur}*Sa-ba-'-a-a;* ^{m}*Am-me-'-ta-'* ^{lú}*Mas-'-a-a* (for the last spelling see p. 58).

379 Cf. Ryckmans, *RNP*, II, 7, 10; K. Conti Rossini, *Chrestomathia Arabica meridionalis epigraphica*, Roma 1931, 165; W. W. Müller, WO 10 (1979), 23-29.

380 Ryckmans, *ibid.;* I, 6-7; idem, *Les religions Arabes préislamiques*^{2}, Louvain 1951, 23.

381 Conti Rossini, *ibid.;* H.B. Huffmon, *Amorite Personal Names in the Mari Texts*, Baltimore 1965, 215-216.

382 Conti Rossini, *ibid.*, 141.

383 Conti Rossini, *ibid.*, 138.

384 I.e.,*'bdd, Dd'b, Ddwsl, Ddkrb, Ḥydd, Ntndd, Sqmdd (RNP*, II, 5); *'ldd, Dd'l, Ddḥsm* (Van den Branden, *TTP*, I, 176; II, 143, 146. Cf. Harding, *Pre-Islamic Names*, 236-237).

385 Cf. for example, Van den Branden, *ibid.*, II, 33, 89, 124. The spelling of *da-ad-da* in K 2802 iii 3, exactly reflecting the ancient Arabic form *dd*, rules out the possibility

^{uru}*Qid-ri-na* (line 37) mentioned among the towns in Bīt Dakkuri may also be connected with the Qedarites,[386] who in the 7th century B.C. lived in the desert near the western border of Babylonia.[387]

The toponyms thus far dealt with are certainly Arab-related; their components have no parallels with the roots of proper names of other ethnic groups in Babylonia. (BM 113203 may yield further Arab-related names such as ^{uru}*Dūr-* ^{m}*Ú-gu-ri* [line 44] and ^{uru}*Dūr-*^{m}*Aq-qi-ia* [line 43].[388] They clearly indicate Arab existence in western Babylonia in the second half of the 8th century B.C.[389] Walled towns with Arab names, surrounded by unwalled hamlets,[390] reflect not only that Arab penetration into Babylonia was extended and intensive but that even if these towns were neither founded nor built but only controlled by Arabs, who in time changed the town names, the process of Arab penetration and settlement in Babylonia began at least some decades before Sennacherib's first campaign.

Two letters almost certainly from the period of Sargon,[391] ABL 88 and 547, support our assumption of the existence of an Arab entity in Babylonia in the 8th century B.C., and contribute further

of its being a miswriting of the name ^{d}*Adad.* The form DINGIR.IM = ^{d}*Adad* in the Rassam Cylinder is apparently an example of folk etymology. For the possibility of reading the name Pirdāda (instead of Birdāda), see Eph'al, *ibid.,* 112 note 25.

386 The toponym ^{uru}*Qid-ri-na* resembles the spellings of the names of the Qedarites in cuneiform inscriptions from the 8th centuries B.C., cf. pp. 223-224.

387 Cf. ABL 350, 811 (on the latter document see pp. 223-224; Rm. viii 30-42.

388 See Eph'al, *ibid.,* 114-115.

389 The designation "Arabs" in this case is based on onomastic and linguistic criteria as well as on way of life.

390 Cf. BM 113203, lines 39, 41, 47, 49: ***ālāni***$^{meš.ni}$***dan-nu-ti bīt dūrāni***$^{meš.ni}$ ***... adi ... ālāni***$^{meš.ni}$***ṣiḫrūti***^{meš} ***šá li-me-ti-šu-nu.*** **Notice also the component BÀD=*dūru*** in their names.

391 ABL 87-99, 396-398, 480-483, 547, were written by Ṭab-ṣil-Ešarra whom Waterman, RCAE III, 44, identified with the eponym of 716 B.C., whose title was *šakin māt Aš[šur];* further confirmation for this identification appears in the beginning of ABL 92 and 397 (cf. also ABL 99): *a-na šarri bēli-ia ardu-ka* ^{m}*Ṭab-ṣil-É-šár-ra šulmu*^{mu} *a-na É-šár-ra*^{ki} *šulmu*^{mu} *a-na ekurāte*^{meš} *šulmu*^{mu} *a-na* ^{uru}*Aššur šulmu ana māt Aššur*^{ki} *lu šulmu*^{mu} *a-na šarri bēli-ia Aššur u* ^{d}*Nin-líl a-na šarri bēli-ia lik-ru-bu;* and also in ABL 480 in which Ṭab-ṣil-Ešarra deals with obtaining land for the temple of Nabû of Dūr-Šarrukīn.

detail. ABL 88 mentions an Arab raid on Sippar,[392] presumably the region, since it seems unlikely that the marauders attacked the walled city itself. The second letter, ABL 547, deals with Arab razzias in the territories of Suḫi and Ḫindānu in the Middle Euphrates region.[393] The insecure conditions in the Sippar region during Sargon's reign are further attested in his annals; see Lie, *Sargon,* 379-384.

Significantly, all the towns associated with Arabs in BM 113203 were in the territories of Bīt Dakkuri and Bīt Amukani, none in Bīt Yakīn. This, as well as ABL 88, suggests that the Arabs penetrated from the Arabian desert into western Babylonia along the main routes — from Wadi Sirḥān via Jauf (=Dūmat al-Jandal, Biblical Dumah), and apparently along the route of Medina-Ḥā'il-Kūfa—which were near an-Najaf in southern Iraq. There is no evidence that they reached the region of the Persian Gulf. Because of the territory in which Arab penetration is attested, and the discovery there (and not in Bīt Yakīn) of most of the inscriptions called "Chaldaean" by W.F. Albright,[394] these inscriptions should be attributed to Arabs and not to Chaldaeans and accordingly called "Old Arabic Inscriptions", as they were designated in the early stages of research.[395]

Shortage of sources makes it impossible to establish the nature of the relations between the Arab settlements in Babylonia and the nomads

392 ABL 88, rev. 3-5: *ma-a a-ta-a* ^{kur}*Ar̂-bá-a-a ḫu-ub-tu ša* ^{uru}*Si-par iḫ-bu-[tú-ni],* "Why did the Arabs plunder Sippar?". The reading ^{Kur}*Ar̂-ba-a-a* instead of ^{kur}*Up-pa-a-a* was first suggested by Deller, *Lautlehre des Neuassyrischen,* Wien 1959, 241.

393 ABL 547 obv.: *[a-na] šarri be-[li-ia] ardu-ka* ^{m}*Ṭab-[ṣil-É-šar-ra] lu šulmu*^{mu} *a-na [šarri bēli-ia] Aššur* ^{d}*Nin-lil*... (5) *ina muḫḫi* ^{kur}*⌜Ar⌝... iš-pur-an-ni...* ^{anše}*gammalē*^{meš} ... *i-ra-'-[u]* ... *ina bu-bu-ti*...... (10) *an-ni-tú a-n[a-ku e-ta-pa]-áš* ^{m}*⌜A⌝-šak-... ina lìb-bi* ... *šá-ak-nu ša šarru be-lí [iš-pur]-an-ni ma-a an-nu-rig a-na* ^{uru}*Ḫi-in-za-ni* (15) *ta-lak ma-a i-si-ka lil-li-ku li-ir-'-u* TA* [UGU] ^{íd}*Tar-ta-ri a-du* ^{kur}*Su-ḫi me-me-ni la-a i-pa-ri-[ik];* rev.: *an-nu-rig a-na ... a-na* ^{kur}*Ḫi-in-za-ni al-lak ta-ḫu-mu ša ú-ka-la-šu-nu-ni ú-ra-mu-u e-ti-qu* (5) *ú-sa-ta-pu-lu i-ḫab-bu-tú a-na* ^{lú}*rab da-a-a-li-ia ša a-pa-qi-du-ni la-a-su la-a i- šá-me-u a-na* ^{lú}*bēl pīḫati ša* ^{uru}*Kal-ḫa li-qi-mu* (10) ^{lú}*rēši-šú i-na pa-an* ^{kur}*Ar-bá-a-a ša qa-ti-šú lip-⌜qid⌝-[du]-nu ta-ḫu-mu... liš-'-lu-u-ni ina lìb-bi* ^{uru}*Ir... i-si-niš úb-bar-ia...* (15) *ina muḫḫi ta-ḫu-me ša ... ša* ^{uru}*Kal-ḫa lu-u ...šu(?)-nu... li-ir-'-u ... i-te-bu* (20)...*i...* URU^{meš} *i-ḫa-bu-tú la-a-šú* UDU^{meš} ^{anše}*gam-mal*^{meš} *[la]-a i-ḫa-bu-tú.* (The transliteration is based on a collation by K. Deller in the files of the *CAD).*

394 *BASOR* 128 (1952), 39-45.

395 Cf. E. Burrows, *JRAS* 1927, 795 ff.

along the western frontier of the country. Thus we cannot determine whether ᵐ*Basqanu,* Sennacherib's opponent, and his sister ᶠ*Ia-ti-'-e* queen of the Arabs were connected with the population of the Arab settlements in Babylonia or with the desert-dwelling nomads. However, judging from later parallels[396] and perhaps even from the relations between the desert nomads and Sennacherib after his first campaign,[397] the Arabs along both sides of the West Babylonian border were probably in close contact. In any case, the settlement of the Arabs in western Babylonia during the Neo-Assyrian period, proceeding from nomadism through the various stages of sedentary life, presents us with a concrete example, so far unnoticed, of a phenomenon well-known in the history of the Near East.

b. The Arabs cooperated with other political groupings in Babylonia against Assyria during Sennacherib's first campaign, as they did later in the same region at the time of the strife between Šamaš-šum-ukin and his brother Assurbanipal (see pp. 142 ff.). Like the political stance of Elam, presumably deriving from and based largely on trade relations, this can be considered general policy. The nomads in Babylonia and its border regions, especially during a period of ferment like Sennacherib's, were threatening Assyrian governance of the country and had to be subdued, and control gained of the desert routes leading to the settled areas of Babylonia. Assyrian activity, at least initially, vis-à-vis the nomads in the northeastern part of the Syro-Arabian desert can be viewed as the continuation and completion of Sennacherib's policy toward Babylonia and not as an end in itself.

Following the organizational and military activities of his first and fourth campaigns (703 and 700 B.C.), Sennacherib was able, at least for a time, to establish control over the settled part of Babylonia and its western approaches, as reflected, *inter alia,* by the receipt of gifts from the people of ˡᵘ́*Te-e-me* and ˡᵘ́*Su-mu-'*-AN (see pp. 124-125). Although the degree of control over the nomads of the desert west of Babylonia is not established, it was evidently incomplete, and a campaign against Adummatu had to be conducted about the time Babylon was destroyed in 689 B.C.

396 Cf. Musil, *Arabia Deserta,* 542, 544, 546.

397 See pp. 124-125.

c. **The military campaign against** ^{uru}**Adummatu**

Sources: Sennacherib Inscriptions: VA 3310, rev. 22-27; K 8544, rev. 5-7[398]
Esarhaddon Inscriptions: Nin. A. iv 1-5; Heidel Prism ii 46-50
Assurbanipal Inscriptions: K 3405, obv. 1 ff.; K 3087, obv. 1 ff.

The campaign against the Arabs is reported in VA 3310 rev., 22 ff., immediately after the description of the eighth campaign (ending in line 21); nothing is said about the destruction of Babylon (689 B.C.). Editions of the Annals which describe all eight of Sennacherib's campaigns, the last in 691 B.C., say nothing, however, about his campaign against the Arabs. His war against them, therefore, had to take place between 691 and 689 B.C.[399]

The two Arab leaders attacked by the Assyrian army were [^{f}*Te-'-el-ḫu]-nu* queen of the Arabs[400] (who dominates VA 3310 rev. 22-23, and whose status is also pointed out in K 8544 rev. 5-7), and Ḫazael, who, according to VA 3310 rev. 23 f., cooperated with [Te'elḫu]nu. His title, not preserved in the damaged lines of the passage, is given as "king of

398 The lines preceding line 5 in K 8544 rev. concern a building project; see pp. 42-43.

399 VA 8248, on the other hand, describes the destruction of Babylon (line 36 ff.), but does not mention the campaign against the Arabs. Musil (*Arabia Deserta*, 480-481) assumed that Sennacherib campaigned against the Arabs in about 688 B.C., after the destruction of Babylon and in the wake of it, in order to vanquish the Babylonian allies. Although we do not have enough evidence to arrive at a conclusion, we must evaluate the relationship between the two events: After so drastic an action as the destruction of Babylon, was a special campaign needed to subdue the Arabs? (Cf., e.g., the report about the people of Tilmun [*ibid.*, lines 39-44], who rushed to send gifts to Sennacherib as soon as they became aware of Babylon's destruction.) Or did Sennacherib exploit his success to achieve what was impossible before Babylon collapsed?

400 VA 3310, rev. 22. According to the inscriptions of Esarhaddon, ^{f}*ap-kal-la-tú/ti šarrat* $^{kur/lú}$*Aribi* and the gods of the Arabs were captured in Adummatu and transferred to Assyria (Nin. A iv 1-5; Heidel Prism ii 46-50); the inscriptions of Assurbanipal refer to *Te-'-el-ḫu-nu,* the former priestess of an Arabian goddess (K 3405 obv. 12; cf. also K 3087 obv. 12). By combining the two accounts R. Borger demonstrated that the exiled queen of the Arabs was named Te'elḫunu, and that *apkallatu* was not her name, but a transliteration of **'fklt,* which in South Arabic means priestess (*Orientalia* 26 [1957], 9-10).

the Arabs" in the inscriptions of Esarhaddon and Assurbanipal,[401] and as "king of the Qedarites" in other inscriptions of Assurbanipal.[402]

As no other toponym except ^{uru}*Adummatu* has survived in VA 3310, the route taken by the expeditionary forces can only be approximated.[403] From VA 3310 rev. 22 ff., it appears that at the outset of the campaign [Te'elḫu]nu queen of the Arabs was camped in tents in the desert (probably at an oasis in the western border regions of Babylonia), where the Assyrian army attacked and captured thousands of camels. From there she (and Ḫazael) fled deeper into the desert to ^{uru}*Adummatu* and another oasis whose name has not been preserved (see line 26). Her last stop was ^{uru}*Adummatu,* where she was overtaken and carried to Assyria with booty and the images of the local gods.[404] This leads us to the consideration of the location of ^{uru}*Adummatu,* a much discussed problem with implications for the study of other historical episodes.

The identity of ^{uru}Adummatu/Adumutu: Sennacherib's war here is referred to in the inscriptions of Sennacherib and Esarhaddon as follows (the date in parentheses refers to the first publication of each):

Sennacherib Inscriptions:

VA 3310 (1904), rev. 25: *ana* ^{uru}*A-du-um-ma-te ... innabtu* (cf. *ibidem,* 26: [^{uru}*A-d]u-um-ma-tu)*

Esarhaddon Inscriptions:

Prism A (=**Borger,** Nin. B^{1}, 1861), ii 55 : ^{uru}*A-du-mu-u*

Thompson Prism (=Borger, Nin. A^{1}, 1931), iv 1	^{uru}*A-du-mu-tu āl*
Hirschberg Prism (=Borger, Nin. B^{6},~1932), iv 10	*dan-nu-tu/te/ti*
Hiedel Prism (=Borger, Nin. B^{7}, 1956), ii 46	$^{kur/lú}$*A-ri-bi.*

The first information about Sennacherib's war against the Arabs came from Esarhaddon Prism A =Borger, Nin. B^{1}, narrating the military achievements of his father, where the toponym was written ^{uru}*A-du-mu-u.* Only decades later was the Sennacherib inscription VA 3310 with the

401 Nin. A iv 6; Heidel Prism ii 51; K 3405 obv. 9 (cf. also K 3087 obv. 9).

402 Prism B vii 93-94.

403 ^{uru}*Ka-pa-a-nu,* which occurs in K 8544 in proximity to "the queen of the Arabs", is apparently not connected with Sennacherib's campaign against the Arabs (see pp. 42-43), and has nothing to do with the campaign route.

404 For references see note 400.

spelling ^{uru}*A-du-um-ma-tu* published, after which the two names were considered coeval variants of the same toponym.[405]

Actually there were no *a priori* grounds for such an assumption, because the same toponym usually has no optional masculine and feminine endings (*-u* and *-tu* respectively).[406] The uniform spelling in the three parallel passages in the inscriptions of Esarhaddon (Borger, Nin. A^{1}, B$^{6-7}$), indicating that the original spelling there of the toponym was ^{uru}*A-du-mu-tu,* does not support such a variant. As Borger acceptedly suggested, ^{uru}*A-du-mu-u* in the Esarhaddon Prism A (=Borger, Nin. B^{1}) is not a variant of the toponym but a scribal error.[407] Consequently, the assumption, accepted by many scholars and leading to varying opinions about Nabonidus' campaign to Tema',[408] that ^{uru}*Adummatu* in the inscriptions of Esarhaddon and *[ ]-du-um-mu* in the Nabonidus Chronicle (i 17) are identical, seems, in fact, invalid.

The Assyrian inscriptions describe ^{uru}*Adummatu,* the Arab strongold conquered by Sennacherib, as a religious center in the desert (far from [Te'elḫu]nu's position at the start of the campaign against the Arabs). It is usually identified with Dūmat al-Jandal (apparently biblical Dumah), the principal oasis in the Jauf depression in Wadi Sirḥān, mentioned by classical and Arab authors from the 1st century B.C. on

405 See, for example, Winckler, *Auszug aus der vorderasiatischen Geschichte,* Leipzig 1905, 71; Albright, *JRAS* 1925, 294; S. Smith, *JRAS* 1925, 508-510; idem, *Isaiah Chapters XL-LX,* 37, 137-139; Hommel, *EGAO,* 581-582, 594; Musil, *Arabia Deserta,* 480, 532; Rosmarin, *JSOR* 16 (1932), 13; R. P. Dougherty, *The Sealand of Ancient Arabia,* New Haven 1932, 71; Montgomery, *Arabia and the Bible,* 62.

406 The singularity of this occurrence, vis-à-vis the *Adumu/Adummatu* identification, has been stressed by V. Scheil, *OLZ* 7 (1904), 70. I found no examples of it in Akkadian or Arabic sources (in names ending in *Tā marbūṭah*), but biblical instances exist in toponyms like יהץ (Isa. 15:4; Jer. 48:34), יהצה (Josh. 13:18; I Chron. 6:63); יזרעאל (I Sam. 29:11; I Kings 21:1; II Kings 8:29, etc.), יזרעאלה (Josh. 19:18). For other biblical examples, see Z. Kallai, *The Tribes of Israel,* Jerusalem 1967, 171-172 (Hebrew).

407 Borger, *Asarhaddon,* 53. The two forms ^{uru}*Adummatu* and ^{uru}*Adumutu* in the inscriptions of Sennacherib and Esarhaddon suggest that the original was ^{uru}*Adummatu,* and ^{uru}*Adumutu* the product of *Vokalharmonie.* This is not unusual in Assyrian proper names, cf. *Arabu - Arubu, Ḫazatu - Ḫazutu;* see Albright, *BASOR* 67 (1937), 27, n. 6; R.T. O'Callaghan, *Aram Naharaim,* Roma 1948, 95.

408 See particularly Albright and Smith above, n. 405. On *[ ]dummu* in the Nabonidus Chronicle see further pp. 185-188.

as an important oasis (spelled Δουμαθα, Δουμαίθα, Domatha, Dumatha, *Dūmah, Dūmat al-Jandal).*[409] Because it was halfway between Syria and Babyonia and had abundant water and orchards it was the most important oasis in all North Arabia and a main stop on the roads to Ḥīra (near Kūfa), Damascus and Medina.[410] Testifying to its size and viable population is the fact that 5000 men were living there at the beginning of the present century, a number that Musil assumes to have been the same or greater when the oasis was economically more important.[411] The economic relations, evinced in Arabic sources between the inhabitants of Dūmat al-Jandal and of Kūfa and Ḥīra in the western border region of Babylonia,[412] might also have existed in the 8th century B.C.

An ancient fortress in Dūmat al-Jandal, called al-Mārid, not yet researched, antedates Mohammed. This is in accordance with Arabic sources, which also refer to the pre-Islamic existence in Dūmat al-Jandal of a temple of the god Wadd, with a larger-than-life-size image of the god.[413] Later sources thus support the conventional identification of ^{uru}*Adummatu* with Dumah = Dūmat al-Jandal,[414] but conclusive proof awaits archaeological investigation, as well as further sources from the biblical period.[415]

409 For the classic sources see J. Tkač, *PW,* V 1790; Musil, *Arabia Deserta,* 532. For the Arabic sources see Musil, *ibid.,* 532-553.

410 For a description of the oasis and its history from biblical times to the 19th century, see Musil, *ibid.,* 472-473, 531-553.

411 Musil, *ibid.,* 537.

412 Musil, *ibid.,* 542, 544, 546.

413 Musil, *ibid.,* 458, 534-535. For a history of the fortress and the possibility of the existence there of a shrine in ancient times, also see Ch. Rabin, *Studi sull'Oriente e la Bibbia offerti al P.G. Rinaldi,* Genova 1967, 306, n. 11.

414 This identification was first proposed in 1890 by Glaser, *Skizze,* 264, 274, when the toponym was known from Assyrian sources only in its corrupt version ^{uru}*Adumû,* and the phonetic grounds for a suggested identification with Dūmat al-Jandal were weak (see p. 120). With the publication (in 1904) of the VA 3310 passage on Sennacherib's wars against ^{uru}*Adummatu,* the hypothesis was corroborated, and since then has been accepted by most scholars; for its acceptance by Winckler, Albright, Musil and Rosmarin see n. 405 above. To these should be added Forrer, *Provinzeinteilung,* 64; Hommel, *EGAO,* 574 n. 1, 594; Landsberger-Bauer, *ZA* 37 NF 3 (1927), 94-95.

415 The ^{uru}*Adummatu* = Dumah identification offers an example of the common

The Outcome of the Campaign: Sennacherib's war against the Arabs was successful: the stronghold of ^{uru}*Adummatu* was taken and the queen of the Arabs captured and, along with booty and divine images, sent to Assyria.[416] These images were later returned to the Arabs by Esarhaddon,[417] who, in his turn, captured the gods of Yauṭa', king of the Arabs, which Assurbanipal returned after their owner had sworn his allegiance.[418] Since the Assyrian kings did not treat other people this way, their behavior toward the Arabs can be explained by the fact that the usual campaign purpose of attacking population centers and permanent settlements and destroying armies had little effect on nomads because of their way of life and avoidance of field battles, to say nothing of the difficulties of repeated campaigns in the desert.[419]

Assyrian sources do not specify that Ḫazael was captured by the Assyrian army, but the Heidel Esarhaddon Prism iii 1-2 shows that he too surrendered to Sennacherib and sent him tribute (see p. 124).

Sennacherib also sought to control the Arabs by taking as hostages and raising in Nineveh ^{f}*Ta-bu-u-a,* who during Esarhaddon's time was made "queen of the Arabs" and returned to her native land.[420] To ensure their loyalty to the king of Assyria, Sennacherib repeated this practice with hostages from other countries as well.[421]

addition of the prefix *A-* to the transcription in Assyrian documents of proper names, cf. ברגש - *mār* ^{m}*Agūsi* (for forms of Assyrian transliteration of this name see Donner-Röllig, *KAI,* II, 207), and perhaps also ^{uru}*A-ru-ma-a* in the list of Galilee cities captured by Tiglath-Pileser III (Lay. 29b:7=Rost, *Ann.* 234), identified by B. Mazar with Rumah of the talmudic sources and Josephus (Maisler, *BJPES* 1 [1933], 4). For other examples for the *A-* prefix (sometimes also *I/U-* in Neo-Assyrian toponyms) see Zadok, *S.E. Loewenstamm Festschrift,* Jerusalem 1978, 164 n. 3.

416 Esarhaddon inscriptions: Heidel Prism ii 46-50; Nin. A iv 1-5; cf. Assurbanipal inscriptions K 3087 obv. 1 ff.; K 3405 obv. 2 ff. The booty taken from Dumah is also listed in K 8544 rev. 5-7, see pp. 42, 123-124.

417 Esarhaddon inscriptions: Heidel Prism ii 51-59; A iv 6-14; Assurbanipal inscriptions: K 3087 obv. 9 ff.; K 3405 obv. 9 ff.

418 Cyl. B (Streck) vii 87-92; cf. VAT 5600 i 3 ff.

419 Cf. also Nebuchadnezzar's identical practice of carrying off Arab divine images (below, p. 171). In this case, however, we have no information about happened afterwards.

420 Esarhaddon inscriptions: Heidel Prism ii 60-62; Nin. A iv 15-16. Cf. Assurbanipal inscriptions K 3087 obv. 13-14; K 3405 obv. 13-14.

421 On this policy towards the Arabs and Ashkelon see Tadmor, *BA* 29 (1966), 98. The

Nin. A iv 15 describes Tabûa as having grown up in Sennacherib's palace (PN *tar-bit êkalli abi-iá*), and the Heidel Esarhaddon Prism ii 60, in Esarhaddon's (PN *tar-bit êkalli-ia*). The available sources do not specify her relationship with Te'elḫunu queen of the Arabs. They are commonly considered mother and daughter,[422] some scholars speculating that Tabûa was born in Nineveh,[423] and even that she was the daughter of Te'elḫunu and Esarhaddon.[424] But since Te'elḫunu was taken to Nineveh in 689/8 B.C. and Tabûa appointed "queen of the Arabs" and returned to her native land in 678/7 B.C. at the latest,[425] making her at most ten years old upon her return, the whole idea is insupportable.

Herodotus II, 141, calls Sennacherib "king of the Arabs and Assyrians" and says that he suffered defeat at the approaches to Egypt (cf. Josephus, *Ant.* X, i, 4). The significance of this information is discussed in pp. 137-142.

2. Tribute and Taxes:

The subjugation of the nomads in the western border region of Babylonia and the extension of Assyrian control over the desert routes had considerable economic as well as politico-military effect. Such luxuries as spices, precious stones and gold, acquired by nomad leaders living along those trade routes, were initially taken along with camels as booty and were later sent as gifts and tribute to the Assyrian king.

a. Following a description of one of Sennacherib's building projects, K 8544 rev. 5-7 preserve the words "[que]en of the Arabs, together with .... *pappardilû*-stones, ...-stones, ... spices of all kinds...,"[426] and thus refer to the booty the Assyrian army took from Dumah.[427] Similar articles, from the gift (*nāmurtu*) of Karibilu king of Sheba, were put in

practice recurs with Bēl-ibni, whom Sennacherib made king of Babylon, see Luckenbill, *Sennacherib,* 54:54; 57:13 (=*AR* II, § 263, 273).

422 J. Lewy, *HUCA* 19 (1945-1946), 420-421.

423 Winckler, *Auszug aus der vorderasiatischen Geschichte,* 71; Hommel, *EGAO,* 582.

424 Rosmarin, *JSOR* 16 (1932), 31.

425 For the date of Tabûa's return to her homeland see pp. 125-126.

426 Lines 4, 8 ff. may also deal with the queen of the Arabs, an unverifiable possibility because of the faulty condition of the inscription, see p. 42.

427 Sennacherib's capture of booty from Dumah is also mentioned briefly in the

the foundation of the Bît-Akîtu Temple.[428] Since this temple was built after the destruction of Babylon (i.e., after 689 B.C.),[429] and apparently after the Dumah campaign as well, the Sabaean king's gifts were obviously motivated by the Assyrian control at the time over the desert routes and their South Mesopotamian termini.

b. When Ḫazael king of the Arabs came to Nineveh to beg for the return of the divine images taken from him by Sennacherib, Esarhaddon demanded tribute in addition to the one levied by his father.[430] Although this suggests that Ḫazael sent tribute *before* the Dumah campaign, we have no evidence of Arabs west of Babylonia sending tribute to any Assyrian king before that campaign. Nor do Assyrian sources suggest that Ḫazael stopped sending tribute to Sennacherib for the at least eight-year period between the Dumah campaign and Esarhaddon's accession.

Esarhaddon demanded as extra tribute only 65 camels,[431] probably because, as the return of the images indicates, he was interested in maintaining Ḫazael's loyalty.[432] Sennacherib, however, must have exacted considerable *maddattu* from Ḫazael, to judge by the substantial tribute — including gold, precious stones, spices and camels — taken by Esarhaddon from the son of Ḫazael.[433]

c. In Sennacherib's time one of Nineveh's gates was called "The Desert Gate through which the Gifts of the People of ^{lú}*Te-e-me* and ^{lú}*Su-mu-'*-AN Enter."[434] It is the only Nineveh gate whose name is

inscriptions of Esarhaddon, cf. Heidel Prism ii 48-50; Nin. A iv 3-5.

428 VA 8248:48-51, cf. note 117. *nāmurtu* indicates a freely given gift to royalty, see Martin, *Tribut und Tributleistungen*, 24-25, 44 ff.; Postgate, *Taxation*, 146-162. Luckenbill's misleading translation, "treasure" (*Sennacherib*, 138; *AR* II,§ 440) says nothing about the circumstances under which these luxury goods reached Assyria.

429 See VA 8248:36 ff.

430 Esarhaddon Heidel Prism iii 1-2: *eli ma-da-at-ti abi-ia maḫ-ri-ti ú-rad-di-ma ú-kin* ṣi-ru-uš-šú. Cf. Nin. A iv 17-18 referring to his "addition to the earlier tribute".

431 Nin. A iv 17 also lists ten asses here.

432 This agrees with the pacification policy adopted in Babylonia as well; see pp. 126-127.

433 Esarhaddon Heidel Prism iii 3-8; cf. Nin. A iv 19-22.

434 *kàt-ri-e* ^{lú}*Su-mu-'*-AN *ù* ^{lú}*Te-e-me* (TM 1931-1932, 2 SH: ^{lú}*Te-e-me ù* ^{lú}*Su-mu-'*-AN) *qí-rib-šá ir-ru-ub abul mad-ba-ri* (BM 103,000 vii 96 — viii 1; cf. Sennacherib Heidel Prism viii 8-9; TM 1931-1932, 2 SH, col. B, 37-38). *kad/trû* means a gift to a king

neither a divine reference, nor an expression of the king's strength in battle and the magnitude of his victory, nor a general designation (such as "The Gate which the Choicest of Grain and Flocks are ever within it");[435] it specifies an actual occurrence. Apparently installed in the Nineveh city wall between 696-694 B.C., some years *before* the Dumah campaign,[436] the event of the time was considered important enough to commemorate its name on a gate.

The tribute-paying tribes named in the Desert Gate are hard to identify, but since it is clear that they can be located neither in the neighborhood of Assyria proper nor in the Tema' region, they were apparently desert dwellers near the western frontier of Babylonia.[437] The desert mentioned in the name of the gate would then be some 600 kilometers from Nineveh. The name itself may reflect the strengthening Assyrian control over Babylonia during the rule of Aššur-nadin-šumi, son of Sennacherib (700-694 B.C.).

B. THE REIGN OF ESARHADDON (681-669 B.C.)

1. The Chronological Framework:

681-676 B.C.	Return of the Arab divine images to Dumah. Return of Tabûa and her appointment as queen of the Arabs.[1]
Not later than Kislev 677	Death of Ḫazael king of the Arabs and the succession of his son Yauṭa'.[2]

as a token of submission (*CAD,* K 33b; *AHw,* 419b: *Begrüssungsgeschenk*) as distinct from *maddattu, biltu,* "tribute" (see also Martin, *Tribut und Tributleistungen,* 20); it demonstrates the extent and nature of Sennacherib's control over the tribes discussed.

435 For the custom of giving to the gates of capital cities names with no historical particularity cf. Dūr Šarrukīn, *AR* II, § 85, 121; and Babylon, E. Unger, *Babylon, die heilige Stadt,* Berlin-Leipzig 1931, 234, 243.

436 This gate is not listed in 1910-10-8, 142, written in 696 B.C. and including 14 gates of Nineveh. It appears for the first time in the gate lists of 694 B.C.; see R.C. Thompson, *Iraq* 7 (1940), 91-93.

437 Some identify ^{lú}*Te-e-me* with the people of Tema' (e.g., Olmstead, *History of Assyria,* 310-311; see also S. Parpola, *Neo-Assyrian Toponyms,* Neukirchen-Vluyn 1970, 350). However, so consistent is the spelling in Neo-Assyrian and Neo-Babylonian inscriptions (always ^{uru}*Te-ma-a;* e.g., III R 10, 2:27; ABL 1404:4; Nabonidus Chronicle ii 5, 10, 23; Nabonidus H_2 i 23; *BIN* I 151:14; BM 117520:4; *GCCI* I 294:6; *YOS* VI 134:4-5; *UET* IV 167:6) that this identification is untenable. On the people of ^{lú}*Su-mu-'*-AN see pp. 165-167, 229-230.

679/8	Conquest of the city of Arṣâ.[3]
677/6	Campaign to the land of Bāzu.[4]
676-673	Rebellion of ^{m}*Uabu* (Wahb) against Yauṭa' and its suppression.[5]
673	Esarhaddon's first Egyptian campaign.[6]
673-669	Revolt and defeat of Yauṭa'.[7]
671	Esarhaddon's second Egyptian campaign.[8]

Notes to the chronological table:

1 These episodes appear in the Heidel Prism (ii 46—iii 2), written in Iyyar 676 B.C., and thus occurred before that date, though not necessarily at the same time (see following note).

2 This episode was likewise reported in the Heidel Prism (iii 3-8). Here the ***terminus ad quem*** for the accession of Yauṭa' is based on the assumption that at least six months had elapsed between the event and its appearance in the Heidel Prism. In this and other prisms the name of Ḫazael's son is written ^{m}*Ia-'-lu-ú,* but this seems merely a corruption of Yauṭa' (see pp. 129-130).

3 Cf. Esarhaddon Chronicle (= Grayson, Chronicle 14), obv. 7-8.

4 According to the Babylonian Chronicle (= Grayson, Chronicle 1), iv 5-6, the Assyrian army conquered the land of Bāzu on the 2nd of Tishri in Esarhaddon's fifth regnal year (676 B.C.); the Esarhaddon Chronicle, obv. 13, on the 2nd of Tammuz of that year. Since the Bāzu campaign was included in the Heidel Prism (iii 9-36) of Iyyar 676 B.C., the dating of it in the chronicles must be disregarded (see pp. 53-54). In our assumption of an error of one year in the chronicles' data (i.e., that the campaign actually took place in Esarhaddon's fourth regnal year), we may in fact have understimated somewhat.

5 The timing of this event, which is reported in Nin. A iv 23-31, but not in the Heidel Prism, is limited by their date of composition.

6 Cf. Babylonian Chronicle iv 16.

7 This episode is not known from the Annals of Esarhaddon (the latest edition of which is dated 673 B.C.) or his other inscriptions, but only from inscriptions of Assurbanipal (VAT 5600, i 3-12; cf. Prism B [Streck], vii 87 ff.; Prism B [Piepkorn], vii 93 ff.).

8 Esarhaddon Chronicle, rev., 2-3; Babylonian Chronicle iv 23-28.

2. The Northeastern Arabian Desert

Esarhaddon's placatory policy toward the inhabitants of Babylonia and its environs, in striking contrast to that of his father, is discernible from the beginning of his reign. Probably because, like his father, he considered control of the desert dwellers west of Babylonia integral to the control system of Babylonia itself, he adopted the same policy toward the Arabs. His policy is implicit in his return of Ḫazael's images taken by Sennacherib.[438] Esarhaddon's gesture by no means indicates Ḫazael's surrender after having been independent of Assyria from the time of Sennacherib's campaign against the Arabs until the recovery of the images; on the contrary, Ḫazael had paid tribute (*maddattu*) to Sennacherib,[439] probably after the campaign against Dumah. Retaining the images of the Arabian gods could have assured the loyalty of the desert dwellers and been a sanction against them even after their surrender, according with his "iron-first" policy in Babylonia and its environs. Esarhaddon's return of the images after their repair,[440] and his refusal to burden Ḫazael further, contenting himself with tribute only slightly increased over that of Sennacherib,[441] all point to his desire to pacify the western border region of Babylonia.

Esarhaddon further enhanced his influence among the nomads by appointing Tabûa queen of the Arabs and returning her and her divine images to their own country.[442] Thus Tabûa, who as a young girl had been deported from Arabia to Nineveh and raised at Sennacherib's court, was given the position that Te'elḫunu queen of the Arabs held before she was exiled from Dumah.[443]

Just as the relationship between Ḫazael and Te'elḫunu is unclear, so is that between Ḫazael and Tabûa. The inscriptions of Esarhaddon may indicate that the return of the images to Ḫazael and the appointment of

438 Esarhaddon inscriptions: Heidel Prism ii 46-59; Nin. A iv 1-14; K 8523 (Borger, Frt. B), rev. 4-5; Mnm. B, 7-12. Assurbanipal inscriptions: K 3405 obv. 9 ff.; K 3087, obv. 9 ff.

439 Heidel Prism iii 1-2: *65 gammalē eli ma-da-at-ti abi-ia maḫ-ri-ti ú-rad-di-ma ú-kin ṣi-ru-uš-šú.* Cf. K 8523 (Frt. B), rev. 5

440 After the divine images were repaired and before they were returned, Esarhaddon ordered his name and "the might of Aššur" to be inscribed on them (Heidel Prism ii 58-59; Nin. A iv 13-14), as he had done with the divine images of Layālê king of Yadi', who was made ruler of the land of Bāzu (Heidel Prism iii 31-32). Only in Esarhaddon's dealings with the Arabs is such a procedure attested; it is without parallel in the history of the Assyrian empire.

441 See notes 431, 439.

442 Heidel Prism ii 60-62; Nin. A iv 15-16; Mnm. B, 12-14.

443 On the affinity between Tabûa and Te'elḫunu, and also on Tabûa's lineage and the circumstances under which she was reared at the court of the king of Assyria, see p. 123.

Tabûa as queen of the Arabs concern two distinct desert groups and two different occasions. It is stated that Ḫazael requested not the return of Tabûa, but of his divine images. Moreover, the inscriptions of Esarhaddon treat the return of *Ḫazael's* gods separately,[444] recording in a new sentence the appointment of Tabûa and her return with *her* gods.[445] Only later, in the inscriptions of Assurbanipal, have the two events been connected, thereby implying that Ḫazael asked that Tabûa be returned.[446]

After the death of Ḫazael, the accession of his son Yauṭa' was approved and supported by Esarhaddon. In return, Yauṭa' had to add to the tribute paid by his father a supplement of 10 minas of gold, 1000 choice gems, 50 camels and 1000 leather bags of spices.[447] Presumably Yauṭa' was prepared to pay so heavily because of his shaky position at the outset of his reign, and his dependence on the Assyrian king. His policy was justified when, at the time that ᵐ*Ú-a-bu*[448] rallied "all the

444 See above, note 438.

445 See above, note 442.

446 The combined text of K 3405 obv. 13-14 and K 3087 obv. 13-14 (M. Cogan, *Imperialism and Religion: Assyria, Judah and Israel in the Eight and Seventh Centuries B.C.E.*, Missoula, Mont. 1974, 16) — ... *ina muḫḫi* ᶠ*Ta-bu-a* ᵈ*Šamaš iš-al-ma um-ma ši-i...it-ti* ᵈ*iš-tar-šú ú-tir-ma [id-din-šú]*, "As for Tabûa, he (i.e. Esarhaddon) inquired of the Šamaš oracle: 'Is she..?' Then he gave him back (Tabûa) together with his goddess" — indicates that Esarhaddon acceded to Ḫazael's request for the return of his goddess, asked Šamaš about Tabûa, and returned the goddess to Ḫazael.

447 On making Yauṭa' king, and the consequent tribute, see Heidel Prism iii 3-8; Nin. A iv 19-22; K 8523 (Frt. B), rev. 5-7; Mnm. B, 14-15.

Note that in the tribute lists of the Assyrian royal inscriptions the spices received from the Arabs are not specified and are generally termed *riqqê kalama*, i.e., "spices of all kinds" (see Tiglath-Pileser III: Rost, *Ann.* 224; III R 10, 2:21, and the parallels to this line; Sargon: *Lie*, line 124; cf. also the general expression *riqqê ṭābūti* in Sennacherib's VA 8248:49, 53.

The spices Esarhaddon received from Ḫazael's son are described in Nin. A iv 21 as: 100 ᵏᵘˢ̌*kun-zi riqqê* (the Heidel Prism has 1000 here instead of 100, and omits the KUŠ = *mašku* determinative), implying that the spices were packed in leather bags. Cf. Pliny who writes that the myrrh of South Arabia was packed in leather bags (*Nat. Hist.* XII, 68) and that Indian spices were marketed in bottles made of camel or rhinoceros hide (*ibid.*, XII, 32).

448 Winckler's suggestion that this is a transliteration of the Arabic name Wahb is commonly accepted.

Arabs" (^lú^*A-ru-bu ka-li-šu*) against him (between 676 and 673 B.C.), an Assyrian expeditionary force intervened, captured Uabu and his people and carried them off to Nineveh to be punished as enemies of the king.[449]

Some time later, between 673 and 669 B.C., when Yauṭa' son of Ḫazael attempted to free himself from Esarhaddon, the Assyrian army campaigned to suppress him.[450] He was defeated and fled, and the images of his gods, including one of Atarsamâin, were captured, to be returned only when Assurbanipal acceded to the throne and Yauṭa' swore a vassal's oath of allegiance. Chief among the reasons for the defection of Yauṭa' may have been the heavy tribute exacted from him by Esarhaddon and the possibility that the Assyrian army was too occupied in Egypt and the northern and northeastern parts of the empire to take counter-measures. On Assurbanipal's encounter with Yauṭa' son of Ḫazael, see below, pp. 147-155.

The name of Ḫazael's successor is given in early Esarhaddon prisms (Borger's Nin. B and Nin. C) as ^m^*Ia-'-lu-u/ú,* and in his later inscriptions as ^m^*Ia-ta-', Ia-ta-a,* or *Ia-u-ti/te-'.*[451] We believe that ^m^*Ia-'-lu-u,* who became king with Esarhaddon's backing, and Ya(u)ṭa', later made king by the Arabs themselves, were the same person.[452] It is more likely that the spelling ^m^*Ia-'-lu-u (=*^m^*Ia-'u-lu-u)* was an error made when the early Esarhaddon prisms were copied.[453] In the treaty between Assurbanipal and the Qedarities the name of Ḫazael's son is written ^m^*Ia-ú-ta-'*, i.e., Yauṭa',[454] the spelling also used in Assurbanipal's Prisms B and C. Because the treaty is an official document (in contrast to the literary character of historical inscriptions) and careful attention had to be paid

449 On the rebellion of ^m^*Uabu* and its suppression see Nin. A iv 23-31; Mnm. B, 16-18; K 8523 (Frt. B), rev. 7-11. We do not know who ^m^*Uabu* was, whether he aspired to the leadership of the Qedarites or was a leader of another tribe and incited various Arab tribes to rebellion (note the expression ^lú^*Arubu kališu).*

450 See Assurbanipal Cyl. B vii 93-98; VAT 5600 i 3-12. For the date of the rebellion, see p. 126.

451 Borger, *Asarhaddon,* 126. On the spelling ^m^*Ú-a-a-te-'* in the later inscriptions of Assurbanipal, see pp. 51-52, 165-168.

452 See, in opposition, P. Haupt, *Hebraica* 1 (1884-1885), 222-223; Hommel, *EGAO,* 582-583; cf. also Smith, *CAH,* III, 84, 125.

453 Streck, *Assurbanipal,* 700. For similar approaches, see Haupt, *ibid.,* 222, n. 7.

454 For this treaty see Deller-Parpola, *Orientalia* 37 (1968), 464-466.

to the correct spelling of the name of the other party to the treaty, the spelling ^{m}*Ia-u-ta-'* is preferable.

3. The Campaign Against the Land of Bāzu

The inscriptions of Esarhaddon devote considerable space to the campaign against the land of Bāzu, which, in the opinion of most scholars, was in the Arabian desert.[455] We shall therefore examine the relevance to our subject of all the information on that campaign. Our sources are:

Esarhaddon Inscriptions: Heidel Prism iii 9-36 (and the parallels in Nin. B); Nin. A iv 53-77; Klch. A 24-27 (and the parallels ND 7097-7100); AsBbE. obv., 4-5; Trb. A 12-13.

Chronicles: Esarhaddon Chronicle, obv., 13; Babylonian Chronicle iv 5-6.

The campaign to Bāzu is included in the Heidel Prism and therefore took place before 676 B.C. According to the chronicles, the conquest of Bāzu took place no later than Tishri 677 (i.e., near the time of the conquest of Sidon). In the Heidel Prism, the Bāzu episode comes immediately after the section on the death of Ḫazael and the installation of his son ^{m}*Ia-'-lu-u* (=Yauṭa'), but this is not sufficient to prove substantive or temporal connection between the two events, since they are separated by a number of other episodes in the later inscriptions of Esarhaddon.

Bāzu is described as a distant country, beyond a salt desert, beyond sandy and thorny land, beyond the sphere of (military?) activity of earlier Assyrian kings.[456] In the course of his war there, Esarhaddon killed eight local kings[457] and many of their warriors,[458] carrying to

455 The location of the land of Bāzu has been widely discussed by scholars, notably: Delitzsch, *Paradies,* 307; Glaser, *Skizze,* 4-8, 264-273; Smith, *BHT,* 17-18; Landsberger-Bauer, *ZA* 37 NF 3 (1927), 74-77; Musil, *Arabia Deserta,* 482-485; E. Forrer, *RLA,* I, 440-441; Hirschberg, *Studien zur Geschichte Esarhaddons,* 57-60; J. Schawe, *AfO* 9 (1933-1934), 59; Bauer, *ZA* 42 NF 8 (1934), 182-184; Weidner, *AfO* 15 (1945-1951), 169-170; 16 (1952-1953), 3-10; Brinkman, *Post-Kassite Babylonia,* 160, n. 970.

456 Heidel Prism iii 9-18; Nin. A iv 53-60.

457 This is the number cited in the annals editions, different from the total in other inscriptions of Esarhaddon; see below, n. 460.

458 Klch. A, 24-27 and its parallels (cf. ND 7097-7100; Trb. A, 12-13) list the names of

Assyria booty which included, as well as men, the gods and property of the Bāzu rulers. The country was subsequently handed over to Layālê (^{m}*La-a-a-le-e*), king of ^{uru}*Ia-di-'*, apparently in or near the land of Bāzu. Layālê initially fled before the Assyrian army, but surrendered when he learned that his gods had been captured, and went to Nineveh to beg for their return. Esarhaddon pardoned him, returned his images after inscribing upon them the strength of the god Aššur, made him ruler and exacted tribute from him.[459] ABL 839, from the reign of Assurbanipal, also mentions ^{m}*La-a-a-li-e šar* ^{lú}*Be-zu* (rev. 8).

The later inscriptions of Esarhaddon — Nin. A; Klch. A and its parallels from Nimrud; Trb. A — list the places conquered in the land of Bāzu; Nin. A includes names of the rulers as well:

Nin. A iv 62-68	**Klch. A, 24-25 and Parallels**[460]	**Trb. A, 12-13**[461]
^{m}*Qí-i-su šàr* $^{\text{uru/kur}}$*Ḫal-di-su*	^{uru}*Ḫa-an-da-su*	^{uru}*Ḫa-an-da-su*
^{m}*Ak-ba-ru šàr* ^{uru}*Il-pi-a-tú/te*	^{uru}*Al-pi-ia-na*	
^{m}*Ma-an-sa-ku šàr* $^{\text{uru/kur}}$*Ma-gal-a-ni*	^{uru}*Ma-ga-la-nu*	
^{f}*Ia-pa-' šar-rat* ^{uru}*Di-iḫ-ra-a-ni*	^{uru}*Di-iḫ-ra-nu*	*[...i]ḫ-ra-nu*
^{m}*Ḫa-bi-su šàr* ^{uru}*Qa-da/ṭa-ba-'*	^{uru}*Qa-ta-bu-'*	^{uru}*Qa-ta-bu-'*
^{m}*Ni-ḫa-ru šàr* ^{uru}*Ga-'-u-a-ni*		
^{f}*Ba-as-lu šar-rat* ^{uru}*I-ḫi-lu(m)*		
^{m}*Ḫa-ba-zi-ru šàr* ^{uru}*Pu-da-'*	^{uru}*Pa-de-e*	^{uru}*Pa-di-'*
	^{uru}*Ú-de-ri/ru,* ^{uru}*Ú-de-e-ri*	^{uru}*Ú-de-ru*

For the nine place-names we have only eight rulers, two of them women, entitled *šarratu.*

seven walled cities in the land of Bāzu and state that they were captured and burned, along with hamlets in their environs. The capture and burning of the cities are not recorded in the annals editions, which are more extensive than Klch. A.

459 Heidel Prism iii 24-36; Nin. A iv 72-77.

460 Seven place-names, six paralleled in Nin. A, are listed in this source, with ^{uru}*Ú-de-ri* unrecorded in Nin. A. Since, however, the eight rulers whom Esarhaddon is said to have vanquished appear in Nin. A (the number also given in Heidel Prism iii 21), the ninth place-name, Uderi, cannot have been omitted, but indicates that both Klch. A and Trb. A (see following note) were based on another source, a premise strengthened by the fact that the spellings vary from those in Nin. A.

461 This inscription is damaged and only five toponyms have survived. In the main it is an exact parallel of Klch. A.

The land of Bāzu is variously spelled:

a. $^{kur/uru}$*Ba-a-zu/ṣú,* ^{kur}*Ba-a-zi/ṣi* (acc.) Heidel Prism iii 9, 33; Nin. A iv 53, 76.[462]

b. ^{uru}*Ba-az/ṣ-zi/ṣí* Klch. A, 26.

c. ^{uru}*Ba-a-su* AsBbE obv., 5.[463]

d. ^{uru}*Ba-az/aṣ-za/ṣa* (acc.?) Bab. Chr. iv 5; Esarh. Chr., obv. 13.

e. (^{m}*La-a-a-li-e šar*) ^{lú}*Be-zu/ṣú* ABL 839, rev., 8.

The land of Bāzu/Bazzu seems to have been associated with *bāṣu/baṣṣu,* "sand", spelled according to each scribe's dialectical particularity.[464] The form ^{lú}*Be-zu/ṣú,* which appears in a non-historiographical document, may, however, hold the key to the original name and therefore be of special importance.

The remoteness of and difficulty of approach to the land of Bāzu are manifestly exaggerated: a distant "arid land, saline ground, a waterless region" (lit. "a terrain of thirst"). The Heidel Prism iii 11-16 records a march of "140 *bēru* (1500 kilometers)[465] covered with sand, thorny plants and 'gazelle-tooth' stones (^{na_4}*šinni ṣabīti*), 20 *bēru* where snakes and scorpions cover the ground like ants, 20 *bēru* through Mount *Ḫa-zu-u,* the mountain of the *ḫašmānu* stones". Nin. A iv 55-57, although reducing the distance by 40 *bēru,* nevertheless describes the same dreadful terrain. Such details are typical of descriptions of other deserts in the literature of the ancient Near East.

Saline ground and a thirsty place is paralleled in Jer. 17:6: "He shall dwell in the parched places of the wilderness, in an uninhabited salt land"; Job 39:6: "(the swift ass) to whom I have given the steppe for his home, and the salt land for his dwelling place"; Ps. 107:33-34: "He turns rivers into a desert, springs of water into thirsty ground (cf. the MT here צמאון = *ṣumāmu*), a fruitful land into a salty waste"; see also Deut. 8:15 below.

Desert snakes and scorpions appear in Deut. 8:15: "Who led you through the great and terrible wilderness with its fiery serpents and

462 The determinative URU occurs here only in Nin. A.

463 As this text contains many spelling errors (see Borger, *Asarhaddon,* 78), the reading *su* is not significant, especially since the *su* and *zu* signs are similar.

464 See *CAD,* B, 134-135; *AHw* 110b.

465 For the determination that a *bēru* was ca. 10,800 meters long, see Weidner, *AfO* 16 (1952-1953), 20-21.

scorpions and thirsty ground where there was no water"; Isa. 30:6: (the way to Egypt) "...through a land of trouble and anguish, from where come the lioness and the lion, the viper and the flying serpent". For fiery serpents cf. also Num. 21:6. Esarhaddon's campaign from Palestine to Egypt in Fragment F rev. 5-7 reports double-headed snakes with lethal breath, and green flying serpents(?). Herodotus (II, 75; III, 109) also speaks of an abundance of flying serpents in the Sinai desert and South Arabia (on the fear of snakes during a military expedition in the Western Desert, see, likewise, Plutarch, *The Life of Young Cato,* 56).

The physical hazards and the length of the journey to the land of Bāzu seem therefore to be literary *topoi* that offer no real clue to its location, despite certain scholarly attempts to utilize them.[466] Definite only is that the land of Bāzu lay beyond a great desert in the neighborhood of Mount Ḥazû.

Bāzu and Ḥazû in the inscriptions of Esarhaddon were considered by Delitzsch, in whose opinion scholars concurred, to be identifical with the Buz (בּוּז) and Hazo (חֲזוֹ) in the list of the Sons of Nahor (Gen. 22:21-22), as well as with the Buz mentioned with Tema' and Dedan and the rest of the "kings of Arabia (מלכי ערב) ...that dwell in the desert" (Jer. 25:23-24), and thus have attempted to use them for locating Bāzu.[467] Hebrew Hazo (חֲזוֹ) does in fact correspond to Assyrian *Ḥazû,* but no such corresp̌ondence can be established for Buz (בּוּז) and Bāzu,[468] because a) *Būz (בּוּז)* in Hebrew demands **Būzu* in Akkadian, where the form has never been encountered, and b) the Hebrew transcription of *Bāzu* would be **Bāz (בָּז*)* not *Būz (בּוּז)*.

466　For such attempts see, for example, Smith, *BHT,* 18; Landsberger-Bauer, *ZA* 37 NF 3 (1927), 76-77; Musil, *Arabia Deserta,* 483-484; Bauer, *ZA* 42 NF 8(1934), 183-184; cf. also Forrer, *RLA,* I, 440.

467　Delitzsch, *Paradies,* 307; cf. Glaser, *Skizze,* 266-267; Musil, *Arabia Deserta,* 484; Hommel, *EGAO,* 558; Forrer, *RLA,* I, 440; Hirschberg, *Studien zur Geschichte Esarhaddons,* 59-60; Albright, *Alt Festschrift,* 8, n. 2.

468　On the discreteness between Buz and Hazo and between the toponyms in the inscriptions of Esarhaddon, see Maisler (Mazar), *Zion* 11 (1946), 6, who, since he was not arguing from a linguistic-phonetic point of view, suggested that biblical Buz might correspond with the land of Bāzu in the Euphrates region known from the Mari documents (cf. note 470). Any identification of Buz with Bāzu is, however, linguistically untenable.

The names of both rulers and territories of Bāzu provide a better clue. Personal names like Yapa', Layālê, Qîsu and Ak/gbaru, and the *-ani/-anu* ending of toponyms are clearly Semitic, in some cases even typically Arabic.[469] The Bāzu of Esarhaddon therefore cannot be identified with similarly named places east of the Tigris or northwest of Assyria,[470] nor located in Dasht-i Kavir in Iran,[471] and consequently must be sought in the Arabian peninsula or the Syrian desert.

The parts of Arabia and the Syrian desert suggested for locating the land of Bāzu include:

i. The northeastern part of the Arabian peninsula and the western part of the Persian Gulf:[472] A proposal first made by E. Glaser, who identified two place-names of tribes said by Ptolemy (VI, 7, 23) to inhabit Arabia Felix (cf. ^{uru}*Magalani* with Μελαγγίται and ^{uru}*Diḫrāni* with Δαχαρηνοί); as well as *Qad/ṭaba', Ga'uani, Iḫilu* and *Puda'* with place-names mentioned by al-Hamadānī and al-Bakri as south of Yamāma. However, except for the one tribal name in Ptolemy — Δαχαρηνοί whose location still cannot be pinpointed[473] — these parallels are no longer supportable.[474]

469 Compare the Arabic names Qais; *'kbrw* (*RNP*, I, 300; Harding, *Pre-Islamic Names, 61); Yf'm, Yf'n* etc. (*RNP*, I, 112; Harding, *ibid.*, 679-680); *Lyl* (*RNP*, I, 121). W. Caskel (*Fischer Weltgeschichte* 4, 209) points out that Ḫābis (compare the name of king ^{uru}*Qa-ṭa-ba-'*) is also a typical Arab name (cf. Harding, *ibid.*, 178).

470 On the land of Bazu northwest of Assyria in ND 4301+4305 obv. 20 f., see Wiseman, *Iraq* 18 (1956), 125, 128. ^{kur}*Ba-a-za*, mentioned in KAH II, 83, rev. 7, which lay near the Ḫabḫi region, in the general area of the mountains northeast of Assyria proper, was attacked by Adad-nirari II. For the possibility that these two places are identical, see Brinkman, *Post-Kassite Babylonia*, 160, n. 970.

471 On the location of the land of Bāzu in Dasht-i Kavir, see Smith, *BHT*, 17-18; Landsberger-Bauer, *ZA* 37 NF 3 (1927), 74-77, whose theory has been refuted by Hirschberg, *Studien zur Geschichte Esarhaddons*, 58; Bauer, *ZA* 42 NF 8 (1934), 183.

472 Glaser, *Skizze*, 4-8, 265-273; Hommel, *EGAO*, 557-561; Thompson, *JRAS* 1933, 891, 895; Schawe, *AfO* 9 (1933-1934), 59; Weidner, *AfO* 15 (1945-1951), 169-170; 16 (1952-1953), 3-6. This view was accepted (without elaboration) by Forrer, *RLA*, I, 441; Albright, *Alt Festschrift*, 8, n. 2. For the difficulties inherent in this view see Bauer, *ZA* 42 NF 8 (1934), 184.

The location suggested above is in fact more strongly supported by such evidence from Akkadian sources as: a) A geographical list from Assur, KAV No. 92 = VAT 8006, describing the boundaries of the realm of Sargon of Akkad, refers to *Ba-za*^ki^ (lines 1, 47).[475] This Neo-Assyrian version is based on Old Babylonian sources containing names of lands like ^kur^*Ḫa-nu-ú,* ^kur^*Subartu* (=KUR.SU.BIR₄. KI), ^kur^*Tuk-riš,* ^kur^*Lul-lu-bi-i* and *Kap-ta-ra*^ki^ which existed in the Old Babylonian period. That Ba-za^ki^ is included seems to indicate the antiquity of this toponym. The first line refers to a bridge(?) of the land of *Ba-za*^ki^ at the end of "the road to the land of Meluḫḫa" ([*ištu*...] *ti-tur-ri Ba-za*^ki^ *šá paṭ ḫarrān* ^kur^*Me-luḫ-ḫ[a*^k^]^i^). Since in the Old Babylonian period the name ^kur^*Meluḫḫa* was primarily confined to the Persian Gulf region,[476] *Ba-za*^ki^ would seem to have been in the north-eastern part of the Arabian peninsula, on the road to ^kur^*Meluḫḫa.* b) ABL 839, which deals with matters clearly connected with southern Babylonia, mentions ^m^*Layālê šar* ^lú^*Be-zu,* suggesting that his territory was in the Persian Gulf region.[477] c) There are proposals to place Bāzu near the land of Tilmun (usually identified with Bahrain)[478] on the basis of the conventional

473 So, for example, Stephen of Byzantium, *Ethnika* (ed. A. Meineke, Berlin 1849), 223, connects the Δαχαρηνοί with the Ναβαταῖοι, who are generally identified with the Nabataeans; that is, far to the west of the area proposed by Glaser.

474 Glaser's assumption of metathesis in Μελαγγίται is groundless; most of his parallels from Arabic sources demand changes in the original spellings.

475 The latest discussions of this document are in Weidner, *AfO* 16 (1952-1953), 1-24; A.K. Grayson, *AfO* 25 (1974-1977), 56-64.

476 For a review of the facts and status of research about the identification of Meluḫḫa during the Old Babylonian period, see Weidner, *ibid.,* 5-11; W.F. Leemans, *The Old-Babylonian Merchant,* Leiden 1950, 159-166; I.J. Gelb, *RA* 64 (1970), 1-8; J. Hansman, *BSOAS* 36 (1973), 554 ff. (esp. 554-557, 559-570). Gelb perceptively distinguishes three possible ranges for locating Meluḫḫa: from the point of view of Mesopotamian military campaigns, of resources and of imports from Iran east of Elam to the Indus Valley. Since we are concerned with the realm of Sargon of Akkad, the most westerly location suits our needs. In Neo-Assyrian royal inscriptions, Meluḫḫa designates southern Egypt, but of course need not be taken into account in discussing the realm of Sargon of Akkad.

477 Schawe, *AfO* 9 (1933-1934), 59.

478 Weidner, *AfO* 15 (1945-1951), 169-170; cf. Albright, *Alt Festschrift,* 8, n. 2.

reading of AsBbE obv. 4-5: *[a]k-šud* ^{uru}*Ba-a-su na-gu-ú šâ a-šar-šú ru-ú-qu eli* ^{m}*Qa-[n]a-a šar*$_4$ NI.[TUK^{ki}] *man-da-at-tú bēlu-ti-iá ú-kin,* "I conquered Bāzu (lit. the town of Bāsu), a district which is far away. Upon Qanâ king of Tilmun I imposed tribute due to me as lord." It should be noted, however, that the reading NI. TUK^{ki} (=Tilmun) is by no means certain, since the text is damaged after the NI sign, as published by Borger who collated the document,[479] and what remains cannot be a TUK sign.[480] The place, therefore, is not certifiably Tilmun, nor can its identity be clarified by its ruler Qanâ, who is known from no other source.

ii. The western part of the Syrian desert (between Wadi Sirḥān and the Valley of Lebanon):[481] Based primarily on attempts to locate Bāzu according to a) the description of the route and the distance to it (Musil); b) the assumption that Abydenus, as quoted by Eusebius when writing about Axerdis, conqueror of Egypt and Coele-Syria,[482] was referring to Esarhaddon and his two most difficult and important campaigns; c) the relation of Buz to the other names in the list of the Sons of Nahor (Hirschberg). A.T. Olmstead's suggestion that Bāzu be identified with "Bazil", where Samsi queen of the Arabs fled to escape Tiglath-Pileser III,[483] is based on Rost's misreading of a non-existent place-name.

That Abydenus really meant Esarhaddon's wars is not proved; the other arguments have already been refuted. Furthermore, according to the inscriptions of Esarhaddon, the land of Bāzu is remote, beyond his forefathers' activity, which was not true of the region between Wadi Sirḥān and the Valley of Lebanon.

iii. The northwestern part of the Arabian peninsula: Based only on the similarity between the names ^{uru}*Ia-di-',* Layālê's country, and the oasis

479 On this document see Borger, *Asarhaddon,* 78, 86, Tafel I.

480 Cf. the form of the TUK.KI signs with the word *sat-tuk-ki* in the document discussed (obv. 15).

481 Delitzsch, *Paradies,* 307; Olmstead, *History of Assyria,* 199, 377-378; Musil, *Arabia Deserta,* 482-485; Hirschberg, *Studien zur Geschichte Esarhaddons,* 57-60. Criticism of this view has been made by Bauer, *ZA* 42 NF 8 (1934), 182-183.

482 In the Chronicle of Eusebius; see J. Karst (ed.), *Eusebius Werke,* Bd. 5, Leipzig 1911, p. 18; and also P. Schnabel, *Berossos und die babylonisch-hellenistische Literatur,* Berlin 1923, 270.

483 Cf. *History of Assyria,* 199, 377-378; and III R 10, 2.

of Yadi' between Fadak and Khaibar,[484] and between the ^{uru}*Il-pi-a-tu/ Al-pi-ia-na* in the list of the kings of Bāzu and the 'Ολαφία mentioned by Ptolemy (VI, 7, 34).[485]

In sum, among the three chief suggestions for locating the land of Bāzu the most acceptable, in spite of inconclusive evidence, is in the northeastern part of the Arabian peninsula, west of the Persian Gulf. The inscriptions of Esarhaddon give no reason for the expedition to this remote country. Although Esarhaddon's motive was presumably economic, the general unitemized reference to the booty taken from the rulers of Bāzu does not support such an assumption,[486] nor are there data about the effect of the surrender of the rulers of Bāzu on the economy of the Assyrian kingdom.

Consequently, the relevance of the Bāzu campaign to the study of nomads in the Fertile Crescent or North Arabia is doubtful, especially since: a) The settlements (or tribes) of that country are not mentioned in biblical sources, and in Akkadian occur only in connection with Esarhaddon's campaign. b) None of the sources for Esarhaddon's campaign against the land of Bāzu states explicitly that the campaign was conducted against *Arabs* , i.e. nomads. The campaign target may, therefore, have been a group of settlements, or tribes, on the western shore of the Persian Gulf.

4. The Arabs as Indispensable to Military Campaigns in Sinai:

a. Esarhaddon, the first Asian king to attack Egypt, was therefore the first to conduct a military campaign across the Sinai desert from Palestine. After telling how water was supplied to his army on the way from Apheq to Raphia, as an introduction to the hazards of the journey through the terrible wilderness, one of his inscriptions says: "When the oracle-command of Aššur, my lord, came to my attention (i.e., a positive answer to the Assyrian king's question regarding the outcome

484 In the Harran inscription (Nabonidus H_2 i 25), with reference to the wars of Nabonidus in North Arabia, the spelling is ^{uru}*Iá-di-ḫu;* see Gadd, *AnSt* 8 (1958), 83-84.

485 A possibility raised somewhat hesitantly by Hommel, *EGAO,* 558-559.

486 Cf. Heidel Prism iii 22-23; Nin. A iv 71-72; Klch. A, 27; Trb. A, 13. The list of booty specifies only gods, general goods (*bušû, makkūru*) and captives.

of the Egyptian campaign), my liver [rejoiced.] Camels of all the kings of the Arabs (*šarrāni*^{meš} ^{kur}*Aribi*) I g[athered and goatskins I l]oaded on them" (Fragment F, rev. 1-2). A parallel passage — Fragment G, 10 — of which only a few signs per line survive, mentions goat- and waterskins as well.[487] Although this is the first reference to the use of Arab camels in military campaigns in the Sinai, it is by no means unique in describing the role of the Arabs in various Sinai expeditions throughout history. To understand the importance of Arab camels in these campaigns, the problems of and solutions for traversing the Sinai desert in wartime must be defined.

The Sinai peninsula, particularly in the north, is a buffer between Egypt and Palestine and the rest of the Fertile Crescent. The paucity of water sources and the boggy sand confined those armies dependent solely on men and animals to specific routes in the region, and limited the size of the armies that could move along them at a given time. Armies generally traveled to and from Egypt along the northern axis ("the Way of the Land of the Philistines"); some, however, did use the central ("the Way to Shur"?) and southern axes ("the Way to Mount Seir"?).[488] Crossing became more difficult when the termini at either end of the transverse routes were controlled by rival politico-military entities. If a single power were in control, the army could be divided into sub-units which moved successively from one water source to the next and were reintegrated at the end of the route.[489] If rival armies were in control, however, division of the expeditionary force became impractical: It was vital for the defender in the settled areas to prevent the aggressor from reorganizing his army units, which had been advancing through the desert about a day or half a day apart. He

487 For the reading ^{ku}*[*^{š}*n]a-a-dí* ^{kuš}*ḫi-in-ti* see *AHw* 346b; Borger, *AfO* 18 (1957-1958), 118.

488 For details of army campaigns along the three axes of Sinai throughout the ages, see M. Gichon, *Carta's Atlas of Palestine from Bethther to Tel Hai,* Jerusalem 1969, maps 35, 36, 38 (Hebrew).

489 Before the camel was adopted for military purposes, the armies of the Pharaohs of the New Kingdom undoubtedly used this system to cross the desert, travelling along the stations of "the Way of the Land of the Philistines". For a list of these stations, including water sources, in the days of Seti I see Gardiner, *JEA* 6 (1920), 99-116; W. Helck, *Die Beziehungen Ägyptens zu Vorderasien im 3. und 2. Jahrtausend v. Chr.*, Wiesbaden 1962, 323-327. Two of the Late Bronze Egyptian

therefore had to attack each unit as soon as it came to the end of the route, destroying the expeditionary force bit by bit. Commanders in this situation had to get their armies (including cavalry) to the approaches of the settled areas in the largest possible blocs, in order to counter the attack of the fresh, generally numerically superior enemy that awaited them at the end of their exhausting journey. An army moving through the Sinai desert had to carry, besides the chief essential, water, all its food (and that of its animals, since there is no grass in the desert), because along the route there were neither supplies nor people from whom food could be exacted. Thus the size of the expeditionary force able to cross Sinai and immediately, in one body, engage in combat at the other end was controlled by the quantity of water and food it could supply to its men and animals. The most suitable beast of burden for such desert transport is, of course, the camel (useless, on the other hand, for pulling wagons, cannon and the like).

We have no details about the number of camels that took part in desert military expeditions in ancient times, nor indication of the ratio of men to horses and how many camels carried water and food. Two well-documented events, however — Napoleon's march from Egypt to Palestine in February 1799, and the Turkish campaign to the Suez Canal in January 1915 — can be used to estimate the number of camels necessary to move armies through Sinai.[490] Since calculations for water, food and personal provisions in these two campaigns were based on minimum requirements, it is hard to imagine that earlier armies managed on less. The data show that in order to support 1000 men (without reference to horses, which consume considerably more food

fortresses in northern Sinai, on the route discussed, have been discovered (Y. Margovski, *Hadashot Archeologiot* 28-29 [1969], 44-45; E. Oren, *Qadmoniot* 6 [1973], 101-103). There is actually no indication during the biblical period that the approaches to Palestine were held by a large army designed to halt and defeat the Egyptian forces upon their emergence from the desert, before they could regroup in the settled area.

490 See Napoleon, *Meine Ersten Siege,* IV^5 (ed. H. Conrad), Stuttgart 1911, 28-36. Instructive material on the decisive importance Napoleon accorded the water supply when planning his campaign in Palestine is also to be found in Gichon, *Yediot* 27 (1963), 195-203. On the Turkish expedition to the Suez Canal see F. Kress von Kressenstein, *Die Kriegführung in der Wüste,* in Th. Wiegand, *Sinai,* Berlin-Leipzig 1920, 1-35; idem, *Mit den Türken zum Suezkanal,* Berlin 1938.

and water than men do), at least 200 camels were needed, on the basis of a three-day water supply, which could presumably be replenished along the road from wells like those at el-Arish and Qatiya.[491] These figures make it clear that, until the mechanization of military transport, water supply was the main problem, and that without wide use of camels it was impossible for armies to cross the desert and join battle on the other side.

The reference to the role of Arab camels in the inscriptions about Esarhaddon's second campaign to Egypt in 671 B.C.[492] and the foregoing discussion of geographic-military matters point to the importance of Arabs in the border regions of Palestine as soon as Asian kingdoms undertook expeditions to Egypt. Cambyses as well, on his way to Egypt in 525 B.C., was supported by Arab camels, loaded with waterskins and awaiting him in the desert (Herodotus III 4, 9).

491 This is calculated mainly from the data about Napoleon's and von Kressenstein's campaigns, as follows:

Crossing the Sinai desert: a march of 8-9 hours a day for 8 days.

Load capacity of a camel: 180 kilograms (von Kressenstein, *Mit den Türken etc.*, 87, estimates it at 120 kgs. In such a case, considering the other figures in this note, about 350 camels would be needed per 1000 men. This estimate of load capacity, however, seems very low, acceptable only for lengthy journeys and in connection with desert-bred camels).

Daily food ration: for a soldier, 600 gms. of black bread plus a handful of olives, dates or raisins; for a horse, 2½ kgs. barley; for a camel, 1½ kg. barley. (The Turkish expedition maintained itself on these rations for four weeks, see von Kressenstein, *Die Kriegführung etc.*, 12. In his later report on this campaign, *Mit den Türken etc.*, 86-87, these rations were erroneously doubled because of a confusion between the *Pfund* (=½ kilogram) and the kilogram, resulting in quantities greater than normal. For example, the barley ration usual for a horse in the Roman and other armies was 3½ kgs. per day, see J. Kromayer-G. Veith, *Heerwesen und Kriegführung der Griechen und Römer,* München 1927, 330, 413).

Daily water ration: for a soldier, 6 liters; for a horse or camel, 20-25 liters.

For a more detailed, and apparently very trustworthy (based on extensive military experience) discussion of the use of camels in military campaigns, see A.G. Leonard, *The Camel,* London 1894.

492 Crossing the Sinai during this campaign was especially difficult because, although most expeditions were undertaken in winter or spring, it becomes clear from the Babylonian chronicles that Esarhaddon's army descended into the desert not before the end of June or the beginning of July, cf. Babylonian Chronicle (=Grayson, Chron. 1) iv 23-26; Esarhaddon Chronicle (=Grayson, Chron. 14) lines 25-26.

Herodotus correctly stresses that "had the Arabs been unfriendly the Persians could never have made their invasion of Egypt" (III 88).

Because of the indispensability of the Arabs, politico-military entities planning to cross the Sinai desert and to control both regions adjacent to it had to assure Arab good-will by dealing fairly and granting them concessions. This was how Herodotus explained the special status of the Arabs in southern Palestine within the general organization of the satrapies of the Achaemenid empire, writing that it was achieved by the help that they gave to Cambyses' army on its way to Egypt (III 5, 9, 88).[493] Similary, the Turkish authorities, rather than confiscating the 20,000-30,000 camels needed for the attack on the Suez Canal, preferred to buy them for as much as ten(!) Turkish gold pounds apiece, to avoid endangering the success of the entire operation by arousing the hostility of the inhabitants, particularly the camel owners.[494]

b. Discussion of the Arab role in Sinai military campaigns brings to mind Herodotus' reference (II 141) to "Sennacherib, king of the Arabs and Assyrians", from whom Egypt was saved when he and an "Arab host" came to Pelusium, because hordes of mice chewed up the leather in his soldiers' weapons. The title "king of the Arabs and Assyrians", as well as "Arab host", gave rise to questions among historians as early as Josephus, who commented that "in speaking of the king of the Arabs and not the king of the Assyrians Herodotus simply erred" (*Ant.* X, i, 4). Certain more recent scholars, in an attempt to justify Herodotus' account, assumed that Sennacherib attacked Egypt after a successful campaign in North Arabia (against ^{uru}*Adummatu*) in the last years of his reign, following which he attached large units of Arabs to his army.[495] Such an assumption, however, fails to consider not only that Sennacherib may have made no second westward campaign,[496] but that the size and aridity of the Syro-Arabian desert prevented a crossing by a large Assyrian (or any other) army from Mesopotamia towards Egypt through Wadi Sirḥān.[497] Equally difficult to confirm, in view of the

493 Economic-administrative considerations, in our opinion, also affected Arab status in the Achaemenid empire; see pp. 206-210.

494 Kress von Kressenstein, *Mit den Türken etc.*, 87.

495 L.L. Honor, *Sennacherib's Invasion of Palestine,* New York 1926, 55-57; Dougherty, *The Sealand of Ancient Arabia,* 72-73. See following note as well.

496 See Eph'al, "Sennacherib", *Enc. Miqr.*, V, 1065-1069 (with bibliography).

497 Musil, *Arabia Deserta,* 482; cf. Smith, *JRAS* 1925, 509-510.

available Assyrian sources, is Sidney Smith's alternative proposal, suggesting that the names in Herodotus (II 141) were switched and that the actual reference was to Esarhaddon's unsuccessful first Egyptian expedition in 674 B.C. (cf. Babylonian Chronicle, iv 16)[498]

Altogether, the historical backgound for Herodotus' statement remains in question. The term "king of the Arabs and Assyrians", however, can be explained without reference to a particular Assyrian king, on the assumption that the tradition about the failure of the invasion reached the ears of Herodotus when he was in Egypt: Because of the scope of the Arab role in military campaigns across the Sinai, the Egyptians thought of any army making such a crossing as "the army of X and the Arabs". Why Egyptian tradition hit upon Sennacherib as the Assyrian king who attacked Egypt exceeds the confines of this study.

C. THE REIGN OF ASSURBANIPAL (668-627 B.C.)

1. Source-Groups Relating to Arabs in the Inscriptions of Assurbanipal:

Since M. Streck's publication of the inscriptions of Assurbanipal in 1916, discussion of the Arabs during Assurbanipal's reign has derived chiefly from the sequencing and reconstruction of events in Streck's historical survey.[499] The description of the so-called "ninth campaign"

498 See Smith, *BHT,* 3-11; and, for the reservation, Landsberger-Bauer, *ZA* 37 NF 3 (1927), 78, n. 2.

499 Streck, *Assurbanipal,* CCLXXIX-CCLXXXV; cf. Smith, *CAH,* III, 123-125; Musil, *Arabia Deserta,* 485-489; Hommel, *EGAO,* 584-589; Rosmarin, *JSOR* 16 (1932), 17-21; Donner, *MIO* 5 (1957), 167 ff., 175; Caskel, in *Fischer Weltgeschichte* 4, 207-209; S.S. Ahmed, *Southern Mesopotamia in the time of Ashurbanipal,* Hague-Paris 1968, 36-39. Olmstead's reconstruction (*History of Assyria,* 426-430) of the chronology of events is more satisfactory than Streck's, even though it errs in various details and in the interpretation of letters.

After the presentation in 1971 of the Hebrew version of my dissertation, on which this book is based, there appeared in *WO* 7 (1973), 39-85, "Die Kämpfe des assyrischen Königs Assurbanial gegen die Araber", a paper by M. Weippert, expanding a chapter of his unpublished dissertation, *Edom: Studien und Materialien zur Geschichte der Edomiter auf Grund schriftlicher und archäologischer Qellen.* In the course of preparing the paper for publication Weippert had recourse to my work (see, for example, his notes 58, 108 etc.). Weipert differs, as do I, from Streck and his followers in interpreting the history of Arab relations with Assyria in Assurbanipal's time. Since our methodology is similar in principle, we have arrived independently of each other at the same conclusions with regard to the

in the Rassam Cylinder (vii 82—ix 114; x 1-5, 21-39) supplies the essence of his survey, with other available sources used only to fill in details not included in the Rassam Cylinder. Recognizing that the events reported could not have taken place during a single campaign, and certainly extended over a number of years, Streck grouped the data under two headings, each connected with one of the two kings named Uaiṭe‘ (ᵐ*U-a-a-te-’*):

The first war (ca. 650-647 B.C.)

Sources: Rm. vii 82—viii 47; Cyl. B. (Streck) vii 93—viii 57 (=B [Piepkorn] vii 99—viii 63); Cyl. C ix 33-49; K 2802 iv-v; VAT 5600 ii-iii; K 4687; K 3096.

The war began during the conflict between Assurbanipal and Šamaš šum-ukin. Uaiṭe‘ I assisted the Babylonian king on two fronts: a) By invading the territories in the western part of the Assyrian empire along with his Qedarite people, and another Qedarite leader named Ammuladi(n). They were defeated by Assyrian units and those of the kings of the regions attacked. Ammuladi and his warriors were taken captive by ᵐ*Ka-ma-as-ḫal-ta-a* king of Moab. Adiya, the wife of Uaiṭe‘, was also captured. Because the Qedarites were starving and recalcitrant,[500] Uaiṭe‘ was forced to flee and seek refuge with Natnu king of Nebaioth. Although his territory was outside of Assyrian control, Natnu, impressed by the might that defeated the Qedarites, sent tribute to Assurbanipal. Uaiṭe‘ (possibly betrayed by Natnu) eventually turned up in Nineveh where he was caged as a punishment;[501] b) By sending a

reconstruction of history and certain basic geographical and chronological matters. We differ considerably, however, in interpreting various episodes, and especially in identifying the Arab kings (see Weippert, 51, n. 58), mainly because Weippert relies wholly on occurrences as they are recorded, without considering, as I have tried to do, the circumstances and temporal developments that conditioned variations in the sources.

500 In some inscriptions this is relegated to the first war (Prism B viii 23-30; VAT 5600 ii 6-20 + K 2802 v 2-3), but in the Rassam Cylinder to the last campaign (ix 53-89). Streck (see preceding note) found impossible to place the episode precisely, and thought in fact that it might relate to both campaigns.

501 Since Streck did not differentiate the punishments of Uaiṭe‘ I and Uaiṭe‘ II, he assumed that both Rm. viii 11-14, and ix 103-111 referred to Uaiṭe‘ II, attributing the description of the punishment of Uaiṭe‘ I to an error resulting from the similarity of the names (*op. cit.*, CCLXXXIII n. 3). Indeed, although both were

force to Babylon under Abiyaṯeʻ and Ayamu, sons of Te'ri. They were attacked and badly beaten before they could join Šamaš-šum-ukin; remnants of the force escaped to Babylon. They tried to break out when famine threatened the city, besieged since 650 B.C., and were again defeated by the Assyrians. Abiyaṯeʻ fled to Nineveh, hoping for mercy from Assurbanipal, who in fact bestowed it and made him king in place of Uaiṯeʻ.

The second war (641-638 B.C.)

Sources: Rm. viii 48—ix 114; x 1-5, 21-30; K 2802 vi 2-43, iii 1-33.

This was a war waged against Arab tribes rebelling against Assyria, led by Abiyaṯeʻ and Uaiṯeʻ II son of Birdāda, who became king of the Qedarites after his uncle Uaiṯeʻ I fell into Assyrian hands. Reinforced by Natnu king of Nebaioth and Ayamu, brother of Abiyaṯeʻ, they attacked the western border regions of the Assyrian empire, at a time when the Assyrian army was involved in war against Ummanaldaš king of Elam. Their action culminated in an Assyrian campaign, conducted on a grand scale, in the desert areas near Damascus and southward. In the course of the war, Abiyaṯeʻ and Ayamu, as well as the members of the family of Uaiṯeʻ, were captured and taken to Nineveh. The fate of Abiyaṯeʻ is unknown; Ayamu was put to death. Uaiṯeʻ and most of the Qedarite force survived the battle, but the severe shortage of food and water caused such bitterness that Uaiṯeʻ was forced to flee.[502] He was captured and carried off to Nineveh, where, after having been displayed at the city gate, he was forced into Assurbanipal's triumphal procession. We do not know what happened to Natnu, who may not have participated in the war, merely sending supporting forces. In any case, the Assyrian army did not reach Nebaioth territory.

This reconstruction, based in the main on what is said of the Arabs in the Rassam Cylinder, and upon the division of sources under two consecutive headings, raises difficulties with the inner logic of the sequence of events as set forth in the sources. Some instances follow:

a. Is it likely that Abiyaṯeʻ, whose men were beaten at Babylon by the Assyrian army, would flee to Nineveh? Or that Assurbanipal would

caged near the same gate of Nineveh, Uaiṯeʻ I was reportedly locked up with a dog and a bear, and Uaiṯeʻ II roped through holes in his cheeks.

502 See note 500.

appoint as king of the Arabs the same Abiyaṭe' who had just helped the Babylonian rebels and fought against the Assyrian army?

b. The inscriptions of Assurbanipal never imply that Uaiṭe' was handed over to the king of Assyria by Natnu king of Nebaioth (a possibility offered by Streck). Rm. viii 5-7 in fact suggests that Uaiṭe' went to Nineveh on his own initiative. Although the Rassam Cylinder says that Uaiṭe' came to Nineveh because of madness inflicted by the god Aššur, this hardly accounts for his arrival so soon after his defeat in the western part of the empire.

c. Of the two kings called ᵐ*Uaite'* in the Rassam Cylinder, which one is connected with episodes whose position in the narrative vary from source to source?[503]

Later publications of additional inscriptions of Assurbanipal enable us to solve these and other problems. In 1933, Th. Bauer pùblished some new Assurbanipal inscriptions and re-edited others. Relating to the Arabs are Prism C x 27-66 and its parallels; K 2664; K 3090; K 3405; K 4687; and an additional fragment from the Letter to Aššur (Th. 1905-4-9, 97).[504] In the same year, R. Campbell Thompson published the inscription from the temple of Ištar in Nineveh, whose important information, especially about the later relations between Assurbanipal and the Arabs, appears in no other sources.[505] In that year also, A.C. Piepkorn published the complete text of Edition B of the Annals, based on parallel cylinders, the earliest of which was written in the month of Ab, 649 B.C. (a year earlier than the copy of Cylinder B at Streck's disposal).[506]

With the publication of these sources, details were added that clarified the development of the historical inscriptions of Assurbanipal which antedated the Letter to Aššur and the Rassam Cylinder (see pp. 46-52). The re-examination, thus made possible, of the episodes relating to the Arabs greatly contributes to more precise understanding

503 See notes 500-501, and also pp. 51-52. On further difficulties in interpreting the sequence of data on Arabs in the Rassam Cylinder, see also Weippert, *op. cit.*, 48-49.

504 *Das Inschriftenwerk Assurbanipals.* For references to the sources mentioned here see pp. 47-49.

505 *AAA* 20 (1933), 80-98.

506 *Historical Prism Inscriptions of Assurbanipal,* 19-94.

of the course and sequence of events. In such a re-examination greater reliance should be placed on the earlier sources, closer in time both to the events and to the early phases of reporting them, than on later ones which sometimes suffered from copying and editing errors, and were affected by varying literary and historiographical approaches. We shall therefore, unlike Streck in 1916, prefer such earlier sources as Cylinders B and C (rather than the Rassam Cylinder and the Letter to Aššur, which are among the later historical inscriptions of Assurbanipal, for those episodes recounted differently in the various sources).

For the purpose of examination, the material concerning the Arabs in the inscriptions of Assurbanipal is classified into 26 episodes, which are listed in the foldout page chart after p. 164. When the textual order of the episodes conforms to the actual chronology of events, they are lettered A to X; the four episodes from later sources only (in our opinion incorrectly inserted) are numbered in Roman I to IV.

On the chart facing the list of episodes in the foldout, the episodes are further arranged according to their occurence in the sources, in order to demonstrate that the sources themselves divide into two groups:

Group A—the early editions (Cylinders B and C), which include a historical survey up to Episode N only;

Group B—the later editions (K 3405; K 2664+3090; Letter to Aššur; K 4687; the Rassam Cylinder; the Slab Inscription from the temple of Ištar), which include the material covered in Group A, plus the Episodes from Q on, as well as I, II, III and IV.[507]

In Group A, the Arab king's name is always written ^{m}*Ia-u-ta-'* and refers only to Uaiṭe' b. Ḫazael (the same orthography is used in the treaty between Assurbanipal and the Qedarites during the period of Episode B,[508] and in the inscriptions of Esarhaddon). In Group B the name ^{m}*Ú-a-a-te-'* is applied both to Yauṭa' b. Ḫazael and Uaiṭe' b. Birdāda.[509] The failure to distinguish between the names Yauṭa' and

507 Episode P has been recorded only in the Letter to Aššur, where the textual damage prevents ascertaining the subject and deciding whether the episode belongs to Source-Group B.

508 For the text of this treaty see Deller-Parpola, *Orientalia* 37 (1968), 464.

509 Compare ^{m}*Uaite' mār* ^{m}*Ḫazailu,* Rm. viii 1, 46; ^{m}*Uaite' mār* ^{m}*Birdāda,* Rm. viii 2; ix 1-2; K 2802 iii 2-3.

Uaiṯe' can be explained by their similarity and by the composition of the sources of Group B (after the defeat of Uaiṯe' b. Birdāda, no earlier than 646 B.C.), which was late enough for various details about Yauṯa' b. Ḫazael (who was defeated no later than 652 B.C.) to have been forgotten.[510] The confusion seems to have occurred first in the Letter to Aššur, the basis for later inscriptions.[511] The spelling of b. Ḫazael's name thus helps to classify references to Arabs in the inscriptions of Assurbanipal into their proper source group.

The chronological classification of episodes illustrates the complexity and irregular sequence of events as they are recorded in the account of the "ninth campaign" in Rm. vii 82-x 39. The accompanying sketch on the following page serves as a visual aid.

Our survey of the history of the Arabs during Assurbanipal's reign is divided into two episode-complexes paralleling the two groups of sources. The first step is a reconstruction of events by internal analysis of the inscriptions; the second an attempt to establish the actual dates through data from other sources.

2. Survey of Events Covered by Source-Group A:

After Assurbanipal's accession, Yauṯa' b. Ḫazael, king of the Qedarites, appealed for the return of the divine images captured by Esarhaddon. When he had sworn allegiance to the king of Assyria, the image of Atarsamâin was returned (Episodes A and B). A treaty fragment (Bu. 91-5-9, 178), published by K. Deller and S. Parpola, mentions Yauṯa' and offers evidence about Qedarite relations with Assurbanipal[512] at that time. Sometime later, under the leadership of Yauṯa', the Arabs revolted,[513] raiding the border regions of Transjordan

510 For the dates see pp. 153-156.

511 See pp. 51-52. The Ištar Temple Slab Inscription, line 119, is exceptional in spelling Uaiṯe' b. Birdāda ^{m}*Ia-u-te-' šar* ^{kur}*Su-mu*-AN. In line 113 the same person is called ^{m}*Ú-a-a-te-' šar* ^{kur}*Su-mu*-AN. The name Yauṯa' appears here probably because the author remembered and wanted to mention an Arab king of that name although knowledge about him was no longer precise. (It should be noted that the inscription under discussion differs from the other late inscriptions of Assurbanipal in the multiplicity of kings' names and changes in style and content; its author must have depended on sources other than the Letter to Aššur).

512 *Orientalia* 37 (1968), 464-466.

513 The common noun ^{kur}*Aribi* is used in the inscriptions of Assurbanipal for various

SEQUENCE OF EPISODES RELATING TO ARABS

ACCORDING TO Rm. vii 82—x 39

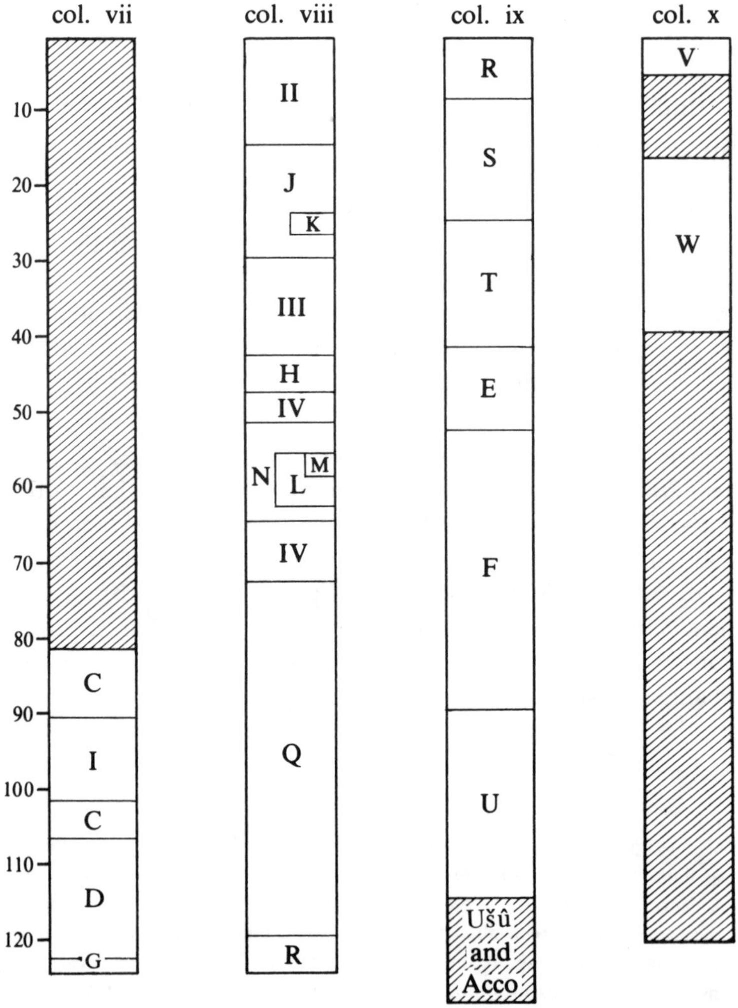

Notes

1. Filled in spaces signify passages unrelated to Arabs.
2. Episodes A and B do not occur in the Rassam Cylinder.

and southern Syria (Episode C). They were repulsed and defeated by Assyrian units stationed at key points along the frontiers from the province of Ṣupite to Edom (Episode D),[514] and by the armies of the border countries themselves, Moab in particular (Episode J). The details and extent of the Arab defeat are described at length in the inscriptions of Assurbanipal: the Assyrian army attacked the Arab camps and burned their tents (Episode D); so much booty was taken — people, donkeys, camels, sheep and goats — that the price of camels and slaves in Assyria dropped drastically (Episode E); the Arabs who survived the Assyrian operations suffered such extreme hunger that they were

groups of nomads (see more about this in pp. 165-168). Nevertheless, since Source-Group A mentions only Yauṭa' b. Ḫazael and Ammuladi(n) in connection with raids to the west, the reference here seems exclusive to the Qedarites.

514 Rm. vii 108-114 lists the following Assyrian military encampments: ^uru^*A-za-ar-an* (or ^uru^*A-za-ar-ilu*), ^uru^*Ḫi-ra-ta-a-qa-ṣa-a-a,* ^uru^ *Ú-du-me, ni-rib* ^uru^*Ia-ab-ru-du,* ^uru^*Bīt-*^m^*Am-ma-ni, ne-gi-e šá Ḫa-ú-ri-i-na,* ^uru^*Mu-'a-ba,* ^uru^*Sa-'-ar-ri,* ^uru^*Ḫa-ar-gi-e, na-gi-e šá* ^uru^*Ṣu-pi-ti/te.* (The words *ina gi-ra-a* head the list. This is a *hapax legomenon* in Assyrian, whose meaning is unknown. Is it possible that the determinative URU was lost, and that here, too, the reference is to a toponym [^uru^]*Gi-ra-a?).*

Among the toponyms in the list some are identifiable with key points along important routes, like Yabrūd Pass (*ni-rib* ^uru^*Ia-ab-ru-du*) and apparently also ^uru^*Ḫa-ar-gi-e.* (The latter may be derived from *ḫrg* = to go out, and may refer to a frontier-post from which a road went out from the border; cf. the names of the oases of Ḫargah = *exit* and Daḫlah = *entrance,* on the western approaches to Egypt). Hommel proposed linking ^uru^*Ḫa-ar-gi-e* with ^uru^*Ar-gi-te,* identified as a road station (*bīt mardīti*) in ABL 414, apparently on the Damascus-Ḥoms road (*EGAO,* 585, n. 5), but we have no certain identifying data. Problems arise with the province of ^uru^*Ḫa-ú-ri-i-na,* which some identify with the putative Ḫaurān province, mentioned in the inscriptions of Shalmanesser III and Tiglath-Pileser III as ^uru/kur^*Ḫa-ú-ra-a-(a-)ni; cf.* 'Αυρανῖτις, Arab. *Ḥaurān* (Forrer, *Provinzeinteilung,* 62-65, 69; B. Oded, *The Political Status of Israelite Transjordan during the Period of the Monarchy,* unpublished Ph. D. dissertation, Hebrew University, Jerusalem 1968, 63-64). This is doubtful, however, since the inscriptions of Assurbanipal use the spelling ^uru^*Ḫa-ú-ri-i-na,* and the shift in ending from *-an(i/u)* to *-īna* is unusual. On the other hand, connecting Ḫaurīna with Ḥawārīn in the environs of Yabrūd makes sense, even though the Assyrian sources do not clearly indicate that it was a provincial center (Delitzsch, *Paradies,* 297; S. Schiffer, *Die Aramäer,* Leipzig 1911, 139, n. 7; Streck, *Assurbanipal,* 65, n. 8; Musil, *Arabia Deserta,* 485; Lewy, *HUCA* 18 [1943-1944], 449 n. 107). Ḥawārīn is known later to have been an important point between Damascus and Palmyra, where military units were stationed and, during the Byzantine period, a diocese was centered (Musil, *Palmyrena,* 37-38, 235;

reduced to eating their children (Episode F).[515] The effect of the defeat on the subjects of Yauṭa' and the influence of Assurbanipal in the border regions near the inner cup of the Fertile Crescent prevented Yauṭa' from taking to the desert and resuming authority. He was forced to flee to the land of Nebaioth, farther than that of the Qedarites from Assyrian-controlled territory, to request sanctuary of their king, Natnu; but to no avail (Episodes G, M). Kingship of the Qedarites was assumed by Abiyaṭe' b. Te'ri, apparently not a member of the same family as Yauṭa' b. Ḫazael. Abiyaṭe' went to Nineveh, received Assurbanipal's consent that he replace Yauṭa', swore allegiance and bound himself to pay annual tribute (Episode H). Augmented Assyrian influence in the desert region impelled Natnu king of Nebaioth also to make an arrangement with Assurbanipal, pay annual tribute and swear allegiance (*adê sulummē epēš ardūti*)[516] (Episode N).

Dussaud, *Topographie historique de la Syrie antique et médiévale,* Paris 1927, 263, 265, 280, 317; cf. also I. Press, *A Topographical-Historical Encyclopaedia of Palestine,* II, Jerusalem 1948, 253, Hebrew).

The list further indicates that Assyrian military units were also stationed in the Transjordanian kingdoms — Edom, Ammon and Moab — either to strengthen these border lands against the nomads, as part of the general defense system of the Assyrian empire, or to serve as garrisons in vassal states (this disposition of the Assyrian army and its purposes were discussed by Oded, *JNES* 29 [1970], 184-186). The determinative URU before the names of the Transjordanian states in this list may indicate only capital cities, suggesting that the Assyrian armies were stationed there to ensure the local leadership's loyalty to the Assyrian king (for designating a capital city by the name of the country cf. עיר יהודה, "the city of Judah," II Chron. 25:28; *āl Ia-a-ḫu-du,* BM 21946 rev. 12, in Wiseman, *CCK,* 72, as synonym for Jerusalem). On the other hand, such punctilio may be unnecessary, given the imprecision of the Assyrian scribes of this period regarding determinatives of countries in the western part of the empire (cf. for example Esarhaddon, Nin. A v 55-62: ^{m}*Me-na-si-i šàr* ^{uru}*Ia-ú-di,* ^{m}*Qa-uš-gab-ri šàr* ^{uru}*Ú-du-me,* ^{m}*Mu-uṣ-ri šàr* ^{uru}*Ma-'-ab/ba,* ^{m}*Pu-du-ilu šàr* ^{uru}*Bīt-Am-ma-na.*

515 It should be pointed out that these statements are characteristic of the literature of the ancient Near East, and are not to be taken literally: some are to be found in ancient Near Eastern political treaties and others in biblical prophecies: For the suckling's unassuaged hunger in spite of seven wet-nurses, cf. D.R. Hillers, *Treaty-Curses and the Old Testament Prophets,* Rome 1964, 61-62; for cannibalism of children during famine cf. Hillers, *ibid.,* 62-63; Oppenheim, *Iraq* 17 (1955), 79, n. 34; cf. also note 531 below.

516 Prism C x (62-63); cf. B viii 59.

Source-Group A further reports the attack made by Ammuladi(n) king of Qedar on the western part of the Assyrian empire, and his defeat by ᵐ*Ka-ma-as-ḫal-ta-a* king of Moab (Episode J),[517] an episode probably depicted as well on reliefs in Assurbanipal's palace (the North Palace) in Nineveh.[518] Since the inscriptions of Assurbanipal refer to Yauṯa' b.

517 The defeat of Ammuladi by Kamasḫalta king of Moab is recorded only in the early group of sources (B viii 39 ff.; C x 36-43), the later sources ascribing the event to Assurbanipal himself (K 2802 v 15-25; K 4687 rev. 1-4; Rm. viii 15-23; *AfO* 8 [1932-1933], 200 No. 79; cf. Ištar Slab, 114). The ascription in later versions to the king of Assyria of personal victories in fact won by others (as recorded in earlier versions) is typical of the historiography of the Assyrian royal inscriptions.

518 The reliefs from Room L ("the Arab Room") in the Palace of Assurbanipal, depicting scenes of war against the Arabs, were recently and comprehensively republished by Barnett, *Sculptures from the North Palace of Ashurbanipal at Nineveh, (668-627 B.C.),* London 1975, pp. 15-16, 45; Pls. XXXII-XXXIII and C (for previous discussions of these reliefs see Opitz, *AfO* 7 [1931-1932], 7-13; J.E. Reade, *Iraq* 26 [1964], 8-9). These (some fragmentary, and others, of which we possess only the drawings made when the reliefs were discovered, lost) make up fewer than half of the reliefs that decorated this room. They can be divided into two (or three) groups: Group I — end of slab 3 and slabs 4-7 (slabs 1-2, and the part of slab 3 contiguous with them that forms the corner of the room, may belong to this group, or may be a separate episode); Group II — slabs 9-12 and perhaps slab 13.

In Group I, of which only drawings survive, three registers can be distinguished. On the middle register of slab 1 camels are kneeling in a line beside Arab warriors, each of whom stands holding a sword and a bow, as though in parade *before* battle. On the lower register, Assyrian soldiers — some in a chariot, some mounted and some on foot — pursue Arabs escaping on camels, reach an oasis and cut down its palm trees. Group II depicts an Assyrian raid — by chariot(s), horse- and foot-soldiers — on an Arab camp, setting fire to its tents, killing its inhabitants (including women) and pursuing those who escape on camels and on foot.

Since the reliefs from Room L, like most of the North Palace war reliefs, have no epigraphs, it is difficult to establish their exact relationship to all the episodes that for years connected Assurbanipal with the Arabs. Nothing links the reliefs with the war against Ammuladi and Adiya. Nevertheless, drafts (or copies) of epigraphs on clay tablets discovered in Assurbanipal's library, do imply the existence of reliefs showing the capture of Ammuladi and Adiya (for a comprehensive publication of these epigraphs see Weidner, *AfO* 8 [1932-1933], 175-203. The Arab-connected episodes are nos. 79-82 [p.200], dealing with the capture of Ammuladi king of Qedar and Adiya queen of the Arabs).

Also to be considered when attempting to date the episodes in the Room L reliefs is the fact that no reliefs relating to the conquest of Susa (in 646 B.C., see note 539) and the period thereafter were found in the North Palace. Furthermore, all the

Ḫazael as "king of the Qedarites" from the beginning of Assurbanipal's reign until the defeat of Yauṭa' in the west, when Abiyaṭe' b. Te'ri replaced him, Ammuladi presumably was another, contemporary, Qedarite king.[519] Ammuladi appears to have invaded the west at or close to the time when Yauṭa' did, and played a role integral to the complex of events reviewed above, which centered upon Qedarite pressure against the arable lands of the Syro-Arabian desert.

Although Source-Group A contains nothing about the Assyrian army assault on the camp of Adiya, her capture and transfer to Nineveh (Episode K), it obviously belongs in the same complex of events because: 1) In the later source-group (Group B) the Ammuladi and Adiya episodes (J and K) are consecutive, two links in a chain of events. In fact, the Rassam Cylinder records that the two were captured at the same time.[520] In the epigraph list (K 3096) the two episodes are also contiguous and the only ones dealing with Arabs.[521] 2) According to Rm. viii 24-25 Adiya was the consort of Yauṭa' king of the Arabs. If she had possessed this title (other inscriptions called her, without further definition, "queen of the Arabs"),[522] its significance would have obtained only while Yauṭa' was king of the Qedarites, until Abiyaṭe' b. Te'ri replaced him. It is possible to explain the absence of Episode K from Source-Group A by assuming that only events whose politico-military essence was clear were reported in this source-group and matters of secondary importance unrecorded.

If it is acceptable to include the Adiya episode in the events described, an interesting parallel can be drawn between that episode and the assault by Sennacherib's army on Te'elḫunu's camp near the Babylonian border.[523] Neither queen is said to have commanded armies

epigraphs published by Weidner antedate the conquest of Susa. On the implications of all this see notes 551 and 563.

519 For the designation of Yauṭa' as "king of Qedar" see Cyl. B (Streck) vii 87-88; cf. B (Piepkorn) vii 93-94; for the connection between Yauṭa' and the Qedarites see also Assurbanipal's treaty with them (see note 512). For the designation of Ammuladi as "king of Qedar" see B viii 39; cf. K 2802 v 15; Ištar Slab, 114; *AfO* 8 (1932-1933), 200, No. 79.

520 Cf. K 2802 v 21-30; K 4687 rev. 1-5; Rm. viii 24-26.

521 See note 518.

522 Cf. K 2802 v 26; *AfO* 8 (1932-1933), 200, Nos. 81-82.

523 Cf. VA 3310 rev. 22 ff.

which were defeated in battle; about both it is written only that their camps were attacked by the Assyrians. Evidently Adiya, like Te'elḫunu in her time, arrived with the nomads to invade the settled area and stayed in a camp sufficiently in the rear to be out of danger in case of defeat.

The nomad pattern of reorganizing at a reasonable distance from their pursuers after they had been defeated is paralleled in Judg. 8:10-12: "Now Zebah and Zalmunna were in Karkor with their army, about fifteen thousand men, all who were left of all the army of the People of the East; for there had fallen a hundred and twenty thousand men who drew the sword. And Gideon went up by the caravan route (lit.:The Way of the Tent-dwellers, דרך השכוני באהלים) east of Nobah and Jogbehah, and attacked the army; for the army was off its guard (והמחנה היה בטח). And Zebah and Zalmunna fled; and he pursued them and took the two kings of Midian, Zebah and Zalmunna, and he threw all the army into a panic (וכל המחנה החריד)." The distance of the rear camp to which the nomads fled on their camels certainly depends on the distance that their camel-less pursuers could cover without resorting to water sources. The fact that Assyrian infantry took part in the attack on the Arab camps along with cavalry and chariots (see the Assurbanipal reliefs) suggests that the camps were no more than 20-25 kilometers from the settled area. It is therefore difficult to countenance Musil's generally accepted identification of Karkor in Judg. 8:10 with Qerāqer in Wadi Sirḥān, which is about 170 kilometers from the edge of the settled region, and more then 250 from Israelite territory in Transjordan,[524] and exaggerates Israelite ability to pursue the Midianites.[525]

A more definite chronology for the episodes reviewed above can be established by further data and arguments:

a) The Šamaš-šum-ukin Chronicle states that he attacked Cutha on the 9th of second Elul, 651 B.C., and took it (BM 96273:7-10).[526] The event appears to be connected with ABL 1117, obv. 6-12, in which

524 Musil, *Northern Ḥeğâz,* 284-285; idem, *Arabia Deserta,* 494-495.

525 Doubt about Musil's proposed identification of Karkor has been raised by Malamat, in *Military History,* 120-121.

526 A.R. Millard, *Iraq* 26 (1964), 25-26; Grayson, *ABC,* 129.

Nabû-šum-lišir announced to Assurbanipal the delivery by Šamaš-šum-ukin of 105 prisoners, slaves of Assurbanipal who were taken at Cutha, by the envoys of Natnu the Nabayatean (the king of Nebaioth of the inscriptions of Assurbanipal).[527] At about the time Cutha was conquered (a few months after hostilities broke out between the kings of Assyria and Babylonia), therefore, contact between Natnu and Šamaš-šum-ukin seems to have been made, a fact brought to Assurbanipal's attention, as indicated by the discovery at Nineveh of the letter under consideration. In Source-Group A, however, Natnu still appears as Assurbanipal's vassal, with no link at all to enemies of Assyria,[528] which confirms Natnu's position vis-à-vis Assurbanipal *before* second Elul 651 B.C., a date that may serve as a *terminus ad quem* for the Arab episodes in Source-Group A.

b) Assurbanipal's siege of Babylon began, according to the Šamaš-šum-ukin Chronicle (line 19), on the 11th of Tammuz in Šamaš-šum-ukin's 18th regnal year (650 B.C.).[529] We know from Rm. viii 30-42 (Episode III) that Abiyaṭe' b. Te'ri and his men went to Babylon to support Šamaš-šum-ukin,[530] were within the city during Assurbanipal's siege and that famine past bearing befell them.[531] When the Arabs at some unknown stage attempted to break out of the city, they were overcome by the Assyrians. It is more logical to suppose that the Arab army entered the city *before* the onset of the siege, rather than that it forced its way into Babylon at the height of siege and famine. This would mean that Abiyaṭe' changed his policy and turned against

527 Millard, *ibid.*

528 Later Assyrian sources also disclose nothing about Natnu's aid to Šamaš-šum-ukin (cf., for example, Episodes I and III) either. The blandishments of the king of Babylon, including the bestowal of captives, seems not to have moved Natnu to join Assurbanipal's enemies.

529 Millard, *op. cit.*, 28; Grayson, *op. cit.*, 130.

530 On the aid Abiyaṭe' extended to Šamaš-šum-ukin cf. also Episode I.

531 The famine is described in the inscriptions of Assurbanipal referring to the "sixth campaign": Rm. iii 128-135, and, more elaborately, in Prism C from Nimrud, see E.E. Knudsen, *Iraq* 29 (1967), 55-56. The severity of the famine is corroborated by Babylonian "siege documents", five of which were discussed by Oppenheim, *Iraq* 17 [1955], 76-77. The dates of these legal documents and that of the Šamaš-šum-ukin Chronicle show that, although the effects of the siege were sorely manifest within a few months after it started, Babylon held out for about two more years.

Assurbanipal rather early — no later than the beginning of 650 B.C. — in the war between Assurbanipal and his brother. Further supporting this is the reference in Prism B (vii 3-29, 43-51) to the revolt of Šamaš-šum-ukin and the aid brought to him by Ummanigaš and Tammaritu, kings of Elam. The Akītu Chronicle (BM 86379:11) indicates that hostilities between Šamaš-šum-ukin and Assurbanipal broke out in January, 651 B.C.[532] Since Episode H in Source-Group A mentions only the beginning of Abiyaṭe' b. Te'ri's reign under Assurbanipal's patronage, and the annual tribute requested, not his collaboration with Šamaš-šum-ukin, Abiyaṭe' must have replaced Yauṭa' b. Ḫazael as king shortly before the beginning of the war between Assurbanipal and Šamaš-šum-ukin.

The Qedarite raids on the border regions of Transjordan and southern Syria under the leaderdhip of Yauṭa' and Ammuladi (Episodes C and J) therefore appear to have taken place prior to the war between Assurbanipal and Šamaš-šum-ukin, no later than 652 B.C. They should thus be viewed as an independent action, not resulting, as has been the common interpretation,[533] from joint initiative on the part of the Arabs and the king of Babylonia to operate simultaneously against the two extremities of the Assyrian empire.

3. Survey of Events Covered by Source-Group B:

The episodes added by this Group to those of Source-Group A fall into two chronological complexes: i) the war between Assurbanipal and Šamaš-šum-ukin (651-648 B.C.) and ii) the period following 646 B.C.

i) **651-648 B.C. (Episodes I, II?, III):** During the war in Babylonia between the two brothers, Qedarite forces led by Abiyaṭe' and Ayamu b. Te'ri, with warriors sent by Uaiṭa' b. Birdāda,[534] proceeded to Babylon to help Šamaš-šum-ukin (Episodes I, III).[535] According to Rm.

532 Smith, *BHT,* 24; Grayson, Chron. 16, *op. cit.,* 131; cf. Millard, *op. cit.,* 24.

533 See note 499.

534 In the inscriptions of Assurbanipal there is no direct connection between the Qedarites and Uaiṭe' b. Birdāda, whose title in the Ištar Slab is *šar* [kur]*Su-mu*-AN. For clarification of his identity see pp. 165-168.

535 Another example of a combined political stance of the Arabs and the inhabitants of Babylonia against Assyrian rule occurs in the days of Sennacherib (see pp. 112-117); it evidently sprang from common economic interests.

viii 30-42, they clashed with the Assyrian army and were defeated, the survivors retreating into the city proper. When they attempted to break out of the city because of the famine, the Arabs were beaten a second time. The Arab force entered Babylon in 651 or the beginning of 650 B.C., close to the start of the battle for the city (above pp. 154-155). Contrary to the general view,[536] this exhausts all the available data in the inscriptions of Assurbanipal regarding the military collaboration of the Arabs and Šamaš-šum-ukin.

It is reasonable to suppose that Yauṭa' b. Ḫazael[537] appeared before Assurbanipal and was punished in Nineveh (Episode II) during the period under discussion. Episode II states that Yauṭa' came but because he was out of his mind,[538] implying that he went to Nineveh on his own initiative, probably to arrive at an agreement with Assurbanipal. He would hardly, even though he had not been given sanctuary by Natnu king of Nebaioth, have gone to Nineveh during the period covered by Source-Group A. Not only was such an action not recorded in this Source-Group, but its proximity in time to his own disloyalty and the enthronement of Abiyaṭe' b. Te'ri, who had initially been loyal to the king of Assyria, makes such a possibility unlikely. It would have been more reasonable for Yauṭa' to have gone to Nineveh when Assurbanipal was at war with Šamaš-šum-ukin, who was at that time supported by Abiyaṭe'. According to this logic, Yauṭa' journeyed to Nineveh hoping that Assurbanipal would restore him to his former position as a counter-weight to Abiyaṭe', now in the rival camp. In any case, Rm. viii 8 ff. asserts that Aššurbanipal was inimical to Yauṭa' and punished his disloyalty, possibly because he thought Yauta' unable to resume his former leadership of the Qedarites.

536 For references regarding the accepted view, see note 499. For the contacts between Šamaš-šum-ukin and Natnu king of Nebaioth, and the question of the latter's political stance, see notes 526-527.

537 In the Rassam Cylinder, the only document containing Episode II, the name is written ^{m}*Ú-a-a-te-' mār* ^{m}*Ḫa-za-ilu* (viii 1). For the change from "*Yauta'*" to "*Uaita'*" in the later inscriptions of Assurbanipal see pp. 146-147 and also pp. 51-52.

538 The insanity of Yauṭa' is also mentioned in the Letter to Aššur (K 2802 v 37-38) but in a context different from that of the Rassam Cylinder. The statement about his condition, because of its position in the Letter to Aššur, interrupts the narrative flow, and the reason for its inclusion is not clear. On this point the literary structure of the Rassam Cylinder seems preferable.

ii) **After 646 B.C. (Episodes IV, Q-X):** This complex describes the Assyrian military campaign against Arab tribal federations led by Abiyaṭe' b. Te'ri king of Qedar, Uaiṭe'(b. Birdāda) king of ^{kur}*Su-mu*-AN and Natnu king of Nebaioth. Certain information and arguments serve to establish the date of this campaign: Uaiṭe' (b. Birdāda), captured in the campaign, was forced into Assurbanipal's victory procession in Nineveh some time after the Arab defeat, as were Tammaritu, Pa'e and Ummanaldaš, the kings of Elam (Episodes U, W). The victory procession had to take place after the destruction of Susa and the capture of Ummanaldaš (in Elamite, Ḫumban Ḫaltaš III). The conquest and destruction of Susa, the last event on Prism F of Assurbanipal, written in 645 B.C., should be set in 646 B.C.,[539] and not in 640 B.C., the date generally accepted before publication of the prism.[540] No mention is made here of the capture of Ummanaldaš, who fled before Susa was conquered and was later handed over to the king of Assyria by the people of Ellipi.[541] The Rassam Cylinder (x 6-16), written about 643/2 B.C.,[542] is the first to note his capture, which must have taken place no later than 644 B.C.,[543] and might have been a year earlier, thus dating the major campaign against the Arabs to 644/3 B.C.[544] This campaign might in fact have occurred as early as 645 B.C., in a way a preferable date (see below). It need not be connected with another extensive campaign against Elam after the destruction of Susa since, as indicated above, Ummanaldaš was not captured by the Assyrians but transferred to them by the people of Ellipi.

The campaign under discussion was fomented by raids on the borders of the Assyrian empire by the peoples of Qedar and Nebaioth (Rm. viii 72). It appears from the line of advance of the Assyrian army that the

539 Prism F was written in the *limmu* of Nabû-šar-aḫḫēšu, the governor of Samerīna, see J.M. Aynard, *Le Prisme du Louvre AO 19.939,* Paris 1957. For dating this post-canonical eponym in 646/5 B.C. see Ungnad, *RLA,* II, 452; Falkner, *AfO* 17 (1955-1956), 113-114, 118.

540 Streck, *Assurbanipal,* CCCXLV; cf.. Malamat, *IEJ* 3 (1953), 26-29.

541 See W. Hinz, *Das Reich Elam,* Stuttgart 1964, 132; cf. Streck, *ibid.,* CCCXLIII ff.

542 See Tadmor, *25th Congress,* 240 (*contra* Streck, Ungnad and Falkner, who date this prism as late as 636 B.C.).

543 See Hinz, *ibid.,* 132.

544 See Tadmor, *op. cit.,* who disagrees with Streck's dating, which ranges between 641-638 B.C. (Streck, *ibid.,* CCLXXXV).

nomads involved dwelt in the Palmyrena region (see below for details of the route) and had been threatening the area from Jebel Bishri to the vicinity of Damascus.

We know from the inscriptions of Assurbanipal that Abiyaṭe' and Ayamu, the sons of Te'ri, as well as Uaiṭe' (b. Birdāda) helped Šamaš-šum-ukin in his war against his brother, but we have no specific information about Natnu's stance in that war. Although initially it seems strange that the inscriptions fail to report that the offending leaders were punished and displaced by the Assyrian king after his victory in Babylon, examination of the state of the Assyrian empire prior to the Arab campaign offers some explanation: Between the conquests of Babylon and Susa the Assyrian army fought in Elam in two campaigns which took place, according to Prism F, in 647 and 646 B.C.,[545] and culminated in the capture of Susa. Because the army was actively occupied in the east between 651 and 646 B.C. — first in Babylonia and then in Elam — it could not undertake large-scale action in other parts of the empire, to the pronounced advantage of the west: Egypt could retain the independence it had recently achieved from Assyrian rule,[546] and the cities of southern Phoenicia could rebel against Assyria.[547] Another by-product may have been the capture of Manasseh king of Judah by the commanders of the army of the king of Assyria,

545 According to Prism F, these are the fifth (iii 33—iv 16) and sixth (iv 17—vi 21) campaigns, paralleling the Rassam Cylinder's seventh (iv 110—v 62) and eighth (v 63—vii 81). On their course see Hinz, *ibid.,* 130-132.

546 The available sources do not specifically mention the liberation of Egypt from Assyrian rule, an event conventionally related in Rm. ii 114 ff. to the assistance Gyges king of Lydia ([m]*Gu-(ug)-gu šar* [kur]*Lu-ud-di*) gave to Psammetichus I (in the Rassam Cylinder [m]*Pi-ša-me-il-ki*) king of Egypt in his revolt against Assurbanipal. In such a case, the *terminus ad quem* for the event is established by the death of Gyges around 652 B.C. Herodotus II, 152, in his account of the assistance given Psammetichus by Ionian and Carian mercenaries, may also be referring to this event. See also Streck, *op. cit.,* CCLXXIX; Smith, *CAH,* III, 115; von Zeissel, *Äthiopen und Assyrer in Ägypten,* 49-50; Drioton-Vandier, *L'Egypte*[4], 574-576; F.K. Kienitz, *Die Politische Geschichte Ägyptens vom 7. bis 4. Jahrhundert vor der Zeitwende,* Berlin 1953, 11-12; R. Labat, *Fischer Weltgeschichte* 4, 87; Kitchen, *Third Intermediate Period of Egypt,* 402, 405-406.

547 In Rm. ix 115-128, following the description of the campaign against the Arabs, there is an episode concerning the punishment of the people of Palaityros ([uru]*Ušû*) and Acco ([uru]*Ak-ku-u*), who offended the Assyrian king by ceasing to pay tribute.

and the fortification of his kingdom *after* his return from Babylonia, as reported in II Chron. 33:11 ff.[548] In other words, Manasseh maintained his anti-Assyrian policy.[549] (In a similar situation Zedekiah was commanded to appear before the suzerain and nonetheless subsequently continued to undermine Babylonian control). Thus, given the situation in other regions in the western part of the empire, the silence in Assyrian sources about punishing of Arabs who had assisted the king of Babylonia can be explained by Assurbanipal's inability to take real action against them, and in fact by his loss of control over the desert dwellers (usually the first group to break away when political hegemony weakens). Since Assurbanipal had no choice but to let them alone, their pressure on the Middle Euphrates and Palmyrena regions increased. Only after victory over Elam could the Assyrian army correct the situation in the west.

The later inscriptions of Assurbanipal report the last campaign against the Arabs,[550] most of it conducted in desert terrain. The report

They probably did so when the chance of reprisal seemed slight, rather than when the Assyrian army was waging a campaign to the west.

Weakening of Assyrian control in the west may have started even earlier and is further illustrated by a deed of sale from Gezer, dated Sivan 17th, eponymy "which is after (*limmu ša arki*) Aššur-dūr-uṣur, governor of Barḫalza" (C.H.W. Johns, in R.A.S. Macalister, *The Excavation of Gezer, 1902-1905 and 1907-1909,* I, London 1911, 25). It points to the fact that two and a half months after the beginning of the year the name of the eponym for 651 B.C. had not reached Gezer; see Eph'al, *WHJP,* IV/1, 281-282.

548 Manasseh's abolition of Hezekiah's cultic and religious reform and his introduction of foreign cults into the Temple (cf. II Kings 21:3-7; II Chron. 33:3-7) are generally considered to illustrate Judah's total dependence on Assyria (see J. Liver, "Manasseh," *Enc. Miqr.* V, 44-45, including bibliography). Accordingly, the report in II Chron. 33:15 that Manasseh later removed the cults seems to prove his anti-Assyrian political stance. For a different approach, which dissociates these cults from Assyria and thus denies their political significance, see Cogan, *Imperialism and Religion.*

549 There are indications that Assyrian power had already begun to decline in the west during the last years of Manasseh's reign, and not, as is generally thought, in Josiah's (for the generally accepted view see F.M. Cross-D.N. Freedman, *JNES* 12 [1953], 56-58; cf. also Liver, "Josiah", *Enc. Miqr.,* III, 417, 420, 424, including bibliography).

550 K 2802 vi 2-43, iii 1-34; K 2664 + K 3090 v 1-13; Rm. viii 48-51, 65-124, ix 1-41, 90-114, x 1-5, 17-39; cf. K 3405 rev. 7-12; Ištar Slab, 113, 118-121, 124-129.

contains two dates which point to the length of the campaign: On the 25th of Sivan the Assyrian army set out from Ḫadattâ for Laribda, which was either in or on the edge of the desert (K 2802 vi 17-21; Rm. viii 96-100; on the 3rd of Ab it left Damascus for Ḫulḫuliti (K 2802 iii 11-13; Rm. ix 9-12) and proceeded to the Mount Ḫukkurina region, where it overcame the nomads by attacking them and seizing all the nearby water sources. The campaign as a whole therefore lasted for about three months. So long a campaign by the Assyrian army against so negligible an enemy is understandable only by reason of Assurbanipal's desire to subdue the nomads once and for all. This could be accomplished only by a combination of frequent assaults on oases and encampments, long-range pursuit of the survivors into the desert, and seizure of the water sources vital to them and their livestock.[551] (Because the campaign took place in the dry season — Sivan-Ab, i.e., July-August — the Arabs had to stay with their livestock near the settled land and could not, as was customary, take refuge in the desert). Assurbanipal's determination to disempower the nomads by burdening his army with so strenuous a campaign reflects the degree of the nomads' threat to the border regions of his kingdom.

Episodes Q to T chart the essential campaign route in a three-part description, each part concerned with a specific section of the route and the attack made on a particular group of nomads. Episode Q outlines the first part of the campaign, starting at Ḫadattâ and continuing through desert terrain between Laribda, Ḫurarina and Yarki and ending in Azalla. The second part (Episode R) proceeds from Azalla to Quraṣiti, from which point captives and booty were transported via the "Damascus Road" (*ḫarrān* $^{uru/kur}$*Di-maš-qa*). The third part (Episode S) begins in Damascus, continues with a night march to Ḫulḫuliti and ends with a final blow to the Arabs in the Mount Ḫukkurina region. Since the line of march to Damascus is described as scarce in water sources, the Assyrian army must have moved from the east through the desert to Damascus, and not along the Ḥama-Ḥoms-Damascus route, where water abounds. Thus Yarki can be identified with Arak, about 27 kms

551 The same combination of elements obtains in the fragmentary reliefs found in Room L ("the Arab Room") of Assurbanipal's palace in Nineveh. The parallelism is typological only, however, since these reliefs appear to deal with episodes earlier than the campaign under discussion; see note 518.

east of Tadmor (Palmyra), but the other points of the march to Damascus and Mount Ḫukkurina are less easily identifiable because our data are not clear enough. The ensuing discussion of the topography of the route draws mainly on Musil, whose survey is the most extensive.[552] Certain of his proposals are based on phonological similarity between contemporary toponyms and those in the inscriptions of Assurbanipal, and others on key points along the desert routes from Damascus to the Euphrates through the Jebel Bishri region (after the probable route is determined from the meager data available).

First Part (Episode Q):

uru*Ḫa-da-at-ta-a:* This is undoubtedly a rendering of the Aramaic toponym חדתא. Musil assumed that the Assyrian army crossed the Euphrates in the Meskeneh region and consequently proposed identifying Ḫadattâ with the al-Jadîdah (the exact Arabic equivalent of Aramaic חדתא) ruins, on the border between the desert and the settled land. E. Honigmann's suggested relationship of Ḫadattâ with the *Adatha* of *Notitia dignitatum,* or. XXXII, 29,[553] is untenable, since Adatha was close to and apparently west of Tadmor (Palmyra),[554] whereas Ḫadattâ of the inscriptions of Assurbanipal was near the Euphrates.

uru*La-ri-ib-da:* This is described as a fortress of unhewn stone, from whose water cisterns the Assyrian soldiers drank deeply before penetrating the desert. Musil suggested locating it either in the Jebb al-

552 Musil, *Arabia Deserta,* 487-489; cf. idem, *Palmyrena,* 76, 86. For exhaustive discussion of the campaign see also Glaser, *Skizze,* 273-278, 309-314; Hommel, *EGAO,* 590-591; and recently Weippert, *WO* 7 (1973), 63-66. Glaser's and Hommel's proposed identifications are valueless, since they are based on erroneous assumptions. (Glaser assumed that Assyrian imperial rule in the 8th and 7th centuries extended to Oman and Yamāma and Jebel Šammar, and therefore located places referred to in Assurbanipal's campaign against the Arabs in the area south of Tema' and Khaibar. Hommel's assumption that the campaign took place along the Kūfa-Jauf-Wadi Sirḥān-Damascus axis is unacceptable, since the Assyrians could not have waged so extensive a campaign without wide use of camels). For a discussion of various details of the campaign (the most important of which will be indicated below), see also Delitzsch, *Paradies,* 298-301.

553 Cf. *PW,* Reihe II, VIII, 1601; Lewy, *HUCA* 19 (1945-1946), 423-424.

554 Thus Dussaud, *Topographie historique,* 270-271, locates Hadatha about five kilometers north of Hawārîn.

Qdeim well region at the edge of al-Labdeh range, or some 40 kms southeast of the oasis of 'Urd (present-day aṭ-Ṭaiyibah) at the southwestern end of Jebel Bishri. The second proposal seems more likely, since the 'Urḑ oasis is on the central thoroughfare between Damascus-Tadmor and the Euphrates, while Jebb al-Qdeim is remote from it, on a side road to Aleppo.

^{uru}*Ḫu-ra-ri-na:* Which Musil proposed identifying with Qal'at al-Ḥurri in the Palmyrena range, some 15 kms northwest of Arak.

^{uru}*Ia-ar-ki:* This is present-day Arak, spelled in Byzantine and later sources *Harac, Yarecca,* and *Aracha,* about 27 kms east of Tadmor, and a key point on the road from 'Urḑ (at-Ṭaiyibah) to Tadmor-Damascus. Armies were stationed there during various periods.[555]

^{uru}*A-ṣa/za-al-la:* Which Musil proposed identifying with al-'Elyaniya at the end of the 'Azzāleh valley.

In a kind of summary, K 2802 vi 29-40 and Rm. viii 107-119 say that the Assyrian troops defeated the ^{lú}*I-sa-am-me-'*, ^{lú}*a'-lu ša* ^{d}*A-tar-sa-ma-a-a-in* ("the confederation of the god Ȧtarsamâin") and ^{lú}*Na-ba-a-a-ta-a-a* in the region between Yarki and Azalla, taking many captives, donkeys, camels, sheep and goats, and, after having travelled a distance of 8 *bēru* (about 86 kms) in the desert, returned to Azalla for water.

It should be noted that the Tadmor (Palmyra) oasis, known from documents from the 18th century B.C. on as the main stop on the principal desert routes from Mt. Lebanon to the Middle Euphrates,[556] is omitted from the campaign report. Since it is unlikely that Assurbanipal's scribe omitted Tadmor out of forgetfulness or error, the probability is that the Assyrian army detoured to one of the secondary routes from Yarki to Azalla. Musil's suggested identification of Azalla provides some support for this view, since al-'Elyaniya can be reached from Arak by a side road from Tadmor. This

555 Benzinger, *PW,* II, 366; H. Hartmann, *ZDPV* 23 (1900), 134; Musil, *Palmyrena,* 86 n. 22; cf. Honigmann, *ZDPV* 46 (1923), 162.

556 Tadmor (*Ta-ad-mi-ir*^{ki}) appears in *ARM* V 23:16 in connection with the attack of the Sutians, and also, as ^{uru}*Ta-ad-mar,* in the descriptions of the wars of Tiglath-Pileser I with the Aramaeans from Babylonia's western border to the Middle Euphrates and the foothhills of the Lebanon (Weidner, *AfO* 18 [1957-1958], 344:31; 350:35). For a list of sources on Palmyra (Tadmor) from the first millennium B.C. on, see Dussaud, *Topographie historique,* 247 ff.; *Musil, Palmyrena,* 233-255; J.G. Février, *Essai sur l'histoire politique et économique de Palmyre,* Paris 1931.

view of course presupposes either that the Arab raiders did not reach Tadmor or managed to get away before Assurbanipal's troops arrived.

Second Part (Episode R):

^{uru}*Qu-ra-ṣi-ti:* Which Musil identified with Bîr al-Baṣîri, the confluence of routes to Tadmor, Qaryatein, Damascus and al-'Elyaniya. K 2802 vi 41-43, iii 1-10, and Rm. viii 120—ix 8 give the distance covered by the Assyrian troops in the desert between Azalla and Quraṣiti as six *bēru* (about 65 kms). In this region the main camp of ^{lú}*a'-lu ša* ^{d}*A-tar-sa-ma-a-in ù* ^{lú}*Qid-ra-a-a ša* ^{m}*Ú-a-a-te-'mār* ^{m}*Bīr-da-ad-da šar* ^{kur}*A-ri-bi* ("the confederation of the god Atarsamâin and the Qedarites of Uaiṭe' son of Birdāda king of the Arabs")[557] was attacked and booty, dispatched via the "Damascus road" (*ḫarrān* $^{uru/kur}$*Di-maš-qa*), was taken: divine images, the mother, sister (Letter to Aššur says "sisters") and family of Uaiṭe', and "all the people of the Qedarites" (*nišê* ^{kur}*Qí-id-ri ka-la-ma*),[558] as well as donkeys, camels and quantities of sheep and goats.

Third Part (Episode S):

At this point the Assyrian army left Damascus and swiftly marched 6 *bēru* (65 kms) through the night to ^{uru}*Ḫul-ḫu-li-ti* (so Rm.; Letter to Aššur has [^{uru}*Ḫ*]*ul-ḫu-li*), which Delitzsch acceptably identified with the village of Ḥulḥuleh in the northeastern part of al-Leja region.[559] The distance between this village and Damascus corresponds exactly to the data in the Assyrian inscriptions. The strenuous Assyrian advance, under cover of darkness, favors the assumption that the nomads against whom they were marching were camped not far from Ḫulḫuliti. At or near Mount *Ḫu-uk-ku-ri/ru-na* the nomads were beaten, Abiyaṭe' and Ayamu, the sons of Ṭe'ri, captured, and booty taken (K 2802 iii 17 ff. and Rm. ix 15 ff.). The surviving nomads sought refuge on Mount Ḫukkurina itself, at all of whose surrounding water points the Assyrians stationed sentries, so that eventually the Arabs succumbed to thirst. The water points, unfortunately unidentifiable, are listed in Rm. ix 27-30: ^{uru}*Ma-an-ḫa-ab-bi,* ^{uru}*Ap-pa-ru,* ^{uru}*Te-nu-qu-ri,* ^{uru}*Za-a-a-ú-ra-an,* ^{uru}*Mar-*

557 In the Letter to Aššur the words *ù* ^{lú}*Qid-ra-a-a,* apparently not part of the original text, are added; about this see note 565.

558 Oppenheim, *ANET,* 299 n. 13, considers that here and in other Neo-Assyrian inscriptions *nišê* means *women.* If this is correct, the characteristics of such a rear camp become even clearer.

559 Delitzsch, *op. cit.,* 299; cf. Musil, *Arabia Deserta,* 489.

qa-na-a, ^{uru}*Sa-da-te-in,* ^{uru}*En-zi-kar-me,* ^{uru}*Ta-'-na-a* and ^{uru}*Ir-ra-a-na.*[560] Since *Ḫulḫuliti* is Ḥulḥuleh the water points must have been on the eastern fringe of al-Leja region, so that Musil's location of Mount Ḫukkurina in the Tulul al-'Iyaṯ area east of Damascus becomes untenable, both because it is far removed from Ḥulḥuleh, and is arid and without springs and nearby settlements.[561]

The success, in all its stages, of the campaign against the Arabs, and fear of further Assyrian action, gave rise to rebellion against Uaiṯa'. He fled, but was captured, possibly even with the connivance of his own people, and taken to Assyria (Episode U).

No further action against the Arabs is mentioned in the Letter to Aššur and the Rassam Cylinder, but in the Slab Inscription from the temple of Ištar, written later,[562] Assurbanipal is said to have turned against Natnu king of Nebaioth also (Episode X; see also note 156). Lines 124-129 refer to a punitive campaign against the people of Nebaioth and the complete destrucation of their settlements.[563] Natnu, his wife and children, and much booty were captured by Assyrian troops. Natnu's son, Nuḫuru, escaped but later surrendered to Assurbanipal, bringing heavy tribute, and was made king in his father's

560 Delitzsch (*op. cit.*, 301) raised the possibility of identifying ^{uru}*En-zi-kar-me* with the village of 'Anz in the South Hauran and ^{uru}*Ir-ra-a-na* with 'Ein er-Rān near Busān in East Hauran. One at least has to be rejected, however, because of the distance between them. Oded's (*JNES* 29 [1970], 185 n. 57) identification of ^{uru}*Ap-pa-ru,* discussed here, with *Afaris* in Wadi Ḥafaris on the southeastern border of the land of Moab must also be rejected, because the places listed in this section of the Rassam Cylinder were in northern Transjordan.

561 See Caskel, in *Fischer Weltgeschichte* 4, 352 n. 11. For a suggested identification of Mount Ḫukkurina in al-Leja region and its link to *ḥlkr* in Egyptian inscriptions see Na'aman and Zadok, *Tel Aviv* 4 (1977), 172-174.

562 Tadmor (*25th Congress,* 240) sets the time of composition at about 640 B.C., two or three years after the Rassam Cylinder.

563 On slabs 5-7 of the Room L ("the Arab Room") reliefs in Assurbanipal's palace, Assyrian soldiers are cutting down palm trees in a captured oasis. The passage in the Ištar Slab, line 125, is the only one of all the Assurbanipal inscriptions to mention devastation of permanent Arab settlements; all other passages seem to refer to temporary camps. As against the possibility of allying the discussed reliefs with Episode U, however, stands the reservation about the *terminus ad quem* of the reliefs of Room L; see note 518.

place. The absence of Episode X from the Letter to Aššur and the Rassam Cylinder and the statement in the Slab Inscription about an assault on oases where permanent settlement existed suggest that the campaign against Natnu was a separate operation from the one described in Episodes Q to V, and took place under different circumstances, along a different route (in the Wadi Sirḥān area or south of it?), some time after the major campaign.

In sum, in the historical inscriptions of Assurbanipal we can distinguish three phases of the war against the Arabs during his reign: against the Qedarites on the border of southern Syria and Transjordan (in 652 B.C. or earlier), against the troops advancing from the desert to Babylon to assist Šamaš-šum-ukin (in 651 or early 650 B.C.) and against the nomad federations in the Palmyrena region (c. 645 B.C.). It is also possible that the campaign against Natnu king of Nebaioth (Episode X) was a later, fourth, phase. At least two of these phases, those involving vaster operations, were connected with nomad incursions from the Syro-Arabian desert and their pressure on extensive border regions in Transjordan, southern Syria and the Jebel Bishri area. These episodes marked the beginning of a protracted struggle in the western half of the cup of the Fertile Cresent. The nomads, repressed in the second half of the 7th and early 6th centuries B.C. by the countries in the region, supported by Assyrian and later by Babylonian armies, so increasingly exerted pressure during the Chaldaean and Achaemenid periods that they finally penetrated the settled areas, including Palestine.

4. Nomad Leaders According to Groupings During Assurbanipal's Reign:

The inscriptions of Assurbanipal differ from other Assyrian royal inscriptions in that they supply names and personal data for the leaders of the various nomad groups in the Syro-Arabian desert, instead of using the general term $^{kur/lú}$*Aribi.* Certain groups and individuals will now be considered.

a. **Yauṭa' king of Qedar and Uaiṭe' king of ^{kur}Su-mu-(')-AN:**

Beginning with the Letter to Aššur (and excepting the Ištar Slab Inscription from Nineveh, on which see note 511) in the inscriptions of Assurbanipal, as listed in the chart after p. 166, the appellation ^{m}*Ú-a-a-te-' šar* ^{kur}*Aribi* designates both Yauṭa' b. Ḫazael[564] and Uaiṭe' b.

564 K 2802 v 37; Rm. vii 83, viii 25; cf. viii 46-47.

Birdāda.[565] In other inscriptions of Assurbanipal, we read ^{m}*Ia-u-ta-' šar* ^{kur}*Qidri/Qadri* for Yauṭa' b. Ḫazael[566] and ^{m}*Ú-a-a-te-' šar* ^{kur}*Su-mu*-AN for Yauṭa' b. Birdāda.[567] The people of ^{kur}*Su-mu*-AN led by Uaiṭa' are undoubtedly identical with those of ^{lú}*Su-mu-'*-AN, who appear with the people of ^{lú}*Te-e-me* in the inscriptions of Sennacherib.[568]

Fr. Delitzsch, followed by R. C. Thompson, reading *Sumu(')*-AN as *Sumu(')il,* interpreted the name as a development of *Ishmael,* the biblical designation for nomadic tribes in the Syro-Arabian and North Sinai deserts.[569] J. Lewy, in agreement, and because of the identical title *šar* ^{kur}*Aribi* applied to both kings, and especially because of the confusion of their names in the inscriptions of Assurbanipal and the statement in Rm. viii 1-2 that the two were cousins, concluded that the titles *šar* ^{kur}*Aribi, šar* ^{kur}*Sumu(')il* and *šar* ^{kur}*Qidri* all refer to the same person (Yauṭa' b. Ḫazael), and hence that the first two are synonymous, applied to the leader whose specific title was "king of the Qedarites".[570] If Lewy were right, the Assyrian sources would demonstrate a clear link, even an identity, between the terms "Ishmaelites" and "Arabs". Given the fact that "Ishmaelite(s)" appears only in biblical sources antedating David's reign, and "Arab(s)" only in sources from mid-9th century B.C. on, and that the Bible makes no connection between the Arabs and Ishmael,[571] such an assumption is of special interest. But it must, nevertheless, be rejected:

565 K 2802 vi 15; Rm. viii 93, ix 1-2, x 21. Although K 2802 iii: (1) ^{lú}*a'-lu šá* ^{d}*A-tar-sa-ma-a-a-in* (2) *ù* ^{lú}*Qid-ra-a-a ša* ^{m}*Ú-a-a-te-'* (3) *mār* ^{m}*Bir-da-ad-da šar* ^{kur}*A-ri-bi* (4) *ù* ^{lú}*Qid-ra-a-a al-me,* "I surrounded the confederation of the god Atarsamâin and the Qedarites, of Uaiṭe' b. Birdāda, king of the Arabs, and the Qedarites," implies that Uaiṭe' b. Birdāda was titled "king of the Arabs and the Qedarites"; the absence of *ù* ^{kur}*Qid-ra-a-a* in the parallel section of Rm. ix 2 suggests that the verbal repetition in the Letter to Aššur was due to the scribal error of copying on line 4 what appeared in line 2.

566 Cyl. B (Streck), vii 87-88; cf. B (Piepkorn) vii 93-94. That Yauṭa' was king of the Qedarites is corroborated by Assurbanipal's treaty with them, published by Deller-Parpola, *Orientalia* 37 (1968), 464 f.

567 *AAA* 20 (1933), 86:113 (cf. line 119: ^{m}*Ia-u-te-' šar* ^{kur}*Su-mu*-AN).

568 BM 103,000 vii 96 (see note 434).

569 Fr. Delitzsch, *Assyrische Lesestücke*^{5}, Leipzig 1912, 183; Thompson, *AAA* 20 (1933), 98.

570 Lewy, *HUCA* 19 (1945-1946), 432, n. 143; cf. also Weippert, *WO* 7 (1973), 669.

571 See pp. 60-63 and also Appendix B.

1. The phonetic development *Yišma''el* > *Sumu'il* is insupportable. Moreover, Yišma''el is a proper name with a verbal construction which, in the *Iqtal, Yaqtal* forms, is found in documents as early as those from Ibla (where it is spelled ^m^*Iš-má-il*),[572] the Akkad period (where it is spelled ^m^*Iš-ma-i-lum,* ^m^*Iš-ma*-AN)[573] and the Old Babylonian period (where it is spelled ^m^*Ia-ás-ma-aḫ*-AN).[574] The names ^m^*Ia-si-me-'*-AN, ^m^*Iš-me*-AN, of the same construction also appear in Neo-Assyrian documents from Gozan and Calah.[575] It is therefore most unlikely that the scribes of Sennacherib and Assurbanipal transcribed Ishmael as *Sumu'ilu,*[576] which is a proper name with a nominative construction. The Hebrew transcription of Sumu'ilu would be *שְׁמֻאֵל or *שֻׁמְאֵל, but surely not ישמעאל.[577]

2. Yauṭa' b. Ḫazael, king of the Qedarites, was succeeded by Abiaṭe' b. Te'ri (episode H), whose leadership ended at the same time as that of Uaiṭe' b. Birdāda (cf. Episodes S and U). They must therefore have been contemporaries.

3. Since we have seen that it is possible to distinguish between Yauṭa' b. Ḫazael and Uaiṭe' b. Birdāda, whatever their titles in the inscriptions

572 G. Pettinato, *BA* 39 (1976), 50.

573 Unger, *RA* 54 (1960), 177-178; I.J. Gelb, *Sargonic Texts from the Diyala Region,* Chicago 1952, 208-209.

574 S.D. Simmons, *JCS* 14 (1960), 27 No. 55:11; Huffmon, *Amorite Personal Names in the Mari Texts,* 64, 249-250. For verbal proper names from the root *šemû* see also J.J. Stamm, *Die akkadische Namengebung,* Leipzig 1939, 147, 166-167, 189, 241, 319; for various examples of this name is West-Semitic sources, see M. Noth, *Die israelitischen Personennamen im Rahmen der gemeinsemitischen Namengebung,* Stuttgart 1928, 28, 198.

575 J. Friedrich *et alii, Die Inschriften vom Tell Halaf,* Berlin 1940, 62, No. 111; J.N. Postgate, *The Governor's Palace Archive,* London 1973, p. 43, No. 14:21, respectively.

576 The reading AN=*ilu* in the name *Su-mu-(')*-AN seems preferable to AN=*il,* since in Assyrian spelling proper names conventionally end with a vowel and not a consonant.

577 Winnett, *AR,* 93-96, suggests connecting ^lú^*Sumu(')-AN with Sm'l,* which occurs in two inscriptions of about the sixth century B.C. from the region of Tema', and is either the name of a place or of a group of nomads. But this would still not support the theory identifying *Sumu(')*-AN and Ishmael, since its validity is based on conjecture unsupported by evidence. For further discussion of this matter, see Eph'al, *JNES* 35 (1976), 229-231.

of Assurbanipal,[578] it seems apparent that the names Qedar and *Sumu(')*AN stand for two groups of differing sizes. *Šar* ^{kur}*Aribi* is the general title for both leaders and provides no clue to their status or the extent of their dominion.

At the same time, since, during the major campaign against the Arabs, the Qedarites and perhaps also the *a'lu ša* ^{d}*Atarsamâin* are said to have been led by Uaiṭe' b. Birdāda (Episode R), he may have had Qedarite connections. In other words, the people of *Sumu(')*AN under his leadership may have been members of the larger Qedarite confederation (for the social implications of this possibility and for other examples of Qedarite ramifications, see Appendix A, 11).

Uaiṭe' b. Birdāda and Abiyaṭe' b. Te'ri, who became chief of the Qedarites after Yauṭa' b. Ḫazael was deposed in about 652 B.C., are known collborators from the time they both dispatched men to help Šamaš-šum-ukin at the start of his war against Assurbanipal (Episode I). They were eventually captured by the Assyrian king, sent to Nineveh, and Uaiṭe' was put on display at the city gate with a rope strung through a hole in his cheek. Later he was forced to take part in Assurbanipal's triumphal procession along with the kings of Elam (Episodes U and W). Nothing, however, is known of the fate of Abiyaṭe'.

b. **Abiyaṭe' and Ayamu, sons of Te'ri:**

The inscriptions of Assurbanipal record two leaders whose father's name was ^{m}*Te-'-(e)-ri.*[579] One, Abiyaṭe', who replaced Yauṭa' b. Ḫazael as king of the Qedarites, appears in Prism B, in the Letter to Aššur and in the Rassam Cylinder;[580] the other, Ayamu, appears only in the later sources.[581] These, although sometimes referring to ^{m}***A-bi-ia-te-'*** ^{m}***A-a-(am)-mu mār*** ^{m}***Te-'-(e)-ri,***[582] never use the plural DUMU.MEŠ =*mārē* or the conjunction *u* between the two names. Two or even three given names, in fact, are not uncommon among South Arabian rulers in later periods,[583] and in some of the passages

578 See pp. 51-52, and also pp. 146-147.

579 For the connection of ^{m}*Te-'-(e)-ri* with the name of the moon god *Šhr*>Ṯhr, see Lewy, *HUCA* 19 (1945-1946), 425.

580 B viii 31; Rm. viii 65 (77, 94), ix 16; K 2802 iii 18-19, v 6; see also note 582.

581 Rm. x 1-2; see also note 582.

582 Rm. vii 97, viii 31, ix 19-20; K 2802 iii 22, 25 (in line 25 the proper names are superfluous, apparently recorded through scribal error).

considered, therefore, Abiyaṭe' Ayamu might indicate one person (Rm. vii 97, viii 31). However, despite the difficulty of explaining the nomenclature appearing above, Rm. ix 19-20, x 1-2 and K 2802 iii 22 make it clear that we are dealing with two brothers. The Qedarite chieftain Abitaṭe' b. Te'ri, was entitled *šar* ^{kur}*Qidri* after he swore allegiance to and concluded a treaty with Assurbanipal (Episode H and Rm. viii 65-68; cf. also K 2802 iii 18-20and Rm. ix 16-17, giving his name to the confederation of ^{lú}*a'-lu ša* ^{m}*A-bi-ia-te-' mār* ^{m}*Te-'-ri* ^{kur}*Qid-ra-a-a).* He was joined by his brother Ayamu in leading the Arab forces to Babylon to support Šamaš-šum-ukin (Episodes I, III) and certainly also in raiding the Assyrian border and in the last campaign against the Arabs. Both were captured during that campaign and taken to Nineveh (K 2802 iii 22-29; Rm. ix 19-24, and Episode V). Ayamu was skinned alive (Episode V), but about Abiyaṭe', supreme Qedarite leader and violator of his oath to Assurbanipal, the Assyrian inscriptions are silent.

c. Natnu and Nuḫuru, kings of Nebaioth:

Assuming that the Ištar Slab covers later episodes of Assurbanipal's reign, the affairs reported in lines 123 ff. seem related to an expedition against Natnu king of Nebaioth,[584] whose throne was given to his son Nuḫuru, who had sworn loyalty to the Assyrian king. Natnu, according to Episode L, had led the people of Nebaioth even before Assurbanipal's accession, thus giving him at least 24 years of leadership at the time of Assurbanipal's major campaign against the Arabs (ca. 645 B.C.).

583 See, for example, J. Ryckmans, *L'Institution monarchique en Arabie méridionale avant l'Islam (Ma'in et Saba),* Louvain 1951, 17, 358-361; J. Pirenne, *Paléographie des inscriptions Sud-Arabes,* I: *Des origines jusqu'à l'époque himyarite,* Brussels 1956, 323-327.

584 On this source, see p. 51.

Chapter VI

THE CHALDAEAN PERIOD (605-539 B.C.)

Our information about the region "Beyond the River" (*Eber nāri*) in the Chaldaean and Achaemenid periods is meager compared with that about the Assyrian period. It is even more restricted vis-à-vis the history of the nomads of that time. The sources merely hint and gloss over events, never describing consecutive actions as do the sources for the Assyrian campaigns (neither annals nor other historical documents like the Assyrian royal inscriptions cover these periods). At the same time, despite their relative paucity, the sources from the Chaldaean and Achaemenid periods vary significantly in type and detail and are independent of each other, allowing data within them to be checked and compared against each other, which is almost impossible when studying the earlier periods dealt with above.

Several decades passed between the collapse of Assyrian rule in Syro-Palestine and the solidification of Babylonian rule there at the end of the 7th century B.C. The political situation changed considerably during this interim period: The provinces in northern Transjordan and southern and central Syria, whose desert borders had been secured by virtue of the Assyrian administration and defense system, and the Transjordanian kingdoms, which were supported by Assyrian army units, were left defenseless as the superstructure of the Assyrian empire disintegrated. Another drastic change was the rise of Egypt and its notable political and military position in western Asia, which in its heyday extended as far as the Euphrates. Such changes should have affected the relations between the nomads and the sedentary populations of the region, but sources for these border regions are too few to specify relationship. Nonetheless, our information about Palestine and its environs at the beginning of the 6th century B.C. leads us to believe that the borders of settled areas were not penetrated by the nomads during the interim period.

The sources for the nomads during the Chaldaean period fall into two geographic and chronological groups: a) The eastern border of Syria and Transjordan during the early years of Nebuchadnezzar's reign. From this period on, nomad penetration into the settled lands of Transjordan and southern Palestine progressed decisively, but, unfortunately, we know nothing of this process until our information about the demographic situation resumes with the Achaemenid period, more than two generations later. b) Nabonidus' sojourn in North Arabia in the middle of the 6th century B.C.

A. THE REIGN OF NEBUCHADNEZZAR (605-562 B.C.)[585]

1. Nebuchadnezzar's war against the Arabs in his sixth regnal year (599/8 B.C.)

Sources: BM 21946 (Grayson, Chron. 5) rev. 9-10; Jer. 49:28-33; cf. Berossus in Josephus, *Against Apion* I 19.

The Chronicle, says: "In the sixth year in the month of Kislev the king of Akkad (i.e. Nebuchadnezzar) mustered his army and marched to the Ḫatti-land. From the Ḫatti-land he sent out his companies, and, scouring the desert, they took much plunder from the Arabs ($^{lú/kur}$*A-ra-bi*), their possessions, animals and gods. In the month of Adar the king returned to his own land".

The significance of the incursions against the Arabs is clarified by the general situation in the western part of the Babylonian empire in the fourth to seventh years of Nebuchadnezzar's reign, as it is reflected in the Babylonian Chronicle and the Bible: Nebuchadnezzar, in Kislev of his fourth year (November 601 B.C.) failed in his attempt to invade Egypt, and his army incurred heavy losses (cf. BM 21946, rev. 5-7). The scope of the Babylonian failure and of the effort to rehabilitate the army is attested by the Chronicle statement that Nebuchadnezzar in his fifth year (600/599 B.C.) embarked on no military campaign, but stayed in

585 Nebuchadnezzar's campaign against the Arabs has been dealt with independently and simultaneously by the author and W.J. Dumbrell (in his Ph. D. dissertation), who published a paper on it in *AJBA* 2/1 (1972), 99-109. We fully agree about the political and historical background of this campaign. Certain aspects, such as the textual and exegetical matters of Jer. 49:28-33, are more broadly handled by Dumbrell.

Babylonia amassing horses and chariots (*ibid.*, line 8). The Babylonian defeat in the confrontation with Egypt and the concomitant military handicaps led Jehoiakim king of Judah to rebel against Nebuchadnezzar in 600 B.C.[586] Until his seventh regnal year (598/7 B.C.), according to II Kings 24:2 and BM 21946, rev. 11-13, Nebuchadnezzar could not counter the rebellion with a massive direct attack against Judah, but had to confine himself to punitive operations, using Chaldaean bands from the western part of the realm, as well as bands of Edomites,[587] Moabites and Ammonites. The Babylonian raids on the Arabs in the winter of Nebuchadnezzar's sixth year (599/8 B.C.) therefore took place at a low point in Babylonian control of the western part of the empire and in its military strength. That Nebuchadnezzar himself went to the Ḫatti-land to direct the raids into the desert testifies to the importance he attached to these operations, though from a purely military point of view they can hardly be regarded as really challenging to a Babylonian commander of Nebuchadnezzar's stature.

Since the publication of the Babylonian Chronicle relating to the early years of Nebuchadnezzar's reign, it has been the accepted view that Jeremiah's oracle "concerning Qedar and the kingdoms of Hazor (ממלכות חצור) which Nebuchadnezzar king of Babylon smote" (49:28-33) refers to the forays during the winter of 599/8 B.C.[588] This oracle and other references in Jeremiah characterize the Arabs as "a nation at ease that dwells securely" (Jer. 49:31); nothing is said or suggested about hostile relations between them and the sedentary population in Palestine and its environs. Nor do the oracles about the Transjordanian kingdoms (Jer. 48:1—49:22) intimate that their destruction by nomads is imminent. It thus appears that these border kingdoms were strong

586 II Kings 24:1 states only that Jehoiakim rebelled against the king of Babylon after having been his servant for three years, but gives no date for the rebellion. For its circumstances and considerations about its date, see Malamat, in *Military History,* 301 ff.; idem, *IEJ* 18 (1968), 142-143.

587 It thus appears that גדודי ארם (bands of Aramaeans) should here be read גדודי אד(ו)ם (bands of Edomites) (for the same occurrence cf. Jer. 35:11, and the Peshitta for both references). It is doubtful whether in the period under discussion "Aram" retained any political significance; see H.L. Ginsberg, *Marx Jubilee Volume,* 356 n. 31.

588 Wiseman, *CCK,* 31-32; Malamat, *IEJ* 6 (1956), 254-256; E. Vogt, *SVT* 4 (1957), 92; Dumbrell, *AJBA* 2/1 (1972), 99-109.

enough to withstand the desert nomads during the early years of Chaldaean rule in Palestine. The Babylonian raids against the Arabs therefore must have taken place not on the Transjordanian frontier but near the more northerly areas of Ḫatti-land,[589] i.e., in the desert borders of the provinces of southern and central Syria, recently reorganized, which depended for their existence on Babylonian forces and not on local authority. In such a case, the military and political situation in the western part of the Chaldaean empire in 600-598 B.C. becomes clearer, and the effect of Babylonian weakness is discernible in two areas: the rebellion under Jehoiakim of the kingdom of Judah, and the nomad pressure from the east on the border of southern and central Syria. These two threats to Babylonian authority in the west compelled Nebuchadnezzar, despite his army's limited fighting power, to take military initiative by making forays into the Syrian desert with small forces which he directed, as well into Judah. Assaulting the Arab encampments, damaging their flocks and taking their gods — all possible with relatively small forces — was apparently sufficient to alleviate the nomad threat to the sensitive region on the Syrian border. Such operations could not, of course, effect the pacification of Judah, which came about a year later when Nebuchadnezzar led his troops to Jerusalem. The echo of the Babylonian raids against the Arabs, heard in Jeremiah's oracles, signals their significance and their decisive and far-reaching impact upon Palestine and possibly the whole Chaldaean empire.

Another echo of the raids against the Arabs seems also to be sounded in the book of Judith (evidently written in the 4th century B.C.),[590] which describes the campaign of Nebuchadnezzar "king of Assyria" to the western part of his kingdom, ending at Judah. Chapter 2 of this book relates, *inter alia:* (v. 23) "... And (he) destroyed Puṭ and Lud, and spoiled all the children of Rasses, and the children of Ishmael, which were against the wilderness to the south of the land of the Chellians[591] ...

589 In the Neo-Babylonian inscriptions the name "Ḫatti-land" encompasses all of Syro-Palestine, thus including Carchemish (BM 21946 rev. 14), Judah (*ibid.,* rev. 11-12) and Ashkelon (cf. *ibid.,* obv., 16-18).

590 Y.M. Grintz, *Sefer Yehudith,* Jerusalem 1957, 3-17 (esp. 15-17); see also D. Flusser, *Kirjath Sepher* 33 (1958), 272-274.

591 Grintz (*ibid.,* 90) relates this region to Χάλον ποταμόν of Xenophon, ***Anabasis***

(25) And he took possession of the border of Cilicia, and slew all that resisted him, and came unto the borders of Japheth, which were toward the south, over against Arabia. (26) And he compassed about all the children of Midian and set on fire their tents, and spoiled their sheepcotes. (27) And he went down into the plain of Damascus ..." (in the R.H. Charles translation). The similarity in detail between the book of Judith and the Babylonian Chronicle concerning Nebuchadnezzar's early regnal years led J.C. Greenfield to conclude that the events recounted in the first part of the book of Judith (chapters 1-3) about Nebuchadnezzar's campaign to the west can be attributed to Nebuchadnezzar king of Babylonia and are evidently based on a Babylonian chronicle.[592] Since, however, the book of Judith condensed all Nebuchadnezzar's western campaigns into a single episode,[593] it is pointless to search there for geographical and chronological clarification of each campaign to which the Babylonian Chronicle refers in passing: that the book of Judith tells of Nebuchadnezzar's war against the nomads in the Syrian desert suffices. Nevertheless, even if Greenfield is correct, the details about the Arabs as described in the book of Judith should not be used as indicative of the actuality of settlement during the Chaldaean period. These details, like the geographic background of the whole book, reflect the late Achaemenid period of the book's composition.[594] Thus, for instance, "Arabia" in verse 25 is identical with the 'Αραβία of the coeval Xenophon, *Anabasis* I, 5, and its appearance in Judith should not be construed as testimony that the Arabs had penetrated the Euphrates region in the 6th century B.C.

I, 4; today it is identified with the al-Quweiq river on which Aleppo lies, on the northern border of the Syrian desert (Benzinger, *PW,* III,2, 2099).

592 Greenfield, *Yediot* 28 (1964), 204-208, provides further examples of this occurrence in the book of Judith, such as the Aramaic paraphrases of historical or semi-historical texts copied during the Chaldaean period from Akkadian sources, which were preserved in literary material from the Achaemenid and Seleucid periods, e.g. the Words of Aḥiqar from Elephantine, and the Prayer of Nabonidus from Qumran. It should be pointed out that many years ago J. Lewy assumed a link between the book of Judith, chapters 1-3, and Babylonian chronicles (*ZDMG* 81 [1927], LII-LIV), but had no concrete support until the publication of the Chronicle by D.J. Wiseman.

593 Greenfield, *ibid.*, 207.

594 For an exhaustive discussion of the geographical background of the book of Judith and its dating in the Achaemenid period, see Grintz, *ibid.*, 29-44.

The nomads who were attacked by Nebuchadnezzar's forces are called in Jeremiah's oracles (49:28-33) (the kingdoms of) Hazor, ([ממלכות] חצור), Qedar, People of the East (בני קדם) and "Those who cut the corners of their hair" (קצוצי פאה). The last three terms and their connection with nomads are clear, but the exact meaning of "kingdoms of Hazor" (ממלכות חצור) presents some difficulty. This phrase and the noun Hazor (חָצוֹר) itself are linked with the nomads only in this oracle. The Septuagint translates לממלכות חצור as τῇ βασιλίσσῃ τῆς αὐλῆς, i.e., "to the queen of a courtyard" (לְמַלְכַּת חָצֵר). The Vulgate, the Peshitta and the Aramaic translation consider חָצוֹר a proper noun. Some modern scholars tend to view it as a collective noun for dwellers in *ḥaṣērīm,* those unwalled settlements with no gates or bars typical to semi-nomads in the desert border regions (cf. Isa. 42:11, "the encampments [חצרים] that Qedar doth inhabit").[595] This interpretation can be provisionally supported by the absence of "Qedar and the kingdoms of Hazor" from the list in the "cup of the wine of wrath" vision (Jer. 25:19 ff.), which includes "all the foreign folk" ((כל הָעֶרֶב), "all the kings of Arabia" (כל מלכי עֲרָב), and "all the kings of the mixed tribes (הָעֶרֶב) who dwell in the desert"; it is also possible that the "kingdoms of Hazor" (ממלכות חצור) in Jeremiah 49 parallels "the kings of Arabia" or "the kings of the mixed tribes" (מלכי [ה]ערב) in Jeremiah 25. Such an assumption, however, does not accord with the literal text of the Bible (see especially v. 33: "Hazor shall become [והיתה חצור] a haunt of jackals, an everlasting waste; no man shall dwell there, no man shall sojourn in her" [fem. sing.: ולא יגור בה אדם]), nor with the fact that Hebrew has no other example of a collective *qātōl* noun deriving from a *qātēl* noun. Until a satisfactory explanation for the form Hazor is found, we must assume that Jeremiah was referring to a place or region unfamiliar from any other source.

595 See Musil, *Arabia Deserta,* 490, 495; W. Rudolph, *Jeremia*[3], Tübingen 1968, 294-295. The Hebrew חצר *(ḥaṣēr)* (likewise Akkadian *ḫaṣārum*) combines two different Proto-Semitic roots: **ḥḏr,* an unfortified encampment, common to nomad groups in the Bible (such as the Qedarites and the Ishmaelites) and in the Mari documents; and **ḥẓr,* an enclosure, a sheep-fold; on this see H.M. Orlinsky, *JAOS* 59 (1939), 22-37; Malamat, *JAOS* 82 (1962), 146-147; idem. *Yediot* 27 (1963), 181-184.

Even the word ממלכות, "kingdoms", (of Hazor) in this oracle is not sufficiently clear. Some scholars presume that ממלכות, "kingdoms", here meant "kings" (for this possible interpretation cf. I Sam. 10:18; Ps. 68:33; *KAI,* III, 14 s.v. ממלכת), i.e., that the phrase "kingdoms of Hazor" (ממלכות חצור) here refers to the leaders ("kings") of the nomads and not to the political entities.[596] However, this explanation still deviates somewhat from the literal meaning, and in any case does not entirely solve the interpretative problem of the expression "kingdoms of Hazor".

2. The Political and Military Background (594-582 B.C.) of Arab Penetration into Transjordan

In 599/8 B.C. the rebellious Jehoiakim faced, among the forces sent by Nebuchadnezzar, bands from the Transjordanian kingdoms (II Kings 24:2; cf. also Jer. 35:11). Their association with Babylonia can be explained not only by the direct territorial advantage to them of incursions into Judah but also by their desire for political stability in the region — provided in this case by Babylonia — without which they would have been the first to suffer.[597] During this period of great Egyptian and Babylonian enterprise in Syro-Palestine, local states presumably could not achieve any real independence, but had to choose between control by one power or another.

A decisive change, however, in the political and demographic situation in Palestine and Transjordan came about between Nebuchadnezzar's 11th and 23rd regnal years (594-582 B.C.). Under circumstances still not clear, though probably arising from Egyptian political and perhaps even military activity during the reign of

596 J. Bright, *Jeremiah,* Garden city, N.Y. 1965, 334, 336; and see Albright, *HUCA* 23 (1950-1951), Part I, 34.

597 Cf. Ginsberg, *Marx Jubilee Volume,* 355 ff., who contends that they were inimical to Judah after Josiah's annexation of Transjordanian territories and fearful of a Judah free of Babylonian control. The texts which, according to Ginsberg, tell of Josiah's conquests in Transjordan are all taken from Isaiah, chapters 1-39. Transplanting them from Isaiah's time to the second half of the 7th century B.C. requires, however, convincing proof, which Ginsberg does not provide. Nor, except for Ginsberg's references to Isaiah, does it appear in the Bible that Josiah tried to recover territory which had once been part of Israel and was annexed to Moab and Ammon, supposedly during the Assyrian period (cf. Zeph. 2:8-9; Jer. 49:1-2).

Psammetichus II (Egypt may not have undertaken actual military operations in Palestine, but certainly committed herself to military support) and the several-years absence of the Babylonian army from Palestine, anti-Babylonian ferment developed in the kingdoms of the region.[598] Represented at the anti-Babylonian conference in Jerusalem were the three kingdoms of Edom, Moab and Ammon (whose bands, in co-operation with the Chaldaeans, had raided Judah five years earlier, during the rebellion of Jeohiakim), as well as Tyre and Sidon (Jer. 27:3). At the start of the revolt in Judah in 588 B.C., however, only Ammon took active part. Ezekiel (21:23-27) gives the impression that Ammon's hostile actions against Babylonia were no less extensive than those of Judah, but since Nebuchadnezzar confronted Judah first, the kingdom of Ammon was spared for a time.[599] Ammon nevertheless maintained its anti-Babylonian policy: the king of the Ammonites gave haven to Judaean refugees, among them Ishmael son of Nethaniah, "of the royal family", and helped them to murder Gedaliah son of Ahikam, whom the Babylonians had installed over the survivors of Judah (Jer. 40:14; 41:1-10, 15).

Since information about Nebuchadnezzar's wars after 586 B.C. is scanty, we cannot determine why the kingdom of Ammon was not subdued by the Babylonians immediately after the conquest of Judah. Nebuchadnezzar may have had to use all his strength for the arduous siege of Tyre, which lasted for years and ended in failure (cf. Ezek. 29:17-18; Josephus, *Against Apion* I, 21; *Ant.* X, xi, 1),[600] and for

598 For extended discussions of the history of the kingdom of Judah and its neighbors during 599-589 B.C. — with detailed information and evaluation — as affected by the political and military position of Babylonia and Egypt in Syro-Palestine, see K.S. Freedy-D.B. Redford, *JAOS* 90 (1970), 462-485; Malamat, *SVT* 28 (1975), 132-145 (including an up-to-date summary of the state of the research).

599 Nebuchadnezzar decided to attack Judah before Ammon apparently because Judah's proximity to Egypt enabled the Egyptian army to entrench itself in Palestine. That Apries indeed sent an Egyptian army to Palestine (Jer. 37:5 ff.) justifies Nebuchadnezzar's decision. The capture of Judah and severance of communication between Egypt and Palestine might have eased the later subjugation of Ammon.

600 The chronological relationship between Nebuchadnezzar's siege of Tyre and the campaign to Transjordan in 582 B.C. is not sufficiently clear: The ambiguous data in *Against Apion* I, 21 about the 13-year siege of Tyre make it impossible to determine whether the siege began in the 7th year of Nebuchadnezzar's reign (598/7 B.C.) and

military emergencies in other parts of his realm as well. *Ant.* X, ix, 7 preserves a report without biblical parallel that, in his 23rd regnal year (582/1 B.C.), Nebuchadnezzar fought the Moabites and Ammonites, subdued them and turned his attention to the Egyptians. Jer. 52:30 records that in the same year Nebuzaradan, the captain of the guard, carried off 745 Jews. It is appropriate, then, to combine the two pieces of information and interpret them as Babylonian reprisal for the assassination of Gedaliah son of Ahikam.[601]

The political existence of the kingdoms of Ammon and Moab seems to have ended with the campaign of 582 B.C. There is archaeological evidence of a wave of destruction over Transjordan during the first half of the 6th century B.C.; population probably decreased on the heels of forced exile and voluntary migration.[602] Such severe upheaval in the sensitive Transjordanian border region, and the concomitant political vacuum, allowed the desert dwellers to penetrate the settled lands whose borders had been breached. Closest to the desert and therefore most vulnerable was Ammon whose land, as indicated for the first time in Ezekiel's oracle (25:1-5), was penetrated by the People of the East. This oracle, dated sometime after 586 B.C. (cf. v. 3: "Say to the Ammonites ... Because you said 'Aha!' over my sanctuary when it was profaned; and over the land Israel when it was made desolate; and over the house of Judah, when it went into exile"), amply reflects the extensive demographic changes in the area at the time. Only this oracle refers to Transjordan, so that we know nothing of circumstances and phases of nomad penetration into its other regions.

continued until his 20th regnal year (585/4 B.C.), or in the 7th year of the reign of Ithobaal king of Tyre (ca. 585 B.C.) and ended about 572 B.C. On the problem of dating the siege of Tyre see Dougherty, *GCCI* II, 22-23; M. Vogelstein, *Biblical Chronology,* 1, Cincinnati 1944, 22-26; H.J. Katzenstein, *The History of Tyre,* Jerusalem 1973, 322 ff. (esp. 325-330). The later date is supported by Ezek, 26:1 ff.; 29:17, and by the fact that the Babylonian Chronicle (BM 21946), which runs to 594 B.C., never refers to a siege of Tyre. The continued anti-Babylonian activity in Ammon and the reason we have suggested for the non-conquest of Ammon immediately after the capture of Judah and the fall of Jerusalem accord with the second possibility but are difficult to reconcile with the first.

601 Ginsberg, *op. cit.*, 367-368.

602 N. Glueck, *The Other Side of the Jordan,* New Haven 1940, Chap. V; cf. A. Van Zyl, *The Moabites,* Leiden 1960, 156-158; G.M. Landes, *BA* 24 (1961), 85-86.

Nevertheless, by the Achaemenid period, when our knowledge of the region is once again documented, the Arabs were already present in large numbers in the territories of the former Transjordanian kingdoms.

Even so, the view, based on Glueck's archaeological survey in Transjordan, that permanent settlement ceased to exist in the area between the first half of the 6th century B.C. and the 4th century B.C., must be rejected. This question and its implications about the ethnic composition of the Transjordanian population during the 6th and 5th centuries B.C. are treated in Chapter VII, about the Achaemenid period.

B. THE REIGN OF NABONIDUS (556-539 B.C.)

It is rare for a king to abandon his country and remain for many years in a remote place, as Nabonidus did when he quitted Babylon for Tema', leaving imperial matters to his son Belshazzar. Economic, religious, military and even medical reasons have been offered in explanation, but available data — although enriched within the last 25 years by sources which rekindled scholarly debate — are too meager to define Nabonidus' behaviour reasonably.[603] We shall therefore use our information only in terms of its significance to the study of the Arabs.

We know about Nabonidus' stay in Tema' primarily from Babylonian sources, with our knowledge of the Tema' region in the 6th century B.C. augmented by some recently published North Arabian inscriptions. But since the dating of these latter cannot be fixed in precise decade, they cannot be related definitively to Nabonidus' residence in that region. The historical discussion below is therefore arranged according to each source group.

603 Besides the sources referred to in page 180, the Aramaic "Prayer of Nabonidus" from Qumran alludes to his stay in Tema' (making no contribution, however, to the study of the Arabs). Of the abundant literature about Nabonidus in Tema', and particularly about the reasons for his stay, see especially: Dougherty, *Nabonidus and Belshazzar,* New Haven 1929, 105-117, 138-160; Smith, *Isaiah Chapters XL-LV,* 36-40, 136-142; Lewy, *HUCA* 19 (1945-1946), 436 ff.; Gadd, *AnSt* 8 (1958), 76-89; W.G. Lambert, *Proceedings of the Fifth Seminar for Arabian Studies,* London 1972, 53-64 (esp. pp. 58-63). (All these studies include additional bibliography).

1. Babylonian Historical Sources

Nabonidus Chronicle (Grayson, Chron. 7), ii 5-23.[604]

Verse Account ii 16-34.[605]

Harran Inscription Nab. H_2 i 22-27, 38—ii 2; iii 4-6, 14-17.[606]

Royal Chronicle BM 34167+ col. v.[607]

When Nabonidus arrived in Tema', the Babylonian documents point out, he made war with the local inhabitants, in which the king of Tema' was killed,[608] and the herds of the inhabitants of the oasis and its environs were slaughtered (Verse Account ii 25-26).[609] Nabonidus thereafter built Tema' into a place fit for the king of Babylonia (*ibid.,* lines 27 ff.). Its walled and sandy ruins, yet to be uncovered,[610] may disclose remains that permit thorough investigation of this interesting affair. During Nabonidus' ten years in Tema' (Nab. H_2 i 26; cf. ii 11), he "went about" North Arabia as far as Dedan (*uruDa-da-nu,* present day al-'Ulā), Fadak (*uruPa-dak-ku,* perhaps al-Ḥuwaiyiṭ), Khaybar (*uruḪi-ib-ra-a*), Yadī' (*uruIá-di-ḫu,* perhaps al-Ḥāyiṭ) and Yathrib (*uruIa-at-ri-bu,* Medina), all important oases in the region south of Tema', an area about 370 kilometers long and, in the open country in its

604 Smith, *BHT,* 111-112; Grayson, *ABC,* 106-108.

605 Smith, *ibid.,* 84-85. For a translation see Lambert, *ibid.,* 56; *ANET,* 313-314.

606 Gadd, *AnSt* 8 (1958), 58-64; Röllig, *ZA* 56 (1964), 220-226.

607 Lambert, *AfO* 22 (1968-1969), 6.

608 *ma-al-ku uruTa-ma-' it-ta-a-ru ina giškakki.*

609 *a-šib āli [u] māti su-gul-li-šu-nu uṭ-ṭa-ab-[bi-iḫ].* This reading, which corrects Smith's original version, was first proposed by Landsberger-Bauer, *ZA* 37 NF 3 (1927), 91.

610 For a description of the Tema' oasis and its immediate environs, with a bibliographical summary of descriptions written by visitors to the site during the last century, see W.L. Reed and F.V. Winnett, *AR,* 22-29. The character of the Tema' "wall" is unclear; today it looks like an extended ridge, 12-15 meters high, mostly covered by sand. Exposed sections at the top reveal a wall about two meters thick. Ch.M. Doughty, one of the early visitors to the site, estimated the length of the "wall" at three miles. Reed and Winnett, driving alongside, found that its southern sector alone measured about three (!) miles. Aerial photographs made after their journey show that the "wall" goes on for miles (*ibid.,* 23). H.St.J.B. Philby's idea, that the wall was meant as a protection not against attack but floods, is hard to accept in view of the high ground that parts of the wall traverse (see, for example, Reed's photographs, *ibid.,* 26, Plate 27). Qurayyah, see P. Parr *et alii, Bulletin of the Institute of Archaeology, University of London,* 8-9 (1968-1969), 219-223, offers another instance of a wall several miles long, partly traversing a ridge.

northern part, about 100 kilometers wide (Nab. H_2 i 24-25).[611] Some of these journeys, at least at the beginning of his sojourn, surely involved military actions to ensure control over the whole region, especially the three principal routes branching off from Medina (Yathrib): two to the north, to Tema' and Dedan; one northeast, to Ḥā'il, east of the Nafūd desert. The fragments of BM 34167+ col. v report that Nabonidus defeated the king of Dedan (line 20: *šarru šá Da-da-nu*), unnamed in the Babylonian inscription. From the inscription JS 138 lih., referring to *krb'l bn mt''l mlk ddn,* "*Krb'l* son of *Mt''l* king of Dedan", but dated no more precisely than between 600 and 450 B.C.,[612] we know that there was in fact a king in Dedan. We cannot be sure whether reference was made in the severely damaged texts to wars against lords of other oases.

The Nab. H_2 Inscriptions twice refer to the Arabs: a) Col. i 38-45 lists "the king(s?) of Egypt, the Medes and the Arabs, and all the kings (who were) hostile" whom the gods Sin and Ištar caused to send envoys to Nabonidus to make peace and establish good relations. b) Cols. i 45 — ii 2 (lines 46-48 of which are damaged) report the repulsion and subjugation of the Arabs (*nišē*^{meš} ^{kur}*A-ra-bi*) attacking "...(the land of) Akkad". Given the place of these passages in the text, the events date from Nabonidus' sojourn in Tema'.

C.J. Gadd, who published Nab. H_2, suggested that the two passages refer to the same episode — beating back the Arab attacks on the oases controlled by Nabonidus in North Arabia and finally defeating them.[613] His view supposes that ... *šá māt Ak-ka-di-[i*^{ki}?] means the soldiers of Akkad who came to Tema' with Nabonidus. Though both passages may indeed refer to the same

611 For identification of the oases discussed see Gadd, *AnSt* 8 (1958), 80-84; Caskel, *Fischer Weltgeschichte* 4, p. 352, n. 18.

612 See Albright, *Alt Festschrift,* 2-6. Caskel, *Lihyan und Lihyanisch,* Köln 1954, 37, 78, in placing the inscription in the 2nd century B.C., adheres to his general historical method, which dates most of the ancient inscriptions about 300 years later than is commonly accepted. For criticism of his method see A. Van den Branden, *BiOr* 14 (1957), 13-16; idem, *Les inscriptions dédanites,* Beyrouth 1962, 42-46. See also Winnett, *AR,* 114-115.

613 Gadd, *ibid.,* 74-78, 84. His opinion about the historical background of the two passages has been accepted by scholars; see Caskel, *Fischer Weltgeschichte* 4, p. 210; Winnett, *ibid.,* 90-92.

episode, they might, on the other hand, suggest that the object of the Arab incursion in passage (b) was not "[the soldiers] of the land of Akkad" but rather "[the people] of the land of Akkad," or "[the border] of the land of Akkad." It is difficult to assume that the "king(s) of the Arabs"—referred to in passage (a) along with the kings of Egypt and the Medes who dispatched messengers to make peace with Nabonidus — were the kings of Tema' and Dedan against whom Nabonidus fought (see above); similary, the invading Arabs referred to in passage (b) probably did not inhabit the region between Yathrib and Tema'. In the latter interpretation, the focus is on the establishment of formal relations between Nabonidus and nomad groups in the Syro-Arabian desert to solidify their mutual interest in controlling the traffic along desert routes (see also p. 191).

The Harran Inscriptions, written after Nabonidus returned from Tema', attempt to contrast his purported successes when he abandoned Babylon for North Arabia with the misfortunes of the people of Babylonia who opposed him.[614] It is in this light that we should evaluate the presentation in these inscriptions of Nabonidus as the savior of the Babylonians who had suffered so severely from Arab raids in the border regions. At the same time, the polemic character of the inscriptions and the very general designation of the enemies of Babylonia who sought peace with Nabonidus suggests that there exists here (especially in passage [a]) only the pretension of superiority over the confirmed enemies of the Babylonian empire, represented by three entities never subjugated by Babylonian kings: Media, Egypt and the nomads of the Syro-Arabian desert. The events reported in these passages may therefore never have taken place.

2. North Arabian Inscriptions:

No early North Arabian inscriptions of special historical value have been found in the oasis of Tema',[615] but about 13 to 30 kilometers to the southwest (in the region of the Jebel Ghunaym summit, al-Khabu

614 On the character of the Harran Inscriptions see Gadd, *ibid.*, 89-91; Tadmor, *Studies Landsberger,* 356 ff.

al-Gharbī, al-Khabu ash-Sharqī and their environs) inscriptions important for our period were found by A. Jaussen and R. Savignac, H.St.J.B. Philby, F.V. Winnett and W.L. Reed. They were recently dealt with and published (some for the first time) by Winnett, who defined their script as a type restricted to the Tema' region and therefore called Taymanite.[616] They have been dated to the 6th century B.C. and are considered the earliest of the inscriptions ever found in the region.[617] The Jebel Ghunaym inscriptions mention the participation of various people in wars (*ḍr,* pl. *ḍrr*) against *Nbyt,*[618] *Ms['*][619] and *Ddn,*[620] and thus enable us, for the first time, to locate in a more or less circumscribed geographical area groups of nomads (Nebaioth and Massa') known from the Bible and Assyrian documents only as dwellers in remote, geographically unspecified regions. The spelling of *Nbyt* in the North Arabian alphabetical inscriptions of the 6th century B.C. strongly supports the opinion that the [kur]*Na-ba-a-a-ti* of the 7th century B.C. Assyrian sources (the biblical people of Nebaioth) are not identical with the Nabataeans known from the Hellenistic period on.[621]

Because of the scriptual and textual homogeneity of the Jebel Ghunaym inscriptions, Winnett believes that they were all written within a relatively short period and are in some way related.[622] He finds it hard to assume that the involvement of the people of Tema' in hostilities against the series of enemies mentioned in the inscriptions was a recurrent phenomenon in a caravan center like Tema', whose

615 Winnett, *ibid.,* 89.

616 Winnett, *ibid.,* 69, 93-108. Some of these inscriptions were published earlier by Van den Branden, *TTP,* II, but were for the most part incorrectly translated, mainly because of errors and inaccuracies in the Philby copies (see further pp. 184-185).

617 Winnett, *ibid.,* 89 ff.

618 Winnett, *ibid.,* 99-101, Nos. 11 (=Ph. 266ag); 13; 15 (=Ph. 266ac).

619 Winnett, *ibid.,* 101, No. 16.

620 Winnett, *ibid.,* 102-103, 105, Nos. 20 (=Ph. 266a); 21; 23; 33. No. 22 (and perhaps No. 20 as well) reads *ḍrr ddn,* "wars against Dedan". The expression *ḍrr ddn* also occurs in a Taymanite inscription from Bani 'Aṭiya (8 kms. north-east of Tema'), published by G.L. Harding, *Bulletin of the Institute of Archaeology, University of London* 10 (1972), 45, No. 39.

621 See in detail Appendix A, 10.

622 Winnett, *ibid.,* 90.

prosperity depended upon peaceful conditions. In his opinion, the inscriptions reflect unusual circumstances, like those obtaining in the same region at the time of Nabonidus' residence. Lack of sufficient data, he emphasizes, however, makes it impossible to determine within decades the dates of the inscriptions.[623]

If the inscriptions in fact date from the middle of the 6th century B.C., the wars against Dedan mentioned there might be identified with those in BM 34167+ col. v, assuming that local residents among the people of Tema' participated in the military operations of the king of Babylonia.[624] Opposed to Winnett's view, however, that caravan trade in North Arabia depended on tranquility in the Tema' region is the possibility that trade could follow the Medina-Dedan (al-'Ulā)-Tabūk route. Thus, those "wars of Dedan" involving the people of Tema' might simply represent competition between inhabitants of two adjacent oases for control of alternative trade routes.[625] As to the other wars mentioned in the inscriptions, we have seen (above, pp. 181-182) that H_2 i 45—ii 2 cannot be used to explain their circumstances. There is nothing in our sources to connect the oases in the Tema'-Yathrib region with the people of Nebaioth and Massa', who apparently lived outside the area.[626] In any case, the Jebel Ghunaym inscriptions make it clear that some branches of these nomad groups did in fact reach the Tema' region. Since there is no information from which to determine the background of the wars with the people of Nebaioth and Massa' or to set them in the Nabonidus period, these wars might well have been fought before or after his sojourn in North Arabia.

Another inscription with a proposed connection with Nabonidus' stay in Tema' is Ph. 279aw from the Khabu ash-Sharqī region, discovered by Philby and published by A. Van den Branden. Each of its two lines is in

623 *Ibid.,* 90-91.

624 *Ibid.,* 91.

625 On these routes, their direction and final termini, see pp. 14-16. The distinction in the Bible between the genealogical connections of these oases should be noted: Dedan is a descendant of Qeturah (Gen. 25:3; I Chron. 1:32), Tema' of Ishmael (Gen. 25:15; I Chron. 1:30). This distinction may also be based upon particular economic conditions (about this see Appendix B).

626 Winnett, e.g. (*ibid.,* 99-100), thinks they dwelt in the Ḥā'il region, in the southeastern part of the Nafūd desert. On the question of their location, see details in Appendix A.

a different script. Some of the signs in the upper line show a similarity to Aramaic letters, but the line as a whole is unreadable. According to Van den Branden, the bottom line is in the early form of Thamudic script, belonging to the 6th century B.C. He reads it: *ṣn.ḫnd(b).(')sl. mlk.bbl.nḏrh,* and translates: "Ḫundab guarded the spear of the king of Babylonia. He dedicated it."[627] Apart from the fact that some signs in his reading, and consequently his translation, do not match the letters in the line-drawing of the inscription in his book,[628] Van den Branden's translation presents syntactical difficulties, suggesting that the copy of the inscription, made by Philby, is not faithful to the original. We must therefore agree with Winnett that it would be unwise to draw historical conclusions on the basis of this inscription until a photograph or an accurate copy is available.[629]

3. Nabonidus' Route to Tema'

A problem of scholarly concern is reconstructing, with only scanty data, Nabonidus' route on his campaign to Tema'. The point of approach to this question is the fragmentary record — only ends of lines and sometimes isolated words — in the Nabonidus Chronicle, col. i 11-12, of his third regnal year. The fragments of lines 11-14 mention a campaign in the month of Ab to the mountain of ^{kur}*Am-ma-na-nu* (line 11), fruit orchards of various kinds (line 12) and the illness and recovery of (probably) the king (line 14). In the even more fragmentary

627 Van den Branden, *TTP,* II, 54-55; idem, *Studia Islamica* 7 (1957), 7, 12-13.

628 The correction of the third word in the inscription is an outstanding example: there, *ssl,* "net", is clearly legible, but Van den Branden deliberately changed it to read *'sl,* "spear", because it is difficult to interpret "guarding the net" of the Babylonian king.

629 Winnett, *op. cit.,* 91, n. 24. All of Philby's copies of the Thamudic inscriptions were prepared carelessly, inaccurately, sometimes even ignoring the division of the letters into words and lines; they must be used with utmost caution (see also Winnett, *ibid.,* 89). This becomes clear, *inter alia,* when Van den Branden's readings of the inscriptions from the Tema' area according to Philby's drawings are compared with those of Winnett, which are based on photographs and new drawings of the same inscriptions (cf. Winnett, *ibid.,* pp. 93-107, Nos. 1-2, 4-9, 11, 14-15, 20, 25a, 26-27, 29-32, 34-35, 38, 43). Albright's proposed version for this inscription (*Von Qumran nach Ugarit* [O. Eissfeldt Festschrift], Berlin 1958, 7) is valueless, since it is not based on the published drawing.

continuation (lines 14-22), the king is said to have gathered his army in the month of Kislev (line 14), and mention is made of the Land of the West (^{kur}*Amurri,* line 16), encamping at *[ ]-du-um-mu* (line 17), a great host (line 18), the gate (?) of the city of *Šin/Ruk-di-ni* (line 19) and other isolated words suggestive of military activity. Regarding the date of the campaign to Tema', only the Verse Account, col. ii 16 ff., tells us that after Nabonidus finished rebuilding the temple of Eḫulḫul in Harran, "as the third year came",[630] he entrusted a military "camp" to his eldest son, and put him in charge of the kingdom, while he, with the forces of Akkad, headed for Tema' in the west (*ana* ^{uru}*Te-ma-' qí-rib A-mur-ri-i iš-ta-kan pa-ni-[šu]).*

These two sources gave rise to the hypothesis that Nabonidus left for Tema' in his third regnal year and in the course of his campaign attacked *[ ]-du-um-mu.*[631] But opinion about *[ ]dummu* is divided, Albright believing it identical with ^{uru}*Adumû/Adummatu* which is Jauf (Dūmat al-Jandal), Smith locating it within the territory of Edom, along the caravan route to North Arabia.[632] In determining the route to Tema', Smith assumed that in his third regnal year, during his campaign in the ^{kur}*Am-ma-na-nu ša-di-i* (the Anti-Lebanon) region, Nabonidus fell ill but recovered in Kislev of the same year to gather an army in southern Syria and summon his son Belshazzar. After giving his son control of the kingdom and part of the army, he himself set out for Tema'. Such a reconstruction thus adds the Anti-Lebanon to Nabonidus' route to Tema' and invalidates the assumption that he passed through Jauf, i.e., through Wadi Sirḥān.

Before we accept these proposals, however, it must be noted that:

a) There is, as we have seen, no connection between ^{uru}*Adummatu* and [^{uru}*A]dummu,*[633] and Albright's opinion thus has no support.

b) The expression "as the third year came", used in the Verse Account for the date of Nabonidus' departure for Tema', seems a

630 *šá-lul-ti šatti ina ka-šá-di.* For this reading see Landsberger-Bauer, *ZA* 37 NF 3 (1927), 91.

631 Smith, *BHT,* 53, 108; Albright, *JRAS* 1925, 293-295; cf. Musil, *Northern Neğd,* 225.

632 Albright, *ibidem*; Smith, *Isaiah Chapters XL-LV,* 34, 36-38, 130, 139-140; cf. idem, *BHT,* 108.

633 See above, pp. 118-121.

literary rather than a hard chronological statement.[634] Since our sources permit us to set Nabonidus' campaign to Tema' between the third and fifth year of his reign, opinion as to the exact year is divided.[635] Any rejection, however, of the assumption that he campaigned to Tema' in his third regnal year contradicts the validity of the statement in the Nabonidus Chronicle, i 11 ff., as a source relevant to the question of the route of the campaign.

c) Even assuming that the campaign to Tema' took place in Nabonidus' third year, there is no evidence for the opinion that he advanced to *[ ]dummu* and Tema' after encamping at Mount Ammananu. The fragmented Nabonidus Chronicle points to two mobilizations and two military operations, the first beginning in Ab, the second in Kislev, five months later.[636] That these were two distinct actions is made clear in BM 34167+, from which we learn that the campaign purpose at Mount Ammananu was to subdue a revolt which had been reported by messengers (rev. 47-64).[637] Since it is hard to believe that the military actions at Mount Ammananu were part of a campaign to take place more than 1000 kms. away, the Chronicle reference to Mount Ammananu cannot serve as a datum for reconstructing the route of the Tema' campaign.

To sum up, since the Babylonian sources appear to contain no data for reconstructing Nabonidus' route to Tema', we must rely on geographical logic: In view of the difficulty of moving a large army through Wadi Sirḥān (even though the campaign was conducted in Kislev, a relatively favorable season),[638] and assuming that Nabonidus'

634 Tadmor, *Studies Landsberger*, 353-356. W.G. Lambert rejects Tadmor's opinion that this expression might be simply a literary device and accepts its literal truth (*Proceedings of the Fifth Seminar for Arabian Studies*, 59). At the same time, he would have it that the campaign might have taken place, according to the sources, at any time between Nabonidus' third and fifth years (pp. 54-58).

635 For the latest summary of approaches to this question see Tadmor, *ibid.*, 351-358; Lambert, *ibid.*, 54-57.

636 The interval increases to as much as 7-8 months if we use the date in the Royal Chronicle (BM 34167+iv 57-58) — Iyyar, Nabonidus' third year — for assembling the Babylonian army for the campaign to Mount Ammananu, and compare it to the Chronicle date — Kislev, the same year — for the campaign to *[ ]dummu.*

637 In MB 34167+iv 60, the determinative URU comes before *Am-ma-na-nu.*

638 Musil, *Arabia Deserta*, 482; cf. Smith, *Isaiah Chapters XL*-LV, 139.

campaign to Tema' had no time limitations, it is reasonable to conclude that he went not through the Syro-Arabian desert, but through the Fertile Crescent, a longer but more convenient campaign route.[639] If the encampment at *[ ]dummu,* whose most likely reconstruction is *[U]dummu,* Edom,[640] was a part of that campaign, it marks a final stage in his march to Tema'.

4. Arabs in Babylonia and North Arabian and Babylonian Connections in the 6th century B.C.

A number of documents attest Arab presence in Babylonia in the 6th century B.C.:

a) BM 117520 (apparently from Uruk), 30 Elul, Nebuchadnezzar's 7th year. An allocation of barley for the support of ^{m}*Ri-mut* ^{lú}*Te-ma-a-a* for the month of Tishri.[641]

b) BIN I 151. Uruk, 21 Nisan, Nebuchadnezzar's 15th year. A list of 25 people charged with seeking(?) or checking(?) something.[642] Line 14 mentions ^{m}*Ri-mut* ^{lú}*Te-ma-a-a,* probably the person referred to in the preceding document. Document (b) indicates that he was a resident of Uruk. The allocation to him (each document allots him two *qa* a day) is not especially large compared to that of other people listed in document (b) (see especially lines 2, 26).

c) Nbk. 287. 20 Adar, Nebuchadnezzar's 35th year (place of origin not indicated). The payment of one mina of silver to ^{lú}*Ar-ba-a-[a]*[643] (an

639 It should be repeated that this consideration is purely geographical, and has nothing to do with whether Dumah-Jauf occurs in the sources for this campaign, a possibility which was independently rejected above by textual arguments.

640 The reconstruction *[U]dummu* proposed by Labat, *Fischer Weltgeschichte* 4, p. 105 (cf. Lambert, *op. cit.,* 55; for this spelling of Edom see Parpola, *Neo-Assyrian Toponyms,* 364-365), accords with the route of Tema'. It might be further emended to [^{uru}*U]dummu,* i.e., "the city of Edom", its capital (cf. BM 21946 rev. 12: URU *Ia-a-ḫu-du,* "the city of Judah", Jerusalem).

641 Dougherty, *Nabonidus and Belshazzar,* Pl. I, p. 117.

642 Lines 27-28: *25 ṣābē*^{meš} *šá a-na eli ḫa-a-ṭu šá ku-up-ru(?) ši-ip-ru.*

643 Since this document also refers to Tyre, E. Unger, *ZAW* 44 (1926), 316-317, read ^{lú}*Ar-ma-a-...,* and attributed it to the people of Arwad. It should be noted, however, that the usual Neo-Babylonian spelling for Arwad(eans) is ^{lú}*Ar-ma-du-[...],* ^{lú}*Ar-mad-da-a-a,* Weidner, *Mélanges Syriens offerts à Mr. R. Dussaud,* II, Paris 1939, 929).

individual name or a collective noun?) for 6 *gur* 120 *qa* of sesame.

d) M(ich.) 422 A letter from Nabonidus (apparently before he became king) to Nabû-aḫḫê-iddina[644] includes instructions to give ^{m}*Te-mu-da-a* ^{lú}*Ar-ba-a-a* several talents of silver.[645] That so prestigious a person as Nabonidus ordered an Arab to be given so much silver suggests that the Arab in question was either employed by the Babylonian authorities or was a merchant to be paid as the letter instructs.

e) YOS VI 59. Uruk, 30 Marheshvan, Nabonidus' 4th year.[646] ^{md}*In-nin-šum-uṣur* son of ^{md}*Šamaš-na-ṣir* descendant of ^{m}*Ar-ba-a-a* sells his house. The Babylonian names of the seller and his father show that the family had lived in Babylonia a long time, at least since the beginning of Nebuchadnezzar's reign.

f) Nbn. 297. 7 Ab, Nabonidus' 8th year. Dates are distributed by ^{md}*Nabû-aḫḫē-*^{meš}*-erība šá muḫḫi Ar-ba-a-a.*

The settlement of *ālu ša* ^{lú}*Arbaya,* apparently located in the Nippur region, is mentioned in two Neo-Babylonian documents:

g) BE VIII/1 26. Written on 16 Kislev, Nebuchadnezzar's 42nd year, at URU *šá* ^{lú}*Ar-ba-a-a.*

h) BE VIII/1 50. Written on 22 Marheshvan, Nabonidus' 9th year, at *bīt* ^{d}*Sin* URU *šá* ^{lú}*Aŕ-ba-a-a.*

Given the variant spellings *Ar-ba-a-a* and *Aŕ-ba-a-a* and the fact that documents (g) and (h) were written by two different scribes, there can be no doubt about the reading of the toponym. But a spelling problem remains: URU *šá* ^{m}AD-^{d}A.A (pronounced *ālu šá* ^{m}*Abi-ila-a-a*) appears in BE VIII/1 51:4; 68:5, 12; 72:12; TMH III/II 90:13 (from Nabonidus' 11th to Cyrus' 8th year), and in BE VIII/1 50 as well, where it is also spelled URU *šá* ^{lú}*Ar-ba-a-a* (lines 5, 15). Since the first four documents are the works of four different scribes, the spelling of the names is not in question. And

644 See E.W. Moore, *Neo-Babylonian Documents in the University of Michigan Collection,* Ann Arbor 1939, No. 67; E. Ebeling, *Neubabylonische Briefe,* München 1949, No. 276. For the date of this letter see Ebeling, *ibid.,* 150.

645 The name Temūdâ is probably connected with the tribe of Thamūd mentioned in the Sargon inscriptions. Similarly, the toponym *Ta-mu-da-',* in Babylonia, appears in BIN I 166:22 (from Neriglissar's second[?] year).

646 See M. San Nicolò-E. Petschow, *Babylonische Rechtsurkunden aus dem 6. Jahrhunderts v. Chr.,* München 1960, No. 57.

since both BE VIII/1 51 and TMH III/II 90 refer to the same temple, *bīt* ^{d}*Sin* URU *šá Arbaya*/AD-^{d}A.A, they (as well as BE VIII/1 50) were both probably written in a place whose name seems to have had alternative forms.

To these data can be added the reference to URU *Ar-ba-a-a* in TMH III/II 147:3 (Darius' 4th year), a settlement close to the *Nār* ^{d}*Sin* canal near Nippur (possibly identical with URU *ša* ^{lú}*Arbaya*).

i) BE VIII/1 65. 20 Iyyar, Cyrus' 5th year. Lines 6-7 have ^{md}*Sin-šar-uṣur* ^{lú}*šanû*^{u} *ša* ^{uru}*Qí-da-ri.*

j) CT XXII 86. Order to deliver wool to ^{m}*Ab-du-'* ^{lú}*Ar-ba-a-[a?].*[647]

Although the existence of Arabs in Babylonia in the 6th century B.C. has thus been ascertained, it is still impossible to determine whether we are dealing with a continuation of the nomad penetration into Babylonia in the 8th century B.C.[648] or with other later political and demographic developments, in the course of which exiles from various lands founded settlements.[649] Especially noteworthy is the incidence in Babylonia of people from Tema' prior to Nabonidus' arrival there (cf. documents (a) and (b) above and UET IV 167).[650] Perhaps their coming was connected with trade with North Arabia (a letter to the king of Assyria, ABL 1404, apparently from the time of Assurbanipal, mentions ^{m}*Am-me-ni-ilu* ^{lú}*tamkaru Te-ma-a-a* and his journey to the king of Babylonia). It is difficult, in any case, to connect the arrival in Babylonia of people from far-off Tema' with the circumstances leading to Arab penetration into Babylonia in the 8th century B.C. Toponyms like URU *Qidari* and URU *ša* ^{lú}*Arbaya,* the titles of the officials in charge of the Arabs (documents (f) and (i) above), and the reference to the people of Tema' (documents (a), (b) and especially UET IV 167) indicate that the Arabs were organized in communities like other ethnic

647 Ebeling, *op. cit.,* No. 86.

648 Regarding this penetration see Eph'al, *JAOS* 94 (1974), 108-115.

649 Cf. Eph'al, *Orientalia* 47 (1978), 80-90.

650 UET IV 167, a damaged letter from Ur, tells of two Temaean families (*2-ta* ^{lú}*qin-na-a-ta šá* ^{lú}*Te-ma-a-a*) in flight(?) from Eridu to the people of ^{lú}*Qu-da-ri* (Qedar?), see Ebeling, *op. cit.,* No. 303 (Ebeling's reading in line 8, *i[ḫ]-t[e(?!)-]il-[q]u,* is uncertain; perhaps another verb should be substituted). A prosopographical examination indicates that the letter should be attributed to the reign of Esarhaddon, see A. Pohl, *Orientalia* 19 (1950), 383.

minorities referred to in documents from the Achaemenid period.[651]

Two documents attest traffic between Uruk and Tema' during Nabonidus' residence in Tema':

k) GCCI I 294. Uruk, 5 Adar, Nabonidus' 5th year.[652] Payment of 50 shekels of silver for a camel and provisions (lit.: *qēmu*, flour) to [md]*Nabû-mušētiq-urra*, son of [m]*Ištar-nadin-aḫi*, who was sent to Tema'.

l) YOS VI 134. Uruk, 19 Ab, Nabonidus' 10th year.[653] A requisition for payment for a camel which carried "the king's food" (PA Ↄ.ḪÍ. LUGAL) from Uruk to Tema'. The nature of the food was not specified, but it was probably of a kind, unavailable in North Arabia, that would keep throughout a trip of at least thirty to forty days.

The name in document (k) indicates that Babylonians as well as Arabs engaged in the caravan traffic from Babylonia to Tema'. The last two documents imply considerable Babylonian control (or at least influence) to ensure regular traffic to Tema' along the desert routes, the routes that were used in trading from Tema' to Uruk and apparently from Tema' to Babylon. Caravans were undoubtedly conducted along the roads encircling the Nafūd desert from east or west — i.e., via Jauf or Ḥā'il—and not along the Fertile Crescent, where the distance is double.

651 Cf. Eph'al, *Orientalia* 47 (1978), 74-90.

652 See Dougherty, *Nabonidus and Belshazzar*, 117.

653 For lines 1-8 see Dougherty, *ibid.*, 114-115.

Chapter VII

THE ACHAEMENID PERIOD (539-ca. 450 B.C.)

Information about Arab movement into and contact with the countries of the Fertile Crescent ceases during the period between Nebuchadnezzar's wars in Palestine and the era of Herodotus and Nehemiah. In the course of this century and more, nomad penetration into the settled areas of Transjordan and southern Palestine, the approaches to Egypt and the Middle Euphrates region developed significantly, but the stages of the process are uncharted and later sources give only a static picture of its termination.

Our historical sources for the Achaemenid period are exclusively contemporary and include the memoirs of Nehemia, who was active in Jerusalem from 445 B.C. on, the works of Herodotus, who toured Egypt and the Persian Empire in the middle of the 5th century B.C. and of Xenophon, who traversed the Euphrates region in 401 B.C. in the famous March of Ten Thousand. We refrain from using later classical authors (of the 2nd century B.C. and afterwards), whose historical value for the Achaemenid period is uncertain. Our consideration of the Arabs therefore ends with the second half of the 5th century B.C., thus obviating the necessity for considering the relationship between them and the Nabataeans dealt with in classical sources for the early Hellenistic period, a subject for special research.

One further remark: The historical writings of the Achaemenid period use the general term "Arab(s)" to designate the nomads between Egypt and the Euphrates region. Our conclusion from the material about the nomads in the Assyrian and Babylonian periods — that the general term "Arabs" was applied to tribes and tribal federations — is valid for the Achaemenid period as well. The "Arabs" therefore cannot be considered a unified political and administrative entity during the Achaemenid period,[654] a time when the nomads spread over more territory than they had earlier. Accordingly, the extent and location of the term "Arabs" in each reference must be determined by internal context alone. This refutes the assumption of a satrapy or other administratively uniform organization encompassing all the nomads in the desert regions adjacent to the settled areas, from the Euphrates to Gaza and Dedan (al-'Ulā) in North Arabia. Thus the term "Arabia" (Pers. *Arbāya,* Bab. kur*Arabi*)[655] in the lists of Darius I and Xerxes must be construed as a certain category of population controlled by the Persian empire, and not as a territory or a specific administrative organization.[656]

Since, as noted, it is impossible to follow the successive stages of nomad penetration into the settled regions of the Fertile Crescent, we must be content with designating the area they occupied at the end of the process. First, therefore we shall deal with the information geographically, and then according to special problems of nomad status in the Achaemenid administrative system in particular regions.

A. DEMOGRAPHY

1. Northern Sinai and the Approach to Egypt: Herodotus, an important source for the demography of mid-5th century B.C. Egypt and the Sinai peninsula, calls the entire region east of the Nile and the Pelusian Branch, from the Mediterranean to the Red Sea, ἡ 'Αραβίη, and its population οἱ 'Αραβίοι (II 8, 15, 19, 30, 75 [cf. note 662], 124, 158). The Gulf of Suez is called 'Αράβιος κόλπος and the mountainous region east of Heliopolis τῆς 'Αραβίης ὄρος (II 8, 124). Daphnae (biblical Tahpanhes, present-day Defeneh) is described as a border town

654 Cf. for example, Olmstead, *History of the Persian Empire,* 56, 243-244, 293; and A.J. Toynbee, *A Study of History,* Vol. 7B, Oxford 1963, 657-659 (who, however, seems hesitant about this matter).

655 See e.g., F.H. Weissbach, *Die Keilinschriften der Achämeniden,* Leipzig 1911, 88-89.

656 The Darius I and Xerxes lists did not accord with the taxable or administrative divisions of the Achaemenid empire and only demonstrated its extent. (On the nature of these sources and the purpose of their composition see Toynbee, *ibid.,* 585-590). This might explain the numerical discrepancy between the 32 names in the Persian royal lists and the 20 satrapies organized at the time of Darius I for administrative and taxation purposes as described by Herodotus III, 89-96.

with a garrison "against the Arabs and the Syrians" (II 30), and the town of Πάτουμος (biblical Pithom) near Bubastis at the approach to Wadi Thumīlāt as 'Αραβίης πόλις (II 158).[657]

Archaeological evidence for Arabs at the approach to Wadi Thumīlāt was provided by the discovery of silver bowls, three bearing Aramaic inscriptions published by I. Rabinowitz.[658] They are votive inscriptions to the Arab goddess han-'Ilāt (cf. her name given as 'Αλιλάτ in Herodotus III 8), one of which says: זי קינו בר גשם מלך קדר קרב להנאלת ("That which Qainū son of Gešem, king of Qedar, offered to han-'Ilāt"), and another: זי קרב צחא בר עבדעמרו להנאלת ("That which Ṣiḥa' son of 'Abd-'Amrū offered to han-'Ilāt"). Although they were not discovered *in situ,* there are convincing indications that they came from the shrine excavated at Tell el-Maskhuṭeh; a hoard of thousands of Attic tetradrachmas found there makes it possible to date the bowls to the 5th century B.C.[659] This date is further supported by the paleography of the inscriptions and the typology of the bowls.[660]

After the Achaemenid period the region east of the Nile delta was called 'Αραβία as well: The Septuagint translates "in the land of Goshen" in Genesis (45:10; 46:34) as ἐν γῇ Γέσεμ 'Αραβιας 'Αραβίᾳ cleary linking the Arabs with the area east of the delta.[661] (On the question of dating the demographic situation reflected in this translation and whether it refers to Geshem king of Qedar, whose name appears in one of the bowl inscriptions, or to Geshem the Arab in the Book of Nehemiah, see pp. 210-214).

All of the preceding proves that during the 5th century B.C. nomads dwelt near the eastern border of lower Egypt and had even settled into

657 For the identification of Pithom with Tell el-Maskhuṭeh see E. Naville, *The Store-city of Pithom,* London 1885, especially 5-8, 29-31, and S. Aḥituv in *Liver Memorial Volume,* 157-160; or with Tell er-Retabeh, see Gardiner, *JEA* 19 (1933), 127.

658 *JNES* 15 (1956), 1-9.

659 The coins are all from the 5th and no later than the first quarter of the 4th century B.C. (Rabinowitz, *ibid.,* 4, n. 24). The shrine seems not to have existed after the cessation of Persian rule in Egypt at the end of the 5th century B.C., after the death of Darius II.

660 J. Naveh, *The Development of the Aramaic Script,* Jerusalem 1970, 42; cf. also Dumbrell, *BASOR* 203 (1971), 38.

661 Rabinowitz, *ibid.,* 6-7.

the approach to Wadi Thumīlāt,[662] probably with the consent of the Achaemenid authorities, as attested by the shrine of the Arab goddess han-'Ilāt in Tell el-Maskhuṭeh. The nomads may have served as the garrison for this important point of entry.[663] This adds to what we already know about Arab habitation throughout northern Sinai in earlier periods (see also p. 196 on Herodotus II 12).

2. The Southern Coast of Palestine: Herodotus' outline of the administrative divisions of the Persian empire at the time of Darius I (III 89-97) includes the fifth satrapy, which extended from Posideium (=al-Mina) at the border of Cilicia and Syria to Egypt, excluding the "Arab district" (μοίρη 'Αραβίων) in the southern part, which was exempt from taxes (III 91; on the significance of this exemption, see pp. 206-210). According to Herodotus, the Arabs of that district were considered "friends" (ξεῖνοι) of the king of Persia, unlike the inhabitants of the other satrapies, who were subjects. Their status is said to have derived from a treaty made by Cambyses with the "king of the Arabs" before the campaign to Egypt in 525 B.C., whereby the Arabs supplied the Persian army with water in the Sinai desert, thus solving the critical problem upon which the campaign's success depended (III 4-9, 88; see above pp. 137-142). Herodotus III 5 states that the district stretched from Gaza (κάδυτις)[664] to Ienysus ('Ιήνυσος)[665] and that its

662 Herodorus II 75 tells of flying snakes that came every year from Arabia to Egypt and were destroyed by ibises before they could penetrate the settled area. Herodotus says that he saw the bones of these snakes in a place defined in his work as one of ἡ 'Αραβίη regions, in the vicinity of the city Βουτο (today Tell Fara'īn in the northwest delta). This geographical designation suggests that Arab territory in the 5th century B.C. extended over most of the northern delta, a proposition difficult to accept in view of all our other information about Egypt for the same period. Βουτο here is apparently an error, written in place of another city (persumably Πατουμος) located in the eastern delta; see W.W. How-J. Wells, *A Commentary on Herodotus,* Oxford 1928, I, 203-204.

663 Rabinowitz, *op. cit.,* 9.

664 The usual Greek form for Gaza was Γάζα; only Herodotus spells it Κάδυτις (II 159; III 5), which reflects the Egyptian pronunciation (written *Gḏt*), as Herodotus apparently heard it when he visited Egypt. For the spellings of Gaza during the biblical period and their reverberations in Herodotus, see Eph'al, "Gaza," *Enc. Miqr.,* VI, 116.

665 Ienysus does not occur in other sources (except in Stephen of Byzantium [*Ethnika,* ed. A. Meineke, 332], who, following Herodotus, spells it 'Ινυσσός and states that

coastal emporia belonged to the king of the Arabs. The fifth satrapy, inhabited by "Syrians",[666] resumed at Ienysus and extended to Lake Serbonis, west of which was the territory of Egypt. Herodotus lists the satrapies of Darius' empire according to the way they were taxed and administered and not according to ethnic or demographic structure.[667] His remarks about the area between Ienysus and Egypt are mainly concerned, like those about Palestine and northern Sinai, with the coast, where he had travelled, and not the interior. His reference to "Syrians" on the Mediterranean coast of Arabia (II 12) implies that the inhabitants of that section of northern Sinai included in the fifth satrapy were also chiefly nomads, and that the "Syrians", i.e., the Phoenicians, dwelt only in coastal trading and shipping stations.

Herodotus' description of the population from Gaza south to Lake Serbonis clarifies several points about Arabian trade operations: i) Herodotus II 12 suggests that the Arabs had no direct interest in maritime activity and were no longer in the spice trade once their goods reached the coast and were shipped out.[668] Accordingly, the "Arab

it is on the road to Mt. Casius). Its location is uncertain. Based on the datum that Ienysus was three days' walk from Mt. Casius and Lake Serbonis (Herodotus III 5), and on the assumption that the emporia of the king of the Arabs between Gaza and Ienysus (Herodotus, *ibid.*,) were numerous, F.-M. Abel suggested identifying Ienysus with el-Arish. He refutes identification with Khan-Yūnis — likely because of the similarity of the names — because he believes that Yūnis, for whom the place was named, was governor of the Gaza region in the 14th century C.E.; see *RB* 48 (1939), 535-539.

666 The "Syrian" territory extended, according to Herodotus III 5, along the coast of the fifth satrapy from Cilicia to Egypt, and included within it the inhabitants of Palestine, who are designated οἱ Συρίοι οἱ Παλαιστίνοι.

667 The system by which the empire was divided for tax purposes is described in detail in Herodotus' introduction to the list (III 89). On the character of the list, delineating the territories of the different satrapies, which did not in all cases coincide with the ethnic structure of the Persian empire, see the Appendix to Toynbee, *A Study of History*, Vol. 7B, 585-597, Tables V-VI. For an all-embracing discussion of the western satrapies listed in Herodotus, see Leuze, *Satrapieneinteilung*, 43-144.

668 Cf. The Words of Aḥiqar xiv 208: "do not show the sea to an Arab or the desert to a Sidonian, for their work is different(?)" (כי עבידתהם פרישה), A. Cowley, *Aramaic Papyri of the Fifth Century B.C.*, Oxford 1923, 219.

district" can be termed a "corridor to the sea", at whose end the Arabs sold their goods. ii) Routing the spices to southern Palestine rather than Tyre reduced the transportation costs of the Arab traders and increased their profits. iii) It is even possible that by routing the spices to the region supervised by the "king of the Arabs", their goods could be marketed through Greek and not only Phoenician merchants, thus improving their economic status and ensuring adequate prices.

3. Idumaea and southern Transjordan: The memoirs of Nehemiah list Arabs among the enemies of Judah who sought to interfere with the construction of the wall of Jerusalem (Neh. 4:1), and Geshem their leader as one of Nehemiah's three adversaries (Neh. 2:19; 6:1, 6). Since the other enemies mentioned in Neh. 4:1 are identifiable as northern, eastern and western neighbors of Judah, and from information given by such classical writers as Herodotus, Diodorus and Polybius about the Arabs in Palestine and Transjordan in the 5th and 4th centuries B.C., these Arabs apparently lived south of Judah,[669] in a region ruled by Geshem. Placing them in southern Palestine and explaining the circumstances of their existence there demand overall comprehension of the demographic developments in southern Transjordan and in the area south of the Judaean hills during the Chaldaean and Achaemenid period.

We have no written information about southern Transjordan for the period between Nebuchadnezzar's war against Ammon and Moab in 582 B.C. and the beginning of the Hellenistic period. The concept of its history in the 150-year-long interim period is based mainly on conclusions drawn from N. Glueck's archaeological survey in Transjordan in the 1930's. It is an all but unique archaeological source for the history of the region, where excavations of Iron Age sites are few. The survey fails noticeably to distinguish any findings from the Achaemenid period (Iron Age III), which is the subject of this chapter, chiefly because at the time the requisite scientific methods and data were lacking. It is not impossible that systematic excavation or even a new

669 Alt, *Kleine Schriften* II, 294, 343-345; M. Avi-Yonah, *The Holy Land from the Persian to the Arab Conquests (536 B.C. to A.D. 640)*, Grand Rapids, Mich. 1966, 26.

survey based on the advances in present-day Palestinian archaeology will change the historical picture.[670]

On the basis of the early survey, Glueck concluded that in the 8th century B.C. material civilization within the territories of Edom and Moab declined considerably and that permanent settlement ceased there in the first half of the 6th century B.C., to be resumed only in the second half of the 4th century B.C. with the first Nabataean habitation.[671] These archaeological conclusions and the complete absence of testimony as to a political structure in Edom and Moab after Nebuchadnezzar's reign suggest that the region was grievously affected by the destruction of its fortresses and the waves of desert people who breached its borders.[672] Although undoubtedly the proportion of nomads in the population gradually increased, the idea of the cessation of permanent settlement and, concomitantly, material culture, is unlikely and would mean that the earlier population was driven *in toto* out of its country as its political system disintegrated. It is more reasonable to suppose that in southern Transjordan two ethnic groups — the earlier inhabitants of Edom and Moab and the Arabs — each with its own culture, existed side by side, intermingling in the course of generations in an extended process whose details are by no means clear.[673]

The list of the builders of the Jerusalem wall (Neh. chap. 3) shows that in the middle of the 5th century B.C. the province of Judah

670 For the failure, until recently, of archaeological research in Palestine to recognize the material culture of the Achaemenid period and for the present stage of such reseach, see E. Stern, *The Material Culture of the Land of the Bible in the Persian Period,* Jerusalem 1973, (Hebrew).

671 For a summary, see Glueck, *AASOR* 14 (1934), 83; 15 (1935), 139.

672 See, e.g., Ginsberg, *Marx Jubilee Volume,* 368; Van Zyl, *The Moabites,* 157-158; Landes, "Ammon", *The Interpreter's Dictionary of the Bible,* I, 112-113.

673 A clear example of the survival of a Moabite cultural element appears in a mid-4th century B.C. inscription from el-Kerak in Moab, published by J.T. Milik, *Studii Biblici Franciscani,* Liber Annuus 9 (1958-1959), 331-341, which mentions the god Chemosh. Even N. Glueck assumes reciprocity and intermarriage between the peoples of southern Transjordan (*The Other Side of the Jordan,* 166-167; *Deities and Dolphins,* New York 1965, 5), thus contradicting his conclusions about the absence of permanent settlements there during the Chaldaean and Achaemenid periods. Glueck's designation of the 6th century B.C. desert people in Transjordan as Nabataean is questionable; see further note 679.

extended to the Tekoa-Beth zur-Keilah line,[674] a border that, according to I Macc. 4:61; 5:65; 14:33, existed until the Hasmonaean wars. The administrative framework of the area south of Judaea[675] in 312 B.C. is described by Diodorus XIX, 95, 2; 98, 1 as an eparchy called Ἰδουμαία. Though Diodorus deals with the beginning of the Hellenistic period, it is possible to assume from his words an identical administrative unit during the Achaemenid period, by what name we do not know.[676]

The name of the eparchy probably derives from the origin of its predominant population at the end of the Achaemenid period. Indeed there are several references to the penetration of Edomites into the southern parts of Judah, which had been wrested from it in the wars of Nebuchadnezzar (cf. Ezek. 35, esp. v. 10; Obadiah, v. 19; III Esdras 4:50),[677] but they are conspicuously absent from the books of Ezra and Nehemiah, which mention only the Arabs in southern Palestine. During the period under discussion, Jews as well might have been living in the "villages with their fields" in the Beer-sheba valley (Neh. 11:25-30).[678]

674 See M. Avi-Yonah, *Historical Geography of Palestine from the End of the Babylonian Exile to the Arab Conquest,* Jerusalem 1962, 18-19, 21, (Hebrew); idem, *The Holy Land,* 17, 20-22.

675 Judah refers to a political entity; Judaea, a geographical one.

676 Cf. Avi-Yonah, *The Holy Land,* 25-26.

677 How and when these parts of Judah were torn away and Edomite penetration began cannot be precisely determined from biblical sources. The oracles of Ezekiel allude to their occurence in the first third of the 6th century B.C. (We cannot accept J. Morgenstern's view, *HUCA* 27 [1956], 101, that the references in Prophets, Psalms and Lamentations to the enmity between Edom and Judah reflect political developments in the Restoration period, since he arbitrarily removes his references from their literary and historical context). For suggestions that the process under consideration began in 598, 586 or 582 B.C., see Alt, *Kleine Schriften* II, 294, 328; Mazar,*'Atiqot,* English Series 5 (1966), 3-4; J.M. Myers, *Near Eastern Studies in Honor of W.F. Albright,* Baltimore-London 1971, 377-392.

678 Since the places listed in Neh. 11:25-30 were undoubtedly not included in the boundaries of the province of Judah (*Yehud*) of the Restoration period, the relationship of this list to the period of Nehemiah is problematic. S. Klein, *Eretz Yehudah,* Tel Aviv 1939, 4-6, held that the list is dated from Nehemiah's time and indicates that Jewish settlement expanded beyond the borders of the province of Judah. Albright thought, on the contrary, that this was a list of settlements saved from Babylonian destruction and composed at the beginning of the Restoration period (*Marx Jubilee Volume,* 364, n. 47a). On the inconclusive problem and dating

The demographic picture in Transjordan, as we see it, suggests that by mid-5th century B.C. the region south of Judaea was not yet socio-ethnically stabilized: Jews may have lived in certain parts of it, but like Edom itself its essential elements were Edomite and Arab in various stages of nomadic and sedentary life.[679]

All of the above makes it clear that, with the collapse in the first third of the 6th century B.C. of the kingdoms of Judah and Transjordan, there was a repetition of what happened in Palestine and its environs after the fall of the kingdoms of Israel and Damascus: waves of nomads penetrated into the settled areas close to the desert borders, this time throughout southern Transjordan and Palestine to the Judaean hills.

To sum up, in the 5th century B.C. the penetration of the nomads into the territory of Palestine and its environs and their absorption into the economic, administrative and military system of the Persian empire were all but completed. This was made possible by the tolerance and multinational structure of the Persian empire, the absence of independent national entities in Transjordan and Palestine, the development of Arabian trade, especially its western branch (for further details see pp. 206-210), and the extensive military undertakings demanding absorption into the Persian army of men from all the peoples under Achaemenid rule. Thus, for example, units of Arabs on racing camels took part in Xerxes' campaign to Greece in 480 B.C. (Herodotus VII 86-87, 184). The extent of Arab absorption into the military system of the western part of the Persian empire is revealed by

of the list, see also Alt, *Kleine Schriften* II, 301-305; W. Rudolph, *Esra und Nehemia,* Tübingen 1949, 189 ff.

679 Our epigraphic evidence indicates that in the mid-4th century B.C., i.e., close to period mentioned in our earliest literary reference to the eparchy of Idumaea, the Edomite-Arab penetration into southern Palestine was complete. Aramaic ostraca from Beer-sheba and Arad contain dozens of names with the Edomite theophorous element Qos, as well as Arabic names like *Whbw, Zydw, Zbydw, Ntynw, Ḥlfw, 'ydw, W'lw, 'mw, Mlkw* (J. Naveh in Y. Aharoni, *Arad Inscriptions,* Jerusalem 1975, 167-204 (Hebrew); idem, in Y. Aharoni (ed.), *Beer-sheba,* I, *Excavations at Tel Beer-sheba, 1969-1971 Seasons,* Tel Aviv 1973, 79-82; idem, *Tel Aviv* 6 [1979], 182-198). Most of the Arabic names are known from the Nabataean onomasticon. This does not attest, however, Nabataean existence in the Negeb in the mid-4th century B.C. and may refer to another "Arab" element; see p. 211.

Diodorus' description of their participation in coastal and overseas operations (in 410 and 386 B.C.).[680]

B. ACHAEMENID RULE IN NORTH ARABIA AND TRANSJORDAN

With the victory over Nabonidus in 539 B.C., Cyrus gained control of North Arabia and its desert routes to Mesopotamia and, of course, Transjordan. The extent of his control over the nomads in the Syro-Arabian desert is demonstrated by his Cylinder Inscription, lines 28-30: "All the kings of the entire world from the Upper to the Lower Sea, those who are seated in throne rooms (*a-ši-ib parakkē*^{meš}), (those who) live in ..., all the kings of the West Land living in tents (*šarrāni*$^{\text{meš kur}}$*A-mur-ri-i a-ši-ib kuš-ta-ri*), brought their heavy tributes and kissed my feet in Babylon".[681]

Dougherty and Smith believed that Cyrus established contact with the nomads in the western part of the empire before the conquest of Babylon in Nabonidus' 17th year (539 B.C.). Since there are no clear sources for Cyrus' activities between 545 and 539 B.C., they assumed that his conflict with Nabonidus lasted several years, beginning with the elimination of Babylonian control in the western part of the empire before he proceeded to Babylon itself.[682] In Dougherty's view, the Persian expeditionary force reached North Arabia, which grew in importance with Nabonidus' lengthy stay there. Smith limited somewhat the actual extent of Persian military operations, but thought that Cyrus had made contact with the nomads and other inhabitants of the Syrian desert, Syria and Palestine, who recognized his dominion even before the fall of Babylon. These opinions are based mainly on Xenophon's report that on the way from Sardis to Babylonia — after overcoming Croesus, king of Lydia — Cyrus subjugated Greater Phrygia, Cappadocia and the Arabs, and was helped by the peoples of these regions to encircle Babylon (*Cyropaedia* VII,

680 Diodorus XIII, 46, 6; XV, 2, 4. Although the first reference does not certify the actuality of the operation, its possibility is sufficient for our purposes.

681 Weissbach, *Die Keilinschriften der Achämeniden,* 6; *ANET,* 316.

682 Dougherty, *Nabonidus and Belshazzar,* 161-166; Smith, *Isaiah Chapters XL-LV,* 42-45, 145-151. For an essentially similar, although generalized, view of events and their sequence, see also Olmstead, *History of the Persian Empire,* 45.

iv, 16; v, 13). They are also based to some extent on the general statement of Berossus (*Against Apion* I 20) that in Nabonidus' 17th year, Cyrus subjugated all the countries of Asia and turned his attention to Babylonia.

But these opinions fail to distinguish Xenophon's exact use of the term "Arab(s)" and misinterpret his testimony.

1. In the description of the campaign of Cyrus the Younger against his brother Artaxerxes II (in 401 B.C.), the name 'Αραβία refers to the Middle Euphrates region, which stretched from the mouth of the 'Αράξης river, i.e., the Khabur,[683] either a five-or an eighteen-day march eastward[684] (*Anabasis* I 5). The Arabs mentioned in *Cyropaedia* VII, iv, 16 in conjunction with Greater Phrygia and Cappadocia along the route from Sardis to Babylon are acceptably placed in the 'Αραβία of Xenophon's geographic picture, as referred to in *Anabasis* I 5; there is no evidence, however, of a political framework linking the Arabs of that region with the nomads in the southern part of the Syrian desert, in Palestine and in North Arabia during the Chaldaean and Achaemenid period.

2. There is dubious historical value in several details about Cyrus II in *Cyropaedia,* which was written as a pedagogic-political and not purely historiographical tract. It is not clear what sources for the events, which antedated the report by 150 years, were available to Xenophon and to what extent he utilized them. The sequence of Cyrus' wars and campaigns against Babylonia and Lydia in this work seems a literary rather than an exact compilation.[685]

683 For this identification, based on the distances recorded in *Anabasis,* and for the geography of the region, see Musil, *Middle Euphrates,* 217, 221-223.

684 'Αραβία undoubtedly extended to the city of Κορσωτή, five days' march from the mouth of the Khabur, and — from Xenophon's report of Cyrus' march beyond that point — possibly as far as Πύλαι, another 13 days' journey (Leuze, *Satrapieneinteilung,* 147).

685 On the question of Xenophon's sources for *Cyropaedia* and on the doubtful value of some of its details, see H.R. Breitenbach, "Xenophon", *PW,* II Reihe, 18 Halbband, 1709-1712; K. Galling, *Studien zur Geschichte Israels im persischen Zeitalter,* Tübingen 1964, 25 ff. For the attribution of military and political victories to Cyrus, which were clearly, as other sources show, achieved by his

3. Neither is there validity in Smith's assumption, based on the opening lines of Herodotus III 88, in themselves not very clear, that both Cyrus and Cambyses subjugated the Arabs, and that the Arabs in southern Palestine helped Cambyses in the campaign to Egypt because they *had been* Persian subjects, though with the special status of ξεῖνοι. Such an assumption is untenable in the face of Herodotus' unusually lengthy report of the treaty with the Arabs made *on the initiative of Cambyses prior to his campaign to Egypt* (III 4, 7, 9).

Furthermore, the Nabonidus Sippar Cylinder and the Ḥarran Stelae, apparently written after Nabonidus' return from Tema',[686] contain no hint of his having been forced out by Cyrus' military pressure and describe Cyrus himself positively, and not as an enemy.[687] These inscriptions indicate that Babylonian control extended to Gaza and the Egyptian border (Sippar Cyl. i 39-42; Nab. H_1 iii 18-23; H_2 iii 18-21), and that, on his return from Tema', Nabonidus was occupied with extensive building and regulation of religious activity in the Harran region. The Chaldaean empire thus seems to have collapsed rapidly rather than over several years of military operations. It emerges that Cyrus gained control over the Arabs in the western part of the Babylonian empire, as he had over all the territory up to southern Palestine, only after his victory over Nabonidus king of Babylonia and *as a consequence of it.*[688]

successors, and for the contradictions between Xenophon and Herodotus about matters concerned with the Arabs, see also Leuze, *ibid.*, 5-7.

686 For the dating of these documents see Tadmor, *Studies Landsberger,* 351-363; on the historical conclusions arising from this, idem, *D. Ben-Gurion Jubilee Volume,* Jerusalem 1964, 450-473 (Hebrew).

687 See particularly the assessment of Cyrus' victory over Astyages ([m]*Iš-tu-me-gu*), his lord, as an act enjoined by Marduk (Sippar Cyl. i 26-35; S. Langdon, *Die neubabylonischen Königsinschriften,* Leipzig 1911, 220-221).

688 The Neo-Babylonian documents from Neirab provided Galling and Smith with diametrically opposed evidence as to Babylonian provenance in the western part of the Chaldaean empire a few years before the fall of Babylon. These documents are, however, irrelevant from the point of view of both chronology and contents, see Eph'al, *Orientalia* 47 (1978), 84-90.

Important evidence of Persian rule in North Arabia is provided by the JS 349 lih. inscription from Qabūr al-Jundi, some twelve kilometers north of the Dedan (al-ʿulā) oasis.[689] The words *b'ym gšm bn šhr wʿbd fḥt ddn* ("in the time of *Gšm b. Šhr* and *ʿbd* the governor of Dedan") *br'[y...],* are a date-formula. Other Lihyanite inscriptions from Dedan point out that the term *br'y,* occurring in date-formulae means "in the reign of ... " and is followed by the king's name.[690] This inscription probably also ended with the name of a king, no longer preserved, to whom Geshem b. Šahr and ʿAbd, governor of Dedan, were subject.[691] Without the king's name the inscription is difficult to date.

Winnett's key study, which classified the Lihyanite and Thamudic scripts according to type and stage and established the chronological relationship between them, defines the script of JS 349 lih. as Early Lihyanite.[692] Based on the argument that the title *fḥt ddn,* "governor of Dedan", in that inscription is Mesopotamian in origin (Akkadian ^{lú}*bēl pīḫati*) and nonexistent in Arabic, and that its occurrence in Dedan can only be explained by the existence there of Persian rule at that time, he concludes that this type of Lihyanite script was common to the Achaemenid period.[693]

689 For the text of this inscription and discussions of its date, see A. Jaussen-R. Savignac, *Mission archéologique en Arabie,* II, Paris 1914, 524-525, Atlas, Pl. CXXXIX; Winnett, *A Study of the Lihyanite and Thamudic Inscriptions,* Toronto 1937, 50-51, Pl. VIII; idem, *AR,* 115-117; Caskel, *Lihyan und Lihyanisch,* 101-102. See also Albright, *Alt Festschrift,* 4, 6; Rabinowitz, *JNES* 15 (1956), 7.

690 Cf. JS lih. 68:4-5: *ṯlt 'ym qbl r'y slḥ*
72:8-9: *snt ḫms br'y ʿbdn hn's*
82:4-6: *snt ṯlṯn wḫms 35 br'y mnʿy lḏn bn hn's mlk lḥyn*
83:6-7: *snt ʿšrn wtsʿ 29 br'y gltqs*
85:2-4: *snt t[sʿ] br'y šmt gšm bn lḏn mlk [l]ḥyn*

These are the transliterations according to Caskel, *ibid.,* 90-93, 114-115, whose reading is different in various details from that of Jaussen and Savignac, the first to publish the inscriptions.

691 Winnett, *AR,* 116, n. 17, thinks it possible that the name of the king was erased because he was foreign. From the drawing of the inscription (a photograph has not been published), it is uncertain whether the name was deliberately erased, was accidentally damaged or the stone itself was worn.

692 Winnett, *Study of Lihyanite and Thamudic Inscriptions,* 50-51.

693 Caskel, *op. cit.,* 101-102 — in accordance with his general chronological system for Dedan and Lihyan — dates the inscription to the second century B.C. and attempts

Our information about southern Transjordan resumes at the beginning of the Hellenistic period with the notable fact that neither this region nor North Arabia was part of the realm of Alexander the Great and his successors. The collapse of Persian rule in these regions signaled the end of Persian control and influence over the trade routes in the cup of the Fertile Crescent, as well as some of the considerable profit derived therefrom. The circumstances of this process cannot be exactly determined: it seems to have taken place after the death of Darius II (404 B.C.) — when Egypt, free of Persian domination, also undertook anti-Persian activities in Palestine, Phoenicia and Cyprus during the period of the XXIXth-XXXth Dynasties — and to have resulted from the rebellions and internal struggles which weakened the central government and dissolved the Achaemenid empire.[694] In establishing the time and circumstances of the end of Achaemenid rule in Transjordan (and North Arabia), it seems necessary to consider the destruction of the settlements in southern Palestine, i.e., Ezion-geber (stratum V) and Kadesh-barnea (stratum III) — which were never resettled — and Arad (stratum V),[695] as well as the great damage done to En-gedi (stratum IV).[696] This was probably the period when the earlier administrative and political structure of southern Transjordan was finally broken down. The northern extremity of the region over which Persia lost control can

to explain that the title *fḥt ddn* was preserved in North Arabia hundreds of years after the collapse of the Achaemenid empire because of the isolation of the region. Neither his system nor his dating can be accepted; see note 612.

Winnett, *op. cit.*, and Albright, *op. cit.*, 4, fix the date at 450-425 B.C.; see also Olmstead, *History of the Persian Empire*, 295, 316; H. Grimme, *OLZ* 44 (1941), 337-343; Rabinowitz, *op. cit.*, 7. Because of their insufficiently supported identification of *Gšm b. Šhr* with Geshem the Arab, Nehemiah's contemporary and adversary, reservations as to such a dating remain; see below, pp. 210-214.

694 For a survey of the political history of the Satrapy "Beyond the River" from the death of Darius II to the end of Achaemenid rule, see A.F. Rainey, *AJBA* 1/2 (1969), 66 ff.

695 Because of the lack of precise data, the termination of each of these strata can be dated only generally to the end of the 5th and beginning of the 4th century B.C. On Ezion-geber Stratum V, see Glueck, *BA* 28 (1965), 87; on Arad Stratum V, Aharoni, *IEJ* 14 (1964), 133, 141, 144; 17 (1967), 243-244; for the date of the destruction of Ezion-geber and Arad, see also Mazar, *IEJ* 14 (1964), 126 n. 8; on Kadesh-barnea Stratum III, see M. Dothan, *IEJ* 15 (1965), 141-143.

696 The discovery of Attic pottery from the first half of the 4th century B.C. in

be determined from the area of Transjordan under the sway of the Ptolemies. It can be said generally to have extended north from the Arnon river (Wadi al-Mujib) and to have included a *cleruchy* (a military colony) in "the Land of Tobiah" to cope with the nomads from the desert.[697] Farther south were the Nabataean Arabs, who were not subjugated until the Roman period.

C. ARAB STATUS IN SOUTHERN PALESTINE WITHIN THE ACHAEMENID ADMINISTRATIVE AND ECONOMIC SYSTEM

In describing the division of the Achaemenid empire for purposes of taxation and administration at the time of Darius I, Herodotus lists twenty satrapies and specifies the annual tax (φόρος) of each (III 89-96).[698] According to Herodotus III 97, the only peoples in the empire exempt from the φόρος were the Persians (who were free of all financial demands), the Ethiopians on the Egyptian border, the Colchians in the Caucasus and the Arabs. Although the last three were in fact not included among the taxed satrapies — whose inhabitants were the majority of the Empire — Herodotus notes that they contributed "gifts" δῶρα at regular intervals. The Arabs' "gifts" are said to have been 1000 talents of frankincense a year. As to Arab territory exempt from the φόρος, Herodotus refers only to the "Arab district" μοίρη 'Αραβίων expropriated from the fifth satrapy along the coast from Gaza to Ienysus, which he mentions explicity as tax-exempt (ταῦτα ἦν ἀτελέα, cf. III 5, 91 and also 88). Since Herodotus locates only the Arabs in southern Palestine and northern Sinai, and none of the others within the Achaemenid empire, it is not clear whether exemption from the φόρος and obligation to give δῶρα applied to other Arabs in the rest of the empire.

Building 234 in En-gedi suggests that, despite the ravaging of the Stratum IV settlement in ca. 400 B.C., it existed until its destruction, about 350-340 B.C. (Mazar, *IEJ* 17 [1967], 138-139).

697 The southern region within the area of Ptolemaic authority in Transjordan was Μωαβῖτις, of unknown extent, whose southern border was possibly the Arnon river (cf. Avi-Yonah, *The Holy Land,* 40-41). About the boundaries of "the Land of Tobiah" and the significance of the *cleruchy* see V. Tcherikover, *Hellenistic Civilization and the Jews,* Philadelphia 1959, 63-65.

698 For literature on the list of satrapies see above, note 667.

The identity of those Arabs and the nature of their "gifts" constitute a fundamental difficulty: In describing the administrative-fiscal situation in the Achaemenid empire during the first half of the 5th century B.C., Herodotus employs Greek terms whose Persian equivalents and means of implementation are unknown. What we know about the regular taxes exacted from subject peoples in the Assyrian empire as well as in Hellenistic and Roman times, the φόρος which Herodotus defines as the main tax of the satrapies, can be generally equated with the *biltu* and *maddattu*. It is, however, not clear whether the word δῶρα used by Herodotus translates an official Persian or Akkadian term or is purely literary, without fiscal-administrative significance. It is doubtful that in the tax system of the Assyrian and Babylonian empires there is a clear parallel to such a procedure as the δῶρα described by Herodotus.[699] On the other hand, there is no sense in attempting to define it by means of its application in the Greek and Hellenistic world, because the fiscal system of that world differed from those of the eastern empires. It therefore appears that the significance of the "gifts" mentioned in Herodotus can be clarified only by the writings themselves.

The accepted method for determining the geographic boundaries of the "Arabs exempt from tax" derives from Herodotus' statement that the Arabs had not been subjugated by the Persians but had achieved the status of "friends" (ξεῖνοι) by virtue of the support given by "the king of the Arabs" to Cambyses in his campaign to Egypt (cf. III 4-5, 7, 9, 88, 91, 97), as well as from geographical arguments.[700] Such an

699 We might compare the δῶρα with *nāmurtu*, meaning "gift" in the Middle-Assyrian period, but becoming during the Neo-Assyrian period a tax whose rate and date of payment were fixed (see Postgate, *Taxation*, 146-162). We have, however, no evidence for payment of this tax by peoples outside Assyrian control, like the Colchians and the Ethiopians referred to by Herodotus. It is also possible to compare the δῶρα with *kadrê* — "gifts", which, besides its general meaning, sometimes refers to a certain kind of tax (occuring with *biltu*) which seems to have been paid regularly, cf. *CAD* K 33, *kadrû*, b. Cf. especially the name of the Desert Gate in Nineveh, during the reign of Sennacherib: "The Gifts (*kadrê*) of the People of ^{lú}*Su-mu-'*-AN and the People of ^{lú}*Te-e-me* Enter through it", see pp. 124-125.

700 These considerations led to disparate conclusions: Leuze, *Satrapieneinteilung*, 103-104, logically assuming that Herodotus meant that only Arabs in the vicinity of southern Palestine helped Cambyses, concluded that they alone and not the other Arabs in the Syrian desert were exempt from tax. In the Appendix to Toynbee,

approach disregards the nature of the "gifts" demanded of the Arabs, clarification of which is vital to the comprehension of the scope and meaning of the δῶρα as used by Herodotus.

When Herodotus states that the Arabs (and likewise the Colchians and the Ethiopians) had to bring δῶρα *of regular amounts at regular intervals,* a definite revenue system is implied, rather than offerings freely and infrequently presented. The specific Arab "gift" of 1000 talents (about 30 tons!) of frankincense *per annum* is an extraordinarily onerous levy, as valuable as those extracted from the wealthiest satrapies.[701] The Achaemenid empire's revenue from the "Arabs" was thus very high, and hardly to be considered a mark of favored status, as Herodotus seems to indicate. The δῶρα can more reasonably be interpreted as a category of regular tax, though collected differently from the φόρος, since those on whom it was levied were beyond reach of the Persian administration.

The value of the Arabs' "gift", in frankincense rather than precious metals or animals, etc., points to involvement in the spice trade and considerable income; it also attests the scope and profit of such trade in the 5th century B.C.

Since Herodotus says that the "emporia on the sea coast" south of Gaza "belong" to the "king of the Arabs" (III 5), it is possible to link his reference to the Arabs' "gifts" (III 97) with that district and the Arabian trade routes that reached it.[702]

Supervising the transport of spices and other luxury goods in southern Palestine was difficult because of the profit from smuggling

A Study of History, Vol. 7B, 658-659, on the other hand, it is suggested that since the nomads lived along the most vital transportation arteries in southern Palestine, in the Middle Euphrates region and in frontier areas with long borders, the Achaemenid authorities exempted from tax all Arabs within imperial limits to ensure their loyalty.

701 Herodotus may not have exaggerated the amount of frankincense contained in the Arabs' "gift", since this datum appears in the list of taxes (III 89-97), probably deriving from an official or semi-official source. He does exaggerate, however, when he writes that at the altar of Bēl in Babylon the Chaldaeans annually burned 1000 talents of frankincense on the god's festival day (I 183).

702 Regarding Gaza as a center of the spice trade in the 4th century B.C., cf. the tradition that Alexander, after capturing Gaza, sent his tutor 500 talents of frankincense and 100 of myrrh (Plutarch, *Alexander,* XXV 4-5); for the Roman

and consequent avoidance of customs duties (a current parallel is the overland smuggling of *hashish* and arms in the Middle East). For this reason, "the emporia on the sea coast" might have been given to the "king of the Arabs" for fiscal purposes in connection with Arabian trade: in other words, the Achaemenid administration, instead of collecting customs itself, may have given the job to the "king of the Arabs", at the same time making him responsible for an annual deposit into the imperial treasury of a specific huge amount of frankincense, effectively equal to whatever duty should have been collected from the Arabian trade (like the tax collectors during the Hellenistic period).

How far, then, did the fiscal responsibility of the "king of the Arabs" extend? Presumably his territory included the routes ending at the Mediterranean coast:[703] from Transjordan (from Petra or vicinity), and perhaps Elath.[704] But it is doubtful whether he could control caravans in areas as remote as the Middle Euphrates region, or even the desert routes leading there from Syria. Accordingly, efficient customs collection became increasingly impossible the farther north from Petra the spice traders travelled. Even if we confine the territory of the "king

period, see Pliny, *Nat. Hist.* XII 32. Archaeological evidence for the connection of Gaza with South Arabian trade can also be found in the monogram — reading *'bm,* "father" — in South Arabic letters on a storage jar, probably from the 3rd-2nd centuries B.C., from Tell Jemme, lying on the road through which South Arabian goods reached Gaza; see G.W. Van Beek, *IEJ* 22 (1972), 246.

703 The "Arab district" south of Gaza seems to have been outside the maritime monopoly of the Phoenicians (cf. Herodotus, II 12; III 5), so that the Arab traders who brought spices there could deal with Greek and Egyptian traders and mariners and get better prices for their merchandise; see also pp. 196-197.

704 In a purely geographically oriented article, Y. Karmon, *Studies in the Geography of Israel* 6 (1968), 53-80, esp. 53-60 (Hebrew), emphasizes the difficulties of sailing in the Red Sea and believes that less time was needed to bring South Arabian goods to Palestine and Syria on the "caravan trail" of the Arabian peninsula than by sea. He therefore assumes that trade in these goods was almost exclusively overland, along roads to Petra and from there to Gaza or perhaps even Suez. We cannot, however, ignore findings from Tell el-Kheleifeh Stratum IV, which point to contact with Arabia (Glueck, *BA* 28 [1965], 86; for dating the 6th century B.C. Minaean monogram found on a jar in this stratum, see Glueck, *Yediot* 31 [1967], 125), and the existence of Achaemenid period settlements in Tell el-Kheleifeh Stratum V and Kadesh-barnea Stratum III (see note 695). Thus we must consider the possibility of transporting goods by sea from Arabia to Elath, from there overland to Gaza and thence both by land and sea.

of the Arabs" to southern Palestine and perhaps southern Transjordan, we are still dealing with a person whose economic-administrative control over an important revenue-producing branch of the Persian imperial economy was considerable. His political significance must therefore be weighed according to the scale of his operations (on this see pp. 210-214).

If we are correct about the nature of the Arabs' "gifts" and their geographical extent, we can, then, differentiate between two issues about the "Arab district", conceived as one by Herodotus:

1. Gaining the sympathy of the Arabs in so sensitive a section of the empire seemed to the Achaemenid authorities essential for the control of Egypt. The water supplied by the "king of the Arabs" to Cambyses in the campaign to Egypt in 525 B.C. reflects this geographical condition, which existed throughout Achaemenid dominion over Egypt. Perhaps Persian dependence on Arab good-will accounted for the grant of such privileges as exemption from the φόρος tax and the status of "friends" (ξεῖνοι).

2. For administrative-economic reasons of efficiency and convenience, the Achaemenid authorities, rather than supervising it themselves, delegated to the "king of the Arabs" supervision of the well-developed western section of the spice trade, carried on from Arabia to the coast south of Gaza. For the privilege of collecting duty for spices, annual fixed amounts of frankincense were returned. These payments by the "king of the Arabs" into the imperial treasury Herodotus calls δῶρα.

D. GESHEM THE ARAB: PROBLEMS OF IDENTIFICATION

Nehemiah's three adversaries when the Jerusalem wall was constructed were Geshem the Arab (Neh. 2:19; 6:1-2, 6), Sanballat the Horonite and Tobiah the Ammonite "servant". The book of Nehemiah does not specify their titles or status, but extra-biblical sources indicate that Sanballat was governor of Samaria in Nehemiah's time[705] and Tobiah a person of high rank in Transjordan and very influential in

705 On the position of Sanballat and his family as revealed by the papyri from Elephantine and Wadi Daliyeh, see F.M. Cross, in D.N. Freedman-J.C. Greenfield (eds.), *New Directions in Biblical Archaeology,* Garden City, N.Y. 1971, 45-69 (esp. 58-62); J. Liver, "Sanballat", *Enc. Miqr.,* V, 1057-1061.

Judah,[706] suggesting status with the Persian authorities and influence in Palestine like that of Nehemiah. Similar qualities can reasonably be attributed to Geshem the Arab. His influence is attested by Sanballat's "open letter" to Nehemiah, which begins: "It is reported among the nations, and Gashmu (גשמו) also says it, that you and the Jews intend to rebel" (Neh. 6:6). Only a person solidly established in the Persian administration could make such a charge against Nehemiah, whose position in Judah was authorized by the Persian court.

The -*û* ending of such names as גשמו (Neh. 6:6), קינו and עבדעמרו (in the Tell el-Maskhuṭeh inscriptions) is common in Nabataean[707] and less so in Palmyrene inscriptions.[708] It is extremely rare in South Arabic and Dedanite and Lihyanite inscriptions.[709] In Ancient Arabic it has survived in the an-Namāra Inscription (328 C.E.) and in the 'Azd dialect in southwestern Arabia.[710] It appears in Akkadian inscriptions in the names ^{m}*Gi-in-di-bu-'u* ^{kur}*Ar-ba-a-a* (the Monolith Inscription of Shalmaneser III, col. ii 24) and ^{m}*Ab-du-'u* ^{lú}*Ar-ba-a-[a?]* (CT XXII 86:7, a Neo-Babylonian letter). These Akkadian inscriptions, evincing the antiquity of this linguistic feature and its occurrence in the Syrian desert area hundreds of years before the other sources, are significant for consideration of the problem of the origin of the Nabataeans and their historical relationship (both chronological and demographic) to the Qedarites. For further aspects of this ending see note 679.

Identifying and characterizing Geshem the Arab strongly depends on clarifying the nature of his rivalry with Nehemiah: While we know that Sanballat and Tobiah were involved with the Temple and with the Jerusalem leadership and were inimical to Nehemiah probably because of his isolationist policy, we have no hint of a link between Geshem and the Temple and Jerusalem. The potential friction between him and

706 See Mazar, *IEJ* 7 (1957), 137-145, 229-238.

707 See e.g., *CIS* II, 2, pp. 228-249. For various proposed explanations of this linguistic feature, see J. Cantineau, *Le Nabatéen*, II, Paris 1932, 165-169.

708 They account for somewhat less than 10% of the names listed in J.K. Stark, *Personal Names in Palmyrene Inscriptions*, Oxford 1971.

709 An outstanding exception is the name *Ḥḏrw* in JS 349 lih. A few additional examples are to be found in Winnett, *AR*, 102 (*Mltw*) 107 (*'tw*).

710 Ch. Rabin, *Ancient West-Arabian*, London 1951, 56-57.

Nehemiah should therefore be reckoned on economic-administrative grounds, not vis-à-vis Judah's internal situation but rather in terms of Arab trading activity, assuming that the region south of Judah (on which see pp.   ) was within Geshem's sphere of influence or even control. From an economic point of view it thus becomes possible to locate him in a territory, not necessarily near Judah and perhaps even remote from Palestine, where, because of his involvement in long-range North Arabian trade, his interests in southern Palestine might be threatened by a too-powerful Judah. This viewpoint provides the basis for the proposed identification of the Geshem refered to in two inscriptions of the Acheamenid period with Nehemiah's rival, Geshem the Arab:

1. The date-formula in JS 349 lih. from Dedan (al-'Ulā) reads: "In the time of *Gšm b. Šhr* and *'bd* governor of Dedan, in the reig[n of ...].[711] The use of *Gšm b. Šhr*'s name as a time-indicator points to a prominent person, of high rank in the Dedan region, and possibly beyond. About his title, however, we know only that he was not *fḥt ddn* (governor of Dedan). Winnett dated this inscription, and consequently the Early Lihyanite script in which it was written, to the Achaemenid period because of the use of the title *fḥh* (Akkadian [ld]*bēl pīḫati*). In seeking to identify *Gšm b. Šhr* with biblical Geshem the Arab, Winnet determined the time of the above inscription quite precisely, at about mid-5th century B.C., a widely accepted view.[712]

2. One of the silver bowls from Tell el-Maskhuṭeh is inscribed: זי קינו בר גשם מלך קדר קרב להנאלת, "That which Qainū son of Gešem, king of Qedar, offered to han-'Ilāt", and is dated archaeologically and paleographically to the second half of the 5th century B.C.[713] Thus Geshem, father of Qainū king of Qedar, becomes contemporaneous with Nehemiah. Accordingly, Rabinowitz and Cross proposed that the Geshem king of Qedar mentioned here be identified with Geshem the Arab in Nehemiah,[714] positing a leader of the Qedar tribal league, whose

711 Regarding this inscription and the meaning of the term *br'y*, see p. 204.

712 See above p. 204.

713 See above, p. 194.

714 Rabinowitz, *JNES* 15 (1956), 9; Cross, *BA* 18 (1955), 46-47. This view had been accepted and further developed by Dumbrell, *BASOR* 203 (1971), 33-44. Caskel (in *Fischer Weltgeschichte* 5, 378), who agrees that the date of the inscription is ca. 400

influence extended from the approaches to Egypt at least as far as southern Palestine, and who may have been "king of the Arabs", controller of Arabian trade in southern Palestine (see pp. 206-210).

Rabinowitz has suggested that the Septuagint translation of "in the land of Goshen" (בארץ גשן) in Gen 45:10; 46:34 as ἐν γῇ Γεσεμ Ἀραβίας/Ἀραβία ("in the land of Geshem of Arabia") reveals that the Greek translators connected Geshem, Nehemiah's contemporary, with the Wadi Thumīlāt region.[715] But the greater likelihood is that they named the district not for a personality who had controlled it hundreds of years before their time, but for a *dynasty,* one of whose progenitors was Geshem king of Qedar, Nehemiah's contemporary. By analogy with such district names as "the Land of Tobiah"[716] and "the Land of Onias",[717] this Egyptian border region, most of whose inhabitants were Arabs, can more reasonably be assumed to have been organized within a special administrative framework in Ptolemaic times as well.

3. These identifications, though chronologically feasible, are tentative and need more proof. Present knowledge demands reservation with regard to Winnett's definite dating of JS 349 lih. (450-425 B.C.),[718] and even stronger reservation regarding the opinion that Geshem, Nehemiah's rival, the king of Qedar and the leader mentioned in JS 349 lih. are one person.[719] Such an opinion depends on assuming a) that the Qedarites controlled Dedan and its environs in the 5th century B.C. (in such a case, why was the title "king of Qedar" not appended to the name of *Gšm b. Šhr* in JS 349 lih.?); and b) that there existed, under Achaemenid rule, an organized, politically influential economic

B.C., unaccountably believes that *Gšm* king of Qedar of this inscription is the *grandson* of Nehemiah's enemy. *Qynw* thus becomes the great-grandson of Nehemiah's contemporary, spanning four generations in the space of 50 years.

715 *Op. cit.,* 6-7. The Septuagint translation of Γόσομ for Goshen (גֹּשֶׁן) in Judea (Josh. 10:41; 11:16; 15:51) makes it clear that they really meant Geshem the Arab when they referred to him in Genesis.

716 Cf. V.A. Tcherikover-A. Fuks, *Corpus Papyrorum Judaicarum,* I, Cambridge, Mass. 1957, 123: ἐν τῆι Τουβίου (P. Lond. inv. 2358 A).

717 ἡ Ὀνίου Χώρα, Josephus, *Ant.* XIV, viii, 1; *War,* I, 1 etc.); ἡ Ὀνίου γᾶ (P.J.-B. Frey, *Corpus Inscriptionum Iudaicarum,* No. 1530, Vol. II, Roma 1952, p. 436 = Tcherikover *et alii, Corpus Papyrorum Judaicarum,* III, 1964, 161).

718 See Winnett and Albright, note 694 above.

719 Cf. note 714 above.

"empire" of tremendous proportions, extending from Dedan to southern Judea and the approaches of Egypt.

Until new data is available, the identity of Geshem the Arab remains an open question.

Direct sources for the Arabs conclude, as stated, at the close of the 5th century B.C. Essentially complete by this time were the demographic, political and economic processes which took place during the 9th-5th centuries B.C., outlined in the Introduction, pp. 1-5, and later developed in detail. The political changes occurring at the end of the Achaemenid period in Palestine and its environs, as well as the emergence of the Nabataeans, considerably altered the political organization and status of the Arabs in the cup of the Fertile Crescent and the nature of their relations with the sedentary populations and political entities in the region. The study of these changes, however, necessitates sources and research tools different from those used in this book.

APPENDIX A

THE NOMAD GROUPS

Appended here is a separate discussion, alphabetically arranged, of the individual nomad groups heretofore dealt with in our historical survey. Along with the heading for each group are the Akkadian and biblical references and identification — which would have interfered with the continuity of discussion in the body of work. Other matters previously set forth in detail are cross-referenced only.

1. **Adbeel:** III R 10, 2:28 refers to the ^{lú}*I-di-ba-'-il-a-a* and other nomad groups in North Arabia and the border regions of Palestine, who surrendered to Tiglath-Pileser during his campaigns in Palestine and its environs. The determinative *lú* bespeaks a socio-ethnic entity, identifiable with the biblical Adbeel (אדבאל) in the list of the Sons of Ishmael (Gen. 25:13; I Chron. 1:29). The Lucianic version of I Chron. 1:29 is Αβδιηλ (cf. also Josephus, *Ant.* I, xii, 4, 'Αβδεῆλος), but the usual Septuagint spelling is Ναβδαιηλ. In Gen. 25:3 the Septuagint adds Ραγουηλ καὶ Ναβδεηλ, i.e. Reuel (רעואל) and Adbeel, to the list of the Sons of Dedan, which suggests some link between Adbeel and the inhabitants of North Arabia. Although we cannot explain the Septuagint substitution of *nun* for *'alef*, neither can we accept Albright's view[1] that the Septuagint spelling connects the people of Adbeel with the people of Nodab (LXX: οἱ Ναδαβαῖοι), which latter are coupled with the Hagarites and the people of Jetur and Naphish, who were defeated by the Israelite tribes of Transjordan (I Chron. 5:19).[2] Such a

1 W.F. Albright, *Levi della Vida Festschrift,* 13-14.

2 On the question of whether the reference to Jetur and Naphish belongs to the period of Saul or later, see p. 67.

view implies that Nadab (נדב) > Nodab (נודב) is simply an abbreviation of *Nadabeel (*נדבאל), but the Assyrian spelling demonstrates that the MT Adbeel (אדבאל) is the original spelling. Moreover, the Septuagint spellings suggest that the translators did not link the two names: while they derived Ναδαβαῖοι from Nadab, they retained the βδ (not δβ) order in their transliteration for MT Adbeel (אדבאל). Lucian and Josephus seem to have etymologized their version from such a name as *'Adbeel (*עבדאל).

Several inscriptions of Tiglath-Pileser (III R 10, 2; K 3751; Lay. 66) refer to the appointment of Adbeel as "warden" on the Egyptian border.[3] Although the name is not uncommon,[4] this Adbeel, because of what we know about the policies of Tiglath-Pileser and Sargon toward the nomads on the border of their realm,[5] can reasonably be connected with the [lú]*I-di-ba-'-il-a-a.*[6]

2. [uru]**Ba-da-na-a-a:** Listed with other nomad groups which surrendered to Tiglath-Pileser during his activity in southern Palestine (K 3751 rev. 3). Concerning their identification see p. 89.

3. **'Ephah:** [uru]*Ḫa-a-a-ap-pa-a-a* Tiglath-Pileser, K 3751 rev. 3; cf. [uru]*Ḫa-a(?)-a...* Lay. 66 (Rost, *Ann.,* 219).

[lú]*Ḫa-ia-pa-a* Sargon, Lie, 22:121; Lyon, 4:20.

Fr. Delitzsch acceptably identifies them with the people of 'Ephah (עיפה) in the biblical list of the Sons of Keturah (Gen. 25:4; I Chron. 1:33).[7] The name generally appears in the Septuagint as Γαιφα,[8] indicating that the original was עיפה (Ghaiphah).[9]

3 [m]*I-di-bi-'-i-li a-na* LÚ.NI.DUḪ*-ú-ti ina muḫḫi* [kur]*Mu-uṣ-ri ap-qid/aš-kun* (for this reconstruction of the text see p. 35). Apparently he is to be identied with *[I]-di-bi-'-ilu* [kur]*A-ru-bu* in Lay 29b (Rost, *Ann,* 240).

4 See, e.g., *RNP* I, 218; II, 79; G.L. Harding, *Some Thamudic Inscriptions from the Hashimite Kingdom of Jordan,* Leiden 1952, p. 44, n. 477; G. Ryckmans, *Le Muséon* 70 (1957), 114-116.

5 For the date of Idibi'ilu's appointment on the Egyptian border, see pp. 24-25. On his status and the significance of his appointment see pp. 93 ff.

6 A Bedouin tribe and its most prominent family (whose head is the leader of the tribe) often have the same name. For a contemporary example, see Musil, *Arabia Deserta,* 478.

7 *Paradies,* 304.

8 Besides this basic form, Γαφερ, Γαιφαρ and Γεφαρ are also attested in the Septuagint; the *rēš* seems to have been added in transcriptions of 'Ephah (עיפה), which appears before 'Epher (עפר) in the list of the Sons of Qeturah.

9 Cf. the spellings of the name of Gaza: עזה — Arab. *Ghazzah* — Γάζα— [uru]*Ḫa-za-tu.*

The people of ‘Ephah are one of the nomad groups (among which are Adbeel, Massa’, Tema’, Sheba’), which surrendered to Tiglath-Pileser following his military activity in Palestine and its environs. In the inscriptions of Sargon they are mentioned with the people of Thamūd, Marsimani and Ibadidi, all said to have been defeated by the Assyrian army, which exiled some of them to Samaria in 716 B.C. Since three of the nomad tribes in the inscriptions of Sargon are not in the biblical purview, and the inscriptions indicate that they lived outside Tiglath-Pileser's sphere of influence, we have to conclude that they were remote from Palestine. At the same time, because ‘Ephah is mentioned in the inscriptions of Tiglath-Pileser, it was, of all the nomad tribes listed in the Sargon inscriptions, presumably the closest to Palestine and to Assyrian governance. The location of the people of ‘Ephah in North Arabia on the Arabian trade route is also implied by Isa. 60:6: "A multitude of camels shall cover you, the young camels of Midian and ‘Ephah; all those from Sheba shall come; they shall bring gold and frankincense..."; and by the fact that ‘Ephah appears as a son of Midian in the Sons of Qeturah list (Gen. 25:2-4; I Chron. 1:32-33). But the available data do not suffice to pinpoint the territory of the people of ‘Ephah; locating it in the Yathrib area (Glazer) or in Ghuafa in the Ḥisma region (Musil)[10] is purely speculative.

4. ^{uru}**Ḫattiaya:** One of the groups which surrendered to Tiglath-Pileser in the wake of his activity in southern Palestine. The spellings include ^{uru}*Ḫa-at-te-a-a* III R 10, 2:28; [*Ḫa-at*]-*ti-a-a* Lay. 66 (Rost, *Ann.*, 220). There is as yet no identifying information.[11]

5. ^{lú}**Ibadidi:** Known only from the inscriptions of Sargon (^{lú}*I-ba-di-di* Lyon 4:20; ^{lú}*I-ba-di-[di]* ND 3411, *Iraq* 16 [1954], 199; [^{lú}*I-ba*]-*a-di-di* Lie 20:120). From our inquiry into Sargon's statement, it can be assumed that this group lived south of Tema' (see p. 89), in a location not precisely determinable.[12]

10 Glazer, *Skizze*, 261; Musil, *Northern Ḥeǧâz*, 289-290.

11 Solely because of the phonetic similarity, Glazer, *ibid.*, 263, located them in the Persian Gulf region. By identifying them with the Hittites of Gen. 26:34; 36:2, Musil, *Northern Ḥeǧâz*, 290-291, proposed the neighborhood of Edom. This cannot be seriously entertained, since it ignores the historical context of those references.

12 The proposals for a more accurate identication of this group (such as Glaser, *ibid.*,

6. [lú]**I-sa-am-me-'**: A tribe mentioned in the inscriptions of Assurbanipal with the people of Qedar and Nebaioth, all of whom were defeated by the Assyrian army in the Palmyrena region (K 2802 vi 33; Rm. viii 111; on this campaign see pp. 161-163).
7. [lú]**Marsimani:** A tribe listed with other nomad groups (Thamūd, 'Ephah and Ibadidi), putatively defeated by Sargon's army, whose "remnants" were brought to Samaria ([lú]*Mar-si-(i)-ma-ni* Lyon 4:20; ⌈lú⌉*Mar-si-ma-[ni]* Lie 22:121). The accepted view, proposed by Delitzsch, is that they can be identified with οἱ Μαισαιμανεῖς mentioned by Ptolemy, *Geographia* VI, 7, 21, with other groups located in the northwestern part of the Arabian peninsula.[13] The same source also lists the people of Thamūd (cf. VI, 7, 4; 7, 21).
8. **Massa':**[14] Assyrian sources: *[ ]Ma-as-'-a-a* III R 10, 2:27 (cf. *[...]-'-a-a* K 3751 rev. 3); PN [lú]*Mas-'-a-a* ABL 260, rev. 3; [kur]*Ma-sa-'* ABL 414, rev. 14.

Massa', listed among the Sons of Ishmael (Gen. 25:14; I Chron. 1:30), is a group to which Agur son of Jakeh the Massa' (Prov. 30:1) and Lemuel king of Massa' (Prov. 31:1) certainly belong.[15]

In 8th to 6th century B.C. extra-biblical sources, the people of Massa' are linked with two regions in the Syro-Arabian desert:

a. They are listed in the inscriptions of Tiglath-Pileser among nomad groups who surrendered to him in the environs of Palestine, most of whom (including the people of Tema', Sheba, 'Ephah and Adbeel) lived in North Arabia or North Sinai.

Bēl-liqbi, who probably served in the Valley of Lebanon or the Damascus-Ḥoms region, responded in ABL 414[16] to the Assyrian king's

259; Hommel, *EGAO*, 600; Musil, *ibid.*, 292) are based on various changes in the spelling of the name in the inscriptions of Sargon.

13 Delitzsch, *Paradies*, 304; Glaser, *ibid.*, 262; Hommel, *ibid.*, 598-599. Musil's attempt, *ibid.*, 292-293, to use classical sources to pinpoint the Marsimani demands substantial spelling changes.

14 For specific discussions of the people of Massa' see Albright, *Levi della Vida Festschrift*, Vol. I, 1-14; Winnett, *AR*, 90-91, 101-102.

15 The Hebrew spelling of Massa' is משא. For the transliteration of Hebrew שׂ *(ś)* as the Assyrian *s*, cf. שְׂנִיר - *Sa-ni-ru* (S. Parpola, *Neo-Assyrian Toponyms*, Neukirchen-Vluyn 1970, 304); הישראלי (the Israelite) — *Sir-'i-la-a-a* (Parpola, *ibid.*, 312).

16 For a translation of this letter and a discussion of its geographical and chronological background, see pp. 95-98.

inquiry about *mār* ^{m}*A-šá-pi,* who had been taken to the land of Massa' (*a-na* ^{kur}*Ma-sa-' ša il-qu-u-ni*).[17] From this we infer that the road to the Massa' territory started in Damascus.

A 6th century B.C. inscription from Jebel Ghunaym in the Tema' region reads *ṯr nṣr bḏ[r] ms(')* (="PN helped in the war against Massa[']").[18]

All this evidence points to North Arabia, but to no specific territory within it.

b. One of the Nabû-šum-lišir letters, ABL 260, reporting an assault by Ayakabaru son of 'Amyaṯa' of Massa' (^{md}*A-a-ka-ba-ru*[19] *māru-šú ša* ^{m}*Am-me-'-ta-'* ^{lú}*Mas-'-a-a)*[20] on a caravan which set out from the territory of the Nabayateans, states that only one man escaped and reached a fortified outpost of the king. The letters show that during the reign of Assurbanipal Nabû-šum-lišir served in the southwestern border region of Babylonia close to the dwellings of various nomad groups,[21] where the territory of Ayakabaru of Massa' should therefore be located.

If the toponyms ^{uru}*Dūr* ^{m}*Ú-gur-ri* and ^{uru}*Dūr* ^{m}*Aq-qí-ia* in the territory of bīt Amukani have any link at all with the names of Agur (אגור) and Jakeh (יקה) "of Massa'" (Prov. 30:1), the people of Massa' led by Agur son of Jakeh might be connected with the southwestern border of Babylonia, where Nabû-šum-lišir served.[22]

9. **Me'unites:** ND 400, referring to Tiglath-Pileser's activities in southern Palestine, notes in lines 22-23 the subjugation of $^{⸢m⸣}$*Si-ru-at-ti* ^{kur}*Mu-'-na-a-a ša šapal* ^{kur}*⸢Mu-uṣ⸣-[ri].* Although the phrase "which is below Egypt" is not very clear, it does indicate that the Me'unites had a geographical connection with the territory of Egypt which in Tiglath-Pileser's time extended to "the Brook-of-Egypt".

17 For this reading see note 322.

18 Winnett, *AR,* p. 101, note 16.

19 The common reading of the name (L. Waterman, R.H. Pfeiffer) is *Ayakamaru.* Albright (*op. cit.,* 5) suggested *Ayakabaru,* which means approximately "where is the greatness". On the spelling of ^{m}*Am-me-'-ta-'* and its meaning, see p. 58.

20 *Sic,* and not *Maš-'-a-a* as in Waterman, Pfeiffer and Albright. For the reading *mas* as well as *maš* see W. von Soden-W. Röllig, *Das akkadische Syllabar*^{2}, Roma 1967, No. 47.

21 On Nabû-šum-lišir's letters dealing with nomads, and the date of his activity, see pp. 56-59.

22 See Eph'al, *JAOS* 94 (1974), 108 ff., esp. 114-115.

References in the book of Chronicles connect the Me'unites with the same region: I Chron. 4:39-41 tells that the Sons of Simeon "registered by name in the days of Hezekiah king of Judah" expanded to the entrance of Gedor, גדֹר (following the Septuagint, this is usually referred to as "the entrance to Gerar", גרר), to the east side of the valley, and they "came ... and destroyed their tents and the Me'unites who were found there and exterminated them to this day".[23] And II Chron. 26:7-8 says that Uzziah's rule extended to "the Philistines and the Arabs that dwelt in Gurbaal and the Me'unites... and his fame spread even to the border of Egypt" (according to the Septuagint "Me'unites", מעונים, should be read instead of "Ammonites", עמונים, in verse 8 as well).[24]

These three sources thus clearly place the Me'unites during the 8th century B.C. in the southwestern border region of Palestine. We can therefore reject Musil's proposal of the Ma'ān region of Edom.[25] J.A. Montgomery's opinion about political and economic connections between the Me'unites and the well-known Minaean kingdom in South Arabia[26] is also doubtful. These views are based essentially on identifying the Me'unites with οἱ Μιναῖοι mentioned in the Septuagint and in classical works of the 3rd century B.C. and later, which reflect the ethno-geographic and economic situation of later times.

The Me'unites are not mentioned in biblical and extra-biblical sources between the 8th century B.C. and the end of the period we are dealing with, nor are they included in the Sons of Ishmael list (on which see Appendix B), suggesting that they disappeared from the Palestine region close to the 8th century, and maintained no contact with it for hundreds of years thereafter.[27]

23 See pp. 65-66.

24 See pp. 68-69, 77-80.

25 *Northern Ḥeğâz,* 243-247.

26 *Arabia and the Bible,* Philadelphia 1934, 182-184. Although ethnic affinity between the Me'unites on the borders of Palestine and the people of the Minaean Kingdom (Ma'īn) is superficially possible, supplementary research, showing that commercial and colonizing activities of the Minaean kingdom in North Arabia did not begin until the Achaemenid period, precludes the political and economic affinity which Montgomery suggested. On this research see F.V. Winnett, *BASOR* 73 (1939), 3-9; J. Pirenne, *Paléographie des inscriptions sud-arabes,* Brussels 1956, 181-183; J. Ryckmans, *JEOL* 15 (1957-1958), 242.

27 For an exhaustive discussion of the references to the Me'unites mentioned in the

10. **Nebaioth:** Assyrian sources (all references except to the letters are from the inscriptions of Assurbanipal):

^{kur}*Na-ba-a-a-te* Rm. vii 124; TM 1931-2, 26 (*Iraq* 7 [1940], 108):14

^{kur}*Na-ba-a-a-ti* Cyl. B (Streck), viii 23, 45; K 2802 v 5, 31, 39; Rm. viii 56, 70

$^{lú/kur}$*Na-ba-a-a-ti-a-a* Rm. viii 95 (gen.)

^{kur}*Na-ba-a-a-ta-a-a* Rm. 48, 95 (var.), 113

^{lú}*Na-ba-a-a-ta-a-a* K 2802 vi 35; Rm. viii 113 (var.)

^{m}*Na-at-nu* ^{lú}*Na-ba-a-tu-ú-a* ABL 1117:7

^{lú}*Ni-ba-'-a-ti* ABL 260 rev. 1[28]

^{kur}*Na-ba-a-a-[ ]* C x 35; *[ ]-a-te* C x 28; *[N]a-ba-a-a-[ti] AAA* 20 (1933), 87:124; *[ ]-a-a-ti AAA* 20 87:123; *[ ]-⌈ba⌉-a-a-ti* ND 5407+ ii 2; *[ ]-a-ti* K 4687 rev. 6

The Bible: נבית Gen. 25:13; 28:9; נביות Gen. 36:3; Isa. 60:7; I Chron. 1:29.

The 6th century B.C. inscriptions from Jebel Ghunaym mention a war between the people of Tema' and the people of Nebaioth *(Nbyt).*[29]

The data for locating the people of Nebaioth are:

a. In ABL 260, from the mid-7th century B.C., they are found in the Babylonian border region near the people of Massa'. This is supported by the statement in ABL 1117 that Šamaš-šum-ukin presented the envoys of Natnu king of Nebaioth with captives from the city of Sippar.

b. In the inscriptions of Assurbanipal, Yauṭa' b. Ḫazael king of the Qedarites is said to have fled after his defeat on the Moab border to Natnu king of Nebaioth "whose place is far away" (cf. B viii 30-31, 51-52; K 2802 v 31-32; Rm. viii 56-58), indicating that Natnu's territory lay outside of Assyrian control and influence.

c. Natnu and the people of Nebaioth were located in the northeastern part of Palmyrena at the time of Assurbanipal's "Ninth Campaign" (K 2802 vi 17-37; Rm. viii 96-115).

d. The Jebel Ghunaym inscriptions, as stated, testify to a war between the people of Tema' and the people of Nebaioth.

Bible and in ND 400, the conclusions of which accord with this study, see H. Tadmor, *Liver Memorial Volume,* 222-230.

28 On this special spelling see p. 58.

29 Winnett, *AR,* 99-101, nos. 11, 13, 15.

e. Gen. 28:9 and 36:3 imply a relationship between the people of Nebaioth and Edom.

Both (d) and (e), and possibly (b), imply that the Nebaioth territory was in the northwestern part of the Arabian peninsula south of Wadi Sirḥān (in the Tema'-Jauf region?); and (a) that in the mid-7th century B.C. some people of Nebaioth ranged the western border region of Babylonia.

The origin of the Nabataeans, who initially appear in Diodorus XIX 94-100, which deals with 312 B.C., is a knotty problem, whose solution is crucial to the study of their history and culture. The idea that the ^{lú}*Nabaitaya* of 7th century B.C. Assyrian documents and the people of Nebaioth (נבי(ו)ת) in the Bible were the ancestors of the Nabataeans (*Nbṭw* in the nominative) has been proffered by a number of scholars,[30] because of: the phonological similarity of the names; the connection of both peoples with the Syro-Arabian desert region; statements in classical sources that the Nabataeans were Arabs;[31] and Pliny's coupling in *Nat. Hist.* V 12 of the *Nabataei* and the *Cedrei*, like that of Nebaioth and Qedar in the Bible (Gen. 25:13 = I Chron. 1:29; Isa. 60:7).

However, it is difficult to identify נבית, *Nabayati*, with *Nbṭ(w)* (Arabic *'Anbaṭ*) because of the extensive spelling changes required: the shift from Assyrian and Hebrew *t* to Nabataean *ṭ*, and the elimination of the consonantal *y* from the earlier form. For these reasons a number of scholars reject the proposed identification,[32] their rejection now reinforced by the discovery of the name *Nbyt* in the Jebel Ghunaym

30 Eb. Schrader, *Keilinschriften und Geschichtsforschung*, Giesen 1878, 99-116 (to which I did not have access); Delitzsch, *Paradies*, 297; S. Schiffer, *Die Aramäer*, Leipzig 1911, 166-167; Musil, *Arabia Deserta*, 492; R. Dussaud, *La Pénétration des Arabes en Syrie avant l'Islam*, *Paris* 1955, 22; E.C. Broome, *JSS* 18 (1973), 1-16.

31 E.g., *Ant.* XIII, i, 2: Ναβαταῖοι Ἄραβες; Diodorus II, 48, 1: Ἄραβες οὓς ὀνομάζουσι Ναβαταίους. It should be noted that Josephus differentiates between the two names: when he mentions the people of Nebaioth in the list of the Sons of Ishmael, he uses Ναβαιώθης as in the Septuagint; when he refers to the environs of the Sons of Ishmael, which ranged "from the Euphrates to the Red Sea", he uses the geographical designation Ναβατηνή, current in his day (*Ant.* I, xii, 4).

32 Glaser, *Skizze*, 409-410; Ed. Meyer, *Die Israeliten und ihre Nachbarstämme*, Halle a/S 1906, 267, n. 2; Hommel, *EGAO*, 193, n. 1; Montgomery, *Arabia and the Bible*, 31, n. 16; J. Starcky, *BA* 18 (1955), 85-86.

inscriptions, in which for the first time the name of the people of Nebaioth is rendered in the ancient *Arab* dialect of the 6th century B.C. Tema' region. This form, which retains the consonants of the Assyrian and biblical spellings, definitively justifies rejection of the *Nbyt* (Nebaioth)-*Nbṭ(w)* identity.[33]

On Natnu king of Nebaioth and his son Nuḫuru, see pp. 150, 153-154, 156, 164-165, 169.

11. **Qedar:**[34] Akkadian references (all the historical sources, except for the first, are from the inscriptions of Assurbanipal):

^{kur}*Qid-ri* Levine, *Two Neo-Assyrian Stelae from Iran,* 19:2 (Tiglath-Pileser).

^{kur}*Qi-id-ri* Cyl. B. (Streck), vii 88; cf. ^{kur}*Qi-id-[ ]* Bu. 91-5-9, 178 obv. 2'

^{kur}*Qí-id-ri* Rm. viii 15, ix 4; K 2802 iii 6

^{kur}*Qid-ra-a-a* Rm. ix 17

^{kur}*Qi-da-(a)-ri* *AAA* 20 (1933), 86:114

^{kur}*Qa-da-ri* B vii 94

^{kur}*Qa-ad-ri* B (Streck) viii 31; B viii 39; K 2802 v 15; *AfO* 8 (1932-1933), 200:69

^{lú}*Qid-ra-a-a* Rm. ix 1; K 2802 iii 2, 4, 20

^{lú}*Qí-dar-ra-a-a* ABL 350:8; ^{lú}*Din-dar-ra-a-a* in ABL 811 obv. 7

33 Winnett, *AR,* 99. In a comprehensive article, Broome (above, note 30) tries to eliminate these difficulties and concludes that ***Nabayati***, Nebaioth and the Nabataeans were the same. He attempts to prove (pp. 3-13) that the original form of the name approximated ****Na-ba-tu*** wherein the *yod* did not appear. He relies for this conclusion upon the spelling ^{lú}*Ni-ba-'-á-ti* in ABL 260 (for a suggestion about the phonetic value of '=*ia* in proper names in this inscription, see p. 58) and systematically ignores the phonetic value *ca-a-a* = *aya* in *Na-ba-a-a-ti/te, Na-ba-a-a-ti/ta-a-a,* which is customary in Assyrian sources. He denies the value of the alphabetic spelling *Nbyt,* considering it secondary, arguing that the Jebel Ghunaym inscriptions reflect a North Arabic dialect from which the biblical spelling is borrowed. As for the *t* > *ṭ* shift, Broome assumes (*ibid.,* 13-16) the development *Na-bā-tu* > *Na-bat-tú* > *Na-ba-ṭú,* taking as his authority "Geers's Law", here irrelevant. But here, too, he relies solely on the spelling *mār Na-bat-ta-a-a* in ABL 305, which does not necessarily refer to the *Nabayati,* eliminating the other sources (Assyrian, North Arabian and biblical), which evidence no change in the pronunciation of the name, but rather the contrary.

34 For conclusions similar in part to mine which appeared after this study was concluded see especially W.J. Dumbrell, *BASOR* 203 (1971), 33-44; idem, *AJBA* 2/1 (1972), 99-109 (cf. also M. Weippert, *WO* 7 [1973], 39-85).

should probably also be read ^{lú}*Qi⌈l⌉-dar-ra-a-a* (thus J.N. Postgate in a letter of 30 September 1971 following a collation made at the request of H. Tadmor).

PN ^{lú}*šanû šá* ^{uru}*Qí-da-ri* BE VIII/1 65:7 (534 B.C.)

cf. ^{lú}*Qu-da-ri* UET IV 167:9

Biblical references: Gen. 25:13; Isa. 21:16-17; 42:11; 60:7; Jer. 49:28; Ez. 27:21; Ps. 120:5; Cant. 1:5; I Chron. 1:29.

The earliest reference to the Qedarites occurs on a stele of Tiglath-Pileser III from Iran (see pp. 23-24), where, following the sentence šarrāni$^{\check{e}}$ *šá* ^{kur}*Ḫat-ti* ^{kur}*A-ri-me šá šiddi tam-ti[m] šá šullum* ^{d}*Šam-ši* ^{kur}*Qid-ri* ^{kur}*A-ri-⌈bi⌉*, "The kings of Ḫatti, the Aramaeans whom I supplanted, of the setting sun, *Qidri, Aribi*", leaders from the western part of the Fertile Crescent are listed. Their names, with one difference, are the same as those who paid Tiglath-Pileser tribute in 738 B.C. (Rost, *Ann.* 150-154), among them Zabibe queen of the Arabs. The king of Qedar, notably, is not included.

Nimrud letter XIV (ND 2773) tells of an incursion into the land of Moab by ^{kur}*Gi-di-ra-a-a.* Although this may also refer to the Qedarites, grave linguistic difficulties minimize the probability (see p. 92).

Yauṭa' b. Ḫazael, whom some inscriptions of Assurbanipal call ^{m}*Ia-u-ta-' mār* ^{m}*Ḫa-za-ilu šar* ^{kur}*Qi-id-ri/Qa-da-ri* (Cyl. B [Streck] vii 87-88; B [Piepkorn] vii 93-94; cf. Bu. 91-5-9, 178), appears in parallel inscriptions as ^{m}*Ú-a-a-te-' šar* ^{kur}*A-ri-bi* (Rm. vii 83, *passim*). Thus Ḫazael, called "king of the Arabs" in the inscriptions of Esarhaddon (Nin. A iv 6; Heidel Prism ii 51, iii 3), also becomes a king of Qedar. Similarly, Adiya, the consort of Yauṭa' king of Qedar, is mentioned in the inscriptions of Assurbanipal as ^{sal}*A-di-ia-a aššat* ^{m}*Ú-a-a-te-' šar* ^{kur}*A-ri-bi* (Rm. viii 24-25) and ^{sal}*A-di-ia šar-rat* ^{kur}*A-ri-bi* (K 2802 v 26). These examples suggest that, in the general designation "king of the Arabs", in the Assyrian royal inscriptions preceding Assurbanipal's, other Qedarite kings might be included. In light of the stele from Iran, this seems especially applicable to Zabibe "queen of the Arabs".

Since the descriptions of Sennacherib's campaign against Ḫazael, who, as we have learned, was king of the Qedarites, and against Te'elḫunu, "queen of the arabs" in the Assyrian royal inscriptions,[35]

35 On this campaign and its destination see pp. 118-121.

suggest an important Qedarite center in Dumah, the Qedarites seem to have lived in the region of the Jauf depression in the eastern part of Wadi Sirḥān. During the 8th and 7th centuries B.C. their territory stretched eastward to the western border of Babylonia, as attested by the walled city named ^{uru}*Qid-ri-na* in the Bīt Dakkuri region during Sennacherib's time (BM 113203:37);[36] by UET IV 167 (apparently from the reign of Esarhaddon) reporting the escape(?) of Temaean families from Eridu to the ^{lú}*Qudari*;[37] by Nabû-šum-lišir's report of his action against the Qedarites (ABL 350);[38] and by the information about the forces sent to Babylonia by Abiyaṭe' b. Te'ri, who had replaced Yauṭa' b. Ḫazael as "king of the Arabs", to help Šamaš-šum-ukin in his war against Assurbanipal (Rm. viii 30-42).

The inscriptions of Assurbanipal clearly indicate that in the 7th century B.C. Qedarites also dwelt in the border regions along the western edge of the Fertile Crescent: In about 652 B.C., led by Yauṭa' and Ammuladi, they invaded the eastern border region of Transjordan and southern Syria;[39] and during the period of Assurbanipal's wars against Babylonia and Elam (651-646 B.C.), the Qedarites, led by Abiyaṭe' and Ayamu, the sons of Te'ri, were among the nomad groups exerting pressure on the settled areas from the Jebel Bishri region to the environs of Damascus.[40] Jer. 49:28 ff. and the Babylonian Chronicle (BM 21946, rev. 9-10) show that in 599 B.C. units of Nebuchadnezzar's army set out to attack Qedarite encampments in the western part of the Syrian desert.[41] For another possible reference to Qedarites on the Moabite border, see Nimrud Letter XIV (=ND 2773), dated between 732-705 B.C., abouf which we expressed serious reservations, see above, p. 92.

36 For the presence of Arabs in the territories of Bīt Dakkuri and Bīt Amukani in the second half of the 8th century B.C. see Eph'al, *JAOS* 94 (1974), 108-115.

37 See note 650 above.

38 The letters of this official indicate that he served in western Babylonia during the time of Assurbanipal. For details of the letters, see pp. 56-59.

39 Yauṭa' was defeated by Kamasḫalta king of Moab. On the Qedarite attacks under the leadership of Yauṭa' and Ammuladi, see pp. 147-155.

40 For nomad pressure in the Palmyrena region and Assurbanipal's campaign against them, see pp. 157-165.

41 On the circumstances of the invasion of the Syrian desert by the Babylonian army, see pp. 171-176.

As the eastern borders of Transjordan collapsed in the 6th century B.C., Qedarite westward expansion continued. Its extent is documented by the votive inscription on a silver bowl found in Tell el-Maskhuṭeh in the eastern approaches to Egypt: זי קינו בר גשם מלך קדר קרב להנאלת, "That which Qainū son of Geshem, king of Qedar, offered to han-'Ilāt."[42] If this inscription actually testifies to the presence of Qedarites in the region (it can be assumed, *prima facie,* that the bowl was brought from afar as a gift to the shrine), then it appears that among the "Arabs", mentioned by Herodotus, who dwelt in northern Sinai and near Egpyt's eastern border (see pp.193-195), Qedarites can be found, perhaps engaged in keeping that border secure for the Achaemenid authorities.

Such breadth of Qedarite distribution suggests a federation of tribes with various sub-divisions. Evidence for the existence of such a social structure figures in the inscriptions of Assurbanipal, where both Yauṭa' b. Ḫazael and Ammuladi, who operated simultaneously in the western territory of the Assyrian kingdom, were designated *šar* ^{kur}*Qidri,*[43] and in Ezek. 27:21, referring to "the Arabs and *all the princes* of Qedar" (ערב וכל נשיאי קדר). Additional evidence for assuming that the Qedarites were a sub-divided federation is the attempt of Wahb (^{m}*Uabu*) to seize leadership of the "Arabs" (certainly the Qedarites) after Ḫazael's death (Esarhaddon Nin. A iv 23-24; see pp. 128-129), and the replacement by Abiyaṭe' b. Te'ri of Yauṭa' as king of the Qedarites (Assurbanipal B viii 32-38; C x 29-35; K 2802 v 6-14; Rm. viii 43-47; see pp. 150, 155, 168-169). Neither Wahb nor Abiyaṭe' seems to have been a member of Ḫazael's family, nor possibly even a member of the same tribe. They could have replaced Ḫazael and his son only if it is assumed that the leadership of the overall Qedarite complex were transferable from one of its components to another.

Following are the Qedarite kings whose identification is unquestioned (vertical lines indicate father-son relationship):

42 I. Rabinowitz, *JNES* 15 (1956), 1—9.

43 On Yauṭa' see: B vii 93—94; Cyl. B (Streck), vii 87—88; Bu. 91—5, 9, 178. On Ammuladi see B viii 39; and cf. K 2802 v 15; Rm. viii 15; Ištar Slab, 114; *AfO* 8 (1932-1933), 200:69.

Ḫazael	First mentioned in connection with Sennacherib's campaign to Dumah (ca. 689 B.C.); reigned until about 676 B.C.
Yauṯa‘	Reigned from ca. 676 B.C. to ca.652 B.C. at the latest. After his father's death, Assurbanipal's troops helped him to oppose Wahb, who tried to seize the Qedarite kingship (not later than 673 B.C.). He was deposed ca. 652 B.C. after his defeat by Kamasḫalta king of Moab. Another Qedarite leader connected with the same war was Ammuladi(n).
Abiyaṯe‘ b.Te'ri	Installed no later than 652 B.C. by Assurbanipal, in place of Yauṯa‘ b. Ḫazael, and removed after having been defeated, ca. 644 B.C., by the Assyrian army.
Gashmū,Geshem	Ca. mid-5th century B.C.
Qainū	Ca. last quarter of the 5th century B.C.

12. **Sheba:** Assyrian references:
^{lú}*Sa-ba-'-a-a* Tiglath-Pileser, III R 10, 2:27
^{uru}*Sa-ab-'-a-a* K 3751 rev. 3
^{kur}*Sa-ba-'-a-a* Sargon, Lie, line 123; Winckler, 100:27
^{kur}*Sa-ba-'* Sennacherib, VA 8248:49

Biblical references: Gen. 10:7, 28; 25:3; I Kings 10:1-13; Isa. 60:6; Jer. 6:20; Ezek. 27:22-23; 38:13; Ps. 72:10, 15; Job. 1:15; 6:19; I Chron. 1:9, 22, 32; II Chron. 9:1-12.

Sheba appears in three biblical genealogical lists: 1) the Sons of Qeturah (Gen. 25:3; I Chron 1:32); 2) the Sons of Cush (Gen. 10:7; I Chron. 1:9); 3) the Sons of Joktan (Gen. 10:28; I Chron. 1:22). The names of the Sons of Qeturah and especially the contextual proximity of Sheba and Dedan (in the Septuagint to Gen. 25:3 Sheba appears with Tema' as well) clearly connect Sheba with North Arabia in the first list. By means of those sons of Joktan who can be identified — Hazarmaveth and Ophir, for example — it is demonstrable that the Sheba of the third list was in South Arabia. While most of the names on the list of the Sons of Cush relate to South Arabia, the contiguity of Sheba and Dedan, both sons of Raamah, suggests locating them in the north.

Modern research in South Arabia, based on the stratigraphy of various sites, with occasional radiocarbon dating, has shown that at the beginning of the first millennium B.C. there were sedentary populations in South Arabia,[44] thus negating the concept that the founders of the South Arabian kingdoms, among them the people of Sheba, were still nomads in North Arabia in the 8th century B.C.[45] There is now an inclination to identify It'amara (*Yṯ''mr*) the Sabaean, of the inscriptions of Sargon, and Karibilu (*Krb'l*) king of Sheba, whose gift to Sennacherib is noted in VA 8248, with two of the Sabaean *mukarribs*,[46]

44 G.W. Van Beek, *BASOR* 143 (1956), 6-9; (cf. idem, *Ḥajar Bin Ḥumeid,* Baltimore 1969, 355-356); Albright, *Von Qumran nach Ugarit* (O. Eissfeldt Festschrift), Berlin 1958, 1 ff.; idem, *Eretz-Israel* 5 (1958), 7*-9*; Bowen, in R. Bowen-F.P. Albright, *Archaeological Discoveries in South Arabia,* Batimore 1958, 43-65.

45 For this concept see Moritz, *Arabien,* Hannover 1923, 91 f.; Hommel, *EGAO,* 142 f., 598. Montgomery, *Arabia and the Bible,* 60-61, also grappled with this question.

46 For this view see particularly K. Mlaker, *Die Hierodoulenlisten von Ma'īn,* Leipzig 1943, 75 ff., 103, 107-108; J. Ryckmans, *L'Institution monarchique en Arabie méridionale avant l'Islam (Ma'īn et Saba),* Louvain 1951, 268 ff.; Albright, *BASOR* 143 (1956), 10. It should be noted that the South Arabian inscriptions refer to various Sabaean *mukarribs* named *yṯ''mr* and *krb'l,* but these sources contain nothing that allows any of these rulers to be synchronized with Assyrian kings. J. Pirenne contradicts Albright's chronology of the South Arabian rulers. According to her system, based on paleographic analysis of South Arabian inscriptions as compared with the development of Greek script, the Sabaean *mukarribs* under discussion date from the 5th century B.C. and therefore cannot be identified with the It'amara and Karibilu of the Assyrian royal inscriptions (see *Paléographie des inscriptions sud-arabes,* vol. I, especially pp. 27-29, 153-154, 279-289). A new criterion crucial to the argument between the Albright and Pirenne schools has emerged with F.M. Cross's study of the development of the alphabet (*Eretz-Israel* 8,[1967], 8*-24*). In a typological analysis of proto-Canaanite script, Cross states (p. 19*) that the proto-Arabic script departed from the proto-Canaanite about 1300 B.C. (With the discovery of shards with letters resembling proto-Arabic in the excavations of Kāmid el-Loz, in a stratum, or strata, close to that in which Akkadian inscriptions of the El-Amarna period were found — see G. Mansfeld, in D.O. Edzard *et alii, Kāmid el-Loz-Kumidi,* Bonn 1970, 29, 32 — unexpected support for Cross's view has turned up). Cross's conclusion, which attests the antiquity of proto-Arabic script, provides some corroboration for the Albright school by indicating the age of the inscriptions of the Sabaean *mukarribs*. In view of the small number of systematic excavations in South Arabia, it is impossible as yet to come to a definite decision or to bridge the gap between the two schools mentioned. For more on the question of the chronology of the Sabaean rulers, with reference to both schools, see H. von Wissmann, *Zur Geschichte und Landeskunde von Alt-Südarabien,* Wien 1964, 27 ff.; idem, *Zur Archäologie und antiken Geographie von Südarabien,* Istanbul 1968, 6.

i.e., rulers whose leadership was based on ritual and religious functions in the period preceding kingship.[47] As against the above-mentioned references to a South Arabian Sheba, other references in the Bible and in Assyrian inscriptions clearly point to Sabaeans in the North: Because all the nomad groups mentioned in the inscriptions of Tiglath-Pileser as surrendering to him were from North Arabia and northern Sinai, the Sabaeans among them cannot have dwelt in the South.[48] Job 1:15, their inclusion in the Sons of Qeturah list and perhaps the Sons of Cush list also imply habitation in North Arabia. It thus appears that besides the sedentary Sabaean population in Yemen we find, in the 8th century B.C. and apparently later,[49] people of the same name in North Arabia or the extended border region of Palestine. Their nomadic character is suggested by the description in Job 1:15 of their raid on his oxen and asses in the land of Uz. At the same time, the economic interests in North Arabia of the kingdom of Sheba may be disclosed by the participation of It'amara the Sabaean in gifts to Sargon in ca. 716 B.C., and by the present of Karibilu to Sennacherib after the latter's campaign to Dumah. It is thus not impossible that the name $^{l\acute{u}/uru}$*Saba'aya* in the Tiglath-Pileser list refers to the people of a Sabaean commercial colony in North Arabia, or to the most important one of a number of such colonies. Some centuries later the Minaeans made a similar practice of establishing colonies in North Arabia to advance the commercial activity of their South Arabian kingdom.

13. **Sumu(')ilu:** Sennacherib inscriptions: $^{l\acute{u}}$*Su-mu-'*-AN (see, e.g.,

47 For a detailed discussion of the meaning of the title *mukarrib* to designate the rulers of Sheba in the 9th-5th centuries B.C. (according to the Albright chronology) and of their political, military and ritual functions, see Ryckmans, *op. cit.,* 51-100.

48 For this extreme view, see Mlaker, *op. cit.,* 107, n. 37 (including a detailed bibliography about the question of locating those Sabaeans mentioned in Assyrian sources, especially the inscriptions of Sargon). It should be pointed out that the distance between the territory of Sheba in South Arabia and Tema', among the southernmost of the groups mentioned in the Tiglath-Pileser list, is more than 1.000 kilometers.

49 This depends on the background and date of the narrative framework of the book of Job, about which there are differences of opinion. In addition to commentaries on the book of Job, see B. Maisler (Mazar), *Zion* 11 (1946), 1-16; A. Guillaume, *Promise and Fulfilment*, Essays presented to S.H. Hooke, Edinburgh 1963, 106-127.

BM 103,000 vii 96); Assurbanipal inscription: ^{kur}*Su-mu*-AN (*AAA* 20 [1933], 86:113, 119).

As suggested by Luckenbill, Olmstead and Heidel, the name can apparently be read *Su-mu-(')-an.*[50] But this is questionable, although the data are too scanty for absolute refutation. The name endings in the Assyrian royal inscriptions whose phonetic value can only be *-an* (e.g. ^{uru}*An-za-an,* ^{uru}*Ša-šá-an,* ^{kur}*Ḫal-ma-an,* ^{lú}*I-ši-an*= ^{lú}*Ia-az-an*), have no penultimate *'a,* whereas in the Semitic names whose ending is *-'l* and whose reading is certain (cf. Ḫazael-חזאל king of Damascus and Adbeel-אדבאל),[51] the penultimate -' is an organic part of the ending. Thus the reading *Su-mu-(')-an* should be rejected for *Sumu'ilu.*[52]

The transcription of this tribal name approximates **Sm'l* or **Śm'l,* and has no connection with *Yšm''l* (Delitzsch, J. Lewy, Thompson and Winnett to the contrary notwithstanding; see above pp. 165-168). The inscriptions of Sennacherib and Assurbanipal locate the tribe in the desert west of Babylonia. Uaiṭa' b. Birdāda, its chief, was a leader of those nomads who raided the Palmyrena region in Assurbanipal's time.

14. **Thamūd:** The inscriptions of Sargon list this tribe with the other Arab tribes of North Arabia who were defeated and whose "remnants" were transferred to Samaria (^{lú}*Ta-mu-di* Lie, 20:120; Lyon 4:20; *Iraq* 16 [1954], 199:18). They can be definitely identified with the people of Thamūd mentioned in classical sources, in the Koran, by Arab geographers and in North Arabian inscriptions.[53] All these sources make it clear that during the period we are dealing with the people of Thamūd lived between Mecca and Tema'.[54]

50 Luckenbill, *Sennacherib,* 113; idem, *AR* II, § 397; Olmstead, *History of Assyria,* 310, 329: A. Heidel, *Sumer* 9 (1953), 170-171.

51 ^{m}*Ḫa-za*-AN, E. Michel, *WO* 1 (1947-1952), 269; ^{m}*Ḫa-za-'*-AN, *ibid.,* 57; 2 (1954-1959), 38, 154; [^{kur}*Bīt-]* ^{m}*Ḫa-za-'-i-li,* D.J. Wiseman, *Iraq* 18 (1956),125; *[I]-di-bi-'-i-lu,* Lay. 29b:13; *[I]-di-bi-'-i-li,* K 3751 rev. 6; ^{lú}*I-di-ba-'-il-a-a,* III R 10, 2:28.

52 For a comprehensive, closely documented study of the Assyrian -AN as transliteration for *-'l, -ilu* in West-Semitic names, see R. Zadok, *On West Semites in Babylonia during the Chaldaean and Achaemenian Periods,* revised edition, Jerusalem 1978, 28-30.

53 For details of all these sources see A.Van den Branden, *Histoire de Thamoud,* Beyrouth 1960, 1-20.

54 Glaser, *Skizze,* 230, 262-263; Hommel, *EGAO,* 598 – 599; Musil, *Northern Ḥeǧâz,* 291-292; Van den Branden, *ibidem.*

APPENDIX B

THE SONS OF QETURAH AND THE SONS OF ISHMAEL

IN THE BIBLICAL GENEALOGICAL LISTS

The ethnographic sector of the biblical genealogical lists includes names of various nomad groups who inhabited the Syro-Arabian and northern Sinai desert. In the Bible and in Akkadian sources from the 9th century B.C. on, they are collectively designated "Arabs" (ערבים, $^{lú/kur}$*Aribi,* etc.). The name עֲרָב (*'Arab*) does not occur in the genealogical lists, and nowhere does the Bible refer to a personage by this name. On the other hand, all the nomad groups known as "Arabs" and mentioned in the genealogical lists appear in the lists of Sons of Qeturah and Sons of Ishmael.

It is commonly accepted that the biblical genealogical lists reflect various historical and ethnographic situations, and that each list defines a specific situation within a given period. The *Sitz im Leben* of some of these lists in fact reflects a comparatively late situation, even though they are connected with the names of such early figures as the progenitors of mankind and the Patriarchs. Thus, for example, the list that includes Gomer, Madai, Tubal and Meshech among the Sons of Japheth (Gen. 10:2; I Chron. 1:5) cannot be dated before the 8th (and perhaps even the 7th) century B.C. because they were unknown in Palestine and its environs before that time. On these grounds we shall attempt to determine the *Sitz im Leben* of the lists of the Sons of Qeturah and the Sons of Ishmael, examining their geographic extent, the characteristics of the groups included and their period.

A. **The Sons of Qeturah** (Gen. 25:1-4; I Chron. 1:32-33)[1]

Gen. 25:(1) "Abraham took another wife, whose name was Qeturah. (2) She bore him Zimran, Joqshan, Medan, Midian, Ishbaq, and Shuah.

1 Besides the commentaries to Genesis, the list of the "Sons of Qeturah" was studied

Joqshan was the father of Sheba[a)] and Dedan.[b)] The sons of Dedan were[c)] Asshurim, Letushim and Leumim. (4) The sons of Midian were 'Ephah, 'Epher, Hanoch, Abida', and Elda'a. All these were the children of Qeturah".[d)]

Notes:
a) The Septuagint adds Θαιμαν between Sheba and Dedan in verse 3.
b) The sons of Dedan are not included in I Chron.
c) In the Septuagint, the list of the sons of Dedan adds Παγουηλ (=רעואל) Ναβδεηλ at the beginning.
d) Toponyms underlined in the usual fashion occur in the Bible other than in genealogical lists; those with broken underlining occur in extra-biblical sources.

Of the "Sons of Qeturah" whose identity is certain, Dedan, Midian and 'Ephah can be located definitely in northern Arabia. In the Bible as well as in Assyrian royal inscriptions Sheba indicates the kingdom of Sheba in southern Arabia (e.g. Gen. 10:28 = I Chron. 1:22; Jer. 6:20; Ps. 72:10; Sennacherib VA 8248:49) and in some cases Sabaean colonies in northern Arabia (e.g. Job 1:15; III R 10, 2:27; K 3751 rev. 3) (see more on this in Appendix A, 12). Shuah (שוח) is identical with the land of [kur]*Suḫi, Suḫu(m)* in the Middle Euphrates region, which appears in cuneiform sources as early as the 18th century B.C. (see, e.g., ARM XV 133 and note 5 below). As to Ishbaq (ישבק), it seems reasonable, as suggested long ago by Fr. Delitzsch,[2] to connect this name with the country of [m]***Bur-a-na-te*** [kur]***Ia-as-bu-qa-a*** who is listed in the Monolith Inscription from Kurkh of Shalmaneser III with leaders of Neo-Hittite kingdoms (among them Pattina, Carchemish, Sam'al, and Que), against which Shalmaneser III fought in 858 B.C.[3] This identity is supported by the spelling Ιεσβοκ in the Septuagint.

The "Sons of Qeturah", whom we have located in northern Arabia, are mentioned in the Bible in connection with trade in such South Arabian

by Glaser, *Skizze,* 445-461; Meyer, *Die Israeliten und ihre Nachbarstämme,* 312-322; Montgomery, *Arabia and the Bible,* 42-45; Winnett, *Translating & Understanding the Old Testament (H.G. May Festschrift),* Nashville-New York 1970, 188-193. Discussion was mainly limited to identifying and locating the "Sons of Qeturah", including groups not referred to in this Appendix because of insufficient data to identify them. There was no attempt, however, to clarify the meaning of the list by determining what was common to all the "Sons of Qeturah", particularly when such remote components as Ishbaq and Shuah were included.

2 *Zeitschrift für Keilschriftforschung* 2 (1885), 92.

3 III R 7, i 54; *ANET,* 277.

products as spices, precious stones and gold (see Gen. 37:25, 36; Num. 31:50; I Kings 10:2, 10 = II Chron. 9:1, 9; Isa. 60:6; Jer. 6:20; Ezek. 27:22; Ps. 72:15; cf. also Judg. 8:21-26; Ezek. 38:13; Job 6:19). Except for the descriptions of the Midianites in Judg. chaps. 6-8 and of the people of Sheba in Job 1:15 — both of which may apply to a specific and relatively short period — the "Sons of Qeturah" are not referred to in later passages in terms of a Bedouin life style wherein livelihood derives mainly from camels and sheep (in striking contrast to the "Sons of Ishmael" in the Bible; see below). The impression that they were connected with international trade is reinforced by the fact that, in biblical references to this trade, groups of names of the Sons of Qeturah appear in such combinations as "Sheba + Dedan" in Ezek. 38:13, cf. also Gen. 10:7 and I Chron. 1:9; and "Sheba + 'Ephah + Midian" in Isa. 60:6. Thus, as Ed. Meyer was the first to note, the name Qeturah appears to be related etymologically to the words קְטוֹרָה (Deut. 33:19), קְטוֹרֶת "incense", and implies a connection with the spice trade originating in southern Arabia.[4]

If we are correct in concluding that international trade was the common denominator for all the "Sons of Qeturah", it must equally apply to Shuah and Ishbaq. The land of ^{kur}*Suḫi* is known to have been an important center of international trade in ancient times, from which, according to the Assyrian royal inscriptions, particularly from the 9th century B.C. on, silver, gold, ivory objects, fabrics, tin and animals of various kings reached Assyria and Babylonia.[5] Nothing so definite can be said about Ishbaq, a country (or people) unfortunately appearing only in the Monolith Inscription. Such distant components as Shuah and Ishbaq were included in the list of the Sons of Qeturah presumably because at a certain period both maintained contacts with Palestine and its environs in the course of their trade relations with the Euphrates region.

B. **The Sons of Ishmael** (Gen. 25:13-15; I Chron. 1:28-31)

Chapter 25 of Genesis reads: (13) "These are the names of the sons of Ishmael, named in the order of their birth: Nebaioth,[a)] the first-born of Ishmael; and Qedar, Adbeel, Mibsam,(14) Mishma', Dumah, Massa',

4 Meyer, *op. cit.*, 313.

5 On the location of the land of Suḫi, its economic importance and its history, see J.A. Brinkman, *Post-Kassite Babylonia*, 183, note 1127 (including detailed bibliography).

(15) Hadad, T̲e̲m̲a̲', J̲e̲t̲u̲r̲, N̲a̲p̲h̲i̲s̲h̲, and Q̲e̲d̲e̲m̲a̲h̲. (16) These are the sons of Ishmael and these are their names, by their villages and by their encampments, twelve princes according to their tribes... (18) They dwelt from Havilah to Shur, which is opposite Egypt in the direction of Assyria (באכה אשורה); he settled over against all his people".[b]

Notes: a) For the tradition that Nebaioth was Ishmael's first-born, see also Gen. 28:9 and 36:3.

b) Toponyms underlined in the usual fashion occur in the Bible other than in genealogical lists; those with broken underlining occur in extra-biblical sources.

1. The stories about Ishmael and the references to the Ishmaelites in the Bible outside of the above genealogical list give a clear enough picture of the way of life and territories of the tribes designated by this name.[6] The *pater eponymos* of these tribes (and his descendants) had a clear connection with the desert regions between Palestine and Egypt: He was the son of Hagar, the Egyptian slave woman (Gen. 16:1, 3 and 21:9); Hagar encountered the angel of the Lord, who told her about the forthcoming birth of Ishmael, of his nature and future greatness, "by a spring of water in the wilderness, the spring on the way to Shur", which was later called "Beer-lahai-roi; it lies between Kadesh and Bered" (Gen. 16); Hagar and Ishmael were rescued by the angel of the Lord in the desert of Beer-sheba, after Abraham sent them away (Gen. 21:14-19); and when Ishmael grew up, "he lived in the wilderness of Paran, and his mother took a wife for him from the land of Egypt" (Gen. 21:21). It is in the same area that we find his descendants, who are described as dwelling "from Havilah to Shur, which is opposite Egypt < in the direction of Assyria >" (Gen. 25:18). This is coterminous with the area where Saul "smote the Amalekites from Havilah as far as Shur, which is east of Egypt" (I Sam. 15:7). The virtual identity of expression in Gen. 25:18 and I Sam. 15:7 enables us to locate Havilah definitively in southern Palestine although not to pinpoint it.

The common translation of the last two words in the geographical definition of the territory of the Ishmaelites in Gen.

6   Treated below are only those characteristics of the "Sons of Ishmael" essential to the understanding of the composition of the list. For a detailed discussion of the biblical data on the Ishmaelites, see Meyer, *op. cit.,* 322-328; Eph'al, "Ishmaelites", *Enc. Judaica,* IX, 87-90.

25:18 — בֹּאֲכָה אשורה – is "in the direction of Assyria". This literal interpretation, whose consequence for the study of the history and geographical extent of the nomad groups in the biblical period is considerable, raises great difficulty vis-à-vis the other biblical traditions on Ishmael. We therefore suggest examining these words orthographically rather than literally, using other biblical references — differently spelled — to the same geographical boundary:

Gen. 25:18: מחוילה **עד שור** אשר על פני מצרים, "from Havila to Shur which is opposite Egypt".

I Sam. 15:7: מחוילה **בואכה שור** אשר על פני מצרים, "from Havila to Shur which is opposite Egypt".

Cf. also I Sam. 27:8: **בּוֹאֲךָ שׁוּרָה** ועד ארץ מצרים, "as far as Shur, to the land of Egypt".

(For the locative suffix הָ after בואך, בואכה, "as far as", "in the direction of", cf. בֹּאֲכָה גררה ... בֹּאֲכָה סְדֹמָה, "in the direction of Gerar ... in the direction of Sodom, "Gen.10:19; and בֹּאֲכָה סְפָרָה, "in the direction of Sephar", Gen. 10:30).

The spelling בֹּאֲכָה אשורה in Gen. 25:18 instead of בֹּאֲכָה שׁוּרָה can, then, be attributed to the phonological error of reduplicating the last vowel of the first word on to the first syllable of the following one.[7] The insertion of both phrases עד שור and באכה אשורה in a single verse (Gen. 25:18) is nothing but a double reading, not unusual in the Bible.[8] Thus there is no point in attempting to identify the אשור* in this verse, or to couple it with the *Asshuri(m)*, אשור(ם), in the list of Dedan's sons (Gen. 25:3) or in Num. 24:2, 24.[9]

A number of biblical episodes imply an Ishmaelite link with the Midianites and other nomad groups in the border regions of Palestine: the Midianites, Amalekites and the People of the East (בני קדם), whom Gideon smote, were said to be Ishmaelites (cf. Judg. 6:3, 33: 7:12; 8:10, 22, 26 with Judg. 8:24); the story of the sale of Joseph mentions a

7 Fr. Delitzsch, *Die Lese- und Schreibfehler im Alten Testament*, Berlin-Leipzig 1920, 134, dealt with this phenomenon in the verse discussed.

8 On double readings in the Massoretic text see S. Talmon, *Textus* 1 (1960), 144-184.

9 This attempt was made in most of the commentaries to the passages discussed and also in Glaser, *Skizze*, 266; H. Gunkel, *Die Psalmen*, Göttingen 1926, 365.

caravan of Ishmaelites on their way from Gilead to Egypt (Gen. 37:25, 27; 39:1); in the same story these same merchants are called Midianites (Gen. 37:28: מִדְיָנִים) or Medanites (Gen. 37:36: מְדָנִים). Both Midianites and Ishmaelites, it should be noted, in addition to their camel-raising and caravan-trade activities, are said to have possessed gold in great quantities (Num. 31:50-54; Judg. 8:21-26).

Since the Midianites and Amalekites were identified with the Ishmaelites, and the descriptions of the territories of the Ishmaelites and Amalekites correspond, it is probable that the Ishmaelites were at one time the leading confederation of nomads in southern Palestine, and that their name was occasionally attached to other groups perhaps not directly related to them.[10] The end of that period cannot have been later than the mid-10th century B.C., after which time there is no reference to the Ishmaelites in the historical or literary sources in the Bible.[11]

2. As early as 1906, in his treatment of the neighbors of the Israelites, Ed. Meyer noted that the "Sons of Ishmael" in the genealogical list in Gen. 25:13-15 (=I Chron. 1:29-31) did not belong to the same historical framework as the Ishmaelites in other biblical sources, but to a later stage in the geographic and ethnological structure of North Arabia.[12] He gave no reasons for this view, contenting himself with the still widely accepted documentary hypothesis which attributes the "Sons of Ishmael" list to Source P and the other Pentateuchal references to Ishmael to Sources JE. For some reason, his opinion was disregarded by scholars, including the followers of the documentary hypothesis. Our information about the "Sons of Ishmael" in the genealogical list from both Assyrian sources and the Bible, however, makes it possible to verify Meyer's view and provides supporting evidence without reference to the documentary hypothesis or its validity:

a) The territory of the groups in the genealogical list greatly exceeded that of the Ishmaelites described in Gen. 25:18. It extended from

10 Calling nomad tribes by the names of larger and better known groups, to whom they may not have been directly related, is common in the Bible as well as in the Mari texts and the Assyrian royal inscriptions. For additional examples of this see M. Anbar (Bernstein), *Biblica* 49 (1968), 221-232.

11 See the table in pp. 60-63.

12 Meyer, *op. cit.,* 326.

northern Sinai (Adbeel) and Gilead (Jetur and Naphish) to the end of Wadi Sirḥān (Dumah) and even east of it.

b) The nomads in the expanse of the Syro-Arabian desert and northern Sinai, including the groups in the genealogical list of the "Sons of Ishmael" are called "Arabs" (ערבים, lú/kur*Aribi,* etc.) in the Assyrian and Babylonian royal inscriptions as well as in biblical sources dealing with the 9th century B.C. and later. In independent sources the name existed simultaneously at both ends of the Fertile Crescent, leading us to conclude that "Arabs" was what the nomads called themselves.

c) On the other hand, no ethnic group is called Ishmael in Assyrian sources nor is there evidence that the nomads mentioned above were so designated.[13]

Biblical references outside of the genealogical list assign the people of Nebaioth, Qedar, Jetur and Naphish a Bedouin life-style, and its attendant sheep and camels (Isa. 60:7; Jer. 49:29, 32; Ezek. 27:21; cf. also the booty list in I Chron. 5:21), tents and unfortified villages (חצרים; Isa. 42:11; Jer. 49:29, 31; Ps. 120:5; Cant. 1:5) and perhaps also with archery (Isa. 21:17). In contrast to the "Sons of Qeturah", the Bible refers to none of these tribes in connection with trade in spices or other Arabian luxury goods. The difference is especially striking when the two groups are mentioned successively:

> Isa. 60:6: "A multitude of camels shall cover you, the young camels of Midian and 'Ephah; all those from Sheba shall come; they shall bring gold and frankincense..." (the Sons of Qeturah);
>
> v. 7: "All the flocks of Qedar shall be gathered unto you, the rams of Nebaioth shall minister to you..." (the Sons of Ishmael).
>
> Ezek. 27:20: "Dedan traded with you in saddlecloths for riding" (the sons of Qeturah);[14]
>
> v. 21: "Arabia and all the princes of Qedar were your favored dealers in lambs, rams and goats, in these they trafficked with you" (the Sons of Ishmael);
>
> v. 22: "The traders of Sheba and Raamah traded with you; they

13 For a detailed discussion of this matter see pp. 165-168.

14 The people of Dedan (דדן) are also mentioned in v. 15 in connection with trade, but the reference there is apparently to the people of Rodan (רֹדן, Rhodes), and not Dedan (see 198).

exchanged for your wares the best of all kinds of spices and all precious stones and gold" (the Sons of Qeturah).

Such hints disclose the nature of the entire "Sons of Ishmael" list,[15] and corroborate the assumption that its compiler included the names of Bedouin groups in the extended border area of Palestine. It should be pointed out that the Assyrian royal inscriptions differ from the Bible in the presentation of some of the groups, mentioning the Qedarites, for instance, in connection with spices and other products of southern Arabia.[16] But the descriptive discrepancies can be cleared up by examining their economic and geographical relations with the eastern part of the Fertile Crescent and with Palestine: The Arabian trade along whose routes the Qedarites dwelt flowed through the Tema'-Dumah-Babylonia axis in one direction only, but did not reach Palestine. (The branch of the inland Arabian trade which did reach Palestine was via the Yathrib [Medina] -Tema' or Dedan [see p. 184] -Tabūk-Ma'ān axis; see pp. 14-15. There is no evidence that Qedarites dwelt along this axis before the Achaemenid period.) For the people of Mesopotamia, consequently, the Qedarites were connected with the Arabian trade, while for the people of Palestine, they were only Bedouin living in the desert and border regions.

Some of the names listed among the "Sons of Ishmael" are not known in other biblical and extra-biblical sources earlier than the 8th century B.C. Such were Nebaioth, Qedar, Adbeel, Massa', Tema' and Dumah, of which the last two are place-names and Tema' a tribal name as well. On the other hand, the list also includes components which can be placed in the ethnological constellation of the end of the second millennium B.C.: Mishma' and Mibsam, which do not appear in extra-biblical sources, are included in the list of the Sons of Simeon (I Chron. 4:25). They may well have been nomads in contact with the tribe of

15 "The caravans of Tema' look, the travelers of Sheba hope" (Job 6:19), givin, 67 Tema' importance in the Arabian trade, is exceptional, since Tema' is listed with "the Sons of Ishmael" and not with "the Sons of Qeturah". Perhaps we have to distinguish here between the people of Tema', who were nomads on the border of Palestine and were referred to as such in the inscription of Tiglath-Pileser III (see above, pp. 87 ff. and the Tema' oasis which was a center of the Arabian trade, and cited thus in Job 6:19.

16 See, for example, the Heidel prism of Esarhaddon, iii 6-7.

Simeon, the southernmost of the Israelite tribes and the closest in its way of life to the nomads. Because of their genealogical association with the tribe of Simeon it is reasonable to locate them in the southern border region of Palestine. Jetur and Naphish are mentioned with the Hagarites in I Chron. 5:19 ff., in connection with the war waged by the tribes of Reuben and Gad and the half-tribe of Manasseh in northern Transjordan. I Chron. 5:10 tells of the Reubenites' war against the Hagarites in the days of Saul. If I Chron. 5:10, 18-22 refer to the same period, at the end of the second millennium B.C. the people of Jetur and Naphish probably lived in northern Transjordan. Because of the linguistic and literary characteristics of the Chronicler, however, notably in I Chron. 5:18-22, it is possible that the reference to Jetur and Naphish in v. 19 is a later addition, reflecting the geographic and demographic situation at the time the book was edited. In that case, the temporal dichotomy between the supposed battle of the people of Jetur and Naphish and the other "Sons of Ishmael" disappears, as does the considerable gap between the first reference to them in Saul's time and the many later references from the 2nd century B.C. on.[17] The inclusion of Mibsam and Mishma' and perhaps also of Jetur and Naphish in the listing in Gen. 25:13-15 suggests that some of the other groups listed there were also connected with the ancient Ishmaelites.[18] But it is difficult to make such an assumption regarding Qedar, Nebaioth and Dumah. (It should be noted that Dumah was a religious center for the nomad tribes in Wadi Sirḥān and perhaps for those as far as in the Syrian desert.[19] There is, however, not a trace of connection between these nomads and Beer-lahai-roi in the neighborhood of Kadesh, apparently the Ishmaelite religious center.) It therefore appears that the list cannot date from earlier than the 8th century B.C.

17 About the date of the war mentioned in Chron. 5:19 ff. see p.

18 In accordance with this, the Ishmaelites, mentioned in Ps. 83:7 as among the enemies of Israel, may have been the people of Jetur and Naphish, who fought against the Transjordanian tribes of Israel (I Chron. 5:19 ff.).

19 The inscriptions of Esarhaddon and Assurbanipal referring to Te'elḫunu and Tabûa, "queens of the Arabs", indicate that Dumah was a religious center of the Arabs in the 8th and 7th centuries B.C. (see pp. 120-121). About the existence of a shrine at Dumah at the emergence of Islam, see Musil, *Arabia Deserta,* 533; Ch. Rabin, *Studi sull'Oriente e la Bibbia offerti al P. G. Rinaldi,* Genova 1967, 306, note 11.

The list of the "Sons of Ishmael" is patterned on 12 names, like other large tribal confederations, such as Israel and Aram (Gen. 22:20-24). This number is also spoken by the Lord to Abraham: "As for Ishmael, I have heard you. Behold I will bless him, and will make him fruitful, and multiply him exceedingly; he shall be the father of twelve princes, and I will make him a great nation" (Gen. 17:20). It is therefore probable that the ancient confederation of the Ishmaelites was also composed of twelve units; when the list of the "Sons of Ishmael" was recorded, however, most of the original components were no longer known, and it is doubtful whether the Ishmaelites themselves were still living near the borders of Palestine. The compiler of the genealogical list, who wanted to include those nomad tribes of his period who lived in the desert areas east and south of Palestine (that is, the "Arabs"), had no biblical tradition about the progenitors of mankind and the Patriarchs for an eponymous *Arab (ערב*), on which to fasten a genealogical-tribal system. But he did have traditions for Ishmael and the Ishmaelites. And since the Ishmaelites were no longer in the Palestinian region, the compiler, by a process of transference, called the Bedouin of his own time the "Sons of Ishmael".

Having examined the lists of the "Sons of Qerurah" and the "Sons of Ishmael" (Gen. 25:1-4, 13-15; I Chron. 1:28-33) we can come to certain conclusions about their nature and composition:

1) The lists are not geographically based, including as they do units removed from each other, like Shuah in the Middle and Ishbaq in the Upper Euphrates region, listed beside North Arabian 'Ephah and Dedan (in the list of the "Sons of Qeturah"). Nor, since the names are not in geographical sequence (remarkable especially in the list of the "Sons of Ishmael"), can various toponyms be identified by means of their proximity in the lists to well-known places.

2) These lists derived from the mode of living, the economic conditions and the nature of the contacts of the listed groups with the inhabitants of Palestine.

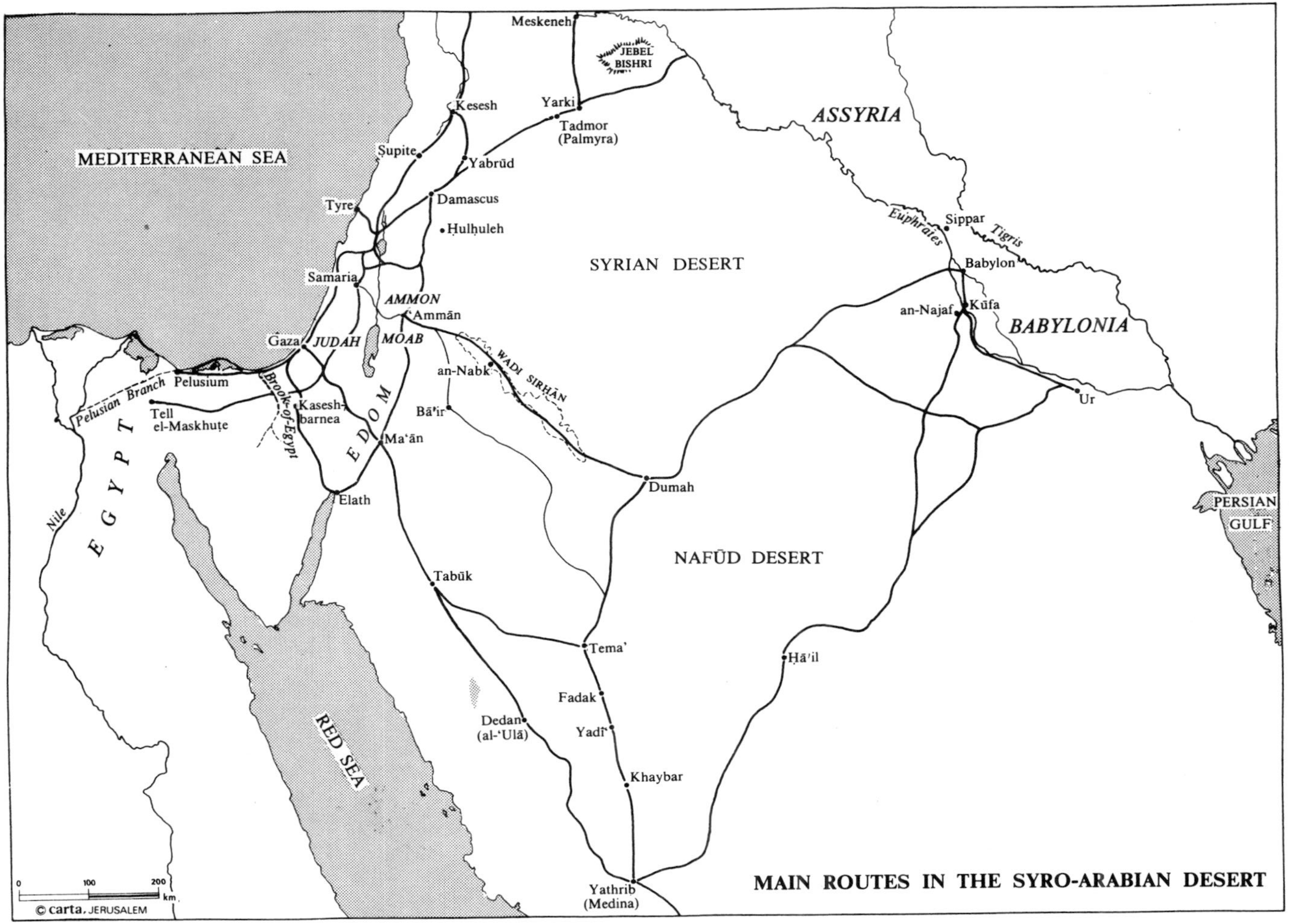

MAIN ROUTES IN THE SYRO-ARABIAN DESERT

ABBREVIATIONS

A.	Tablet signature of the Oriental Institute University of Chicago
AAA	*Annals of Archaeology and Anthropology*
AASOR	*Annual of the American Schools of Oriental Research*
ABL	R.F. Harper, *Assyrian and Babylonian Letters,* I-XIV, London-Chicago 1892-1914
ADD	C.H.W. Johns, *Assyrian Deeds and Documets,* I-IV, Cambridge 1898-1923
AfO	*Archiv für Orientforschung*
AHw	W. von Soden, *Akkadisches Handwörterbuch,* Wiesbaden
AJBA	*Australian Journal of Biblical Archaeology*
Alt, *Kleine Schriften*	A. Alt, *Kleine Schriften zur Geschichte des Volkes Israel,* I-III, München 1953-1959
[A.] Alt Festschrift	*Geschichte und Alttestament,* Tübingen 1953
ANET	J.B. Pritchard (ed.), *Ancient Near Eastern Texts relating to the Old Testament,* Princeton 1969[3]
AnSt	*Anatolian Studies*
APN	K.L. Tallqvist, *Assyrian Personal Names,* Helsingfors 1914
ARM	*Archives royales de Mari* (Paris)
ArOr	*Archiv Orientální*
BA	*The Biblical Archaeologist*
BASOR	*Bulletin of the American Schools of Oriental Research*
BE	*The Babylonian Expedition of the University of Pennsylvania, Series A: Cuneiform Texts* (Philadelphia)
BIES	*Bulletin of the Israel Exploration Society* (1951-1962, Hebrew) (continuation of *BJPES)*

BIN	*Babylonian Inscriptions in the Collection of J.B. Nies* (New Haven)
BiOr	*Bibliotheca Orientalis*
BJPES	*Bulletin of the Jewish Palestine Exploration Society* (1933-1950, Hebrew)
BM	Tablet signature of the British Museum
Borger, *Asarhaddon*	R. Borger, *Die Inschriften Asarhaddons, Königs von Assyrien,* Graz 1956
Brinkman, *Post-Kassite Babylonia*	J.A. Brinkman, *A Political History of Post-Kassite Babylonia (1158-722 B.C),* Roma 1968
BSOAS	*Bulletin of the School of Oriental and African Studies*
CAD	*The Assyrian Dictionary of the Oriental Institute of the University of Chicago*
CAH, III	*The Cambridge Ancient History,* III: The Assyrian Empire, Cambridge 1925
CIS	*Corpus Inscriptionum Semiticarum*
25th Congress	*Proceedings of the 25th International Congress of Orientalists,* I, Moscow 1962
CT	*Cuneiform Texts from Babylonian Tablets, etc. in the British Museum* (London)
Delitzsch, *Paradies*	Fr. Delitzsch, *Wo lag das Paradies?,* Leipzig 1881
Donner-Röllig, *KAI*	H. Donner-W. Röllig, *Kanaanäische und aramäische Inschriften*², I-III, Wiesbaden 1966-1968
Enc. Judaica	*Encyclopaedia Judaica,* Jerusalem 1971-1972
Enc. Miqr.	*Encyclopedia Miqrā'īt* (Encyclopaedia Biblica), Jerusalem (Hebrew)
Fischer Weltgeschichte	*Fischer Weltgeschichte,* Frankfurt a/M. 4: *Die erste Hälfte des 1. Jahrtausends,* 1967; 5. *Griechen und Perser,* 1965
Forrer, *Provinzeinteilung*	E. Forrer, *Die Provinzeinteilung des assyrischen Reiches,* Leipzig 1920
GCCI	*Goucher College Cuneiform Inscriptions* (New Haven)
Glaser, *Skizze*	E. Glaser, *Skizze der Geschichte und Geographie Arabiens von den ältesten Zeiten bis zum Propheten Muḥammad,* II, Berlin 1890
Grayson, *ABC*	A.K. Grayson, *Assyrian and Babylonian Chronicles,* Locust Valley N.Y. 1975

Abbreviations

Harding, *Pre-Islamic Names*	G.L. Harding, *An Index and Concordance of Pre-Islamic Names and Inscriptions,* Toronto 1971
Hommel, *EGAO*	F. Hommel, *Ethnologie und Geographie des alten Orients,* München 1926
HUCA	*Hebrew Union College Annual*
IEJ	*Israel Exploration Journal*
ITP	H. Tadmor, *The Inscriptions of Tiglath-Pileser III King of Assyria,* Jerusalem (in press)
JAOS	*Journal of the American Oriental Society*
JARCE	*Journal of the American Research Center in Egypt*
JBL	*Journal of Biblical Literature*
JCS	*Journal of Cuneiform Studies*
JEA	*Journal of Egyptian Archaeology*
JEOL	*Jaarbericht van het Vooraziatisch-Egyptisch Genootschap "Ex Oriente Lux"*
JNES	*Journal of Near Eastern Studies*
JQR	*Jewish Quarterly Review*
JRAS	*Journal of the Royal Asiatic Society*
JSOR	*Journal of the Society of Oriental Research*
JSS	*Journal of Semitic Studies*
K	Tablet signature of Kouyunjik Collection in the British Museum
Kohler-Ungnad, *ARU*	J. Kohler-A. Ungnad, *Assyrische Rechtsurkunden,* Leipzig 1913
Lay	Plate number in A.H. Layard, *Inscriptions in the Cuneiform Character from Assyrian Monuments,* London 1851
Levi della Vida Festschrift	*Studi orientalistici in onore di G. Levi della Vida,* I-II, Roma 1956
Leuze, *Satrapieneinteilung*	O. Leuze, *Die Satrapieneinteilung in Syrien und im Zweistormlande von 520 bis320*, Halle/Saale
Lie, *Sargon*	A.G. Lie, *The Inscriptions of Sargon II, King of Assyria,* I :The Annals, Paris 1929

Liver Memorial Volume	*Bible and Jewish History*, Studies in Bible and Jewish History dedicated to the memory of J. Liver (ed. B.Uffenheimer), Tel Aviv 1971
Luckenbill, *AR*	D.D. Luckenbill, *Ancient Records of Assyria and Babylonia*, I-II, Chicago 1925—1927
____, *Sennacherib*	D.D. Luckenbill, *The Annals of Sennacherib*, Chicago 1924
MAOG	*Mitteilungen der altorientalischen Gesellschaft*
Martin, *Tribut und Tributleistungen*	W.L. Martin, *Tribut und Tributleistungen bei den Assyrern*, Helsinki 1936
Marx Jubilee Volume	*A. Marx Jubilee Volume*, New York 1950
Military History	J. Liver (ed.), *The Military History of the Land of Israel in Biblical Times*, Tel Aviv 1964 (Hebrew)
MIO	*Mitteilungen des Instituts für Orientforschung*
Nbk.	J.N. Strassmaier, *Inschriften von Nabuchadonosor, König von Babylon (604-561 v. Chr.)*, Leipzig 1889
Nbn.	J.N. Strassmaier, *Inschriften von Nabonidus, König von Babylon (555-538 v. Chr.)*, Leipzig 1889
NBN	K.L. Tallqvist, *Neubabylonisches Namenbuch*, Helsinki 1905
ND	Tablets excavated at Nimrud (London and Baghdad)
Olmstead, *History of Assyria*	A.T. Olmstead, *History of Assyria*, New York-London 1923
____, *History of the Persian Empire*	A.T. Olmstead, *History of the Persian Empire*, Chicago 1948
OLZ	*Orientalistische Literaturzeitung*
PBS	*Publications of the Babylonian Section, University of Pennsylvania, the Museum* (Philadelphia)
PEQ	*Palestine Exploration Quarterly*
Pfeiffer, *SLA*	R.H. Pfeiffer, *State Letters of Assyria*, New Haven 1935
Postgate, *Taxation*	J.N. Postgate, *Taxation and Conscription in the Assyrian Empire*, Rome 1974
PW	Pauly-Wissowa, *Realenzyklopädie der klassischen Altertumswissenschaft*
R	H.C. Rawlinson *et alii*, *The Cuneiform Inscriptions of Western Asia*, I-V, London 1861-1909
RA	*Revue d'assyrologie et d'archéologie orientale*

RB	*Revue biblique*
RLA	*Reallexikon der Assyriologie*
RNP	G. Ryckmans, *Les noms propres sud-sémitiques,* I-III, Louvain 1934-1935
Rost, *Tiglat-Pileser*	P. Rost, *Die Keilschrifttexte Tiglat-Pilesers III,* Leipzig 1893
Smith, *BHT*	S. Smith, *Babylonian Historical Texts,* London 1924
—— , *Isaiah Chapters XL-LV*	S. Smith, *Isaiah Chapters XL-LV: Literary Criticism and History,* London 1944
Streck, *Assurbanipal*	M. Streck, *Assurbanipal und die letzten assyrischen Könige bis zum Untergang Niniveh's,* I-III, Leipzig 1916
Studies Landsberger	*Studies in honor of B. Landsberger on his seventy-fifth birthday* (H.G. Güterbock, Th. Jacobsen, eds.), Chicago 1965
SVT	*Supplement to Vetus Testamentum*
TMH	*Texte und Materialien der Frau Professor Hilprecht Collection* (Leipzig)
UET	*Ur Excavations Texts* (London)
VA, VAT	Tablet signature of Staaliche Museen, Berlin
Van den Branden, *IT*	A. Van den Branden, *Les inscriptions thamoudéennes,* Louvain 1950
—— , *TTP*	A. Van den Branden, *Les textes thamoudéens de Philby,* I-II, Louvain 1957
VDI	*Vestnik drevnei istorii*
Waterman, *RCAE*	L. Waterman, *Royal Correspondence of the Assyrian Empire,* I-IV, Ann Arbor 1930-1936
WHJP, IV/1	*The World History of the Jewish People,* IV/1: *The Age of the Monarchies: Political History* (ed. A. Malamat), Jerusalem 1979
Winckler, *AOF*	H. Winckler, *Altorientalische Forschungen,* Erste Reihe, Leipzig (1893-1897)
—— , *Sargon*	H. Winckler, *Die Keilschrifttexte Sargons,* I-II, Leipzig 1889
Winnett, *AR*	F.V. Winnett, W.L. Reed *et alii, Ancient Records from North Arabia* Toronto 1970
Wiseman, *CCK*	D.J. Wiseman, *Chronicles of Chaldaean Kings (626-556 B.C.) in the British Museum,* London 1956

WO	*Die Welt des Orients*
YOS	*Yale Oriental Series, Babylonian Texts*
Yediot	*Yediot bahaqirat Eretz-Israel weatiqoteha* (1962-1967, Hebrew) (continuation of *BIES)*
ZA	*Zeitschrift für Assyriologie und verwandte Gebiete*
ZDMG	*Zeitschrift der deutschen morgenländischen Gesellschaft*
ZDPV	*Zeitschrift des deutschen Palästina-Vereins*

GENERAL INDEX

INDEX OF SOURCES

A. SCRIPTURE REFERENCES

B. CUNEIFORM SOURCES

C. CLASSICAL SOURCES

D. NORTH ARABIC AND ARAMAIC SOURCES